ZBrush® Digital Sculpting
Human Anatomy

Scott Spencer

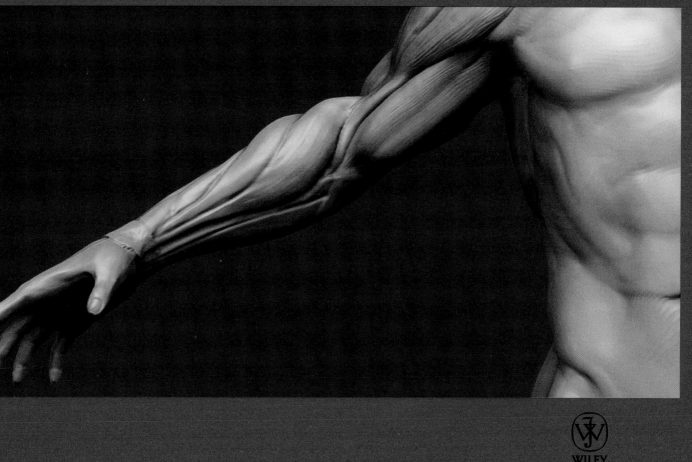

WILEY

Wiley Publishing, Inc.

Acquisitions Editor: Mariann Barsolo
Development Editor: Jim Compton
Technical Editor: Paul Gaboury
Production Editor: Dassi Zeidel
Copy Editor: Kim Wimpsett
Editorial Manager: Pete Gaughan
Production Manager: Tim Tate
Vice President and Executive Group Publisher: Richard Swadley
Vice President and Publisher: Neil Edde
Media Associate Project Manager: Jenny Swisher
Media Associate Producer: Shawn Patrick
Media Quality Assurance: Josh Frank
Book Designer: Mark Ong, Side by Side Studios
Compositor: Kate Kaminski, Jim Kramer, and Chris Gillespie, Happenstance Type-O-Rama
Proofreader: Kathy Pope, Word One New York
Indexer: Ted Laux
Project Coordinator, Cover: Lynsey Stanford
Cover Designer: Ryan Sneed
Cover Image: Scott Spencer

Library of Congress Cataloging-in-Publication Data

Spencer, Scott, 1975-
  ZBrush digital sculpting human anatomy / Scott Spencer.
    p. cm.
  ISBN 978-0-470-45026-0 (paper/dvd)
  1. Computer graphics. 2. ZBrush. 3. Human figure in art. I. Title.
  T385.S65975 2010
  006.6'9—dc22

                          2009035138

Dear Reader,

Thank you for choosing *ZBrush® Digital Sculpting Human Anatomy*. This book is part of a family of premium-quality Sybex books, all of which are written by outstanding authors who combine practical experience with a gift for teaching.

Sybex was founded in 1976. More than 30 years later, we're still committed to producing consistently exceptional books. With each of our titles, we're working hard to set a new standard for the industry. From the paper we print on, to the authors we work with, our goal is to bring you the best books available.

I hope you see all that reflected in these pages. I'd be very interested to hear your comments and get your feedback on how we're doing. Feel free to let me know what you think about this or any other Sybex book by sending me an email at nedde@wiley.com. If you think you've found a technical error in this book, please visit `http://sybex.custhelp.com`. Customer feedback is critical to our efforts at Sybex.

Best regards,

Neil Edde
Vice President and Publisher
Sybex, an Imprint of Wiley

To Richard and Tania:
Thank you for your friendship, inspiration, and support.

Acknowledgments

There are so many people who bring a book like this to life, and I would like to try to thank each of them here. They include those with a direct hand in the editing and layout, those whose inspiration drives me to continue working and learning, and those whose support makes this kind of endeavor possible. First I'd like to thank Richard Taylor and Tania Rodger for their cherished friendship, Karl Meyer of Gentle Giant Studios for opening so many doors and being a genuine and good friend, and Jim McPherson for his friendship and expert artistic guidance. Thanks to all the artists at Weta Workshop for their kindness and sharing. I would also like to thank Andrew Cawrse of Anatomytools.com. Were it not for his hospitality and guidance, this book would be far less useful and my own knowledge and experience far more limited. I would also like to extend very special thanks and acknowledgments to Andy Chamberlin and the Samuel Merritt Medical School anatomy lab for access to the facilities and for the dissection time.

Special thanks to Digital Raster for access to NEX tools and tips along the way on how to make the most of this amazing tool. For the many wonderful photographs of reference models in this book, I must thank 3d.sk, the premiere source of high-resolution figure reference photos online. Every photo shoot is a team effort, and they had the full 3D.sk team involved, including Veronika Jaskova aka Kristin (project manager for the anatomy websites and manager of models and photo shoots), Tomas Babinec (project manager for Environment Textures and 3D.sk), Tomas Pondelik (project manager for 3D Tutorials), and Jiri Matula (photographer).

Thanks to Paul Gaboury for serving as the technical editor of this book and a constant source of information. I can say with certainty this book would not exist without Paul's input and assistance. Thanks also to Ofer Alon, Jaime Labelle, and Martin Knapp at Pixologic, and Alex Alvarez, Ryan Kingslien, David Caplan, and everyone at Gnomon.

I'd also like to thank Rick Baker, Zack Petroc, Jamie Beswarick, Dave Meng, Greg Tozer, Andrew Baker, Gino Acevedo, Steven Lambert, Greg Broadmore, *3D World* magazine, Imagine FX, Eric Keller, Meats Meier, Scott Patton, Neville Page, Cesar Dacol, Ian Joyner, Mitch Devane, JP Targete, Eric Keller, Javier Soto, Gary Hunt, Bill Spradlin, Bill Johnson, Paul Hudson, and all the artists and teachers who have inspired me to keep working and learning.

A very special thanks to Mariann Barsolo, Jim Compton, Dassi Zeidel, and the wonderful team at Wiley who helped me get this book to print and were always professional, patient, attentive, and helpful to the process.

Thank you to Meredith Yayanos for her love, support, and reassurance, especially when the deadlines were piling up. Thanks to my brother, Bill Spencer, for his help and fun times at the Magic Castle. And finally I want to thank my parents for being the most loving, patient, and supportive mother and father anyone could hope for. Thank you.

About the Author

My name is Scott Spencer, and I work as a creature and character designer in the entertainment industry. My experience started in a makeup effects studio called Lone Wolf Effects, where I worked for Bill "Splat" Johnson. Bill's incredible design sense and attention to detail were a huge early influence.

After several years working in the shop, I left to attend the Savannah College of Art and Design, where I studied animation, sculpture, drawing, and anatomy (SCAD). After SCAD, I studied for a summer in Florence, Italy, at the Florence Academy of Art. After returning to the entertainment industry, I worked as the art director at Gentle Giant Studios, a resident artist at Anatomytools.com, and a freelancer sculpting for a variety of film, commercial, and collectable studios. Most recently, I have relocated to New Zealand, where I have the good fortune to work at the Weta Workshop among some of the most amazing artists I have ever met.

I am a firm believer that you should never stop learning, so I took it upon myself to seek out other artists and try to learn as much as possible from them. I had one such opportunity working with Andrew Cawrse of Anatomytools.com, where I was fortunate to be allowed more than 50 hours of dissections in a medical school. This exposure to real anatomy was a once-in-a-lifetime experience, and I am indebted to Andrew for this.

Along the way, I have made a lot of sculptures, taught a lot of classes, and met some amazing artists who continue to inspire and influence me. Overall, I consider myself very fortunate to have the opportunity to do what I always dreamed of doing—creating characters for a living. I also feel fortunate to have the opportunity to share some of what I have learned with readers around the world. It is my sincere hope you find this book, and the information I can share, useful.

Contents

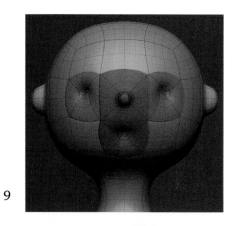

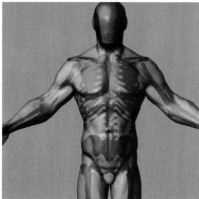

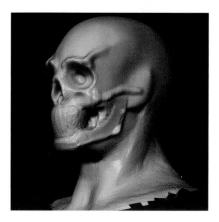

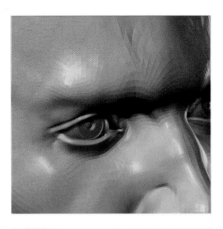

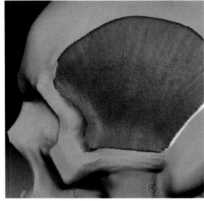

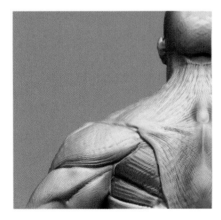

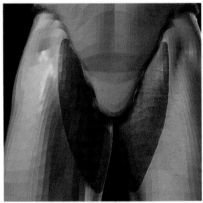

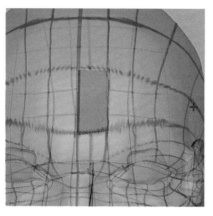

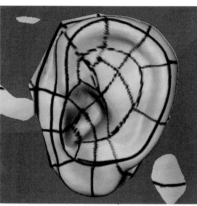

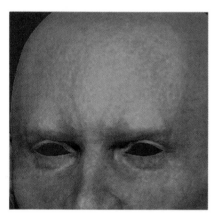

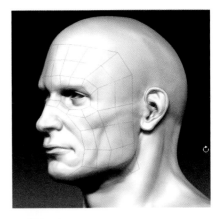

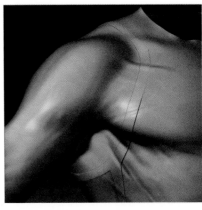

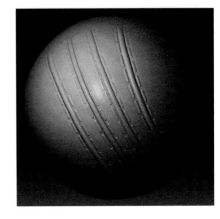

Introduction

Since you have picked up this book, it is apparent you have an interest in learning more about sculpting the human form. It may be to improve your digital sculptures for film, games, and other commercial applications; you may be exploring digital sculpting as a fine-art medium; or perhaps you just are just curious about an approach to creating figures in ZBrush. All of these are valid reasons to learn more about sculpting the human body.

The human form is so infinitely complex and full of subtleties that it can take a lifetime to master its many nuances. To me, the process of learning about the figure is like climbing a mountain. The mountain looks massive from afar, but once you start the journey, you reach a series of plateaus where a concept or shape suddenly becomes clear. Each of these moments of clarity is infinitely valuable, and each forms the basis for the next stage in your learning.

Learning anatomy provides a powerful way to support our work as sculptors. I say *support* because it is important to remember the difference between knowing the name and function of every muscle and knowing how to represent that form in your chosen medium, be it polygons, pixels, clay, or pigment. It is never enough to just have knowledge of muscles and the skeleton. You must strive to understand how to represent the shapes they make and to represent them in an aesthetically pleasing manner. This is where the art of the figure comes into play and where your true creativity can shine.

It is my goal in this book to guide you through sculpting one of the most popular subjects in commercial fantasy art, a heroic male figure. The heroic figure can be the basis for a space marine, a barbarian, a gallant knight, a hardened sci-fi tough guy... the variations are endless. I chose this style of figure because it is such a versatile and common figure archetype that manifests in film, video games, and collectables. It also has the added benefit of providing a clearly defined physique on which I can illustrate important points on the figure. A more understated body type would involve more subtle forms that can be tricky when trying to illustrate different muscle groups.

As I show how to sculpt this character throughout the book, I will take special care to examine each body part and how it is constructed as well as how it relates to the whole. I will further examine sculpting costume elements such as drapery, which have dynamics all their own that are directly influenced by the form beneath. I will then show how to take your final sculpture and prepare it for a variety of media including film, video games, and digital output. This kind of process allows you to focus on the sculpture first and foremost and then prep the final model to fit into whatever pipeline the final product may be. This kind of freedom is one of the strengths of current digital tools like ZBrush.

Even though I am showing how to sculpt a popular fantasy archetype, I will take special care to inform the work with the same tenets that have guided sculptors and other artisans for centuries. It is this attention to the foundations of artistic discipline that will make your character stand out and feel alive. You will learn about gesture, form, and proportion and how to consider these aspects as you work. You will also learn about breaking complex shapes into more manageable basic forms, which will help to lend your sculpting a true sense of structure and form.

Along the way, you will learn ways to conceptualize and remember the complex shapes that combine to create the human body. If you approach something like the arm and break it down into more simple geometric shapes, it becomes far easier to understand and reproduce. By understanding the basic forms that combine to create the figure, you have a powerful tool to help create compelling and realistic figures.

I wrote this book as a means of sharing some of the information I have gathered over the past several years of working as a sculptor in the effects industry. In my view, this book is as much a guided tutorial as a journal charting many of the lessons I have learned in my own continued study of the human body. I believe the joy of learning about the human figure is the journey itself, the process of discovery, and watching your own work grow with each new milestone of understanding. The human form is vastly complex and varied, and the ways of representing the form artistically in an aesthetically pleasing manner introduce another whole world of options. As the old saying goes, the journey is the reward, and in art I find this particularly true. You never stop learning and you never stop growing—well, that's the hope at least. For me this is a continuing process, and this book is a collection of what I have learned in my own exploration of the world of digital sculpting. I hope that this information is valuable to readers and proves useful as a guide to one method of sculpting the figure. This is only one approach, and you should not feel confined by the demonstrations that follow. There are as many varied ways of approaching sculpture as there are individual artists. It is my hope that this book will help illustrate the way I personally approach figure sculpting and will open the door for your own exploration of this vibrant and exciting subject matter.

Essential Anatomy Resources

Although I have tried to make this book as useful as possible to you on its own, no single book can communicate the whole of human anatomy, nor every process of approaching the figure. So, here are some of the finest reference books on anatomy I have encountered. I recommend having one or two of these handy as a reference. They will serve you well. This list could be several pages long, but I have narrowed it down to the five books I reference the most often. I have tried to take the visual information you will gain from anatomy texts such as those listed here and illustrate how to apply it in a sculptural approach in this book:

Human Anatomy for Artists: The Elements of Form by Eliot Goldfinger (Oxford University Press, 1991)

Modelling and Sculpting the Human Figure by Edouard Lanteri (Dover Publications, 1985)

Artistic Anatomy by Dr. Paul Richer and Paul Beverly Hale (Watson-Guptill, 1985)

Atlas of Human Anatomy for the Artist by Stephen Rogers Peck (Oxford University Press, 1982)

Modeling the Figure in Clay by Bruno Lucchesi and Margrit Malmstrom (Watson-Guptill, 1996)

There are other extremely helpful resources available to artists interested in sculpting the figure. Zack Petroc is a friend and an inspiration to me as an artist. Zack offers several videos and digital models on his website: www.zackpetroc.com. Zack also has an extremely useful DVD on figure sculpture from The Gnomon Workshop (www.thegnomonworkshop.com) as well as a life sculpting class he offers in California taught in ZBrush. Zack's work is phenomenal, and his influence has been huge on me and my work. I recommend readers explore Zack's website for more reference materials.

Photo reference is important to any artist, and when it comes to finding high resolution reference photos of the human body you can't beat www.3d.sk. 3d.sk is a subscription based website with an amazing array of photo references of all kinds of bodies and poses. I cannot recommend it highly enough.

When sculpting, it can be very helpful to have physical models on hand as a reference; www.anatomytools.com offers a full range of artist reference models, which are, in my opinion, the best in the world. See their website for a full range of models, reference charts, and instructional DVDs. The most recent releases from AnatomyTools.com include a female anatomy figure, a male figure, a human skull model, and several traditional sculpting DVDs. I have products from AnatomyTools.com at home and work for constant reference and inspiration.

Who Should Read This Book

This book is for anyone who wants to improve their digital sculpting and design skills with ZBrush. In the tutorials I assume some familiarity with the ZBrush tools I covered in my first book, *ZBrush Character Creation: Advanced Digital Sculpting* (Sybex, 2008). I have tried to keep the selection of brushes and tools to a minimum because that's how I prefer to work. Every artist will find the tools in ZBrush that best suit their needs. Do not feel constrained by the brush selections I cite in the text. Part of growing as an artist is finding the tools that work for you and a method of applying them. If you have other brush preferences, by all means use them. It is my hope that the tutorials will be valuable as a document of process as well as a guide to how you can see and re-create human anatomy in the medium of digital sculpting.

For a more foundational introduction to the tools, I recommend looking at my earlier book and at Eric Keller's *Introducing ZBrush* (Sybex, 2008).

What You Will Learn

This book focuses specifically on sculpting a heroic-styled character. This figure has been influenced by the work of Frank Frazetta and other classic fantasy artists in the presentation of this character. The proportions I will use are within a heroic canon and are well suited to many different applications.

In this book, you will learn how to work with the ZBrush sculpting and painting tool set to create a believable human figure. In each chapter I will isolate a part of the body, and I will demonstrate an approach to sculpting that takes into account the underlying anatomical forms, the overall gesture of the figure, and the fundamental basic shapes you are trying to create.

For each part of the body, you will see the skeletal structure underlying the part as well as the major muscle groups that combine to describe the ultimate form. In each section I will refer to a version of the final model with skin and fat removed and the muscles sculpted in to help illustrate the concepts.

I will discuss some basic anatomical terminology as well as how to read and interpret the text in your favorite anatomy books. You will learn how to identify and communicate about specific muscles and bones. You will also learn about the skeletal structure of the figure and where the skeleton creates major surface landmarks on the outer form.

You will also learn how to build an animation-ready mesh over the final sculpture so that your work can be translated into games or film pipelines as well as how to export for 3D printing and prototyping. The book also covers how to create costumes and accessories for the figure as well as how to paint realistic texture maps for use in a subsurface shading material rendered in Maya.

Hardware and Software Requirements

To complete the core exercises of this book, you need ZBrush version 3.1 or newer. Some sections also include material related to Photoshop and Maya and using these programs together with ZBrush. Hardware requirements are a PC or Mac running ZBrush with a gigabyte or more of RAM. The more RAM you have, the better results you can get with ZBrush.

It is also imperative that you have a Wacom tablet. Although it is possible to use a mouse with ZBrush, it is like drawing with a brick. A Wacom or other digital tablet will open the doors for you to paint and sculpt naturally. Personally I recommend a Wacom Cintiq. There are two variations of this tablet screen available at the time of this writing: one is a desktop model with a 21″ screen, and the other is a smaller, 12″ portable model. The Cintiq allows you to sculpt and paint directly on the screen and can vastly improve the speed and accuracy with which you can use ZBrush. It is essential to use some form of Wacom tablet, be it a Cintiq or a standard Intuos with ZBrush.

How to Use This Book

I have structured this book to be a single linear tutorial on sculpting, remeshing, painting, and costuming a human figure. It is best to work through the lessons from the very beginning with the possible exception of Chapter 1. In Chapter 1, I cover how to build the base mesh I supply on the DVD, and you will gain some important insight on proportion as well as gesture by working through the tutorial before you progress to the sculpting phase.

This book should be used in conjunction with other anatomy tools and texts. There is a plethora of material available on human anatomy in your local bookstore, and I recommended the five most useful books in my own collection earlier. I recommend that, as you follow the tutorials in ZBrush, you try to supplement your work with as much other experience working with the figure as possible. This includes life drawing and sculpting classes as well as videos on sculpting the figure. Every source of information you can find will offer some new aspect that you can learn from. I would like to especially stress the importance of working from a live model. You will absorb volumes of visual information by simply working with a life model and trying to re-create what you see on paper or in clay. I consider this a process of building up a vocabulary of shapes and solutions that you can then pull from when you are sculpting without a model in the room.

Chapter 1, "Blocking In the Mesh," builds a base mesh to use for the remainder of the book. You will examine proportions as well as modeling techniques using polygons and ZSpheres.

Chapter 2, "Gesture and Masses," explores bringing a sense of life to the base mesh by quickly blocking in the general form of the character with an eye for the weight and pose of the figure. Concepts such as rhythm and gesture are introduced.

Chapter 3, "The Head and Neck," isolates the head of the figure. You'll look at facial structure and proportion as you sculpt the hero's head from the base mesh.

Chapter 4, "The Torso," examines the form and structure of the core of the figure. You'll examine the two movable masses of the torso, the rib cage, and the pelvis, and you'll look at how to sculpt the underlying muscular anatomy of the center of the figure. Special attention is given to transitional areas at the shoulders and hips.

Chapter 5, "The Arms," looks at the skeletal and muscular anatomy of the arms. You'll start by looking at prominent bony landmarks on the skeleton and flesh out the arms from the bones to the skin. You'll also look at how to accurately represent the forearm and its complex underlying flexor and extensor muscles.

Chapter 6, "The Pelvis and Legs," continues the appendicular skeleton by examining the lower extremities from the skeleton out. Special attention is given to understanding surface features like the knee in particular.

Chapter 7, "Hands, Feet, and Figure Finish," takes the figure to a finish. Separate hands and feet are sculpted to illustrate an entire process of sculpting these features from a simple block mesh. The hands and feet are examined in terms of the underlying skeletal structure as well as the basic forms that will help you understand the shapes you are trying to create. The chapter closes with a final sculpting pass over the entire figure, where a layer of skin and fat is applied to give the figure a more natural appearance.

Chapter 8, "Remeshing," looks at two different approaches for generating an animation mesh for the hero figure: using the built-in ZBrush topology tools and using a third-party plug-in for Maya called NEX.

Chapter 9, "Texturing," illustrates a workflow for creating color texture maps of human skin for use in an SSS shader. This process includes both phototexturing and hand-painting textures.

Chapter 10, "Creating a Costume," shows how to create a superhero costume for our character. This process uses ZBrush retopology tools, painted masks, Maya polygon modeling, and specialized sculpting techniques to help create costume elements for any kind of character quickly and efficiently.

The Companion DVD Videos

On the DVD I have included several support files for each chapter. Many tutorials have video files accompanying them. In addition to videos, I have included supplementary text materials expanding on certain concepts as well as sample meshes, materials, and brushes. The video files were recorded using the TechSmith screen capture codec (www.techsmith.com) and compressed with H.264 compression.

I hope the videos included will help further illustrate the sculptural approach I take in ZBrush. Seeing a tool in use can better illustrate the concepts than still images alone. On my website, www.scottspencer.com, you will find more tutorials expanding on the content of this book. Please also check the Sybex website for this book (www.sybex.com/go/ZBrushAnatomy), where I have posted exclusive content beyond what you find on the DVD here. You may also want to check www.gnomonology.com for more video tutorials by myself and many other artists.

How to Contact the Author

I welcome feedback from you about this book or about books you'd like to see from me in the future. You can reach me by writing to scott@scottspencer.com. For more information about my work, please visit my website at www.scottspencer.com.

Sybex strives to keep you supplied with the latest tools and information you need for your work. Please check the book's website at www.sybex.com/go/ZBrushAnatomy, where we'll post additional content and updates that supplement this book if the need arises.

In conclusion, thank you for buying this book. It is an honor for me to share some of what I have learned with you. I hope you enjoy the lessons as you progress through the chapters. As you work, remember: the journey is the reward!

one

Blocking In the Mesh

In this chapter we will create *a sculpting mesh. This is a very simple blocked-in model to serve as a foundation on which to sculpt the figure. We will look at two different methods of creating a mesh upon which to sculpt our figure. The mesh we create will be a very basic armature, which represents the most basic proportions of the figure. The idea is to create the most versatile base possible to support the sculpting in subsequent chapters. By making a complex base mesh you can lock yourself into certain shapes too early. By taking the approach we use here, which creates an extremely simple blocked-in model, we will be able to sculpt nearly anything we want on the mesh. If your ultimate needs demand more specific topology, Chapter 9 deals with rebuilding the underlying mesh while retaining all your sculpted details. This workflow of sculpting first and remeshing later is the standard approach that I have used professionally for the past several years for multiple clients.*

The first section of this chapter addresses a standard polygon modeling approach to generating the mesh. This takes place in Maya and assumes a certain familiarity with Maya's modeling tool set. These tools and approaches are universal and can easily be applied to any polygon modeling package, as the tools utilized are standard between all polygon modeling applications.

The second section offers an interesting alternative to standard polygon modeling. This section is geared toward those users unfamiliar with traditional modeling or who may desire to learn a new approach. In this section we will create our base mesh using ZBrush exclusively, utilizing the mesh-generating tool known as ZSpheres.

I have included both models on the DVD, and you are welcome to skip this chapter and move on to sculpting; however, I recommend building a base mesh using these methods at least once. This is not so much for the technical experience but because this is the very first place in which we address the overall gross proportions of the human figure. In the case of this book we will be using a proportion of eight heads high. We will talk in more detail about proportions later in this chapter.

Sculpting the Figure

In this chapter we will look at some of the core precepts that guide me while I sculpt any human figure. Figure 1.1 shows the human figure that we will create in this book. It is a heroic male figure realized in the eight-head proportion, which we will discuss in the next section. It is my goal to share with you the workflows, thought processes, and technical approaches I take to sculpt this figure. In this first chapter we will lay the groundwork for the remainder of the book. In terms of creating the base mesh, we will discuss the ideas of gesture, form, and proportion as well as ways of thinking about sculpting in a digital environment. In terms of the tutorial itself we will be creating the very basic sculpting blocked-in mesh that will be the foundation of the next several chapters. In this first chapter we will be addressing the overall proportion of the human figure as well as starting to think about how to create a mesh that is in line with our chosen proportional canon.

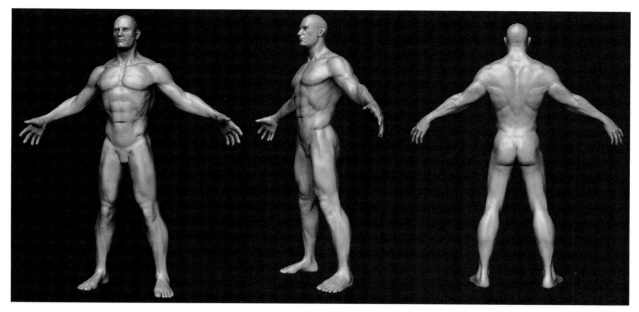

Figure 1.1 The final figure

Gesture, Form, and Proportion

When sculpting, I always try to consider three points as I work: gesture, form, and proportion. These three concepts are the foundation of my workflow. If each element is addressed in the sculpture, they combine to create a solid, effective sculpture. If any of these is omitted or addressed inadequately, the work as a whole suffers.

Let us look in depth at what these three words mean.

Gesture

Gesture is the overall dynamic curve or action line that can be traced through a figure. Figure 1.2 shows the gesture line superimposed on a sculpture. A gesture drawing is one that does not attempt to describe the outline of the figure but the energy or direction of the action. Figure 1.3 shows an example of gesture drawings.

Figure 1.2 The gesture line superimposed on a sculpture

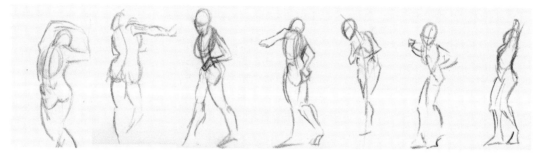

Figure 1.3 An example of gesture drawing

Gesture is just as important in sculpting as it is in drawing. A figure without a clear gesture will seem stiff and dead. Even if it is a well thought out sculpture with accurate anatomy, if there is no gesture, the sculpture will fail to excite the viewer. Gesture is apparent even in a neutral pose. The bones of the body have a gesture that telegraphs out to the final fleshed figure. Without this gestural quality, characters would appear to be composed of tubes with no overall rhythm.

Closely linked to the idea of gesture is *rhythm*. Rhythm refers to the alternating curves or shapes present in the figure. Figure 1.4 shows how rhythm can be seen in the alternating masses of the head, chest, and pelvis. Notice how the masses are offset and rotated against each other to create the alternating flow of mass distribution. Figure 1.5 shows the rhythm in the curves of the skeleton. Notice how each level, from the most basic representation to the most complex, echoes the same general rhythm.

These rhythms that are present in the skeleton influence the muscle forms and finally telegraph out into the final fleshed figure (Figure 1.6). Notice the rhythmic curves of the skeleton leg and how they are echoed in the final fleshed leg in Figure 1.7.

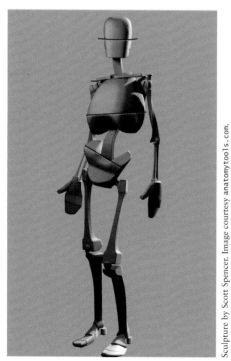

Sculpture by Scott Spencer. Image courtesy anatomytools.com.

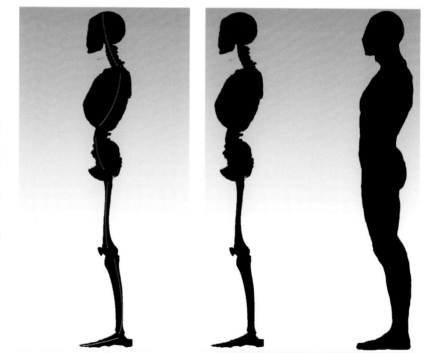

Figure 1.4 Rhythm expressed in the alternating of masses

Figure 1.5 The rhythm of curves visible in a skeleton

Figure 1.6 Rhythm in silhouette

Gestural rhythms can be difficult to spot on the fully lit figure. For this reason, in Chapter 2 you'll learn how to turn off surface shading in ZBrush and look just at the silhouette of the figure (Figure 1.8). When you look at the figure in outline, the gesture and rhythm comes into easier focus. By removing the distraction of interior forms, you can address the silhouette. This has a vast impact on the effectiveness of the rest of the figure.

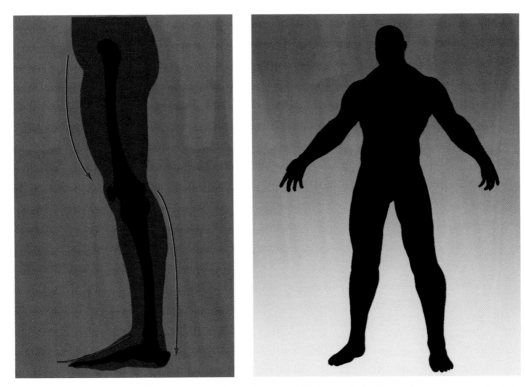

Figure 1.7 *Curves in a skeleton leg and a fleshed leg in silhouette*

Figure 1.8 *The whole figure in silhouette, shaded*

Form

Form is the external shape of an object. Form is represented by light and shadow and the gradients between. There is a hierarchy of form:

1. Primary form
2. Secondary form
3. Tertiary form

Throughout this book as we address different parts of the body, we will break complex shapes down into their simpler parts. By dissecting them into basic forms we render them easier to understand and reproduce. For example, let's look ahead to the rib cage. By breaking it down into a simple egg and slicing off planes, we come to the more subtle complex form of the rib cage (Figure 1.9).

This approach allows us to recognize and address changes in planes and nuances in form that we might otherwise overlook when trying to sculpt a finely detailed rib cage from the start.

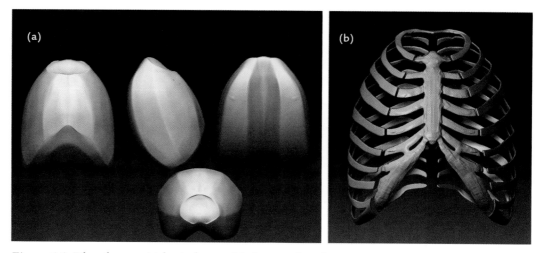

Figure 1.9 The rib cage: (a) basic forms, (b) the complete form

Form and Light

The perception of form is made possible only by the use of light and shadow. Figure 1.10 shows a figure (a) with no lights and (b) with lights. Notice that when light is off there is no form, only silhouette. It is helpful to understand that when you are sculpting, you are manipulating the effects of light and shadow on a surface. This is different than painting, where you are creating light and shadow by directly applying them to the surface. Figure 1.11 shows how a shape can be changed and the resulting highlight and shadow are altered as well. This is particularly important in the final stages of a sculpture when you are refining the surface quality, the nuances of fat, muscle, skin, and bone. Often it is helpful in remaining subtle in your approach if you remember that, at this stage, you are catching light and casting shadow more than you are adding materials or carving away. Moving your light can also illustrate the transitions between forms. Figure 1.11 shows two different transitions between the same shapes. Notice the difference between them. While they may be subtle, little details like this can add up to a great character sculpture.

Because of the importance of light and shadow to the subject of form, you will want to be able to move your light as you work. There is a handy utility for this built into the ZBrush interface. This tool is found under ZPlugin>Misc Utilities and is called Interactive Light.

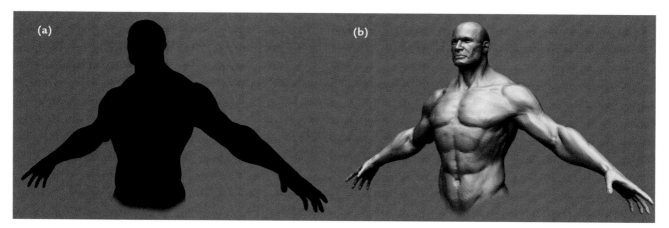

Figure 1.10 Form and light

Figure 1.11 Note that the shadow in this image was darkened by adding volume to the adjoining surfaces.

The Interactive light button allows you to move the currently selected light with the mouse. Simply press the button and move the mouse, and the currently selected light will move around the sculpture. I usually set a hotkey for this tool by holding down the Control key and clicking the Interactive light button. ZBrush will ask you to assign a hotkey for the tool.

I use Interactive light often as I work, and I encourage you to do so as well. As you sculpt take time to move the light and see how different lighting conditions change your perception of the shapes you are making. By observing the highlights and shadows on the figure from different lighting conditions, you can build a more complete picture of the shape in your mind. This will be invaluable for picking out areas that may need more work, which may have been missed otherwise.

By doing this you will ensure the sculpture is accurate under all lighting conditions. Be aware that interactive light only works with the Standard Materials and will not function when using Matcap Materials.

Proportion

Proportion refers to relative sizes between parts. There are several systems of proportion for dealing with the human figure. All of these systems, known as *canons*, strive to create a general set of rules that help create a natural-looking figure. In reality no canon of proportion is always correct for all people. The importance of the canon is that it provides the artist with a standard set of measurements to keep the figure looking natural.

View Blur

When working on the figure it can be useful to look at the surface in terms of shadow shape and value. By value, I mean the relative lightness or darkness of the shadow. When working with traditional media for centuries, artists have used the trick of squinting at the model to reduce the amount of visual information into a fuzzy generalized image. This helps you judge the shadow shapes and form. ZBrush has a feature built in to help you replicate this effect. It is called View Blur. View Blur is located under the Preferences → Draw menu. Simply set the slider to a value above 0 and press the VBlur button. This will apply a Gaussian blur to the entire canvas, helping you pick out the general shape of the forms and the patterns of highlight and shadow on the surface. With the view blurred, it is often easier to find shadows that are too dark or too hard, or areas where the highlight appears wrong. This is a telltale sign that something is wrong with the sculpture in this area.

In this book we use the *eight-head canon*. This means we will create a figure that can be evenly divided into eight head measures in height; that is, the head is 1/8 of the total. I chose this canon for several reasons. First, it is one of the easier to remember because the head measures fall on specific bony landmarks. Figure 1.12 illustrates another reason I chose this canon—the grace of the figure it produces. Compared to a 7 ½-head figure, the eight-head model is longer and more graceful. The 7 ½-head figure, although it's more accurate, can have the appearance of being somewhat "dumpy." An eight-head figure gains length in the legs and arms and can lead to a more graceful and heroic-looking figure.

Remember that canons are sets of rules to help you create a figure that looks right; once you understand these rules you can break them. But at the outset it is important to have a set of guidelines like this to help keep the figure within acceptable ranges of proportion. This assists you in trying to find areas that may not be working and determine why not. Being able to refer to your canon of proportion and correct the figure based on that is a better approach than simply tugging at the overall proportion until it "looks right."

In the eight-head canon, measures fall on the following points:

Landmark	Head Measure
Chin	Head 1
Nipples	Head 2
Navel	Head 3
Pubic bone	Head 4
Lower thigh	Head 5
Bony protrusion of the knee (Tibial tuberosity)	Head 6
Lower shin	Head 7
Bottom of feet	Head 8

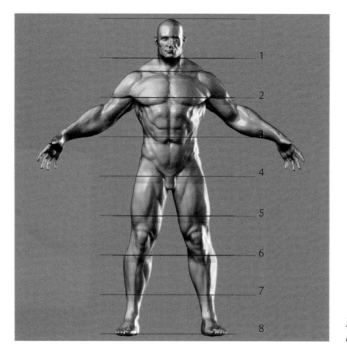

Figure 1.12 The eight-head canon

Once your figure is established you can manipulate proportions to change the perception of the character. See Figure 1.13 for examples of how subtle changes to the figure's proportion can alter the character. Notice how simply lengthening the arms or enlarging the size of the head can vastly affect the perception of the character.

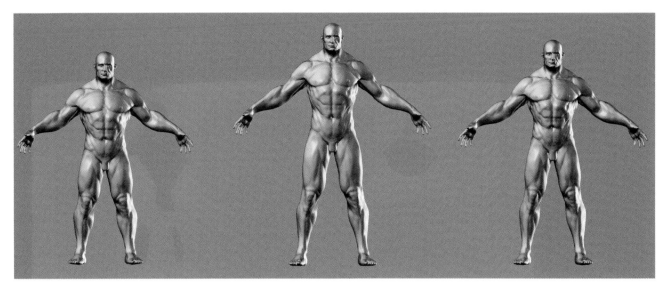

Figure 1.13 *Proportion and character versions*

From Basic Forms to Complex Shapes

How do we apply the tenets of gesture, form, and proportion to sculpting? First we will establish the figure gesture within a set of proportions, in this case eight heads. Then we move on to each part of the body, each time readdressing the gesture, forms, and proportions of the figure in relation to the whole.

By carefully considering each as we progress through the character sculpture, we can ensure that we stay on track and sculpt with direction, not mindlessly moving digital clay in the hopes it will "look right."

In this section we will look at some of the approaches we will take in developing this character sculpture. We will look at each part of the figure, from the most basic aspects down to the more complex, sequentially creating a more and more realized form. By establishing the most basic shapes first, we will make the final figure all the more realistic, because the details live on a shape that is solid and feels accurate.

Ultimately I consider gesture the most important aspect of making a sculpture or drawing feel compelling. Without it, the figure is still and less than lifelike. Gesture is followed closely by form, the effective representation of a shape in space. Bad form creates anatomy that looks mushy and ill defined. The final tenet, proportion, insures that the figure looks realistic within a generally acceptable set of rules for its relative size. If you have good gesture and form but proportion is tweaked, your work will not look wrong but stylized. To create the sense of a shorter figure you may adjust the proportions of the head and hands to the body, for instance. If the gesture and form are correct, proportion is a visual guide to the size and sometimes the character of the figure.

Anatomical Terminology

I will be using anatomical terms throughout the book where they are applicable. While it is beyond the scope of this book to offer an in-depth study of the physiology of the human body, it is important to have a basic understanding of anatomical terminology. Understanding anatomical terminology assists us in communication about the human form. By understanding what the names are and mean, we can decipher valuable information from other sources like textbooks and anatomical reference materials. Figure 1.14 shows the figure with skin and fat removed, revealing the major muscle groups we will be looking at in this book.

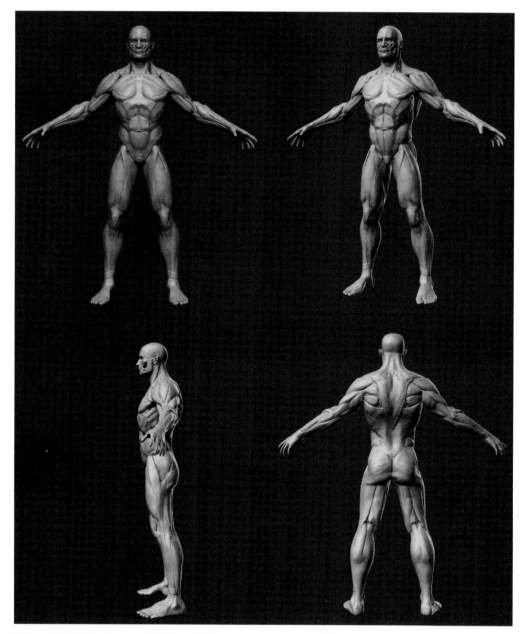

Figure 1.14 *The figure with its underlying anatomy revealed*

Understanding names also helps identify the placement and function of a part. For example, if we know that *distal* means distant from the centerline of the body and *head* refers to the end of a bone, then when we read "the distal head of the humerus," we know it refers to the end of the upper arm bone farthest from the shoulder.

Many anatomical names have Latin or Greek roots, because the earliest anatomists named them using these ancient languages. In modern times it has the added benefit that two doctors of any nationality with different languages can refer to the same part and be understood. They may look complex, but the words have very simple meanings. Once you understand these meanings you will be able to decipher a wealth of information.

The reason I give most often for why it's valuable to learn the names of parts is that it gives you a kind of mental box in which to put information about a part. If I know the name of a muscle, it is easier to remember its placement, shape, and function. Without the name of the muscle, you are dealing with a volume of information about some abstract shape. Again I should also stress that names often carry hints to placement and function in them.

There are some standard anatomical directions, movements, and regions that we will look at first. What follows is a selection of some of the more commonly encountered. These names may seem daunting at first, but just become familiar with them. You will find them used over and over when describing different muscles and bones.

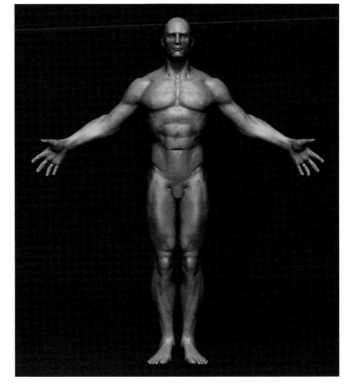

Figure 1.15 *The default position*

Figure 1.15 shows the human body in the default anatomical position. That is standing feet together palms out. We will sculpt our character in a more relaxed pose but it is important to understand that most anatomy books will refer to bones and muscles in this state.

When in this position anything toward the front of the body is called *anterior,* while anything toward the back is called *posterior.* The direction up is called *superior,* while the direction down is called *inferior.* Figure 1.16 shows how these and other directional terms are used in practice.

Let's look at an example of how the naming of a skeletal feature can clue us in to important information. In Figure 1.17 you see the pelvis. The marked bony landmark is an important measure on the figure; it serves as the point from which the front leg muscles radiate. It is called the *iliac spine.* It is more specifically referred to as the *superior anterior iliac spine.* This simply means that it is the superior, toward the top, anterior, toward the front, iliac spine. Once you understand how this apparently abstruse terminology works, the inherent meaning is quite simple.

By knowing this name we can also now infer that there must be a superior posterior iliac spine as well as inferior anterior and inferior posterior iliac spines. Otherwise, there would be no need to name one "the iliac spine on top and in the front." Figure 1.18 shows the posterior superior iliac spine, which is also seen on the surface of the body making dimples at the base of the spine.

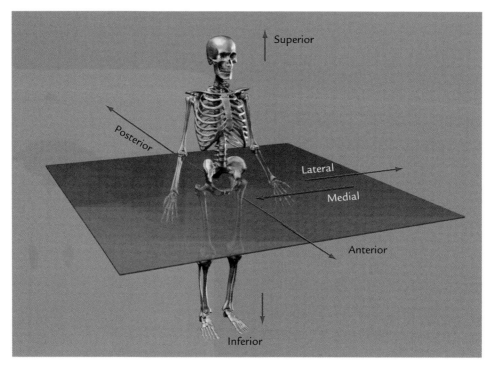

Figure 1.16 The directional planes

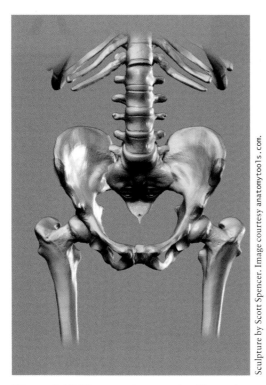

Figure 1.17 The superior anterior iliac spine

As a rule of thumb, if a landmark is defined as being superior, you can infer there is a counterpart that is inferior. The same is true of posterior and anterior. Anatomical names for the bone landmarks can also influence the names of the associated muscles.

Let's look at the scapula. In Figure 1.19 you see the back of the shoulder blade—the posterior surface. The landmark marked on the image is called the spine of the scapula. This is an important landmark on the back of a fleshed figure (Figure 1.20).

The muscles that lie above and below this bone feature are named *Supraspinatus* and *Infraspinatus*, respectively (Figure 1.21). The names simply mean that the Supraspinatus is superior to or above the spine of the scapula, and the Infraspinatus is inferior to or below it. Again we see how the seemingly complex naming translates into very simple terms. Once you understand anatomical direction, you find many muscle names are extremely simple to remember based on this fact.

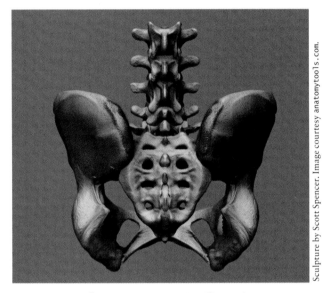

Sculpture by Scott Spencer. Image courtesy anatomytools.com.

Figure 1.18 *The superior posterior iliac spine*

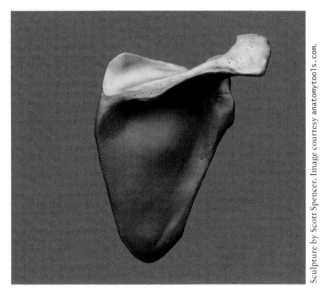

Sculpture by Scott Spencer. Image courtesy anatomytools.com.

Figure 1.19 *The scapula*

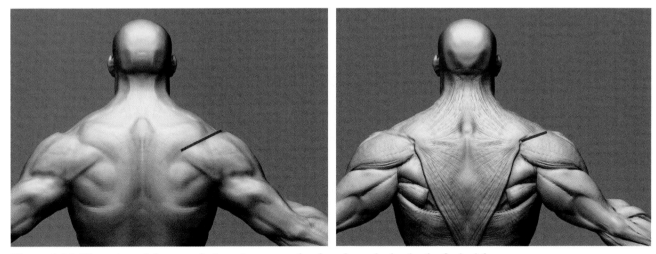

Figure 1.20 *The spine of the scapula is an important landmark on the back of a fleshed figure.*

When talking about muscles we will often refer to origins and insertions, as shown in Figure 1.22.

The *origin* of a muscle is the point at which it originates on the skeleton. Muscles pull toward their origin. An easy way to determine the origin of any muscle is to find the point at which the muscle moves the least. For example, see Figure 1.23. The Pectoralis muscle originates on the sternum and inserts on the humerus or upper arm bone. The head that attaches to the arm has the most range of motion, so it is the *insertion*. The shape of a muscle may change as it moves, but the origin and insertion never change; they are attached to the skeleton. So by knowing these points you understand how to place the muscle in any pose. You also know what direction the muscle pulls in and what its function is. If you know the start and end points of a muscle, deciphering its function is rather simple. Just remember that muscles pull toward the origin, and you will quickly realize the purpose of the muscle in question. Combine this with useful clues contained in the muscle name, and you have a wealth of information about the form in question.

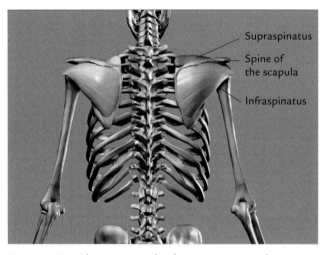

Figure 1.21 The supra- and infra-spinatus muscles

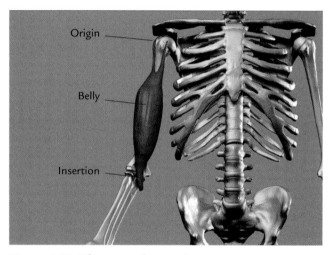

Figure 1.22 The parts of a muscle

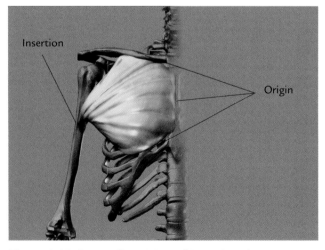

Figure 1.23 Pectoralis origin and insertion

As we discuss each part of the body in this book, we will be looking at the major muscle forms including their origins and insertions. It's important to understand what these terms mean and how they apply, so as we come across them later you will understand their importance. A simple way to remember the difference between origins and insertions is that a muscle pulls in the direction of its origin.

One last point I want to mention here about muscles. As we start sculpting, I will often refer to planes and plane breaks. This is simply a way to define a structure and apply an angular quality to the surface of the figure. For years I considered the muscles to be somewhat soft forms inside the body pressed against each other. It wasn't until I started doing cadaver dissection that it came to my attention that the muscles are very structural bodies that maintain their shapes independent of each other.

The muscles have these specific independent shapes even to the point of having defined angles and planes. Bear this in mind as we work since you want to avoid having a soft blobby figure at all costs. As we refine the muscle forms we will continually give attention to the planes and structural quality of each. This is part and parcel of being aware of the form in our sculpture.

Creating a Base Sculpting Mesh

We are now ready to begin creating our character. To start we will block in a polygon mesh in the proper proportion. This is a very simple block mesh which will serve as a base for all our sculpting. Later in this book we will look at methods of retopologizing this mesh for film or games, as an animation-ready mesh. For now we are only concerned with sculpting and creating a base suitable to support the forms we want to create.

A sculpting mesh differs from an animation mesh in that the topology is not laid out for animation. Instead, a sculpt mesh features evenly spaced, efficient polygon edges that allow for consistent subdivision in ZBrush without allowing the base mesh to define any form on its own. The only aspects we want the sculpt mesh to address are gesture and proportion.

This mesh is purely for sculpting. It is not an animation-ready mesh as seen in Figure 1.24. I find that starting from the most basic mesh allows me the most freedom in sculpting. Sometimes if you have a muscle form edge looped in your base model, it can fight you as you sculpt.

Figure 1.24 *An animation mesh is prepared with edge loops and topology that facilitates UV layout and animation.*

Building a Sculpt Mesh in Maya

In this section we will create our simple base sculpt mesh, using very simple polygon modeling techniques that are applicable to nearly every modeling package on the market as well as Maya. This simple base mesh layout is based on a modeling approach used by Zack Petroc. I thank him for permission to reference it here. See the DVD for a video demonstration of this process. This tutorial describes the key points, but you will gain a much deeper understanding by watching the process in real time in addition to reading these steps. While I recommend following along to better understand how landmarks are placed in space, I have also included the final mesh on the DVD so you may move directly into sculpting in the next chapter. See Figure 1.25 for an idea of just how simple the resulting mesh will be. Figure 1.26 shows how even from a very simple base, complex shapes can be sculpted with ease.

1. Begin by loading your polygon modeling software. In this case we will use Maya, but the same simple steps apply to nearly all packages on the market. From the DVD load the `measurePlanes.obj` file. This object consists of eight planes, corresponding to each head measure (Figure 1.27). This will guide us in placing major forms in the base model as well as making proportional decisions for the remainder of the project. I have added the measure planes to a layer in Maya so I can show and hide them for clarity as we work.

The instructions in this procedure assume that, like most ZBrush users, you're also familiar with Maya and basic polygon modeling techniques.

---

2. Save your file.
3. Create a polygon cube by selecting Create → Polygon Primitives → Cube. Make sure Subdivisions Width, Height, and Depth are set to 1 so each side has only one face. Move this cube up so it lies between the planes marked 4 and 5. You will need to scale it down so the top vertices lie on the line marked 5. This cube will represent the pelvis of the figure, and we will extrude all other geometry from it (Figure 1.28).

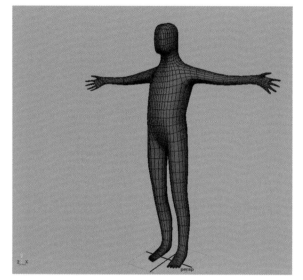

Figure 1.25 The final base mesh

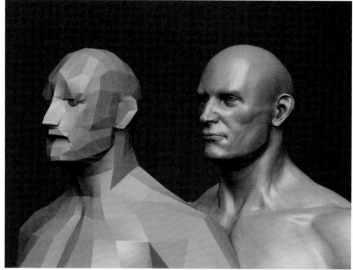

Figure 1.26 This image illustrates how much form can be sculpted from the simplest base mesh.

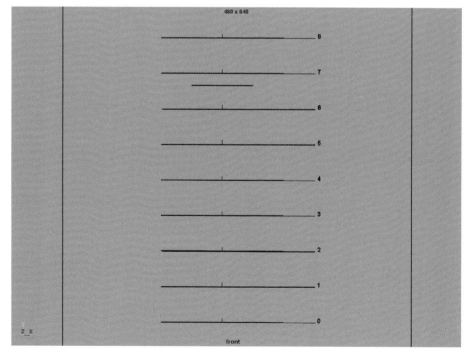

Figure 1.27 Measure planes

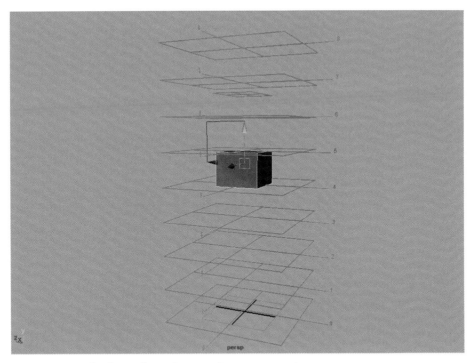

Figure 1.28 *The first cube in front and perspective view*

4. Keep the bottom of this cube aligned with the fourth head measure. This is the midline of the figure and is equivalent to the ischium or pubic bone of the skeleton (Figure 1.29). Select the top face and extrude up twice, ending at the shorter line between lines 7 and 6. This shorter line is one third of a head measure from the top. This is the highest point of the neck, on the back of the figure, corresponding to the 7th cervical vertebra and, on the front of the figure, to the first rib. These can be seen in Figure 1.30. Scale down this last extrusion. This will be the start of the neck.

5. As shown in Figure 1.31, extrude this face up to the bottom of the first head measure and then again to the top. This will represent the neck and head of the figure.

6. We will now cut a centerline for the body. Select one of the edges running lengthwise down the body (Figure 1.32).

7. Control-right-click and select Edge Ring Utilities from the Marking menu. From the second menu select To Edge Ring and Split, using the Marking menus for splitting edge rings in Maya as shown in Figure 1.33. So we can mirror the model across the middle, and cut a centerline down the model, as seen in Figure 1.34. Using the Edit Mesh → Insert Edge Loop tool, insert a loop on either side of the center edge (Figure 1.35).

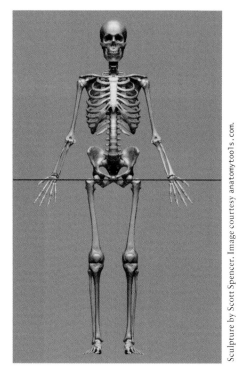

Figure 1.29 *The skeletal ischium and the 4th head measure line*

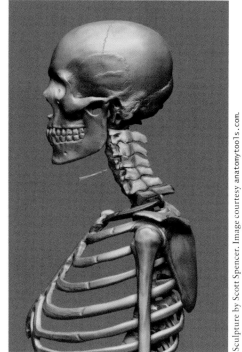

Figure 1.30 *The 1st rib and the 7th cervical vertebra*

Figure 1.31 *Extruding and scaling the neck*

Figure 1.32 *Selecting an edge to form the centerline*

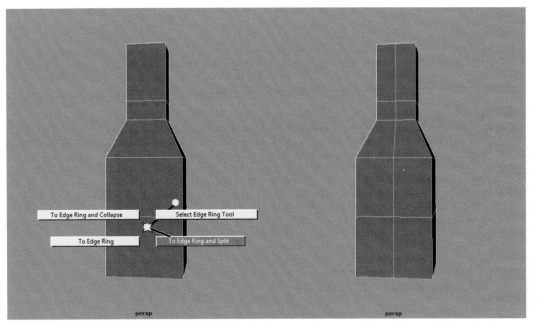

Figure 1.33 *Marking menu sequence*

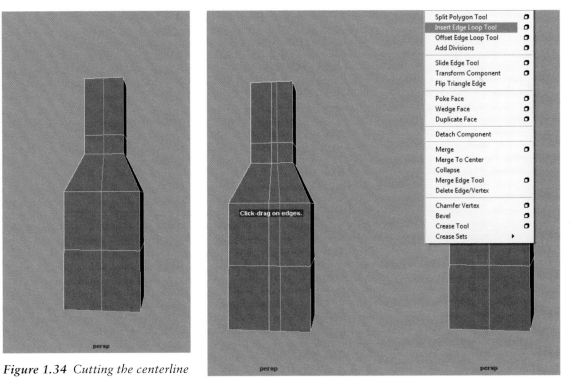

Figure 1.34 *Cutting the centerline*

Figure 1.35 *Adding loops*

8. Extrude the legs down by selecting the face pictured and extrude to the ground plane (Figure 1.36(a)). Repeat the extrusion in the area pictured in Figure 1.36(b). The two edges at the knee are important. The bottom edge at the second head measure represents an anatomical landmark called the *tibial tuberosity* (Figure 1.37). This is the bottom-most border of the perceived structure of the knee, although it is part of the shin bone. We will talk more about the knee in Chapter 6.

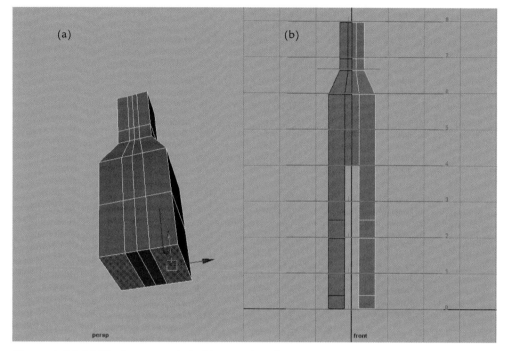

Figure 1.36 *(a) The legs extruded, (b) repeating the extrusion*

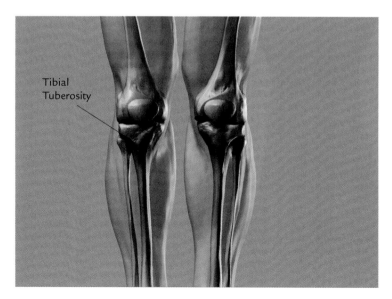

Figure 1.37 *The tibial tuberosity on the skeleton and overlay*

9. At this point cut an edge along the side of the body. This will bisect the form from the side view as seen in Figure 1.38(a). Select the vertices of the leg from the knee down, and scale and move them back in the Z axis as shown in Figure 1.38(b).

10. To create the foot, arrange the existing edges so there are three faces toward the front of the foot, as shown in Figure 1.39(a). This configuration will allow us to extrude five toes from the minimal number of edges and is a technique I learned from Zack Petroc. Select these three faces and extrude them forward, as shown in Figure 1.39(b). See the chapter video for an in-depth look at this process.

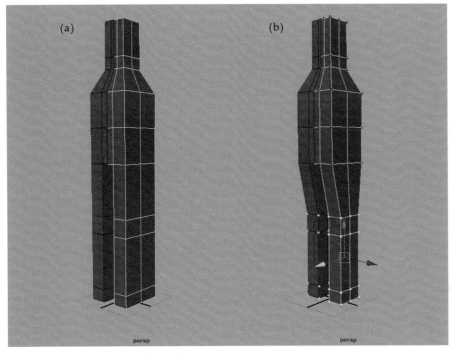

Figure 1.38 *(a) Adding edges, (b) moving verts*

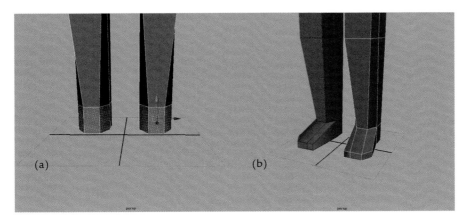

Figure 1.39 *(a) Foot faces, (b) extruding the foot*

At this point we have the base geometry for the trunk and legs, but if we look at the figure in profile, you can see it is essentially a column (Figure 1.40). We will start now to edit the positions of the vertices in Z to start to suggest the profile of the figure.

1. Add edge loops and move the points only in the Z direction to start shaping the body (Figure 1.41). By selecting and moving points back, we can create the taper of the legs. At this stage also note the S curves and alternating rhythms of the body, which are starting to take shape. To see this process in full, be sure to watch the accompanying DVD.

2. We will now add a loop in the crotch area. By adding this in the geometry it helps us define the tricky transition from the legs into the pelvis later on as we sculpt. This is the simplest approach and allows the most freedom later down the line. Cut two edges at the pelvis as seen in Figure 1.42. Delete the loops shown in Figure 1.43. Now draw a connecting edge to allow the faces at the centerline of the body to turn (Figure 1.44).

3. At this point, even out the edges to continue to define the volumes of the body (Figure 1.45). The idea is to use the least number of edges possible to define shapes and volumes. More edges now means fewer subdivisions later in ZBrush.

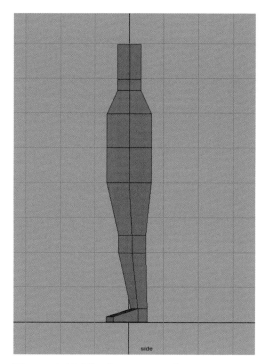

Figure 1.40 The figure as a column

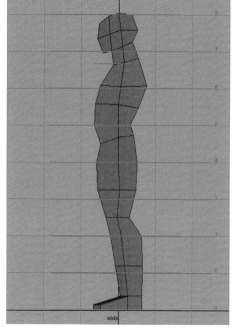

Figure 1.41 Shaping the body in profile

4. Adding the arms is as simple as selecting the face pictured in Figure 1.46. The placement of our vertices so far creates a convenient edge that will run from the bottom of the pectoral muscles in the front of the figure to the back of the armpit (also shown in Figure 1.46). We will extrude the arms out to the sides now but relax them a bit later in the sculpting phase. This will keep the figure in a "neutral pose," but also allow us to add some gesture and spring to the arms.

An important thing to note: The arm span on a eight-head figure is equal to the height (Figure 1.47).

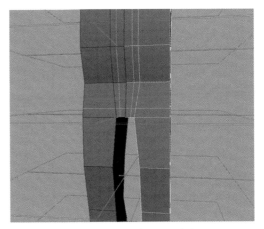

Figure 1.42 Creating the crotch loops

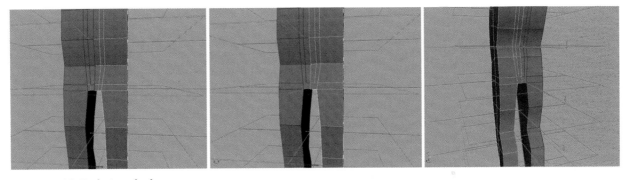

Figure 1.43 Deleting the loops

5. The arms are built in the anatomically neutral position knows as *supination*. An easy way to remember this position is the way you position your arm to hold a bowl of soup. In this position the flexors and extensors of the forearm are relatively straight as opposed to their position when rotated (Figure 1.48). In this phase I extrude the fingers and toes, taking care to place edges at each knuckle. This process is best shown on screen rather than described in text. I encourage you to watch the accompanying video to see this in action.

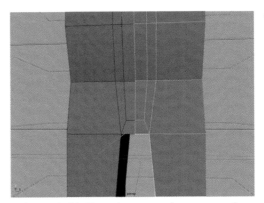

Figure 1.44 Drawing new edges at crotch

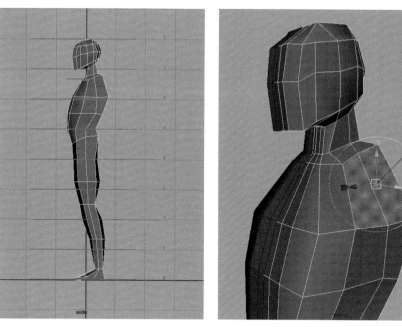

Figure 1.45 *Distribute edges*   **Figure 1.46** *Select this face to extrude arms*

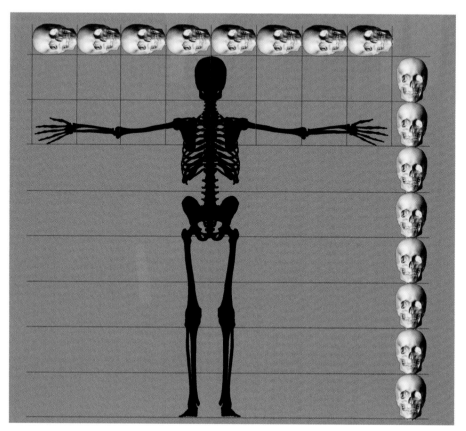

Figure 1.47 *Arm span vs. height*

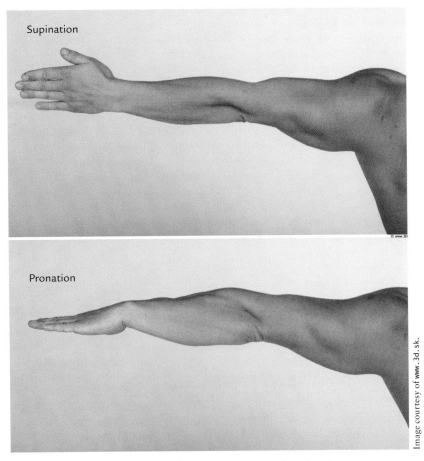

Image courtesy of www.3d.sk.

Figure 1.48 *The forearm muscles in pronation and supination*

6. It is important to be sure the geometry is as clean as possible. If we export a mesh to ZBrush with holes or otherwise erroneous geometry that went unnoticed, it can be very difficult to fix once we have started sculpting. Use the custom polygon display to check for border edges and unmerged polygons. In Maya click Display → Polygons → Custom Polygon Display. Make sure Border Edges is checked (Figure 1.49). This will highlight any unmerged edges or holes in the mesh.

7. To resolve any other geometry problems, use the Cleanup function, found under the Polygons menu. Cleanup will remove lamina faces and other problematic geometry errors that may have cropped up while we model. Figure 1.50 shows the Cleanup Options window.

8. Now delete the instance and duplicate again as a copy. Merge the two halves and make sure all vertices along the edge are wielded. Average the vertices by going to Mesh → Average Vertices to display the window shown in Figure 1.51. This operation helps smooth the forms and soften any remaining facets.

Figure 1.49 *The Custom Polygon Display Options window*

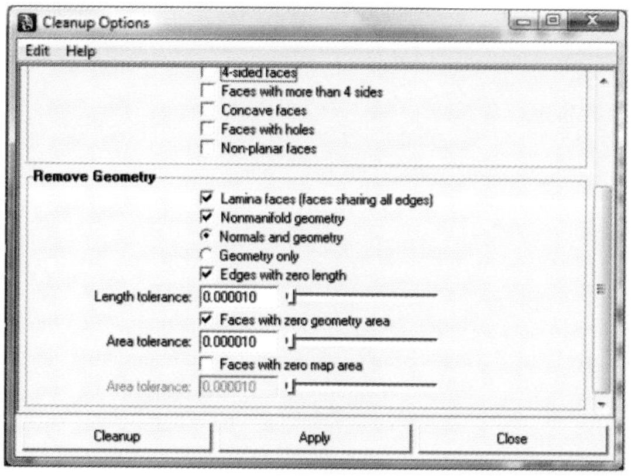

Figure 1.50 *The Cleanup Options window*

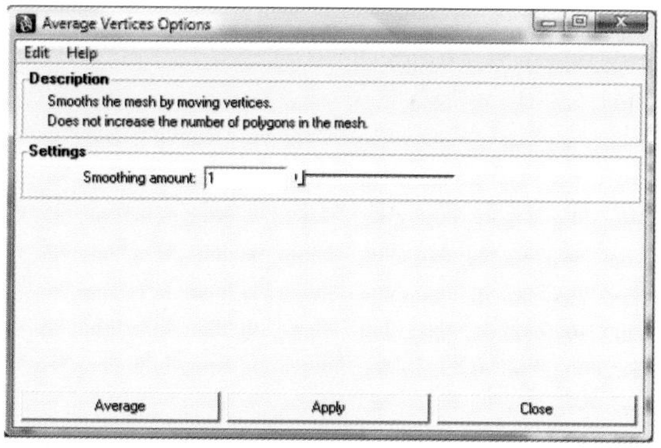

Figure 1.51 *The Average Vertices Options window*

We are now ready to export this model to ZBrush and begin sculpting.

If you would rather jump right into sculpting, I have included this base mesh on the DVD, but I highly recommend following the process of building the model at least once. At this stage you are ready to move on to Chapter 2. However, if you prefer to generate your base mesh in ZBrush, the following section illustrates this process using the ZBrush mesh-generating tool known as ZSpheres.

Building a Sculpt Mesh in ZBrush

In this section we will look at a method of starting your sculpt mesh entirely in ZBrush using its powerful polygon model-generation tool, called the ZSphere. Instead of moving points and edges in space as one would do in Maya or other 3D applications, in ZBrush meshes are built by creating and connecting spherical volumes (Figure 1.52). For more information on ZSphere modeling please see my *ZBrush Character Creation: Advanced Digital Sculpting* (Sybex, 2008). ZSpheres in ZBrush 3.5 has been vastly improved from previous versions. There have been some significant changes in the way ZBrush calculates the skin from your ZSphere model. While the new version, called ZSpheres2, creates a model more accurate to the shape of your ZSphere chain, the original skinning method is still included in ZBrush 3.5 since it is still more effective for some applications like making topology loops for eyes and mouths. We will look at how to create both types of skins in this section, examining their relative strengths.

To help us place the masses and maintain accurate proportions, we will use the head measure guide ZTool included on the DVD. To load this into ZBrush, follow the demonstration video of this process, also on the DVD.

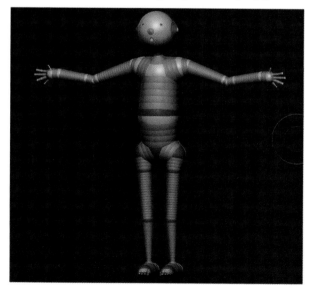

Figure 1.52 *An example of a ZSphere model*

ZSpheres have the benefit of being a fast and efficient method of creating your base mesh. They are easy to create, faster than polygon modeling, and they will automatically polygroup the model into logical sections. ZSpheres are also easier to re-pose and adjust than a polygon mesh in Maya. Things like fingers and toes are far easier to create with ZSphere chains than standard polygon extrusion.

The drawback to ZSpheres is that they can be limiting when you are trying to exert more specific control over edge placement. In our example this is apparent where the legs meet the torso. In the Maya model we have the ability to create a more even transition of edges from the trunk into the legs, while the ZBrush model simply splits into two legs extruded from the body. Both will work fine for sculpting, but as you start building more characters and sculpting in ZBrush, you will discover the kind of base model you prefer to work with.

For this section we will use the head measure guide as a subtool to help us place the ZSpheres and create a figure in the correct general proportion. Each line represents a head measure on an eight-head tall figure. The first set of lines represents the head itself. Each mark down represents one more head measure. The shorter line between the first and second head measures marks the point of the shoulders on the figure.

1. From the Tool menu load the `measureguides.ztl` ZTool. We will use this model as a guide to help keep the figure's basic proportions in line. Each line represents a head measure from the floor to eight heads tall. The smaller line represents the level of the shoulders (Figure 1.53).

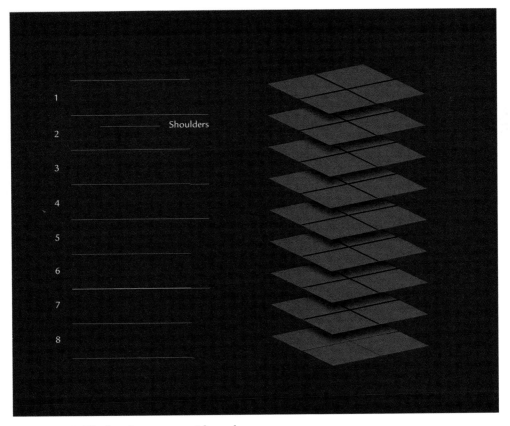

Figure 1.53 *The head measure guide tool*

2. With the tool loaded, go to Tool → Subtool and click the Append button. Select the ZSphere tool from the popup menu to append it as a subtool of the head measure guide. Make sure the ZSphere is the active subtool by clicking on it before you proceed. Also, make sure perspective is off by pressing the P hotkey. We will want to build this mesh in orthographic view.

   You will now have the eight-head measure guide loaded as a ZTool with a ZSphere as a subtool.

5. Move the ZSphere so it lies on the 3rd head measure. You can move the ZSphere by pressing the W hotkey to enter move mode, or by selecting Move from the top of the screen. You will also want to scale the ZSphere down so it is about the size of one head unit or the spaces between the lines on the head measure guide. Scaling is preformed by selecting Scale from the top of the screen or pressing the E hotkey.

   Make sure you are in draw mode by pressing the Q key or selecting Draw from the top of the screen. Press the X key to enter X symmetry mode. This will turn your cursor into two green dots. You know you are centered on the ZSphere when the two dots become one. Rotate to the bottom view of the ZSphere. You will need to enable transparency on the right side of the screen to see through the head measures to the ZSphere. As of ZBrush 3.5, you can adjust the transparency effect by going to Preferences → Draw, and turning off GhostClearTransparency. There are also several sliders here that can further refine the transparency effect to your liking. Make sure your two dots join into one on the surface of the ZSphere, and draw a new ZSphere on the bottom of the floor by click-dragging on the first sphere. If you press Shift while drawing, the sphere will become the same size as the original. Rotate to the top view and repeat the process (Figure 1.54).

6. Press the A key to preview the mesh. Your mesh should look like Figure 1.55. Press A again to exit preview mode, and move the bottom sphere to the 4th head measure line and the top sphere to the shoulder line as seen in Figure 1.56. If you have problems seeing the head measure lines, turn off transparency so they become opaque again.

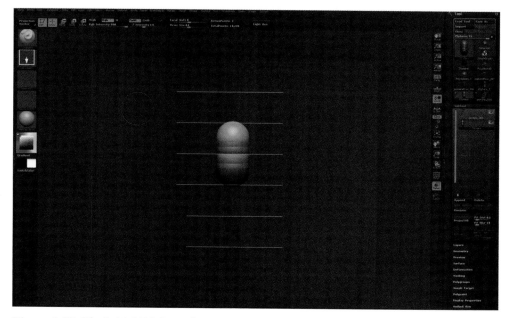

Figure 1.54 The initial ZSphere chain

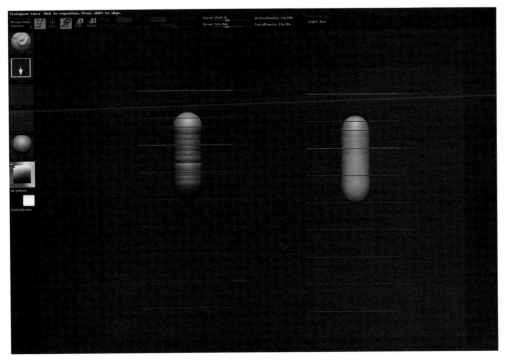

Figure 1.55 The capsule mesh after moving the ZSpheres to the correct head measure lines

7. Under Tool → Adaptive Skin, turn on Classic Skinning. Set Density to 4, Ires to 3, Mbr to 91, and Mc to On. This insures the best results from the polygon skin. Feel free to experiment with these values and use anything that you feel makes your volumes better. The important thing in this tutorial is that the proportions remain consistent.

8. Add child spheres for the shoulders and pelvis as seen in Figure 1.56. Be sure to check your progress with the A key. Since we are using the new ZSpheres2 skinning, by default the mesh should conform exactly to the spheres you see on screen.

9. Draw ZSpheres for the hands, feet, and head. Switch to move mode with the W key and pull them away from the body (Figure 1.57). Drag the foot spheres down to the 8th head measure. Drag the wrist spheres to just below the 4th head measure. Once the wrists are placed at the point just below the waist, we know the arm length is accurate. Switch to rotate mode with the R hotkey, and clicking between the shoulder and wrist spheres, rotate the arms up as seen in Figure 1.57b. This is because the arm span is equal to the total height of the figure. If we place the wrist just below the waist then rotate them up into position, we can be sure the arms are the correct length once the hands are added.

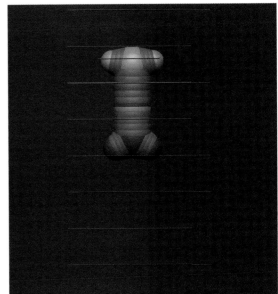

Figure 1.56 Creating the shoulders and pelvis

10. Press the A key and check your progress. Your figure should look like Figure 1.58.

11. Add spheres for the elbows and knees so your figure looks like Figure 1.59. Make sure to place the knee ZSphere just above the 6th head line. Scale down the wrist and ankle ZSpheres slightly to give a taper to the limb. At this stage you may want to turn off visibility on the head measure subtool so you can see the fingers and toes as you work on them. Visibility is disabled by clicking the eyeball icon next to the subtool in the Subtool menu (Figure 1.60).

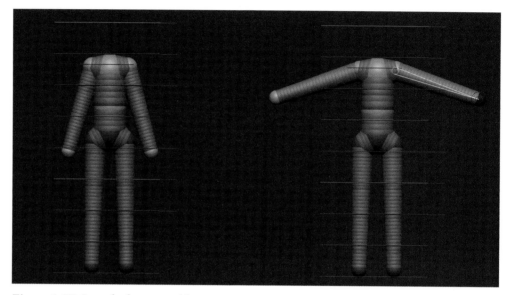

Figure 1.57 Stretched arms and legs

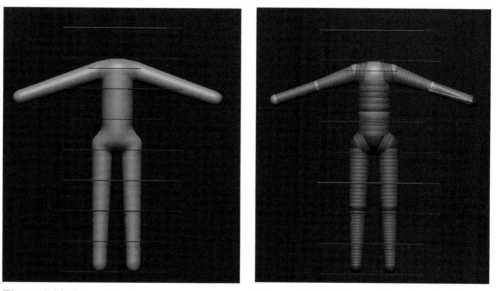

Figure 1.58 Figure preview

Figure 1.59 Adding spheres for the elbows and knees

12. Create a ZSphere chain for the foot and heel (Figure 1.61).
13. To add fingers, draw five small child spheres on the end of the arm as seen in Figure 1.62.

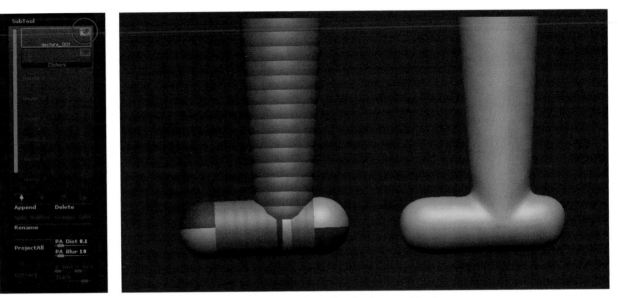

Figure 1.60 Click this icon to turn off visibility on the head measure subtool.

Figure 1.61 Creating a ZSphere chain for the foot and heel

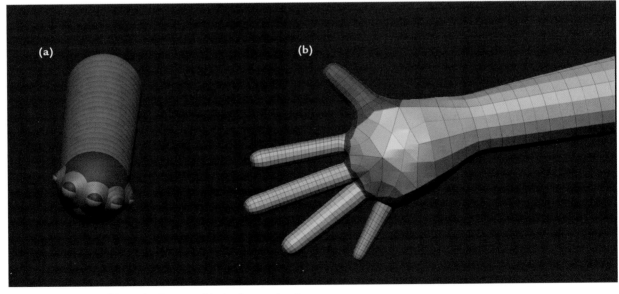

Figure 1.62 (a) Adding the fingers; (b) the fingers in place

14. Move the thumb down and arrange the finger spheres in a natural position. Add another sphere to the end of each finger and pull them out. Remember, you can press Shift while dragging to make a new sphere the exact same size as its parent. Add a ZSphere to the wrist, and scale it down slightly so the arm tapers before the start of the hand. Press A to preview your mesh. Your hand should look like Figure 1.62b.

15. Repeat the same process for the toes (Figure 1.63). The shape may look strange now, but the odd forms can be corrected in seconds with the Move brush once we start sculpting. In addition it is far easier to pose and create gesture in the figures using ZSpheres than it is when extruding faces in Maya.

    Now we want to add the head and neck.

16. Restore the visibility on the measure guides. Turn on transparency, and from the top view add a neck ZSphere on the shoulders. Draw another ZSphere on the neck and move it up to the first head measure as shown in Figure 1.64.

17. At this stage add two ZSpheres between the head and shoulders by clicking between them. Scale these two spheres down to create a neck. Add small spheres for the eyes, nose, and mouth as seen in Figure 1.65.

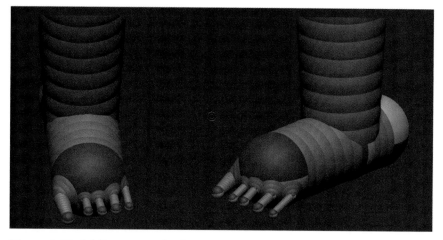

Figure 1.63 Adding toes to the feet

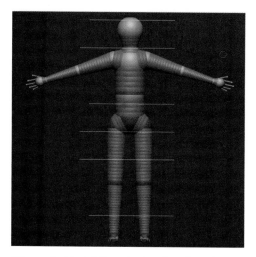

Figure 1.64 Adding the head and neck

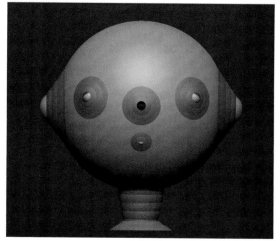

Figure 1.65 Adding spheres for the facial features

These smaller spheres will create topology loops to represent the inner eyes and mouth as well as the nose and ears. If you preview this mesh, you will have something like Figure 1.66.

The effect of these spheres differs from what you can do using Classic Skinning. Under Adaptive Skin enable Classic Skinning mode, set Ires to 3 and Mbr to 9. Move the eye and mouth spheres in slightly so they become holes in the ZSphere head (Figure 1.67). Now when you preview, you will have recessed loops in the mesh for the eyes, nose, and mouth.

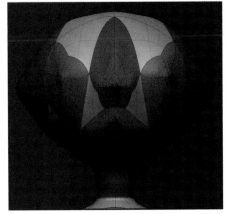

Figure 1.66 *The ZSpheres2 facial loops skinned*

When adding geometry for facial features, as we have just done, this is where you must decide on which skinning method works best for you. The default skinning in ZBrush ZSpheres2 will look much closer to the ZSphere chain you create for your figure, but it will not handle the countersunk ZSpheres in a predictable manner. That is one reason why there is a Classic Skinning button under the Adaptive Skin menu. Experiment with both skinning methods. For this tutorial I used Classic Skinning with the following settings to make the edge loops for the facial features.

If you use the new ZSpheres2 skinning method, make sure you do not countersink the spheres for the facial features into the head. ZSpheres2 does not support countersink, and this may cause undesirable behavior.

Figure 1.68 shows this ZSphere model under both skinning methods in ZBrush Classic and ZSpheres2. Notice that the Classic Skinning gives you more accurate facial loops for sculpting the eyes, nose, and mouth while the default ZSpheres2 skinning seen on the left follows the ZSphere chain more accurately but does not recess the topology for the face. The edge loops are still there in ZSpheres2; you will just have to manually press them into the head when you start sculpting. Both skins will work fine; it is entirely up to your own preference when working with the base mesh. Figure 1.69 shows the facial topology of Classic Skinning and ZSpheres2 so you can see how the underlying loops are conformed to the surface.

Remember, if you use Classic Skinning, the volume of the limbs will no longer follow the ZSphere chain as you have made it. To rectify this, simply add more Zspheres between the joints to help define the forms as seen in Figure 1.70. It is also important to note that the hands and feet will generate topology differently between the two skinning methods. Try both and decide which mesh is more appealing to you as a base on which to sculpt. Please see the DVD for a video demonstrating both ZSphere approaches and the nuances of each skinning method.

18. Save your Zsphere model by clicking Tool → Save As. make sure to save the Zsphere model as well as the Adaptive Skin separately. We will now generate a polygon mesh from the ZSphere model. Under the Adaptive Skin menu, click the Make Adaptive Skin button. You will notice a new ZTool listed in the tool menu prefixed with the name Skin. Select this tool. This is the polygon mesh generated from the ZSphere model. Save this tool separately from the ZSphere model in case you want to revisit the original ZSphere chain for further edits in the future. By using the Move brush you can quickly move the mesh into a more accurate shape of a basic human, as seen in Figure 1.71. Notice the eyes and mouth have been pressed in and the hands and feet shaped. This is done entirely with the Move brush to help refine the figure for the next chapter. The very simple Zsphere model can quickly be refined into a more accurate human form using the Move brush alone (Figure 1.72). Please see the DVD for copies of all the ZSphere and Adaptive Skin models as well as multiple variants of the ZSphere skeleton.

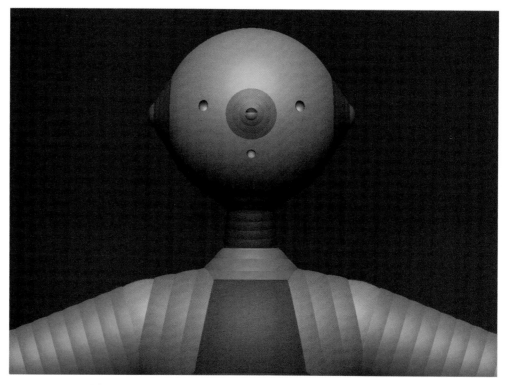

Figure 1.67 *Adding spheres for the eyes, nose, ears, and mouth*

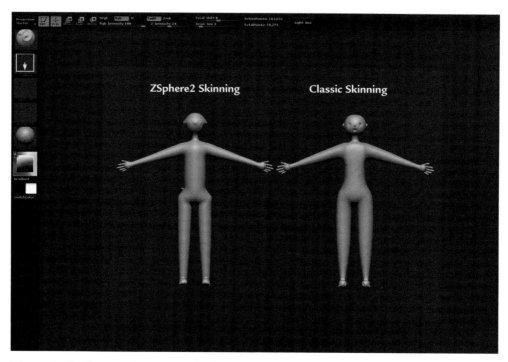

Figure 1.68 *The two skinning methods, Zspheres2 and Classic*

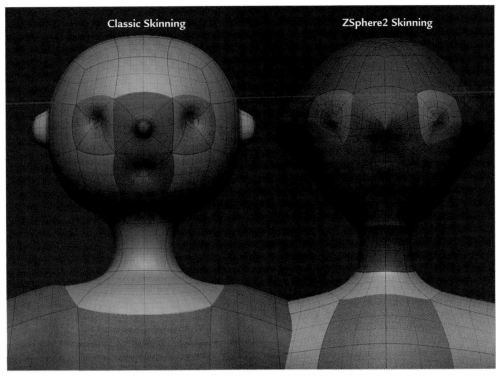

Figure 1.69 *The facial topology seen under both skinning methods*

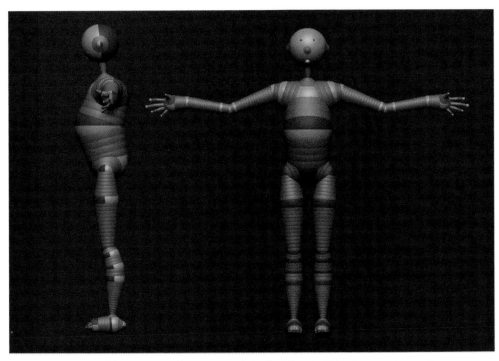

Figure 1.70 *By adding more spheres to each limb, Classic Skinning can be made to more accurately represent the volumes of the figure.*

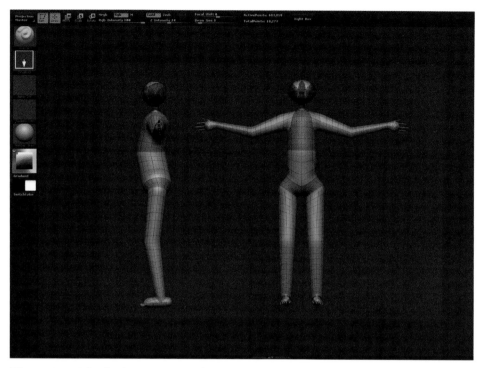

Figure 1.71 *The final armature mesh*

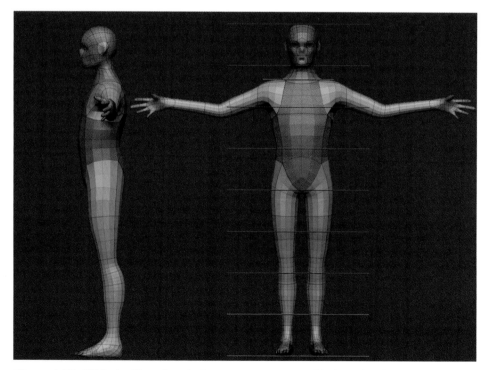

Figure 1.72 *With the Move brush the armature can quickly be refined into a human shape.*

For more information about using ZSpheres, see *ZBrush Character Creation*.

See the video for this lesson on the DVD for a complete walk-through of this process. This represents the most basic form on which to start sculpting. It doesn't look special now, but it will be very useful to us since our base is built with accurate proportions in mind.

ZSketching

ZBrush also includes a new ZSphere based mesh tool called ZSketching. While this is a unique and powerful tool for generating models with a medium level of surface form quickly, I do not use it in this chapter to generate the sculpting model. This is because the tool is stroke based and lends itself to a more involved process of building up muscle forms with strokes rather than generating a quick and simple gesture figure. ZSketching also requires you take extra steps to generate an Adaptive Skin with multiple subdivision levels. I feel that we will learn more in the next two sections by sculpting our shapes directly in the simple block in mesh. ZSpheres and Polygons lend themselves to forcing you to think in very simple global terms about the overall gesture and proportion of the figure. If you would like to take a more stroke-based approach to creating an ecorche base mesh, I recommend checking out the videos on ZSketching available from www.pixologic.com.

What's Next?

In the next chapter we will discuss sculpting silhouettes, planes, and plane breaks. By looking at the figure in terms of its external profiles, we can establish important landmarks without being distracted by too much detail too early. We can also take this opportunity to strengthen the gesture and rhythm of our figure.

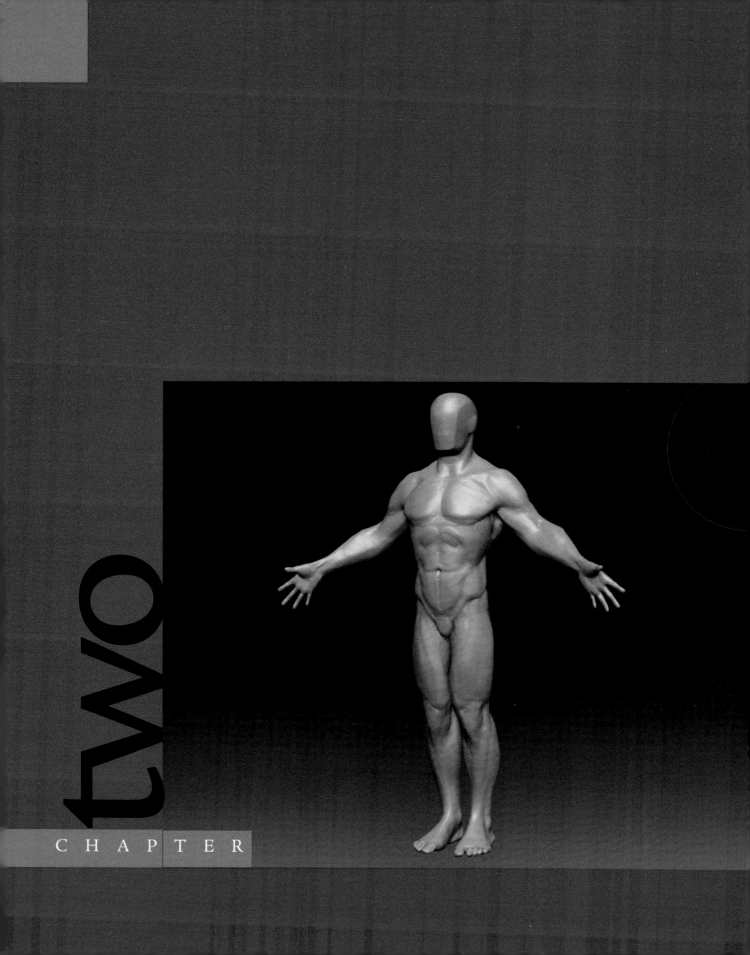

two

Gesture and Masses

As this book progresses, *you will be examining the body of our character by specific parts. That is to say, you will look at the arm independently of the leg in different chapters. Although this is necessary for a survey of sculpting the figure in detail, it is important to understand the figure as a whole before you begin. Think of this as a jigsaw puzzle. When you start a puzzle, you don't begin examining individual parts; instead, you look at the picture on the front of the box. This chapter is about that overall picture. Once you have a grasp of this overall form, you can move on to examining the aggregate parts of the body. Just as you focus on big shapes first and then work down into the finer details, you need to be able to see the figure as its overall outline.*

In this chapter, you will be looking at the figure as a whole unit together. Instead of looking just at the relationships between bone and muscle landmarks, you will sculpt the shape the entire figure makes.

Note that I will avoid most proper names of muscles and bones in this chapter. When discussing the clavicles, for example, I will defer to common usage and call them collar bones. This is so as not to overwhelm you if you're not fully comfortable with some of the more technical names for the parts of the body. As we progress into later chapters, I'll introduce the proper nomenclature for bones and muscles, but I thought that this chapter was best left simple so you can focus on the process of making shapes.

Looking at the Figure as a Whole

You must understand the overall shapes and major mass relationships of the normal human anatomy before you can push that into a heroic figure (Figure 2.1). You can stretch the limits even further into fantasy but keep your work grounded in some realism, as shown in the werewolf in Figure 2.2.

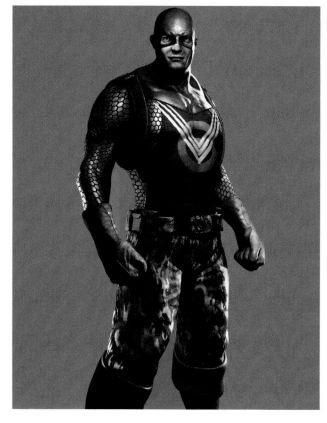

Figure 2.1 A heroic figure

Figure 2.2 Fantasy characters like this werewolf work best when the anatomy has some basis in reality.

Crests and Valleys

Crests and valleys are the points in the figure outline that are high or low. By knowing where on the outline the lines crest or valley, you can more quickly and accurately sculpt a human figure. Figure 2.3 points out the *crests*, or points where the silhouette is highest, and points out the *valleys*, the points where it is the lowest. The place where two lines meet in a crest or valley I call a *break*. By sculpting a figure with attention to the silhouette, you are working from the biggest shapes down to the smallest. The most valuable piece of advice I have been given as an artist is to always focus on the most basic aspects of the figure first and foremost, and only then refine finer and finer forms until you arrive at the final figure. It is a natural inclination to jump into details too soon, and we have to make a conscious effort to avoid that.

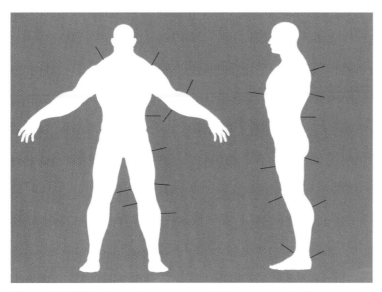

Figure 2.3 *This figure shows many of the crests and valleys as seen in the silhouette of the figure.*

These crests and valleys will guide your hands as you place anatomical forms internally. For example, in Figure 2.4 you can see the crest and valley in the shoulder. It is important to understand the gesture and inclination of this line. If you look further at the shaded view of the same sculpture, you can see how a valley is created by the Deltoid, or shoulder, muscle inserting in front of the Triceps muscle at the back of the arm (Figure 2.5). These muscle insertions are internal forms that combine to create the silhouette you are accustomed to seeing. By keeping an accurate silhouette in mind, you can maintain a direction while you sculpt. Having a goal in mind always makes the process of sculpting flow easier. There are times when many artists, including me, may find themselves moving points around on the surface, trying to "make it look right." Often in these moments it is best to step back and examine the figure from the silhouette inward.

Figure 2.4 *On the shoulder of the figure, note the crests and valleys in the outline.*

Figure 2.5 *The same figure in shaded view; see how the internal forms combine to create the outline shown in Figure 2.4.*

Plane and Profile Analysis

By examining the planes and profiles of the figure, you can further understand how the different basic shapes interlock and form the figure. In Figure 2.6, you see a basic eight-head model human rendered in a planar form by simply using the Pinch and Flatten brushes in ZBrush. You may also use the Clay Finish and Polish brushes to accomplish this process. I do not recommend trying to use the Planar brushes for this tutorial, as they are more suited to creating chiseled edges based on a specific normal and do not lend themselves to the sketching quality of this process.

As you are working, always be aware of the crests and valleys of the silhouette as well as the crests in the internal forms, because the plane changes on the three-dimensional forms of the body.

Keep in mind as you work how the skeleton influences these forms. Figure 2.7 shows the same planed figure with the skeleton visible as an overlay. Notice how the clavicles, knees, anterior crests of the pelvis, and rib cage come close to the surface and influence the shape of the body directly. We will be examining these skeletal landmarks in detail throughout the book.

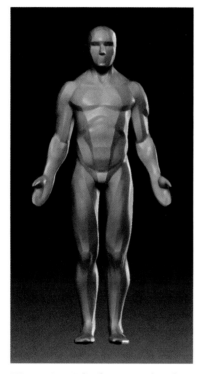

Figure 2.6 The figure rendered in planes

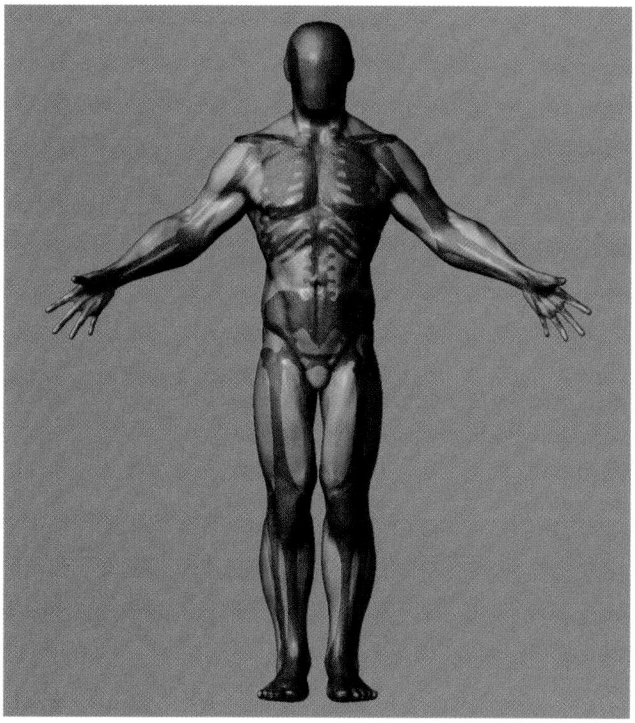

Figure 2.7 The planed figure with a skeleton overlay

Sculpting a Basic Figure

This tutorial is intended to guide you through sculpting a rough representation of the figure. This model will be the basis for all the following chapters in the book. You shouldn't be as concerned with the internal forms here as you are in establishing a relationship between the masses of the body and the interlocking of their shapes. As you work, constantly try to maintain an accurate silhouette. Also note that an exercise like this needs to be repeated often to be the most beneficial. Learning about sculpting the figure is so fascinating for me because of the many layers of understanding you can gain each time you work. If you return to this exercise and sculpt the rough figure again after having completed the book, you will find you understand the shapes you create in a different way and ideally learn more from your own work in the process.

Please be sure to check the DVD for a complete video of this entire chapter's tutorial.

For this tutorial, you will use the Maya base mesh created in the first chapter. Load the Maya mesh you created and use this as a starting point. I have created a a ready-to-load ZTool with the measure planes as a subtool to help check proportions as you work. You can load this from the Chapter 2 folder on the DVD.

You will use a limited palette of ZBrush brushes in this tutorial. Table 2.1 lists the brushes to be used along with each one's function.

Table 2.1: Brushes Used in the Gesture Sculpt

Brush	Description
Standard	The Standard brush pulls the surface straight out from the center of the brush radius. It is a popular general-purpose tool.
Move	The Move brush allows you to shift areas of the mesh as if pulling on taffy or clay. It is valuable for making large shape changes, especially to the silhouette. Tip: Hold down the Alt key to pull directly along the surface normal.
Claytubes	The Claytubes brush is a variant of the Clay brush. It adds material in a flattened, rough application, much like lumping wet clay on the surface. I find this brush valuable for building up a form. Make sure to adjust the brush embed setting. I work between 0 and 10.
Flatten	The Flatten brush flattens the area beneath the brush falloff. This is valuable for adding planes and other structural forms to the surface. Dial down the ZIntensity to between 15 and 20.
Pinch	Pinch pulls edges in toward the center of the brush. It is useful especially in conjunction with Flatten to create sharp plane breaks.
Inflate	The Inflate brush pulls faces out along their surface normals. This makes for an "inflated" look to the brush stroke. This brush can be useful especially for making shapes that swell against each other, but be careful because overuse can create a bloated-looking surface.
Clay Finish	The Clay Finish brush is a hybrid between Flatten and Polish. It is particularly good for introducing planes and taking down the noise created on the surface by the Claytubes brushes.
Clay polish	The polish brushes are similar to the Flatten and Clay Finish brushes. They take down surface noise and help to create planes in the sculpt.

Getting Started

Take the following steps to get started sculpting a basic figure:

1. Import the Maya mesh by going to the Tool menu and selecting the Polymesh Star tool from the Tool palette. This is a generic 3D mesh tool that allows you to import other models into ZBrush. With the star selected, click Tool ➤ Import, and browse to the CD or the folder where you saved your Maya export. This will import the model into the Tool palette.

2. Draw the mesh on the canvas, and enter edit mode with the T hotkey (Figure 2.8).

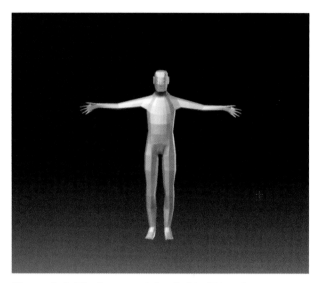

Figure 2.8 *The base mesh loaded in ZBrush*

You will be using the Claytubes brush extensively in this exercise, so you will want to begin with several subdivision levels. Claytubes is one of the Clay brushes that come with ZBrush. These brushes add to the surface in a very gestural manner, similar to soft clay on a sculpture. They don't have the same bloating effect as the Standard and Inflate brushes. For this reason I like to use the Clay brushes to build up form. They tend to work best with several subdivision levels rather than at the lower divisions.

3. Add three subdivisions to the ZTool by selecting Tool ➤ Geometry ➤ Divide or by pressing the Ctrl+D hotkey.

4. Select the Claytubes brush from the Brush palette, and you are ready to begin sculpting.

As you can see from the silhouette view (Figure 2.9), there is little detail in the outlines of this figure. If you build based on the image planes provided, the proportion will be correct, but the profiles will be as simple as possible. This tutorial will show you how to sculpt with attention to the profiles.

Throughout this tutorial you will switch to silhouette view often. To do this, you'll use the Flat Color material (informally known as a *shader*). One of the standard ZBrush Startup materials (Figure 2.10), Flat Color, will remove all shading information and show just the flat color of the object.

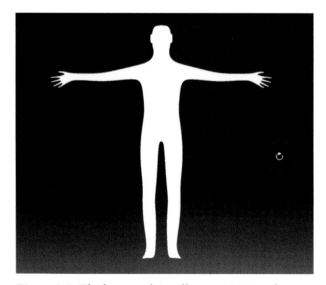

Figure 2.9 *The base mesh in silhouette. Notice the relative lack of profile detail.*

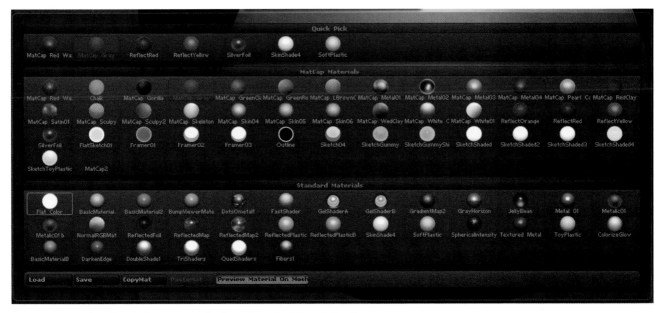

Figure 2.10 *The Flat Color material selected in the Material palette*

5. To select the Flat Color material, simply click the Material palette icon on the left dock, and from the flyout menu select Flat Color.
   To simplify moving quickly between the Basic Material and Flat Color, it's a good idea to use a hotkey for both Flat Color and Basic Material.
6. To set up a hotkey, open the Material palette from the left side of the screen, and while holding down the Ctrl key, click the Flat Color material icon. At the top of the screen you will see ZBrush asking you to set a hotkey: "Press any key combination to create hotkey –or– Press ESC or Mouse button to cancel."
   Any key you press now will be assigned to this material; for this exercise, press Alt+Q.
7. Repeat this process for the Basic Material, and assign it Alt+W. Now you can quickly switch between materials as you work, checking the progress of the silhouette.

Sketching in the Torso Masses

You will begin with the central pillar of the human body, the head and torso. This is also known as the *axial skeleton*. The torso is composed of three movable masses: the head or cranial mass, the rib cage or thoracic mass, and the hips or pelvis mass. You will begin by sketching in the masses of the rib cage and the pelvis because these will be the central pillar of the body from which you will build all the other forms. Figure 2.11 shows the three masses as basic geometric shapes.

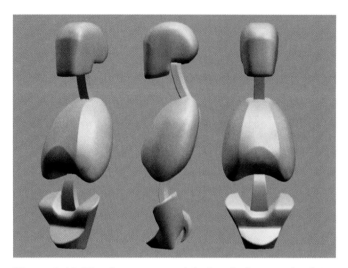

Figure 2.11   The three masses of the head, chest, and pelvis

1. Start by sketching in the outline of the rib cage from the front (Figure 2.12). Use the Claytubes brush to create the egg shape of the rib cage. Make sure to continue the form around the sides and back. At this point, quickly block in a box for the pelvis, as shown in Figure 2.13.

Using the Transpose Tools

At this point, you'll want to lower the arms into a more relaxed posture. To do this, you will use the transpose tools. These are valuable tools for adjusting gesture and proportions as you work because they allow you to quickly pose and orient the mesh like you would bend a wire armature or pose a puppet.

You can access the transpose tools by clicking the Move, Rotate, or Scale buttons at the top of the screen, as shown here.

2. To use the transpose tools to rotate the arms down, press the R key to enter rotate mode, or click the Rotate button at the top of the screen.

   The transpose tools work by affecting unmasked parts of the mesh, so you need to make sure the body from the shoulders in is masked and immovable. You could manually paint a mask by holding down the Ctrl key while you sculpt, which would place your brush in masking mode. But this can be a difficult approach, especially when you have a large area to mask. The easiest way to accomplish this is with the transpose feature Mask By Topology.

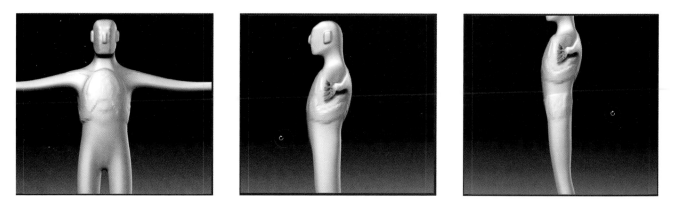

Figure 2.12 *Sketching in the rib cage with the Claytubes brush*

3. Hold down the Ctrl key, and drag from the shoulder toward the arm.
4. A mask will grow from the center of the body toward the arm. Release the mouse and Ctrl key, and the mask is complete.

   This approach is easy to master and helps you quickly and gesturally mask large or small parts of the mesh for the purpose of posing the figure. It works based on the underlying edge loops, which makes ZSphere meshes or simplified box models like our mesh ideal.
5. Mask the mesh as described earlier, and draw a transpose line from the shoulder to the wrist by clicking and dragging the mouse. The transpose line looks like an orange line with three circles along its length (Figure 2.14).
6. Click the Rotate button at the top of the screen; then click in the last circle by the wrist, and drag to rotate around the first circle.
7. When the arms are rotated down, click the Move button at the top of the screen, or use the W hotkey, and click in the center circle and drag to place the arms in relation to the shoulders.

The transpose tools can be challenging for new ZBrush users, particularly with their masking options. Be sure to check the video of this chapter's tutorial on the DVD to see how I've used them.

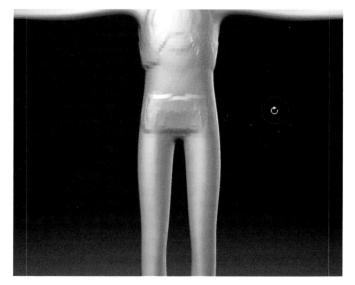

Figure 2.13 *Massing in the pelvis block*

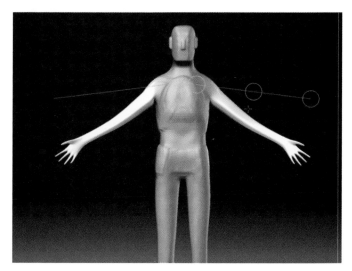

Figure 2.14 *The transpose line*

The Legs

At this point, you will start to establish the major shapes of the legs. The legs are, of course, composed of several interlocking muscle groups, but for this chapter you should be concerned only with the most basic internal shapes and the silhouette. For this rough sculpture, you will establish this basic form and then in later chapters refine it into the individual muscle shapes.

1. Turn on the measure line's subtool to help guide the placement of these basic shapes. Using the Claytubes brush, rough in an oval teardrop shape, as shown in Figure 2.15. Notice that the bottom of the teardrop shape dips just below the fifth head measure from the top. Eventually this will be the muscle bulge just above the knee, as you can see in Figure 2.16.

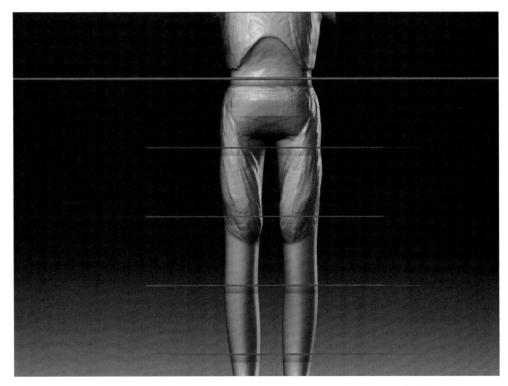

Figure 2.15 The upper leg muscles have an oval or teardrop shape from the front.

2. Still using the Claytubes brush, rough in a box form for the knee, as shown in Figure 2.17. This box shape will span from the bottom of the teardrop form to the sixth head measure line down. This will represent the form of the knee area that takes on a box shape because of the close proximity of the bones of the leg to the surface of the skin in this area. I also make a curved stroke from the bottom of the knee to the foot. This will represent the curvature seen in the shin.

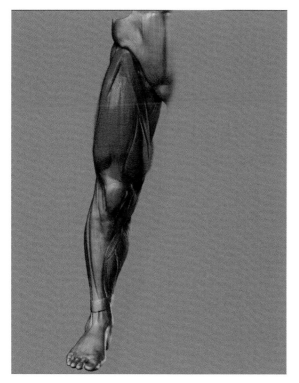

Figure 2.16 *This teardrop shape represents the leg muscles.*

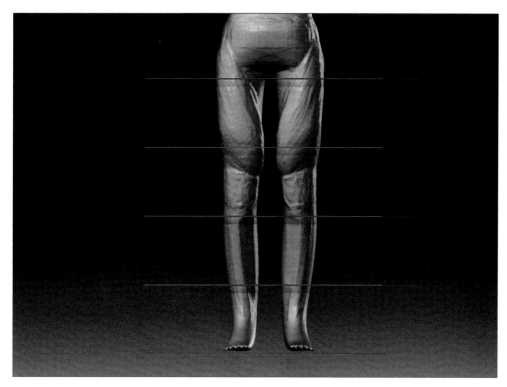

Figure 2.17 *Building a box shape for the knee*

3. Now move to the side view. You want to create the characteristic curvature of the leg in silhouette. Use the Move brush to pull the upper leg out and the back of the lower leg, the calf, back. You can see this change in Figure 2.18. In this figure I have marked the signature curves you will want to establish. These alternating curves create a rhythm in the shape of the leg.

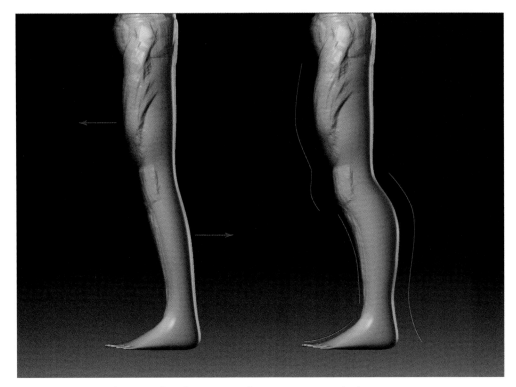

Figure 2.18 Use the Move brush to create this curvature on the leg.

4. Move to the back of the legs. With the Claytubes brush selected, mass in an oval form, as shown in Figure 2.19(a). Then on the back of the upper leg, mass in a shape like that shown in Figure 2.19(b). You will also want to indicate the bottom. This can be as simple as creating a volume for each side of the rear. These shapes will represent the muscles of the back of the leg. Notice how the lower leg muscles wedge into the upper leg muscles (Figure 2.20). As you work, you may want to step down in subdivision levels and smooth the geometry to reduce some shapes and generally have more control over the sculpture. When smoothing the geometry, make sure to adjust the intensity of the Smooth curve so as not to destroy the form you have already sculpted.

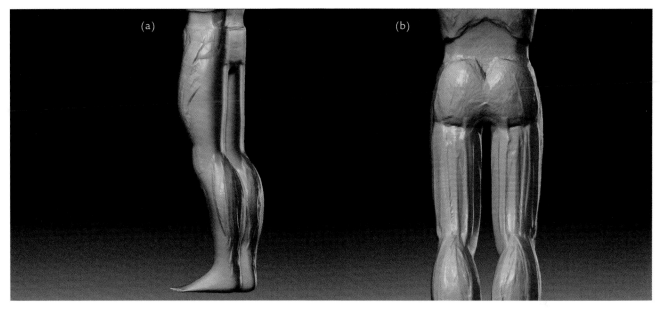

Figure 2.19 *Sculpting the back of the legs: (a) the calf muscles, (b) the back of the upper leg*

Figure 2.20 *Notice how the shapes of the upper and lower legs wedge into each other on the final figure.*

Using the Smooth Brush

As you build up forms, you'll need to use the Smooth brush to push back when the shape is becoming too inflated. At its default setting, the Smooth brush is very strong and will obliterate your sculpture, as shown here.

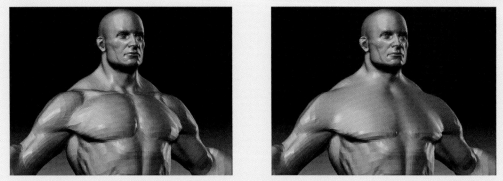

You need to adjust the smoothing curve to reduce the overall strength of the Smooth brush. This allows you to have a full range of 0 to 100 ZIntensity, while reducing the intensity of the 100 percent setting.

1. To reduce the smoothing curve, click the Brush palette at the top of the screen, and scroll down to Curve. While holding Shift down, click in this menu to open the Curve control. When Shift is depressed, the curve will control the Smooth brush.

   In ZBrush you cannot select the Smooth brush directly. Changes you make to the brush controls while holding Shift affect the selected Smooth brush. In the Brush palette, there is a selection of Smooth brushes available, from the normal smooth to smooth peaks, which only smoothes high points, and smooth valleys, which only affects the low points. When a Smooth brush is selected, it will become active only when the Shift key is pressed.

2. Click Reset, and then drag the rightmost point down.

   The left point represents the strength of the Smooth brush in the furthest outer rim of the brush, while the right point represents its strength in the center. The curve between the two points represents the falloff over the course of the brush's effect, as shown here. You can also adjust the ZIntensity of the brush while holding Shift to further soften the effect of the smooth.

5. Moving up the back, sculpt in two pillars from the buttocks to the base of the skull (Figure 2.21). These will be clear in later chapters as major muscles of the back. For now they will serve to link the pelvic mass and the rib cage, as well as to help establish the profile of the torso as seen from the side by transitioning between the pelvis and the rib cage.

6. Move to the side view. Here you will add a transitional shape between the ribs and the pelvis again. This S-shaped form, shown in Figure 2.22(a), flows from the back of the rib cage to the front of the hips. This form is a simplification of the flank muscles of the torso shown in Figure 2.22(b). The point here is to unify the torso with the pelvis, linking the two basic shapes together.

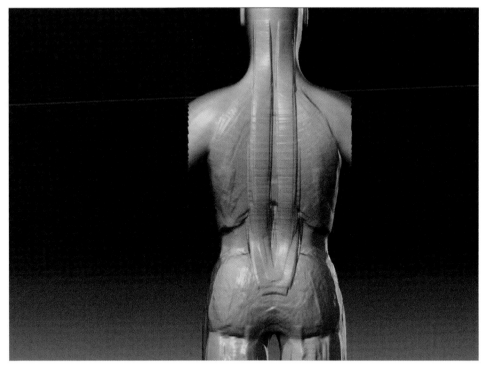

Figure 2.21 *Sculpt two pillars from the base of the spine to the skull.*

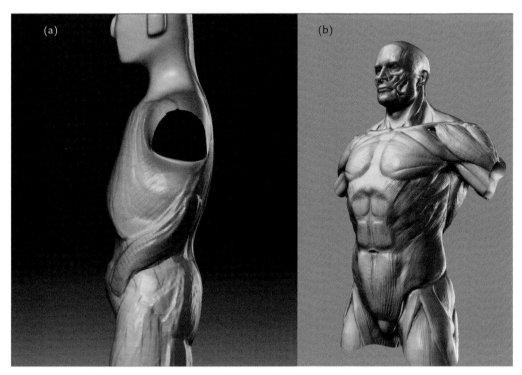

Figure 2.22 *Unifying the torso with the pelvis: (a) sculpting the flank of the figure, (b) the S-shaped flank form representing the Oblique muscles*

The Chest and Shoulders

Now you will move up to the chest and shoulders. Figure 2.23 shows the rough figure at this stage from a full-body view. Remember to keep checking your work against the measure guide subtool as you sculpt, and check the profiles often in flat shade view.

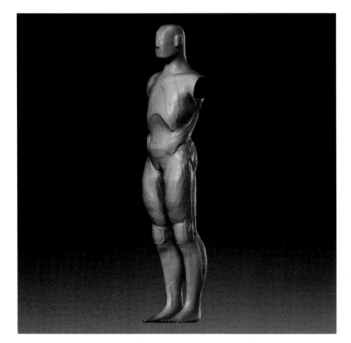

Figure 2.23 The rough figure sculpture at this stage

1. From the front view, sculpt the shape of the chest muscles, as shown in Figure 2.24. These look like two steaks that taper toward the armpits. They will start right on the collar bone line of your measure guide. This is because these chest muscles originate from the ribs as well as the collar bones or clavicles.

2. Once the chest muscles are established, tip the figure forward, and sculpt the collar bones, as shown in Figure 2.25. Notice the sweep the shapes take as they flow out to the shoulders. Collar bones are very much like the handlebars on a bicycle. Make sure to end the collar bone at the center of the shoulder.

3. Using a mask, isolate the area for the shoulder muscle, as shown in Figure 2.26. This muscle will start on the last third of the collar bone and continue around the back of the figure. Notice how the muscle looks somewhat V-shaped and tapers to a point in the middle of the upper arm. This muscle is called the *Deltoid* because it looks like the Greek letter delta (Δ) upside down. For modern people, it's easiest to think of it as a triangle wrapped around the shoulder.

4. You will now sculpt the shape of the shoulder blade on the back. Isolate the area for the shoulder blade, as shown in Figure 2.27(a). Create it using the Claytubes brush. You will notice here that the back of the shoulder muscle overlaps the shoulder blade. You will look at this attachment in detail in Chapter 4. The shoulder blade is important enough to include in this very rough model because it influences the shape of the back as seen from the side (Figure 2.27(b)). It is also important, because even in this simplified figure, it serves as a central point of attachment for the shapes of the back of the arm and back of the neck.

5. You will now add the muscles of the back of the neck. This muscle form is called the Trapezius, and you will look at it in more detail in the next two chapters. For now, you want to isolate its shape with a mask and sculpt the form using the Claytubes brush, as shown in Figure 2.28(a). In the silhouette view in Figure 2.28(b), notice that it flows from the base of the skull to the line where the shoulder muscle, or Deltoid, overlaps the shoulder blade.

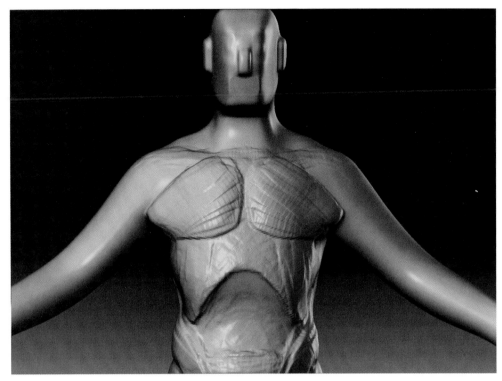

Figure 2.24 *Sculpting the chest muscles*

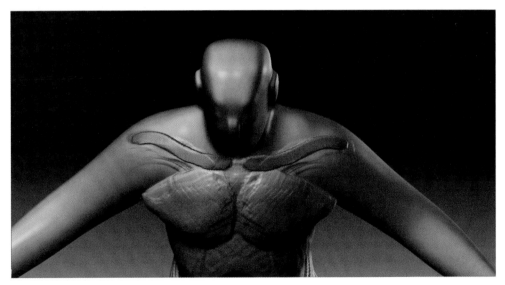

Figure 2.25 *Sculpting the collar bones*

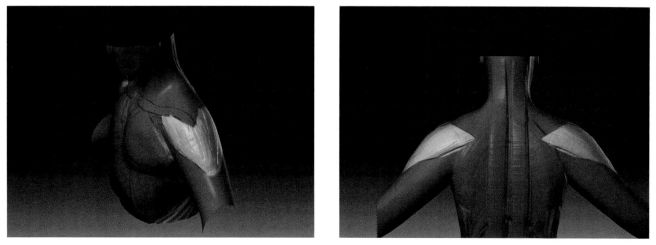

Figure 2.26 *Sculpting the shoulder muscle*

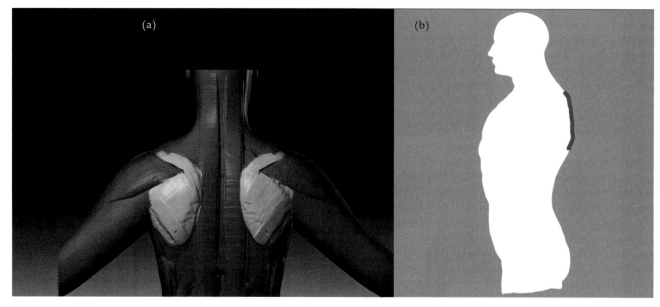

Figure 2.27 *Sculpting the shoulder blade: (a) isolating the shoulder blade, (b) a plane break in the silhouette of the figure created by the shoulder blade and its associated muscles*

6. To finish off the shoulder area, rotate to the front, and add in the two neck muscle shapes shown in Figure 2.29(a). These are called the Sternomastoids, and you will be looking at them in more depth next chapter. For this sculpture, simply make sure the form flows around the neck starting from the base of the skull to the point between the collar bones, as shown in Figure 2.29(b).

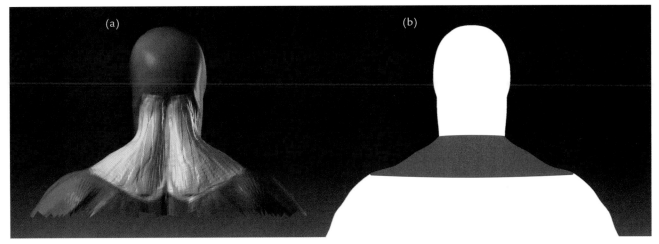

Figure 2.28 *Sculpting the back of the neck: (a) isolating the back of the neck, (b) the shoulders taking a trapezoid shape in front- or back-view*

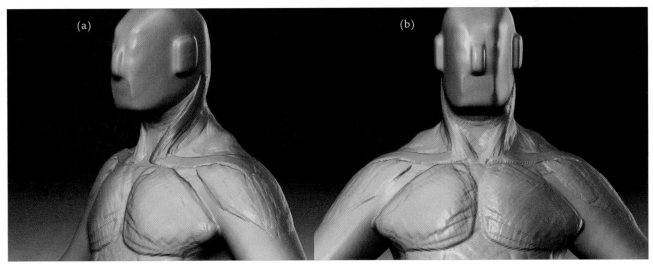

Figure 2.29 *Sculpting the neck muscle forms: (a) adding the two shapes, (b) the form flowing from the base of the skull to the point between the collar bones*

7. At this stage, take a look at the overall figure again. Turn on the measure guide sub-tool, and make sure the measures fall where they should. Remember, the midpoint of the figure should be at the fourth head line, and the sixth line should fall just below the knee. Notice as well that the collar bones fall on the smaller line just below the first head measure. At this stage, make any adjustments to the silhouette in flat color view before you move on to the arms.

The Arms

Now that you have worked up the figure from the legs to the neck, you will look at the arms. Just as with the legs, you should be most concerned with the overall profiles of the arm and the way in which the upper arm wedges into the lower arm. Be careful not to become too involved with smaller forms. In this sculpture, you will represent the arm with the minimum of simple volumes.

1. You will start the arm by addressing the silhouette from the front. As you can see in Figure 2.30(a), the arm is a very simple tube shape at the moment. Using the Move brush, pull the outline into the shape shown here. Be sure to notice the angle between the crests of the silhouette on the outside of the arm as it relates to the crest on the inside. A common error is to make these crests even when they should be offset, as shown in Figure 2.30(b).

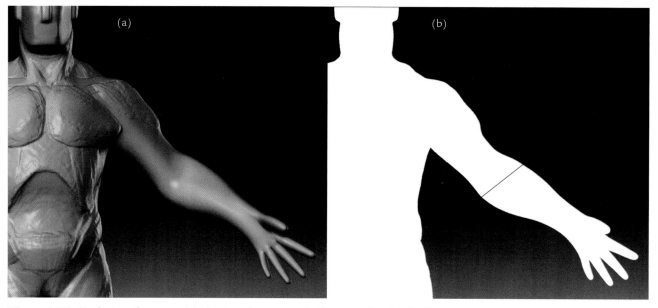

Figure 2.30 *Sculpting the arms: (a) shaping the arm with the Move brush, (b) the crests in the silhouette of the forearm on an angle*

2. You will now sculpt the Biceps muscle. Using the Claytubes brush, mass in the rectangle of the Bicep from the armpit down to the forearm (Figure 2.31). Be sure to continue it into the forearm slightly because this is part of the interlocking between the upper- and lower-arm shapes. You can see this interlocking of form in Figure 2.32.

3. Now rotate to the back of the arm. You are going to sculpt an oval shape here that will taper from the armpit to the elbow. This will represent the Triceps muscle, which encompasses the entire back of the arm. Isolate the area, and mass in the shape using the Claytubes brush (Figure 2.33).

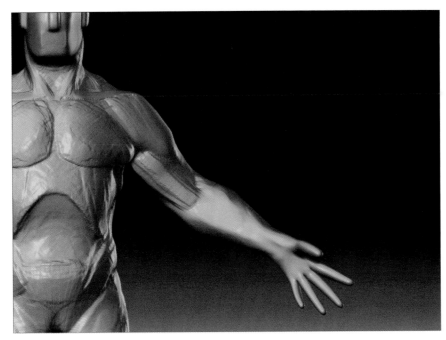

Figure 2.31 *Sculpt the Bicep with the Claytubes brush.*

Figure 2.32 *You can see the interlocking between the shapes of the upper and lower arm in this image.*

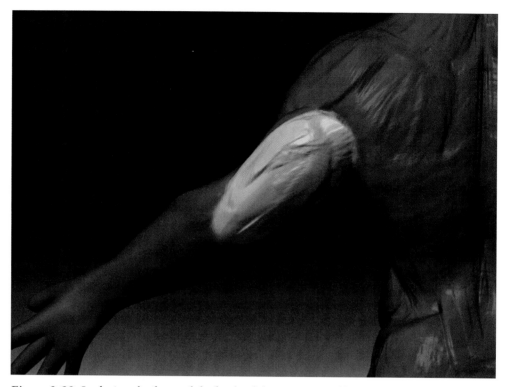

Figure 2.33 Sculpting the form of the back of the arm created by the Triceps muscle

4. To better define the joint between the upper and lower arm, you will now bend the elbow. Use transpose masking to mask down to the elbow. Draw a transpose rotate line that ends at the point of the elbow, as shown in Figure 2.34. Hold down Alt and drag in the last circle to bend the elbow.

The Hands

You will now rough in some basic hands for this figure. As in the previous sections, you are most concerned with the gross form and overall shapes. The hands themselves will be addressed in detail in Chapter 7.

1. Use the Smooth brush to reduce the volume of the fingers until they are even, narrow tubes (Figure 2.35(a)). Isolate the thumb with a mask, and using the Inflate brush with a low ZIntensity setting, mass in the fleshy portion of the base of the thumb (Figure 2.35(b)).

2. Moving to the back of the hand, start to indicate the bones of the back of the hand with a few strokes of the Standard brush. These don't have to be overstated, just simple lines leading to the base of each finger (Figure 2.36).

3. Use the Claytubes brush to refine the back of the hand. As shown in Figure 2.37, pull the webbing between the fingers up on the palm side of the hand. This is an important form feature of the hand. The fingers attach at a bevel, not straight on.

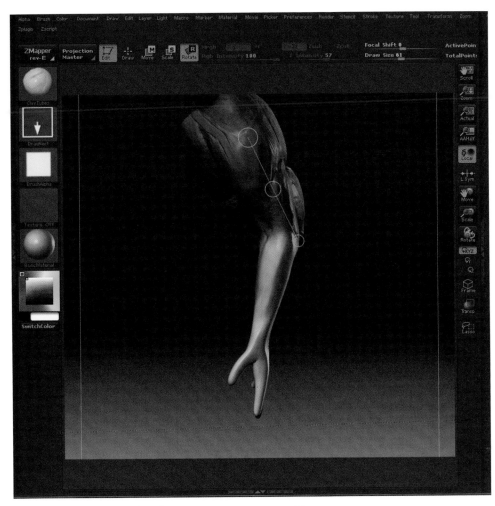

Figure 2.34 *Bending the elbow using transpose masking*

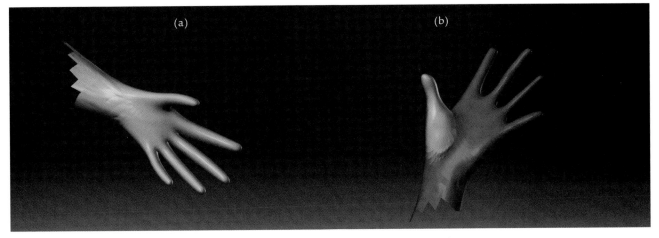

Figure 2.35 *Roughing in some hands: (a) smoothing the fingers to reduce their volume evenly, (b) using the Inflate brush to mass in the thumb*

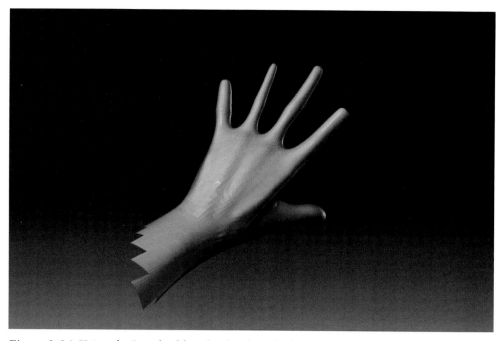

Figure 2.36 Using the Standard brush, sketch in the bones of the back of the hand.

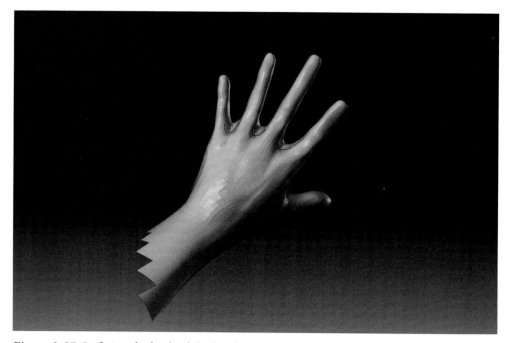

Figure 2.37 Refining the back of the hand and indicating the webbing of the fingers

4. Rotate to the palm of the hand, and mask out the wrist. Using the Inflate brush, create the masses of the palm, as shown in Figure 2.38(a). Be sure to rotate around the hand and check the shapes from many angles (Figure 2.38(b)). Do not become too involved with the fingers at this stage. You can indicate the knuckles with a slight touch of the Inflate brush.

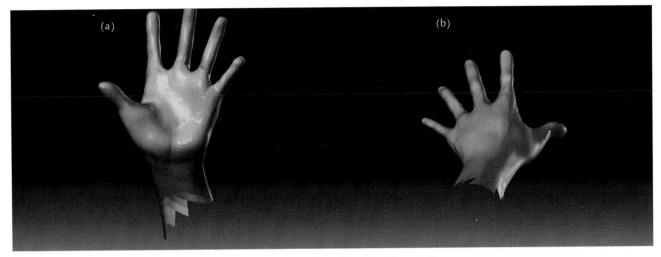

Figure 2.38 *Creating the masses of the hand: (a) using the Inflate brush to indicate masses of the palm, (b) rotating around the hand to check it from multiple angles*

Final Stages

You are now in the final stretch, and the gesture sculpture is almost done. All you have left now are the head, abdomen, and toes. In the following steps, you will begin by filling out the abdomen of the figure:

1. Returning to the front of the figure, isolate the abdomen with a mask, as shown in Figure 2.39(a). Use the Claytubes brush to mass in a column of muscle from the ribs to the pubic bone (Figure 2.39(b)). Be sure to check your work here from the side view as well (Figure 2.39(c)).

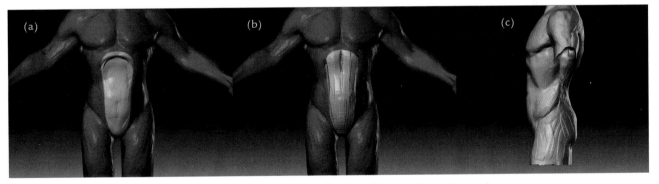

Figure 2.39 *Filling out the abdomen: (a) isolating the area for the abdominal muscles with a mask, (b) massing in a column of muscle with the Claytubes brush, (c) checking the abdomen from the side view*

2. Use a mask to isolate six areas, as shown in Figure 2.40. These are the abdominal muscles commonly called the *six-pack*. There are actually eight of these muscles, but only on very rare and fit people are all eight visible. Use the Claytubes brush to indicate these muscles. Turn on the measure guides, and place the navel at the third head measure down (Figure 2.41).

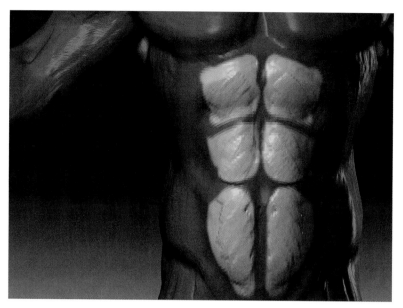

Figure 2.40 Adding the abdominal muscles

Figure 2.41 Placing the navel

3. Move down to the legs, and turn on flat shade mode (Figure 2.42). Make sure your silhouette is correct and you have the crests and valleys in place.
   Since you'll be working on the feet next, I will point out one very important angle. In Figure 2.43, notice the angle between the anklebones. Make sure the inner anklebone is higher than the outer one.

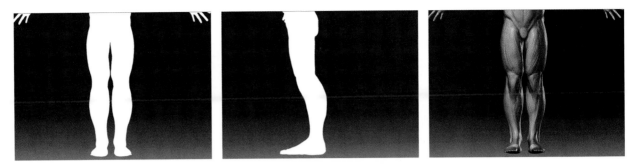

Figure 2.42 Check the legs in silhouette as well as shaded view.

Figure 2.43 Be careful to include the angle between the inner and outer anklebones.

4. Rotate to the top of the feet. Notice that the toes are somewhat evenly spaced and all the same size (Figure 2.44(a)). You will correct this by stepping down to the lower subdivision levels. Select the Move brush, and adjust the points of the toes so they follow an arc, as shown in Figure 2.44(b).
5. Use the Move brush and the Inflate brush to refine the toe shapes. Note the gap between the big toe and the other digits. Also note the arc created by the front of the foot (Figure 2.45).

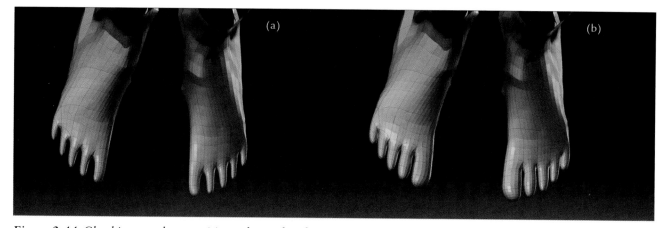

Figure **2.44** *Checking out the toes: (a) evenly sized and incorrectly placed, (b) using the Move and Inflate brushes to move the toes into an arc and increase the size of the big toe*

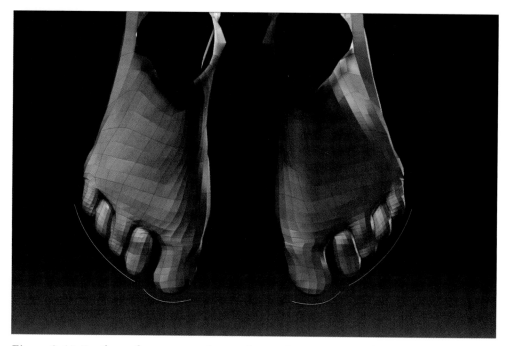

Figure **2.45** *Further refinements to the toe shapes. Be sure to note the arc of the toes.*

The Head

With the abdomen and toes complete, you are at the last stage. Now you will create the most basic head form possible for this figure. This will be a primitive head shape that contains the volume of the skull but with no features. You will sculpt the head in detail in the next chapter.

From the front and side views, smooth back the extrusions for the ears and nose, as shown in Figure 2.46. Be sure to adjust the smoothing curve, the intensity of the Smooth brush, or both, to keep from smoothing away the head form. The topology created by these extrusions will remain and be helpful for pulling shapes out of these areas later in the sculpting process.

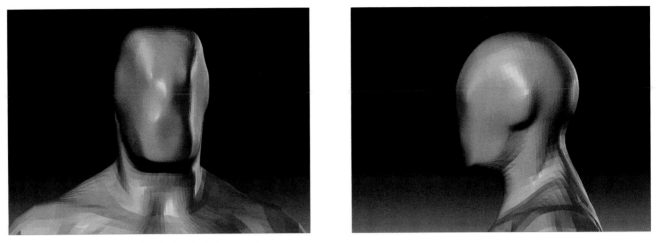

Figure 2.46 Smoothing back the facial extrusions

Use the Pinch brush with Lazy Mouse to pinch the line, as shown in Figure 2.47(a). You can activate Lazy Mouse by pressing the L hotkey. This plane change will represent the side of the skull. Repeat this process for the front of the skull, as shown in Figure 2.47(b). Check the shape of the head in flat color mode. Figure 2.48 shows the sculpture with flat shade (silhouette) on.

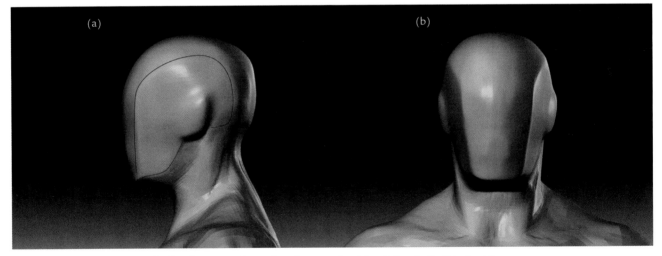

Figure 2.47 Working on the head: (a) pinching the plane at the side of the skull, (b) pinching the sides of the skull from the front view

That completes the rough gesture sculpture (Figure 2.49). Check your work in flat shade mode as well as with the perspective camera on and off.

Congratulations, you have completed the gesture sculpture tutorial. You have now finished sketching in a figure with attention to the silhouette and basic forms of the body. This may not seem vital now, but it is one part of the foundation on which the rest of this book is built. You will move on now and begin to look at the parts of the body in more detail, focusing on how muscle flesh and bone forms combine to create the human body.

At this point, save your ZTool. You will be using it again for the remaining chapters.

Figure 2.48 *The head in flat shade view*

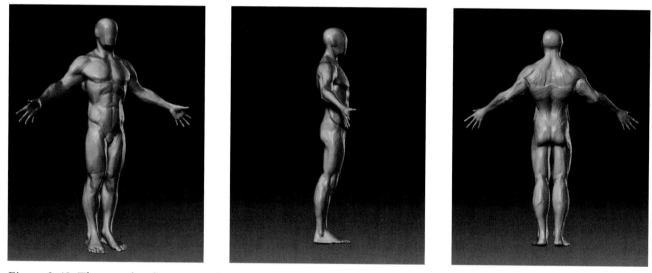

Figure 2.49 *The completed gesture sculpture*

Analyzing Planes

Before you move on to Chapter 3, I would like to call your attention to a bonus tutorial available as a narrated video on the DVD. Now that you have a rough figure sculpture, you can take it a step further by addressing the geometric planes created by the internal forms of muscle and bone (Figure 2.50).

Planes are important in sculpture because they define the quality and placement of the shadows on your figure. A sculpture with poorly defined planes will appear soft. By sculpting with attention to the planar breakdown of the forms, you can give your work a more solid structural integrity and make it feel like flesh and bone rather than soft lumps of polygon clay blended together.

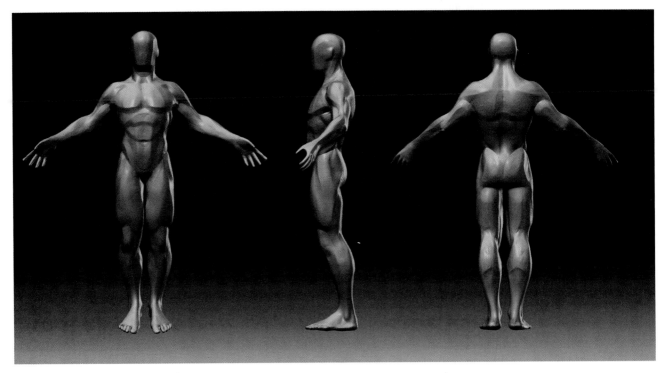

Figure 2.50 *The final planes figure*

I have chosen to include this as a video since the process may be difficult for you if you have never sculpted the human form or are unfamiliar with many of the muscle and bone landmarks referenced. In these cases, I recommend working through the remainder of the book and then revisiting this tutorial to help develop your sense of structure and form when dealing with the figure as a whole.

What's Next?

Congratulations, you have completed this tutorial in sketching a human body. You have learned about the importance of the silhouette as well as plane breaks and crests in both the outline and the muscle form. Much of what we did this chapter is the foundation for the rest of this book. What you learned here will inform the sculptural decisions you make for the rest of the figure. Without understanding plane crests, breaks, and profiles, all the muscle knowledge in the world won't help.

Let's move on to sculpting the head and shoulders using what you have learned so far!

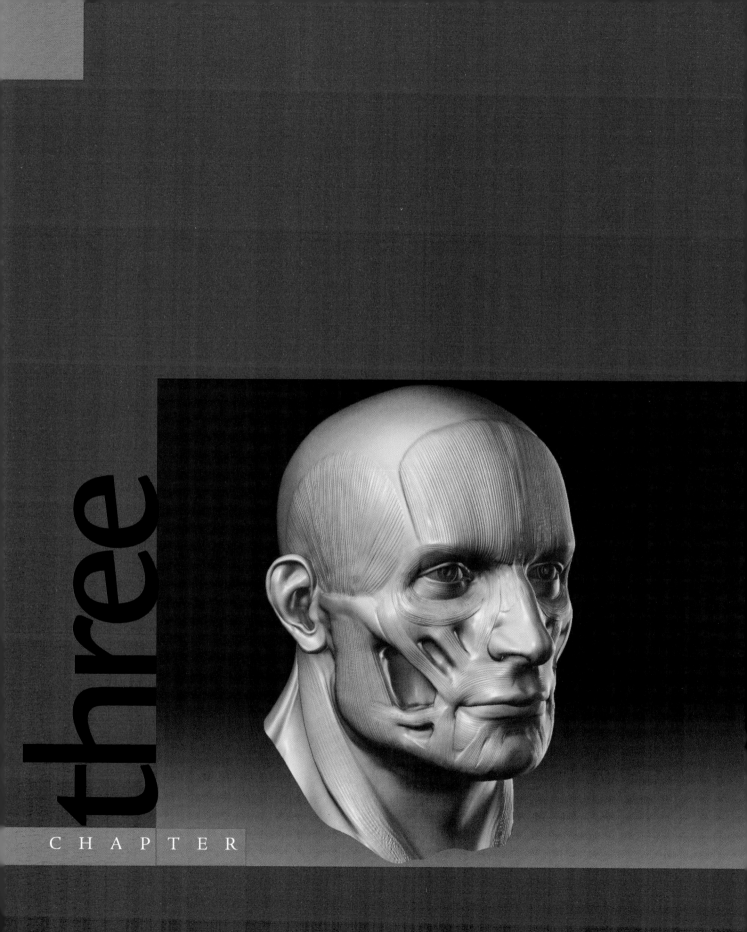

three

The Head and Neck

In this chapter, you will work *on the head and neck of the figure you've been building in previous chapters. You will establish the head by first sculpting the form of the skull on the established basic shape. From there, you will begin to address the major bony forms of the skull by looking at how they influence the face. As you work the sculpting steps in this chapter, I will illustrate how certain muscles, as well as the bony protrusions of the skull, are influencing the final fleshed form.*

You will address the neck by its major muscle forms and points of attachment to the torso, that is, the spine of the scapula and the clavicles. There is some overlap here with the work you will do on the torso in the next chapter, but that is good since it is difficult to address the full figure as just its aggregate parts. You must consider each in relation to the whole. Because of this, you will find that I revisit certain areas in relation to the parts around them.

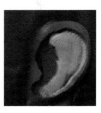

You will be using a limited number of brushes in this chapter: the Claytubes, Rake, Move, and Standard brushes with a few instances of Flatten, Masking, Pinch, Inflate, and Smooth. You will also be using the M, or Material, modifier on the brush to add surface materials as you sculpt. I'll explain this process in the "The Facial Muscles" section.

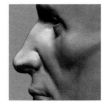

The Skull

The skull represents the entire bony structure of the head (Figure 3.1). It consists of several distinct parts, but for the purpose of artistic representation and understanding the masses, you can divide it into two major shapes: the *cranial mass* and the *facial wedge* (Figure 3.2). These two masses joined together create the basic form of the skull.

   The cranial mass is the cranium, the protective casing of the brain, which has an ovoid form. The facial mass consists of the eye sockets, zygomatic bones, maxilla or upper jaw, and the mandible or lower jaw. Figure 3.3 shows multiple views of the head in rotation.

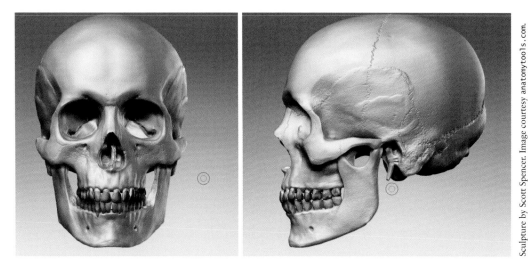

Sculpture by Scott Spencer. Image courtesy anatomytools.com.

Figure 3.1 The skull forms the base structure of the head.

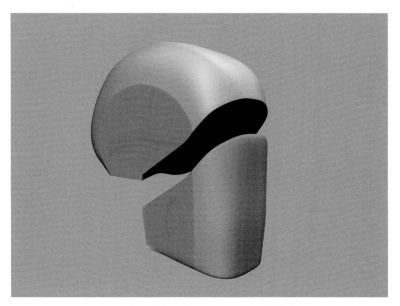

Figure 3.2 The cranial and facial masses in exploded view

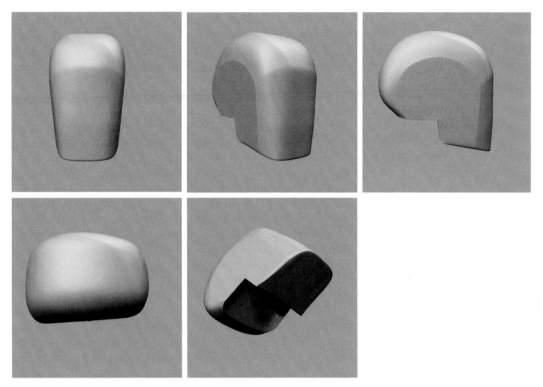

Figure 3.3 *The basic form of the human head shown in rotation*

You can further simplify the forms of the head. Figure 3.4 shows the head and facial features broken down into basic geometric shapes. This model has a somewhat humorous robotic look, but what it represents is important to understand.

By seeing the head in these basic blocks and cylinders, you can understand the basic shape of each area and the kinds of shadows cast. Remember that when you sculpt, you are most concerned with the shape and quality of the shadows cast on the surface of the form. Notice how the eyes are simple spheres deep set in a wedge-shaped recess. Also notice the mouth represented by a cylinder. These shape analogies can be very helpful as a tool to help build up the sculpture from a solid base.

Because of this high concentration of bony landmarks in the head, you will approach this chapter slightly differently than you will the rest of the figure. In other chapters, you will take a more fluid approach, sculpting muscle and bone together. However, since the skeletal framework of the head is so visible, you will take a more layered approach here with the head sculpture. This approach is called *écorché*, French for "flayed."

This is a learning device in which a human figure is displayed with fat and skin removed so the muscle and or bones are exposed. Many art classes use *écorché* as a teaching exercise. The figure is built up starting with the skeleton, and then major muscles are laid over until a final figure is achieved.

Figure 3.4 *The head and facial features broken down into their most basic shapes*

Before you begin, you need to examine the skull and its major landmarks. Figure 3.5 shows a human male skull in rotation with major landmarks called out. You will refer to these points in the course of the first part of this chapter. Refer to this image for reference. These points are typically visible on the surface of the fleshed head and easily felt through the skin.

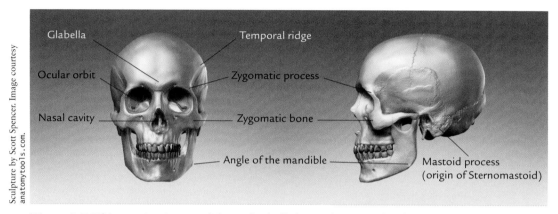

Sculpture by Scott Spencer. Image courtesy anatomytools.com.

Figure 3.5 This rotation image of the male skull shows the major landmarks and their names.

Proportions and Placement of Facial Features

As you sculpt the head, you need to be aware of the relative placement of the facial features. To do this, you will adopt a canon of measurement just as you did for the figure. By having a set of rules to follow as you work, you will ensure the features lie in acceptable spaces relative to each other. Without guidelines like this, it is very tricky to sculpt a convincing human head.

Placing the Features

You can plot the features by using the rules described in this section. From the front view, mark off the top and bottom of the head. Now place a mark for the hairline. The rest of your measures will be based on this line (Figure 3.6).

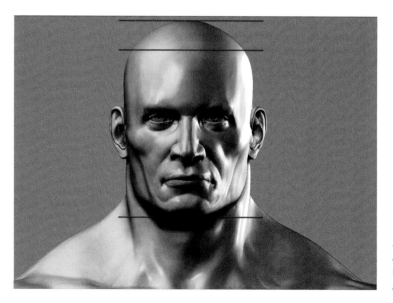

Figure 3.6 The top and bottom of the head marked off and a line added for the hairline

If the rest of the head is divided into thirds, you can see how the first third marks the brow line, while the second is the bottom of the nose (Figure 3.7).

The space between the bottom of the nose and the chin can be divided again into thirds. The first line represents the line between the lips, as shown in Figure 3.8. Notice that the inner corners of the eyes are on the same line as the wings of the nostrils, while the inner edge of the iris falls on the same line as the corners of the mouth.

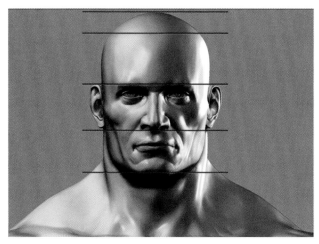

Figure 3.7 The face divided into thirds to find the brow line and bottom of the nose

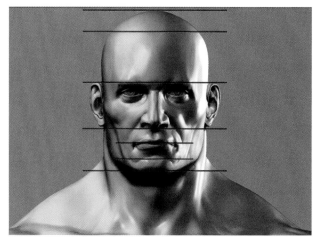

Figure 3.8 The first third of the bottom of the face represents the lip line.

From the side view, the ear should be at an angle just behind the midline of the head. It falls between the brow line and the bottom of the nose (Figure 3.9). On this image also note the important angles that have been marked in red. These include the angle of the ear, the angle between the brow line and the cheekbone, the angle of the jawbone, and the plane break present at the hairline.

These rules are not to be taken as law but merely as guidelines to direct you as you sculpt. What makes a likeness or character is how much these rules are actually deviated from. It is important to have these as a road map to place your features since it helps create a head that feels rooted in reality. You'll need to refer to these measures a little later in this chapter, so keep them in mind. Now let's talk about sculpting the bony and muscle masses of the head.

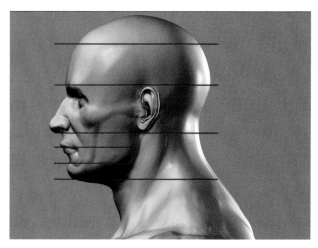

Figure 3.9 From the side, the placement of the ear falls between the brow line and the bottom of the nose.

Sculpting the Basic Skull

To begin, you will load the final gesture sculpture from Chapter 2. This is the iteration before the planes were sculpted in. The basic shape of the skull should appear as shown in Figure 3.10. This is the overall mass of the skull, including both the cranial and facial sections discussed earlier.

1. Begin by sketching in the location of the major landmarks, starting with the eye sockets and nasal cavity. Place the eye openings approximately in the center of the head.

You can see these measures on the head in Figure 3.11. On the final head, the pupils will lie on the midline of the skull. Take this into account when sketching in the sockets. Use the Standard brush with ZSub to etch these openings into the head.

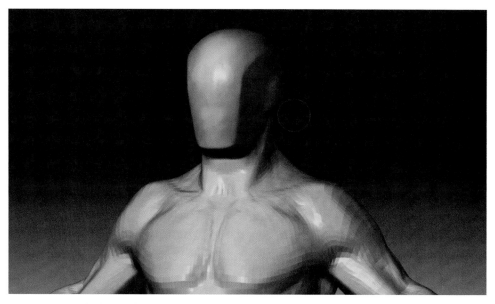

Figure 3.10 *The basic form of the head*

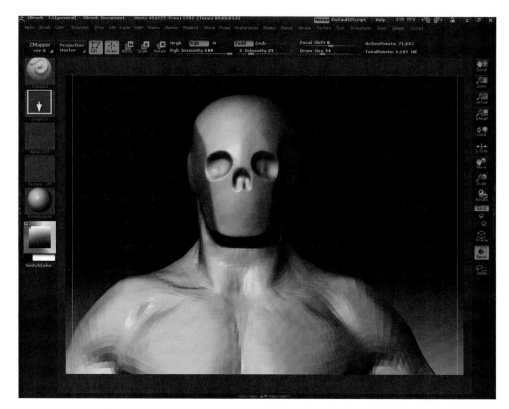

Figure 3.11 *Sculpting the eye sockets and nasal cavity*

2. Using the Claytubes brush, rough in the shape of the zygomatic bone. Commonly called the *cheekbone*, this consists of the zygomatic bone as well as the zygomatic process (Figure 3.12). These form the bony structure of the eye sockets and cheeks, landmarks that are visible on the fleshed surface of the figure. The zygomatic bone ends at the center of the ear. Take notice that the zygomatic bone is not a straight line but more of a zigzag shape. A common error is to make the zygomatic bone a straight line pointing back to the middle of the ear.

3. Figure 3.13 shows the zygomatic bones as well as the angle of the jawbone roughed in with the Claytubes brush. Also start to mass in a bulge for the mouth. It is important not to let the mouth remain a flat plane, as you will see shortly. Figure 3.14 shows the temporal region of the skull isolated and scooped in using the Claytubes brush with ZSub.

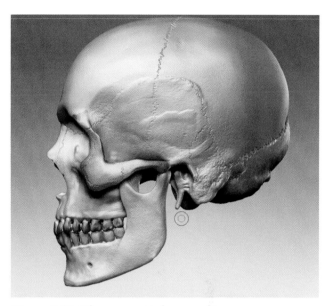

Figure 3.12 *The zygomatic bone and process are highlighted; the zygomatic process is shown in blue.*

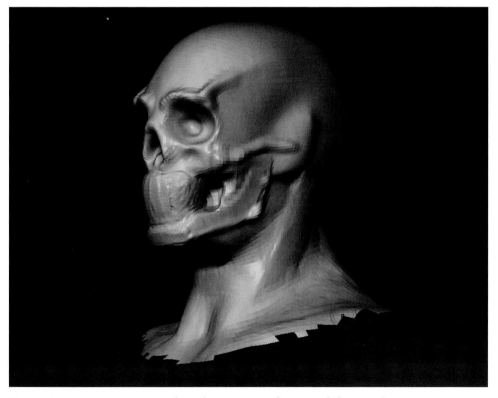

Figure 3.13 *Beginning to rough in the zygomatic bones and the mouth*

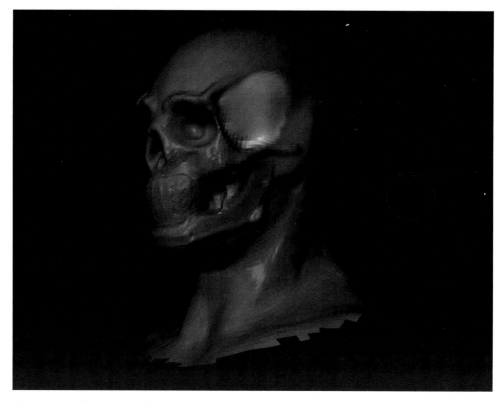

Figure 3.14 Pressing in the temporal region of the skull

4. Using the Move brush, adjust the shape of the eye sockets to match Figure 3.15. Notice that the eyes of a skull have an almost plaintive or sad look with their upward slant. At the center of the eyebrows, create the trapezoid shape of the glabella of the skull (Figure 3.16). This bony protrusion forms the raised planes just above the nose and between the eyebrows. This landmark influences the shape of the brows considerably and is important to address. A common error for beginners is to make the brow line a single uninterrupted ledge.

5. Make sure to pull the zygomatic process out in a crest to the sides of the sockets (Figure 3.17). There should be a consistent angle or plane from the zygomatic process down to the sides of the zygomatic bone (Figure 3.18). This plane helps set the foundation for an important plane change in the finished head. This form manifests as the line down the side of the face where highlights catch or a shadow starts to turn on the cheek of the head.

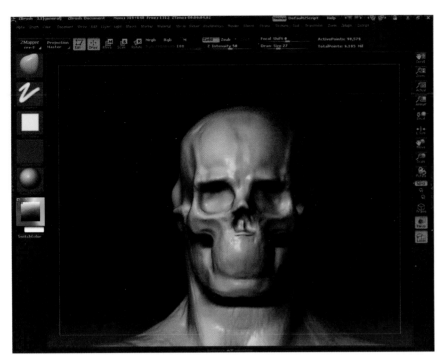

Figure 3.15 The general outline of the eye sockets

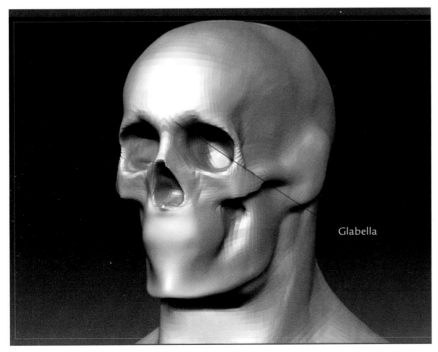

Figure 3.16 Sculpting the glabella

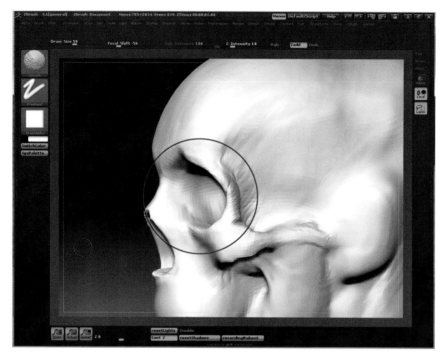

Figure 3.17 Sculpting the zygomatic process

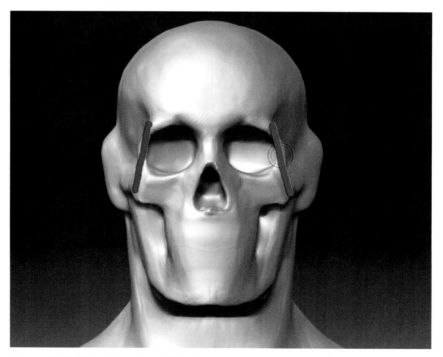

Figure 3.18 The plane formed by the zygomatic process and the zygomatic bone at the side of the eye socket

6. Rough in the jawline using the Claytubes brush. Add negative space for the division between the mandible (jawbone) and maxilla (upper teeth). Notice the angle of the jawline from the front view (Figure 3.19).

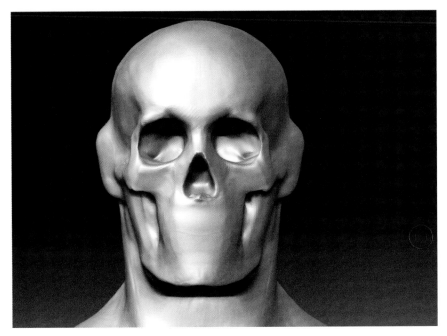

Figure 3.19 *Resolving the jawline from the front view*

7. From the side, continue to work the jawline, taking care to maintain a sharp delineation. This is also a good time to build up the cylinder of the mouth. While I will not go into the details of sculpting individual teeth, note that the most important aspect of the mouth area to get right is the barrel shape the maxilla and mandible create (Figure 3.20). A common mistake is to make this area too flat, which creates a very unnatural mouth and lips on the final head. The lips should be curved as if lying over a cylinder. Using Claytubes, build up this cylindrical form. You will be building the lips around this shape, so having an accurate base is a huge step toward making a realistic mouth (Figure 3.21).

8. Adjust the angle of the ear in relation to the jawline and zygomatic bone. The ear follows the same angle created by the mandible (Figure 3.22). Using the Move brush, shift the base of the ear into place. Do not worry about sculpting details at this phase, because I will address the ear specifically later in this chapter. For now, you just want to make sure it sits at the correct angle and general placement on the head.

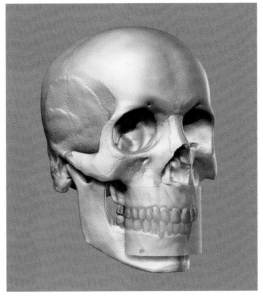

Figure 3.20 *You can see the barrel shape of the mouth overlaid on a finished skull. This shape is very important to guide the effective placement and form of the lips.*

Sculpture by Scott Spencer. Image courtesy anatomytools.com.

9. Switch to silhouette mode by changing to the Flat Color material (Figure 3.23). Using Flat Color here will allow you to check the general angles of the skull and profile as well as the smaller, subtler angles of the individual parts of the profile. I cannot stress enough how important it is to be sensitive to these details early on in the process. By keeping these angles accurate, you'll make the final sculpture all the more natural, realistic, and effective. Often when I have almost completed a sculpture, I will return to the flat shade mode and deliberately refine the profiles, adding the sharp breaks and curves that can often get lost in the process of finishing a sculpture.

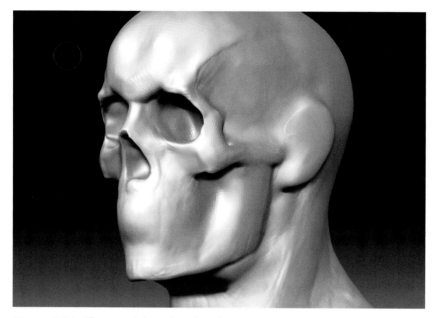

Figure 3.21 The mouth barrel sculpted in

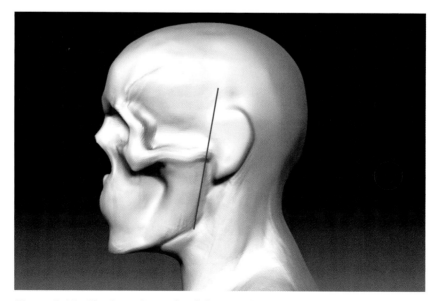

Figure 3.22 Checking the angle of the ear relative to the jawbone

Figure 3.23 *Checking the profile of the skull with the Flat Color material*

10. Check the skull and head from the front and side views. See Figure 3.24 for the major angles you should be sensitive to. From the side, check the nasal bone and the angles of the overall profile. Although there is a lot of character that can be developed in a sculpture by experimenting with these angles, for this exercise you want to maintain them in a more natural and general range.

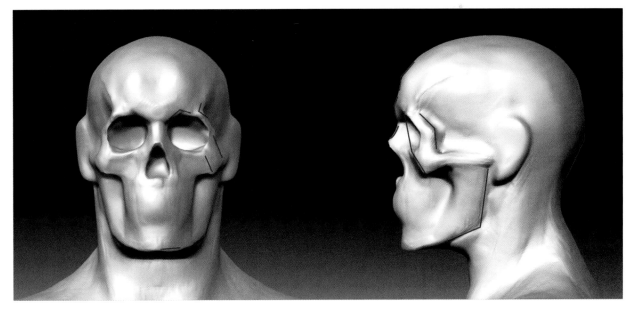

Figure 3.24 *These front and side views of the head show the angles you are trying to maintain.*

Refining the Initial Sculpt

In the final pass, I typically use the Clay Finish brush to reinforce the planes created between the bone forms sculpted so far:

1. Select Flatten, and turn down the intensity to about 50. You want to establish the plane changes in the skeletal portions of the face to help guide you as you work. Remember that crests, planes, and angles all influence light and shadow. The way light and shadow react on the surface of your sculpture is what adds visual interest and a sense of structure. Figure 3.25 shows the planes of the zygomatic bones.

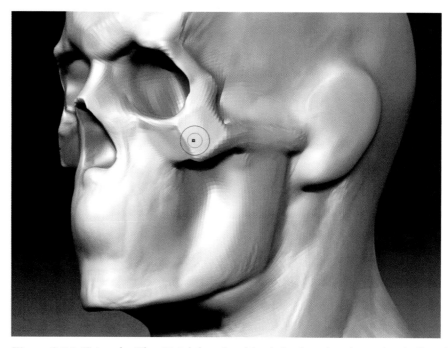

Figure 3.25 *Using the Clay Finish brush, add subtle plane breaks to the skull sculpture.*

2. At this point, you are ready to place the eyes in the skull. The eyeball should not fill the entire eye socket; instead, it rests within the socket and is held in place by a combination of fatty tissues and muscle. From the DVD, load the file eyeballs. ztl (Figure 3.26). This is an eyeball model that you will place in the head model. Remember that the pupils will lie on the centerline of the head (Figure 3.27).

3. Load the eyeball ZTool into ZBrush, and switch back to the figure ZTool.

4. Append the eyeball ZTool into the mesh using Tool → Subtool → Append. Make sure the eyeball subtool is active, and press the W key to activate the Move Transpose tool. Using the Transpose tools Move and Scale, move the eyeball into place in the eye socket. When placing the eye, be aware of the diagonal line created between the brow and the cheekbone (Figure 3.28). You may want to activate transparency by clicking the Transparent button on the right side of the screen to make it easier to see the eye in relation to the head (Figure 3.29).

Figure 3.26 *The eye ZTool*

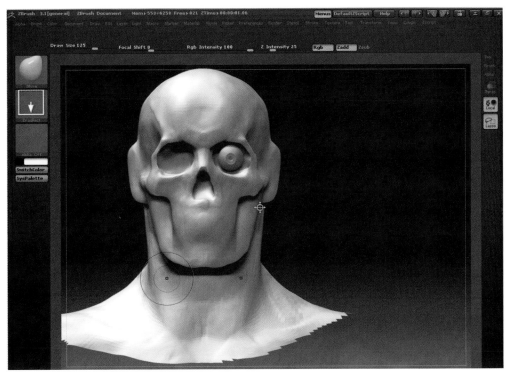

Figure 3.27 *Eye placed on centerline*

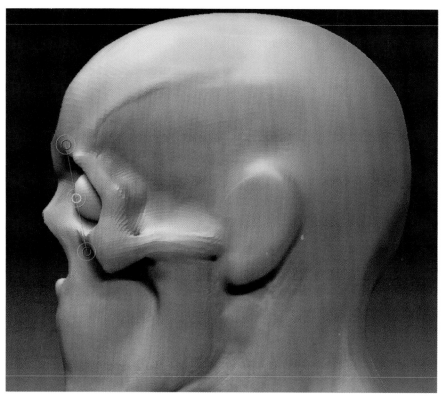

Figure 3.28 *Moving the eye back so it sits on the diagonal line shown between the brow ridge and zygomatic bone*

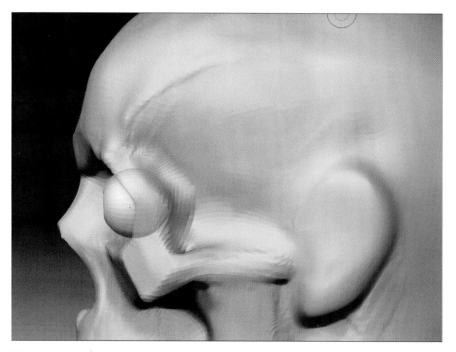

Figure 3.29 *Using transparency can help you move the eyes in relation to the head.*

5. Once the eye is properly placed and scaled, you will want to duplicate it to the other side of the head. The simplest method is to use the SubTool Master script, a plug-in developed by Pixologic and available for free download from the Pixologic website:

   `http://www.pixologic.com/zbrush/downloadcenter`

   You can install the plug-in by extracting the files into the `ZStartup/ZPlugs` folder.

6. SubTool Master allows for a number of operations to be performed on multiple subtools. Since you want to mirror-duplicate the eye across X, make sure the eye is selected.

7. Run SubTool Master by clicking the button under ZPlugin → SubToolMaster. This will open the SubTool Master menu (Figure 3.30). Click the Mirror button. In the Mirror subtool options (Figure 3.31), select the Merge Into One Subtool option and the option to mirror across the x-axis.

8. This will create a single new subtool of both eyes mirrored across the x-axis. You will now want to create lips for your head. Instead of simply sculpting them from the surface, you will want some form of mouth bag to facilitate later work when you want to turn this head into an animatable mesh.

9. Switch to wireframe by pressing the Shift+F hotkey, and you will be able to see the edge loops you placed for the mouth in Chapter 1 (Figure 3.32).

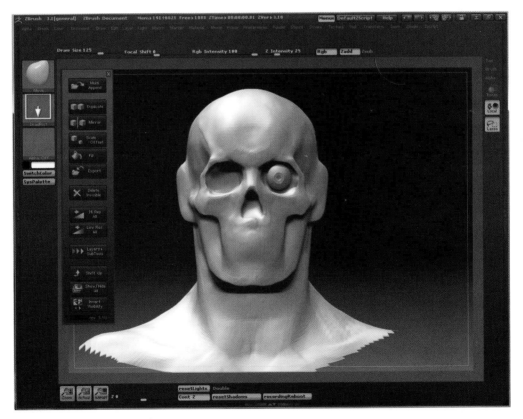

Figure 3.30 *The SubTool Master menu options*

10. Using the Standard brush with ZSub on, press the interior of the mouth in to create a cavity for the teeth and tongue (Figure 3.33). Don't press too deeply because it will stretch the face in the area of the lips where you will want more detail later.

11. Use the Move brush to tug the mesh back together (Figure 3.34). You will further refine the lips later in this chapter, but for now you just want to establish a general location and depth to the cavity of the mouth.

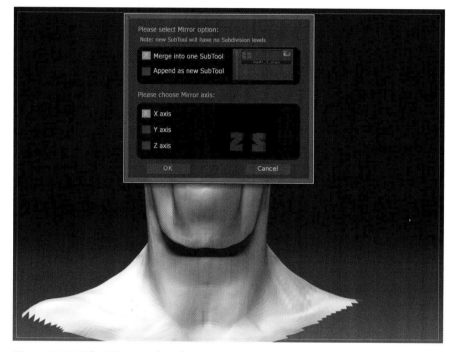

Figure 3.31 The Mirror subtool options

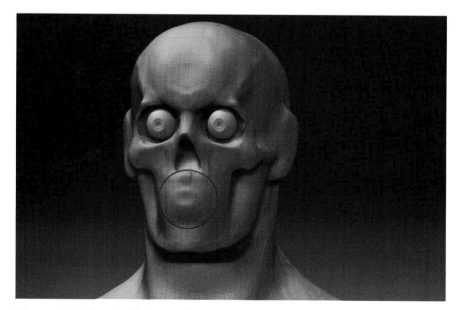

Figure 3.32 The mouth in wireframe

Figure 3.33 *Using the Standard brush to push the mouth cavity in*

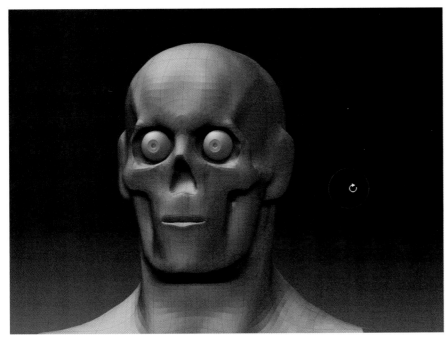

Figure 3.34 *Pull the lips together over the mouth cavity.*

The Facial Muscles

The muscles of the face can be broken down into two groups: the muscles of expression and the muscles of mastication. *Mastication* means to chew, so those muscles are most directly involved in closing and grinding the jaw. Muscles of expression are involved in displaying emotion with the face, one of the most telling parts of our bodies. So much of our nonverbal communication is accomplished with subtle facial cues, as muted as the twitch of a brow or the turning of a corner of the mouth. We are all intensely attuned to the subtleties of the human head, so it is no wonder that animating realistic humans is such a difficult task.

For sculpting the muscles, you will rely mostly on the Rake and Claytubes brushes. The Rake brush in particular is well suited to this task since it creates the muscle striations as it builds up form, helping you to spot the direction and flow of the muscle fibers (Figure 3.35).

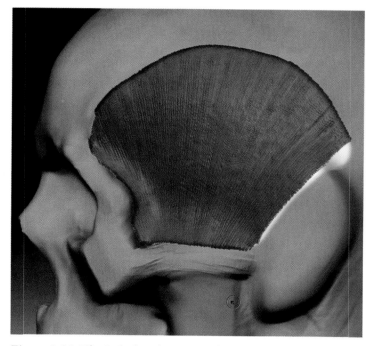

Figure 3.35 The Rake brush is particularly good for sculpting muscle fibers.

As a visual guide while you work, you will be using the brush to add material as well as form. This means that, as you sculpt, each new stroke will display as a new material on the model, specifically the Red Wax shader.

To make it clear where you are sculpting the muscle forms, you will use the Material functionality of ZBrush's brushes. You can sculpt paint as well as add material using a sculpting brush in ZBrush. By adding a material while you work, you'll make it clear where each muscle is placed. To do this, you need to make sure the Basic Material is selected and the M modifier is turned on at the top of the screen.

1. Click Color → FillObject. This will fill the model with the Basic Material, allowing you to switch to a new material and have it added as you sculpt.

2. From the Material menu, select the Red Wax material. Since you have filled the model with Basic Material, it will not change appearance at this time; however, any strokes you make on the model will also apply this new material. Select the Claytubes brush, and make sure both M and ZAdd are on. Now when you sculpt the muscles, they will appear in the new material (Figure 3.36).

The muscles you will be examining in this chapter are only a few of the muscles of the face. They are, however, the major muscles that influence the surface form of the most basic planes of the head, and for that reason alone they are valuable to know and understand. Figure 3.37 shows these muscles labeled on the skull, and Table 3.1 lists the muscles and describes the origin, insertions, and functions of each one.

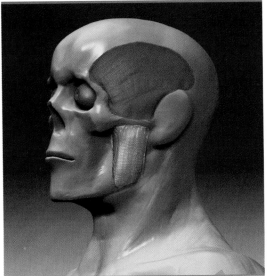

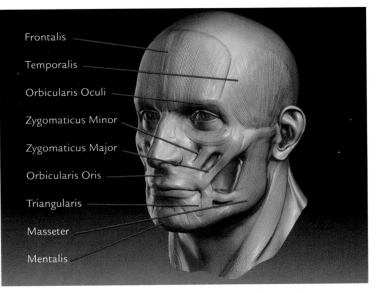

Figure 3.36 A muscle sculpted with the Red Wax material turned on

Figure 3.37 The muscles you will be addressing in this chapter

Table 3.1: The Functions, Origins, and Insertions of This Chapter's Muscles

Muscle	Function	Origin and Insertion
Frontalis	Raises the eyebrows	Origin at top of the forehead; inserts at skin of eyebrow
Temporalis	Closes the jaw	Origin at the temporal ridge; inserts at angle of the jawbone
Masseter	Clenches the teeth	Origin at the bottom of the zygomatic bone; inserts at the angle of the jawbone
Zygomaticus major and minor	Pulls the angle of the mouth upward	Origin at zygomatic bone; inserts at nodes of lips
Orbicularis oris	Opens and closes mouth	Attaches at nodes of the lips
Orbicularis oculi	Opens and closes eyes	Outer border of the eye socket
Triangularis	Pulls the angle of the mouth down	Origin at bottom edge of jaw; inserts at the nodes of the lips
Buccinator	Pulls the corners of the mouth back	Origin on the jaw; inserts at the nodes of lips
Mentalis	Raises the chin	Origin at the bottom of the lower teeth; inserts into skin of the chin

Laying the muscles on the skull in this manner helps you see how the primary planes of the face are composed. It is my hope that this exercise will help you learn not only about the structure of facial anatomy, but also how the underlying muscle and bone combine to create the very specific highlights and shadows on the human face; this understanding is in many ways more important. Remember, all form is merely light and shadow. To be a good sculptor, you need to learn how to manipulate the way a surface is affected by the light falling on it.

The Masseter and Temporalis Muscles

You will begin by sculpting the Masseter and Temporalis muscles. These are muscles that are concerned primarily with moving the jaw. They also fill out the hollows under the cheekbone and the temporal regions of the skull (Figure 3.38).

Figure 3.38 The Masseter and Temporalis from the front view

1. Mask out the area for the Temporalis, as in Figure 3.39. The Temporalis fills the hollow at the temple of the skull. It originates at the temporal ridge and inserts on the jawbone. Using the Rake brush, mass in the Temporalis muscle.
2. The Masseter is masked in much in the same way as the Temporalis. Start by using Ctrl-click masking to paint the shape of the muscle; then Ctrl-click the background to invert the mask so you can sculpt the muscle. Figure 3.40 shows the Masseter sculpted in place.

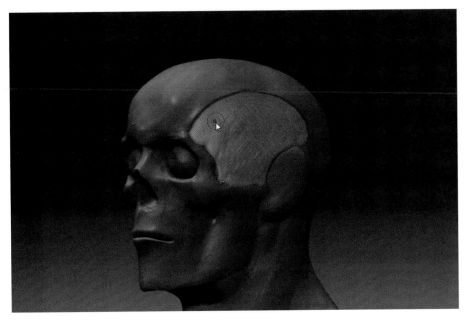

Figure 3.39 *The Temporalis sculpted in with the Rake brush*

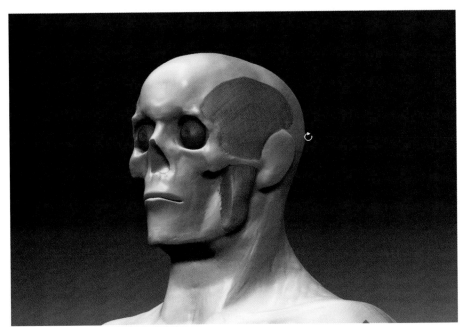

Figure 3.40 *Sculpting the Masseter muscle*

The Zygomaticus Major and Minor

Next you will place the Zygomaticus major and minor muscles. These muscles raise the lips and, most important, form the long edge of a major plane on the face. This plane is called the *infraorbital triangle* because it is inferior, or below, the orbital or eye socket (Figure 3.41). The Zygomaticus minor is the top, shorter muscle; the major is the lower, longer muscle (Figure 3.42). The minor originates on the front of the cheekbone, while the major originates on the side. Both muscles weave into the Orbicularis oris, or circular mouth muscle, which you will sculpt next.

1. Mask out the area for the Zygomaticus muscles. Invert the mask so the surface is ready to sculpt.
2. Using the Move brush, pull the form out so it creates a triangular planed area. You can further refine the form with the Rake brush.

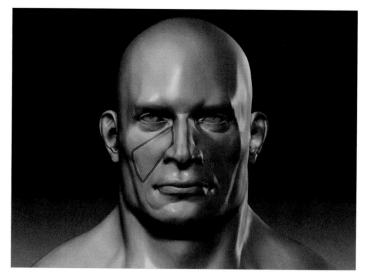

Figure 3.41 The infraorbital triangle as seen on the finished face

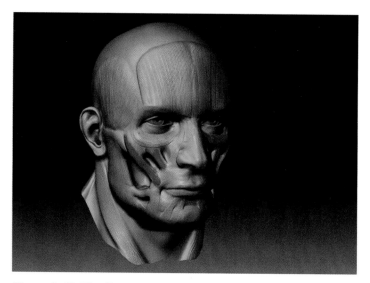

Figure 3.42 The Zygomaticus major and minor muscles

The Orbicularis Oris

The Orbicularis oris is the circular muscle that surrounds the mouth and allows you to express many emotions by changing the shape of the lips; it also assists in speech and eating.

1. Mask out the shape, as shown in Figure 3.43.

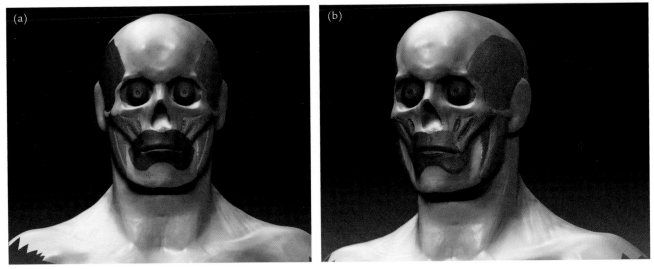

Figure 3.43 *Masking out the shape: (a) the area for the Orbicularis oris masked, (b) the sculpted Orbicularis oris*

2. Invert the mask by Ctrl-clicking the background, and then use the Rake tool to sculpt the muscle as shown on the right. Take care not to make it too thick because the muscles of the face, with the exception of the Masseter and Temporalis, are actually extremely thin. The Orbicularis oris has an appearance similar to a frowning clown mouth. The two dips on the sides of the chin are important to note since they are always visible on the fleshed surface of the figure (Figure 3.44).

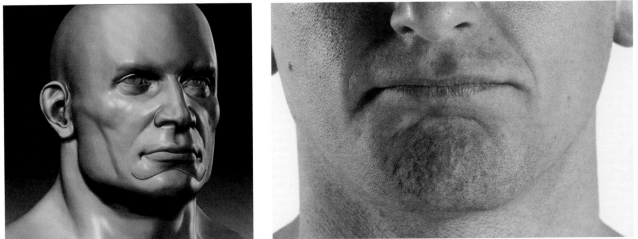

Photo courtesy of www.3d.sk.

Figure 3.44 *The Orbicularis oris muscle: (a) the W shape of the Orbicularis oris muscle marked, (b) the Orbicularis oris clearly visible*

The Triangularis and the Mentalis: The Chin

For the chin, you will add two muscles, the Triangularis and the Mentalis. The Triangularis muscles are on either side of the chin. Needless to say, the Triangularis muscle has a triangular shape. It is extremely thin and not often noticeable on the face except by its effect on expression. Figure 3.45 shows the Triangularis sculpted in place.

The Mentalis is a small oval muscle at the center of the chin. It is often visible on the surface as a subtle bump, and it merits mention for the way its shape interlocks with the W form of the Orbicularis oris (Figure 3.46). Interestingly, the Mentalis is a rare muscle that turns out to connect to the skin instead of bone. When you grimace, as if eating a sour lemon, the small crevices on your chin are created by the fibers of the Mentalis muscle where they are attaching to the deep tissues of the chin.

1. Isolate the area for the Triangularis muscle with a mask. Select the Rake brush, and sculpt its form into place. It weaves into the corners of the lips.
2. Using the Rake brush, sculpt in a circular form for the Mentalis muscle. These two forms are very thin, so take care not to mass them out too much. The effect on the surface of the face is apparent but subtle.

Figure 3.45 Sculpting the Triangularis

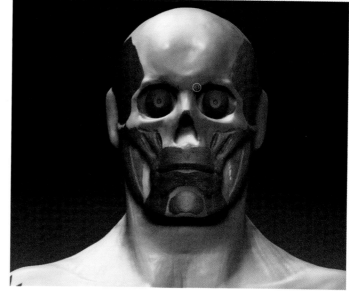

Figure 3.46 The Mentalis is a small oval muscle at the tip of the chin.

The Frontalis: The Forehead

The forehead is covered by a thin sheet of muscle called the Frontalis. The Frontalis furrows the brow and also pulls up on the eyebrows. It is extremely thin except for the small tail that inserts into the eye socket.

1. Using the Masking brush, paint in the shape of the Frontalis, as shown in Figure 3.47(a).
2. Once you are satisfied with the shape, invert the mask, and then use the Rake brush to add the muscle. Be sure not to make it too thick; the Frontalis is extremely thin, and its shape is more defined by the frontal eminence of the underlying skull than the muscle, as shown in Figure 3.47(b).

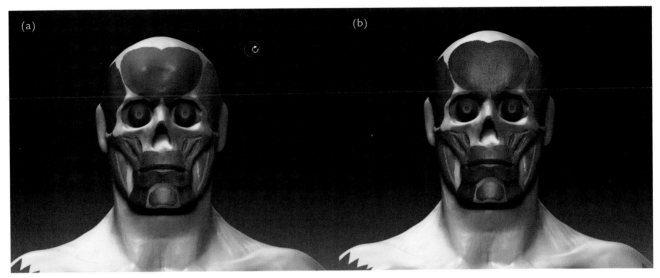

Figure 3.47 Adding the Frontalis: (a) the area for the Frontalis isolated, (b) the Frontalis sculpted in

The Orbicularis Oculi

You will now turn your attention to the muscles of the eye. These muscles are circular in form, similar to the Orbicularis oris. The eye muscles are called the *Orbicularis oculi*. They lie like goggles over the eye sockets and form the eyelids (Figure 3.48).

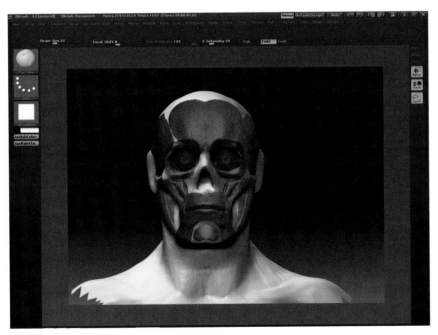

Figure 3.48 The Orbicularis oculi isolated and ready for sculpting

1. To create the Orbicularis oculi, mask into the eye sockets. Invert the mask, and then use the Claytubes brush to fill out the hollows and bring the faces to the front. It may be helpful to turn on transparency in order to see through the eyeballs while you work.

2. Using the Rake brush, sculpt the muscle using a circular stroke around the circumference of the eye socket (Figure 3.49).

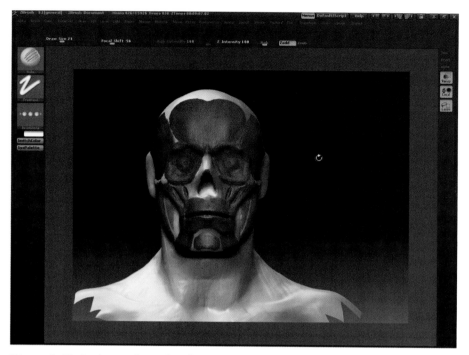

Figure 3.49 Sculpting the Orbicularis oculi

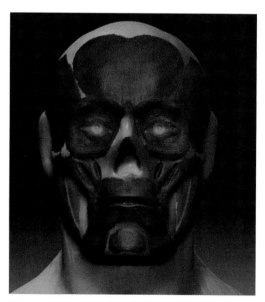

Figure 3.50 Creating the eyelids. Use the Claytubes brush with ZSub to press the eyes in.

3. To create the eyelids, first mask the shape of the interior of the eye (Figure 3.50). Invert the mask, and then use Claytubes with ZSub to press the unmasked faces into the head. On the right you can see that activating transparency makes it easier to move the eyelids in relation to the sphere of the eyeball.

4. Isolate the eyes and mask the bony areas of the eye socket, as shown in Figure 3.51(a). It is important to preserve the bony shape of the orbit because you want to retain a sense of soft fatty areas as well as sharp bony areas around the eye. Using the Move brush, pull the lids forward so that they lie against the surface of the eyeball. The upper eyelid should lie over the lower. To facilitate this, mask out the lower lid, and then use the Move brush to gently pull the upper lid out slightly, as in Figure 3.51(b).

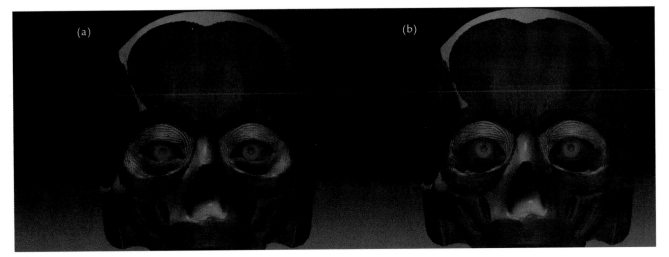

Figure 3.51 Masking the bony areas of the eye socket: (a) pulling out the eyelids, (b) pulling the upper lid out

When working on the eyelids, it is important to understand their shape. The two corners of the eyes are called the *canthus*. The one on the side is the *lateral canthus*, while the one in the center is the *medial canthus*. Notice in Figure 3.52(a) that the lateral canthus is slightly higher than the medial. In Figure 3.52(b) you can see the rhythms of the eyelids. Notice how the crest of the upper lid is toward the center, while the crest of the lower lid is toward the outside.

5. Continue to sculpt the eyelids, using transparency mode to facilitate manipulating the faces inside the eyeball and pulling them out to the surface. Don't forget that the eyelids have thickness. If you make them too thin, it will be difficult if not impossible to catch a highlight on the lower lid, which will make the eye look unnatural.

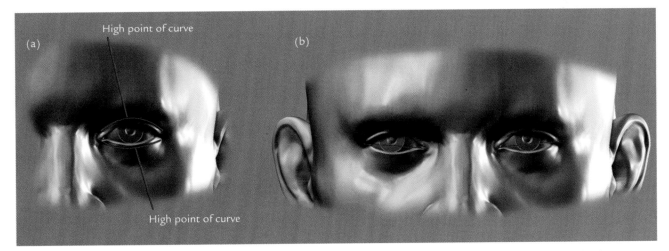

Figure 3.52 Working on the eyelids: (a) the angle of the eyelid from the lateral to medial canthus, (b) the rhythms between the curve of the upper eyelid and the lower lid

The Buccinator Muscle

At this stage, you will add the Buccinator muscle. The Buccinator is a deep-layer muscle and is not apparent on the surface of the face, but I chose to add it in here to help fill in the hollow area of the cheeks. This muscle originates on the jawbone and inserts into the corner of the mouth at the Orbicularis oris muscle (Figure 3.53).

Use the Claytubes brush to mass in the muscle and fill out the deeper areas of the cheeks. Do not bring it to the same level as the Masseter, however, because there is fatty tissue covering both of these muscles that will fill out the side planes of the cheeks.

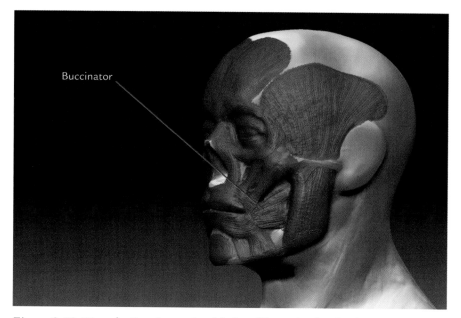

Figure 3.53 *Here the Buccinator is added to fill out the depth of the cheeks.*

The Facial Features

So far, you have built up the skeletal and muscular anatomy of the face. In the interest of making this look more like a human, you need to add the facial features like the nose, lips, and ears. You will start adding these features now, as well as the muscles of the neck, so you can better evaluate the head sculpture as you move into finer forms.

The Nose

The nose is a complex shape when taken as a whole. Much like the ear, which I'll address later in the chapter, it is primarily cartilage and composed of many subtle planes. For ease of understanding, Figure 3.54 shows the four parts of the nose: the tip, or *alar cartilages*; the wings of the nostrils; and the lateral cartilages at the bridge of the nose.

1. To start sculpting the nose, mask out the inside of the nasal cavity. Invert the mask, and use the Claytubes brush to fill out the cavity (Figure 3.55). Use the Move brush to pull the nose out from the face and start to establish it in silhouette.

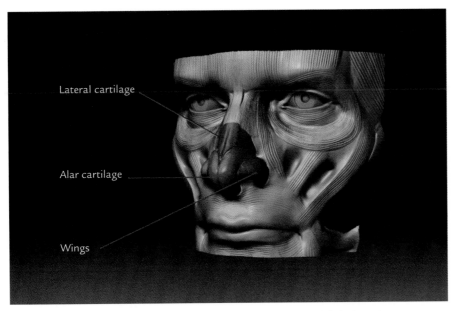

Figure 3.54 This sculpture of the nose in écorché *view is labeled to show its major parts.*

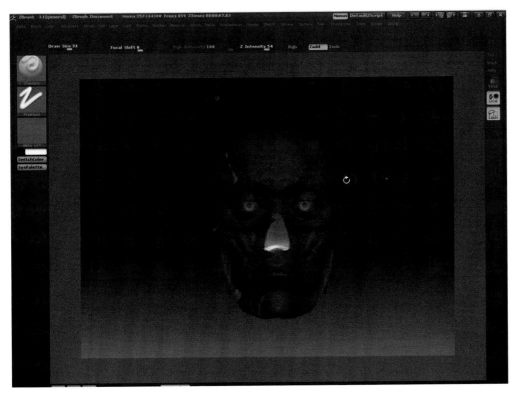

Figure 3.55 Filling out the nasal cavity

2. Move to the front view, and start to pull the wings of the nostrils out from the sides (Figure 3.56(a)). The nose takes patience; just as with the mouth, very tiny changes here can drastically alter the appearance of a character. With the bridge of the nose and wings in place, use the Standard brush with ZSub to press the nostrils in (Figure 3.56(b)).

3. From the side view, pull the septum down, and curve it into the upper lip. The septum is the bit of skin and card ledge between the nostrils.

   At this point, you have the general shape of the nose, but you will need to use the Flatten brush to introduce the hard planes that give the nose its characteristic and complex shape.

4. Start by establishing the planes of the alar cartilage. The alar looks like a diamond on the top of the nose, as shown in Figure 3.57(a). Moving up, flatten the bridge of the nose and the sides that meet the face. Figure 3.57(b) shows the nose refined on the final sculpture.

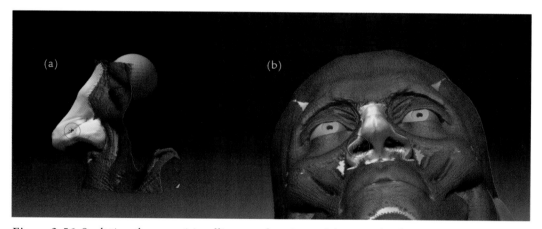

Figure 3.56 *Sculpting the nose: (a) pulling out the wings of the nostrils, (b) pressing in the nostrils*

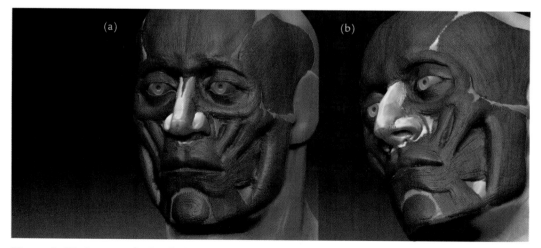

Figure 3.57 *Creating the hard planes of the nose: (a) using the Flatten brush to plane in the alar cartilage and bridge of the nose, (b) planing the underside of the wings of the nostrils*

Closing the Mouth

To facilitate ease of sculpting the mouth, you will want to isolate the upper and lower lips into separate polygroups. *Polygroups* are sets of faces in ZBrush that you can easily hide or display by Ctrl+Shift-clicking them. They are visible in PolyFrame mode as different-colored mesh segments. Figure 3.58 shows the mouth with the upper and lower lips polygrouped.

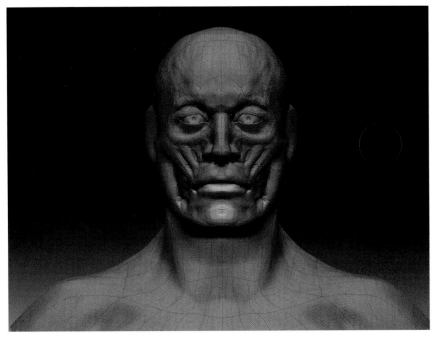

Figure 3.58 An example of colored polygroups

1. Begin by storing a *morph target* of the mouth in its current closed position. To do that, choose Tool → Morph Target → Store MT. This keeps a copy of the current mesh position and shape stored in memory. This shape can be recalled at any time by returning to the subdivision level where the morph target was stored and clicking the switch button. Only one morph target can be stored at a time per subtool. You may also find that you cannot access the switch button if you are either on a different subdivision level than the target was stored or if you have part of the mesh hidden.

2. Using the Smooth brush, smooth the mouth to separate the lips (Figure 3.59).

3. To mask the lower jaw, click the Lasso button on the right side of the screen to turn on lasso mode, and then hold down Ctrl while dragging a masking marquee around the lower jaw (Figure 3.60). Anything inside this gray region will be masked when you release the mouse, while anything outside will be unmasked.

4. With the lower jaw masked, select Tool → Morph Target → Switch. The mouth will now close again, but the lower jaw will remain fully masked (Figure 3.61).
   To avoid having to repeat this process each time you want to mask the upper or lower lips, you will use the polygroups function in the next steps.

5. With the lower jaw still masked, click Tool → Masking → HidePt. This will hide the unmasked faces of the rest of the body, leaving the lower jaw isolated (Figure 3.62).

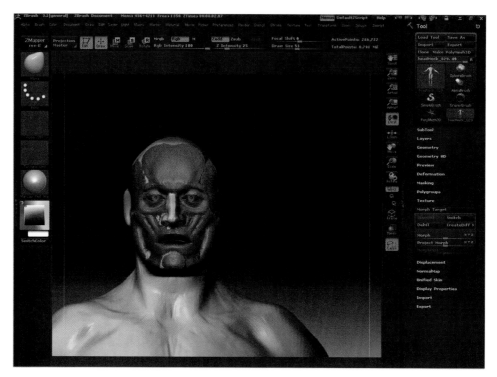

Figure 3.59 *Using the Smooth brush to separate the lips*

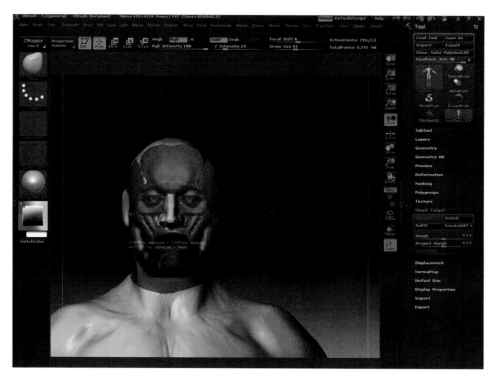

Figure 3.60 *Drawing a mask lasso around the lower jaw*

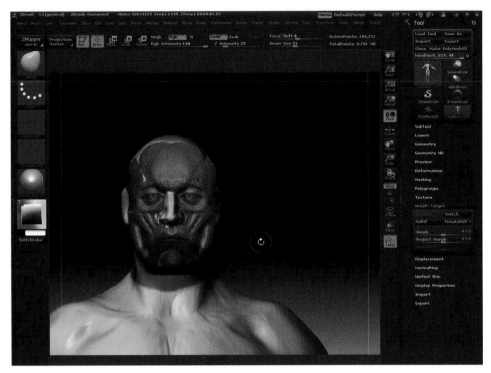

Figure 3.61 The lower jaw closed and masked

6. With only the lower jaw visible, select Tool → Polygroups → Group Visible. This will polygroup the lower jaw faces currently on the screen. Ctrl+Shift-click the backdrop to reveal the rest of the model again.

7. Press Shift+F to see the model in PolyFrame view. You will notice the lower jaw is now a different color (Figure 3.63). Ctrl+Shift-clicking the jaw will now isolate it and allow you to mask it quickly.

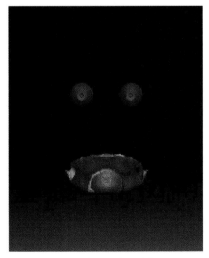

Figure 3.62 The isolated lower jaw

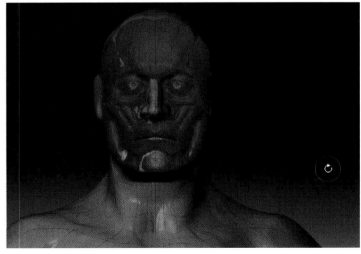

Figure 3.63 The polygrouped jaw

You can now move the lips of the upper mouth without affecting the lower.

8. Simply isolate the jaw polygroup with Ctrl+Shift-click and mask it; then reveal the rest of the model again.

9. Using the Move brush, pull the lips together.

10. To invert your mask, Ctrl+click the background. This will allow you to move the lower lip.

At any point now you can Ctrl+Shift-click the jaw to isolate it and mask it independently of the rest of the head. Figure 3.64 shows the lower lip masked to facilitate pulling the upper lip over it.

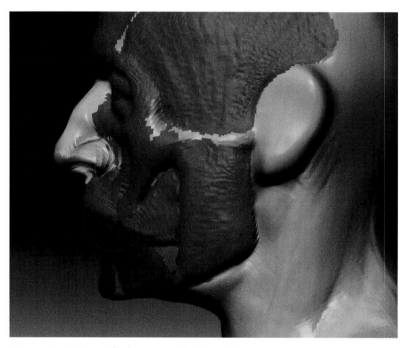

Figure 3.64 Here the lips are pulled together

The Neck Muscles

At this point, the head is at a level of form that you can start thinking about the neck. In this section, you will move away from the face and start to refine the muscles of the neck so you can anchor the head to the shoulders and make it look more natural. It is also good to move around often as you work, so by moving to the neck now, you can take a break from the face before you return for a final pass of refinements.

You will begin the neck with the Sternomastoid muscles. The Sternomastoids originate behind the ear and insert at the pit of the neck. They specifically attach to the clavicles. Consider them as ribbons of muscle wrapping around the cylinder of the neck (Figure 3.65).

1. Rough in the Sternomastoid with the Rake brush, as shown in Figure 3.66. Try to stroke in the direction of the muscle flow; this will help establish the rhythm of the

muscles of the neck as they interlock with the chest. The Sternomastoid has two heads; one connects to the sternum at the pit of the neck, and the second head branches off and attaches to the back of the collar bone.

It is important to note that the Sternomastoid should be visible from the back of the figure, as shown in Figure 3.67. If this is not the case, then they are too thin or the Trapezius is too large.

2. The Trapezius muscle originates at the base of the skull and flows down to the scapulas and the posterior border of the scapula (Figure 3.67). Use the Claytubes brush to build these up.

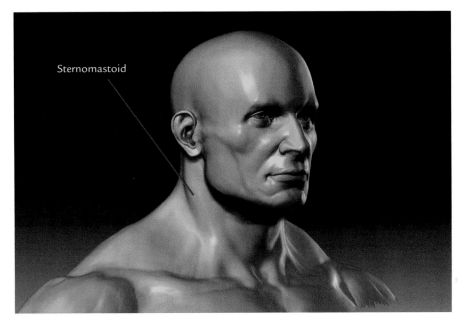

Figure 3.65 *The Sternomastoid muscles*

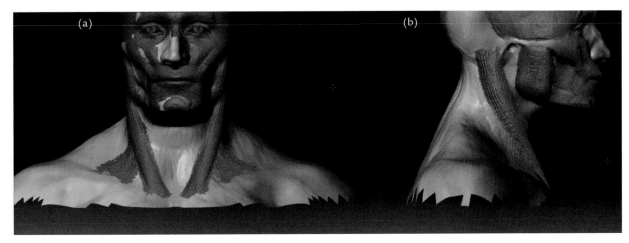

Figure 3.66 *Sculpting the Sternomastoid muscles from the front and side views*

3. Because you are working on a heroic figure, you'll want to adjust the silhouette to make the traps appear bulkier. This increases the apparent mass of the shoulders as well as makes the head appear smaller. This helps give the impression of a more massive and heroic figure (Figure 3.68).

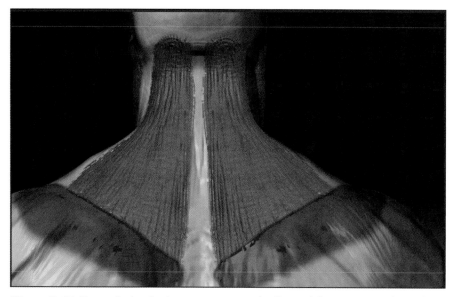

Figure 3.67 From the back view, you can see the flow of the Trapezius from the base of the skull to the spine of the scapula. (Note as well that the Trapezius also attaches to the clavicles, as shown in Figure 3.68.)

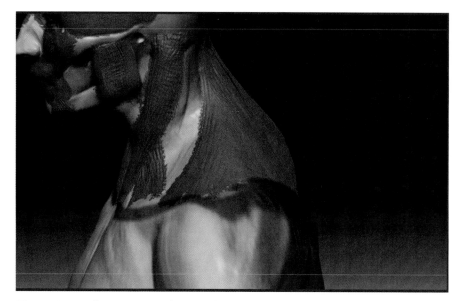

Figure 3.68 The Trapezius also attaches to the back of the clavicle.

4. At this point, you can use the Claytubes brush to reinforce the clavicles, which sweep back from the center of the chest much like handlebars on a bicycle. Figure 3.69 shows these shapes. Notice that there is a definite step or sweep back to the bone.

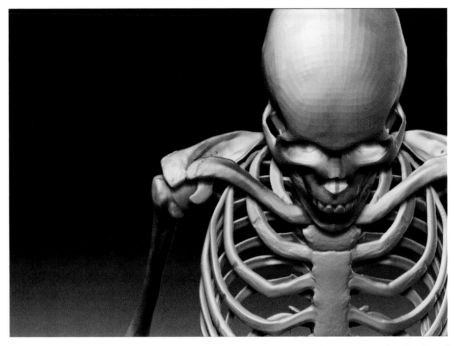

Figure 3.69 The clavicle as seen on the skeleton. Notice the sweeping back of its form.

Refining the Surface

You have now filled in many of the major muscles of the face that have a direct impact on the gross shape or form. There are indeed many more muscles that I could discuss, but they do not have such a visible effect on the shape you know as the head.

At this point, you will fill in the red color of the muscles and start to reinforce the planes that these muscles create. I want to stress again that it is important to understand not just the muscles, but also the planes and shapes they combine to create.

1. Make sure the Basic Material is selected, and select Color → Fill Object to fill the head with the Basic Material.
2. Using the Smooth brush, take down the strokes of the Rake brush. You will now start to suggest the skin and fatty tissues that cover the muscles of the face. Begin with the cheek. With a mask, isolate the area shown in Figure 3.70. As mentioned earlier, this is called the *infraorbital triangle*. You will mass in the fatty tissues of the front of the face in this area.

The infraorbital triangle is the location of a small deposit of fat that creates a fold of skin called the *nasolabial fold*. The nasolabial fold becomes more pronounced with age as the fatty tissues are pulled down by gravity. Figure 3.71 shows the head with the addition of the nasolabial fold as well as some fatty tissues filling out the cheek area.

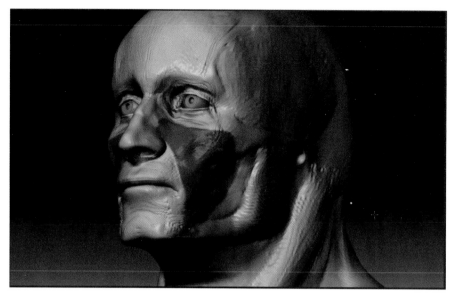

Figure 3.70 Masking the infraorbital triangle

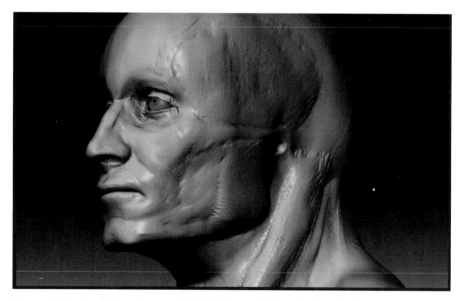

Figure 3.71 Sculpting the nasolabial folds and filling in the cheeks

Sculpting the Ear

The ear is a shape similar to the nose in complexity, and it becomes much easier to sculpt when broken into its aggregate parts. Figure 3.72 shows the ear labeled. The parts of the ear can be quite easy to remember because they mostly consist of a name and its inverse.

For example, you have the *helix* on the outside of the ear as well as the *antihelix* directly inside the helix. Another example is the small nub of flesh and cartilage that covers the auditory *meatus*, or ear hole; this part is called the *tragus*. Directly opposite the tragus is the *antitragus*.

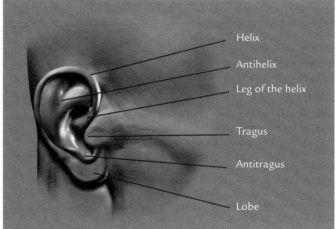

To sculpt the ear following the steps below, you will use a combination of masking, the Standard brush, and the Flatten brush to create the ear. Because you have some geometry in the base mesh to support this form, you should be able to get fine detail and sharp planes quite easily.

1. Begin by moving the edge loops for the ear into position. The top of the ear should line up with the brow ridge, while the lobe should line with the bottom of the nose. Make sure the ear tips back on the head at the same angle as the jawbone. Figure 3.73 shows the outside of the ear masked to facilitate pulling the helix up and out over the rest of the head. You will be able to see the edge loops of the base mesh by turning on PolyFrame mode with the Shift+F hotkey.

Figure 3.72 The parts of the ear

2. Once the ear is in place, use Claytubes to mass in the form of the ear. You will also want to use the Move brush to pull the general shape of the ear out from the head. Use Claytubes with ZSub to scoop out the inside of the helix, making room for the antihelix and conch (Figure 3.74). Right now don't worry about anything but creating the outermost form, or helix and lobe of the ear.

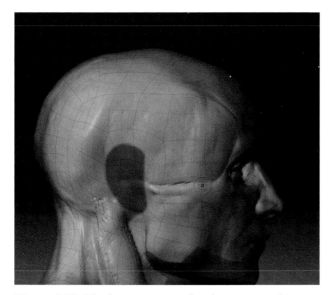

Figure 3.73 The base geometry for the ear moved into position and isolated with a mask

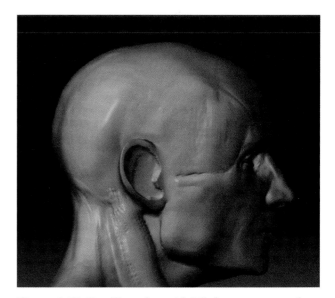

Figure 3.74 Use Claytubes with ZSub to scoop out the inside of the ear.

3. With the interior of the ear scooped out, clear the mask by holding down Ctrl and dragging on the background. Mask the interior of the ear, and invert the mask. Using the Claytubes brush, rough in the shape of the antihelix. Notice that it continues down to join the tragus in the antitragus (Figure 3.75).

4. Using the Standard brush with ZSub, press in the hollow basin of the ear known as the *conch*. At this stage, you also sculpt the *leg* of the helix, which is the terminating point of the helix that dips into the ear (Figure 3.76). Pull out the tragus using the Move brush.

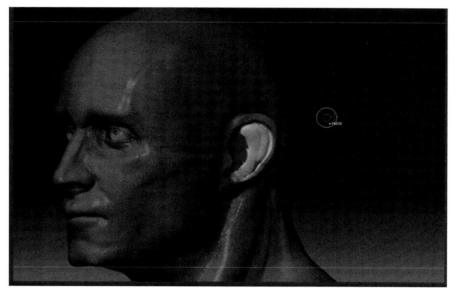

Figure 3.75 *The antihelix sculpted in place*

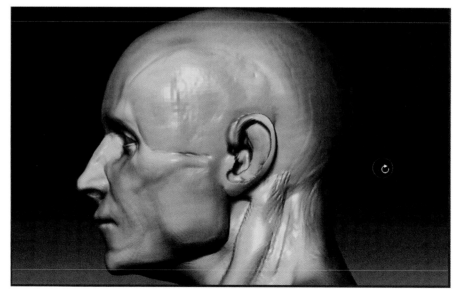

Figure 3.76 *Sculpting the conch and leg of the helix*

5. You can further refine the ear with the Pinch brush and Lazy Mouse. Try to establish the planes and structural form of the ear by pinching with a low intensity. I usually keep the brush between 15 and 20 ZIntensity.

6. From the front view, make sure the antihelix extends out from the helix (Figure 3.77(a)). Also check the angle of the ear in relation to the skull from the back (Figure 3.77(b)). It is rare that the ear lies perfectly flat against the head; this tends to look awkward and should be avoided. Figure 3.77(c) shows the final ear.

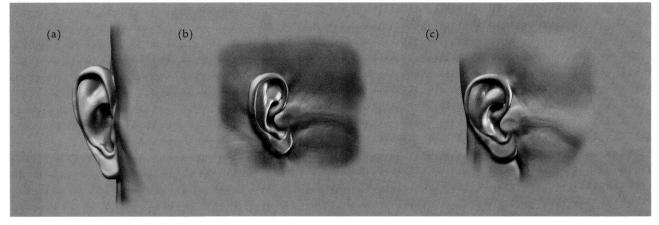

Figure 3.77 *Sculpting the ear: (a) the antihelix seen from the front extends out from the helix, (b) checking the angle from the back, (c) the final ear*

Adding Character and Refining Forms

At this point, you will return to the face to make subtle adjustments to help create a sense of character.

Refining the Lips

The lips are roughed in at this stage but still incomplete. You need to address the pillows of fat that compose the lips themselves as well as a very important surface feature called the *nodes* of the lips.

The nodes of the lips are small, doughnut-shaped areas of fat and skin at the corners of the mouth. They are created by the lower lip tucking under the upper lip as well as by the tension in the area generated by the Zygomaticus and other muscles pulling on the corner of the mouth.

1. With the Inflate brush set to 10 intensity, mask the corners of the lips, and sculpt in the nodes, as shown in Figure 3.78. This is a subtle and tricky area, so move the light as well as the camera often as you work.

2. The lips are also defined by a sharp division along their border where the fatty tissue abuts the rest of the face. This again is a subtle area best approached with low ZIntensity settings and from many angles. Sculpt in the shelf of the upper lip, as shown in Figure 3.79, with the Standard brush and alpha 41. This helps create a fine, sharp line to delineate the plane change.

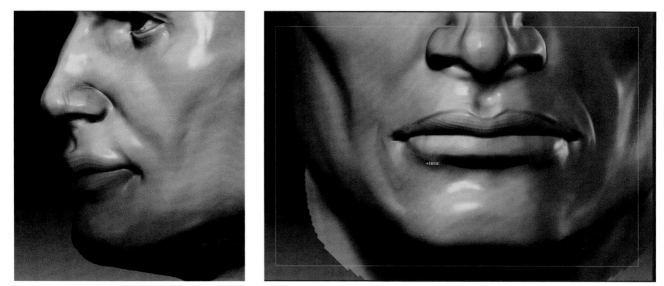

Figure 3.78 Sculpting the nodes of the lips   *Figure 3.79 Sculpting the line for the upper-lip ledge*

3. The lower lip has a similar plane change, but notice in Figure 3.79 how the shelf is most pronounced at the center just above the chin. As you move out from the center of the lower lip, the plane change becomes much more subtle as the lip feathers into the W shape of the Orbicularis oris discussed earlier.

4. Lastly, the *philtrum*, or "cupids bow," is the little division just below the septum of the nose. To create it, use the Standard brush with a ZIntensity of 10. You can further sharpen the lips using the Pinch brush with Lazy Mouse on. Keep your intensity low, between 10 and 20 to avoid creating too harsh a line. Figure 3.80 shows the final lips in detail.

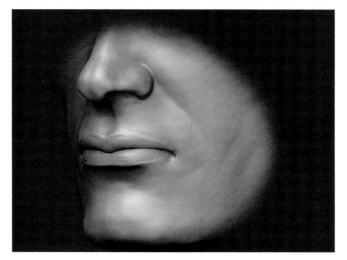

Figure 3.80 The final lip sculpture

Correcting Problematic Geometry

When sculpting the nose and lips especially, you may find that the underlying geometry has become stretched to a point that unappealing artifacts are occurring on the surface of the sculpture. Figure 3.81 shows an example of this. Luckily, ZBrush has a built-in tool for eradicating these problem areas. It is called Reproject Higher Subdivision level.

Figure 3.81 also shows the wings of the nostrils in wireframe. Notice how the edges are pulled far to the left and cause a pinch at the nostril.

1. To correct this issue, step down to a middle subdivision level; in this case, I have moved to level 4. Select the Smooth brush, and set ZIntensity to 20. You want to gently smooth the edges to bring them back into alignment.

2. Smooth the problem area. Take care not to destroy all the sculpted form, but merely massage the edges back into line (Figure 3.82).

3. Under the Tool → Geometry menu, click the Reproject Higher Subdiv button. This will reproject the higher subdivision level onto the newly smoother edges, reintroducing the form without the awkward pinch.

ZBrush will now calculate for a few moments, and when complete, the model will return to the highest subdivision level. You can repeat the projection process again if needed to further correct the problem area. Figure 3.83 shows the wireframe of the nose area after the reprojection. Notice how the severely tweaked edges are gone and the form of the nostril is still there.

Figure 3.81 Pinching in the mesh is a common problem in protruding areas

Figure 3.82 Smoothing the bad edges to bring them back into order

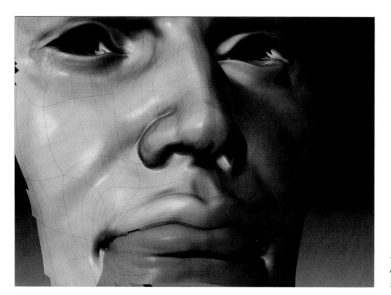

Figure 3.83 The problem area has been remedied with the reprojection.

Equalize Surface Area

As of ZBrush 3.5, a new feature has been added to help correct areas where the underlying faces have become stretched. This feature is located under Tool → Geometry and is called Equalize Surface Area. This button will automatically examine the mesh and locally subdivide areas where the underlying mesh is stretched. Simply step down to the lowest subdivision level and press the Equalize Surface Area button to locally subdivide the mesh. While this can be useful, be aware that local subdivision can create seams on the model which interfere with some brushes. For this reason I find it is best to only locally subdivide when the sculpture is almost complete, just to get that last level of resolution to finish the forms.

Final Adjustments

At this stage, you will adjust the placement of the features to fall more accurately within the canon discussed at the start of this chapter. For this purpose, I have created a ZTool with the head measures marked. You will load this as a subtool and shift the features to line up with the correct lines.

This ZTool is on the DVD. If you have followed to this point with the base mesh provided on the DVD, the guide ZTool will load correctly oriented to the head of the ZTool. If you created your own base mesh, there is a chance it will not align. In that case, use the transpose tools to shift it into place, making sure the top mark aligns with the top of the head.

1. Begin by loading the facial landmarks ZTool into ZBrush. Select your sculpture, and append the landmarks ZTool by clicking the append button under Tool → Subtools. You will now see the landmarks guide (Figure 3.84). Turn off Perspective if it is on by pressing the P key.

2. Select the Move brush, and step down to subdivision level 4. You want to be at a subdivision level where the forms are apparent but there are not so many faces that large changes are difficult to make.

3. Shift the eyes down so the brow line falls on the first measure line below the hairline (Figure 3.85). You will also want to shift the eyeballs again so they line up correctly with the pupils on the centerline of the head.

4. At this stage, you will refine the lids of the eye. Zoom in on the eyelids, and isolate them with a show marquee. Select the Standard brush and alpha 01. Etch in the fold of the upper eyelid, as shown in Figure 3.86.

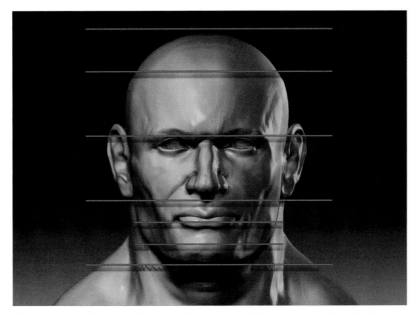

Figure 3.84 The facial landmarks guide tool loaded as a subtool of the figure

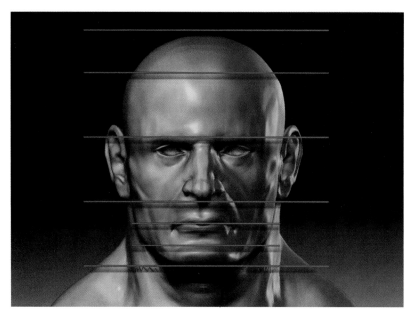

Figure 3.85 Shift the brow ridge down with the Move brush.

Placing Eyeballs

Getting the eyeball placement just right can be challenging. Tiny variations in how much of the iris is visible and which parts are covered can make huge changes in the nature of the character's gaze. When placing the eyes, I like to make the lower eyelid just barely overlap the bottom of the iris. This helps create a natural, relaxed gaze (`eyeplaced.tif`).

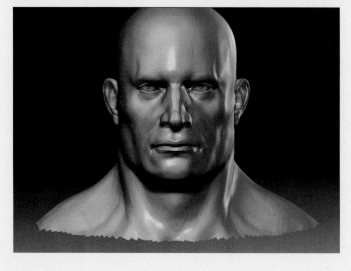

5. Select the Pinch brush, and press L to activate Lazy Mouse. Pinch the edges of the eyelids to sharpen the ledge where they meet the eyeball (Figure 3.87(a)). Select the Standard brush, and turn down the draw size. You need to add the small bump of flesh seen inside the medial canthus of the eye; this small pink piece of flesh is called the *lacrimal carnucle*. You can see this in Figure 3.87(b).

6. With the Move brush, move the bottom of the nose down to coincide with the second measure line, as shown in Figure 3.88, where you can also see that the bridge of the nose is adjusted. Notice that the plane break at the bridge of the nose should fall even with the eyelids. Move to a side view, and check the silhouette of the nose. Further adjust the bridge from the side view, as shown in Figure 3.89.

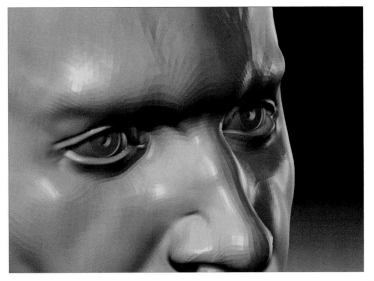

Figure 3.86 Etch in the fold of the upper eyelid with the Standard brush.

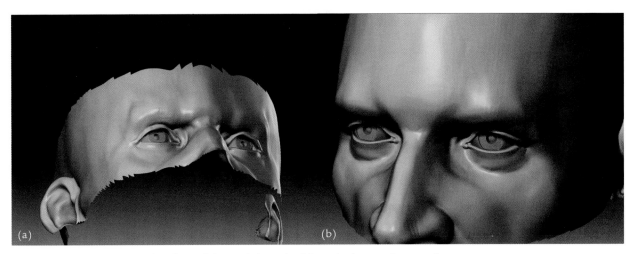

Figure 3.87 Pinching the borders of the eyelids and adding the lacrimal carnucle

7. Move the lips down so the line between them falls on the first of the smaller lines dividing the bottom of the head into thirds, as shown in Figure 3.90. There you can also see that I have reinforced the nasolabial fold again. At this stage they appear too strong, which ages the head, but you will reduce their mass and therefore the shadow they cast as the head is refined.

8. Mask out the lower lip to allow the upper lip to be shifted out and over it. You do this at the lower subdivision levels so there are fewer points to shift to make the change. By moving points at a lower level, the lips will not appear lumpy as they might if you tried to move their shapes at the higher subdivision levels (Figure 3.91).

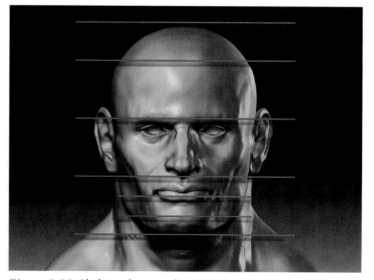

Figure 3.88 *Shifting the nose down to the second measure line. Notice the break in silhouette at the top of the nasal bone.*

Figure 3.89 *The bridge of the nose adjusted from the side view*

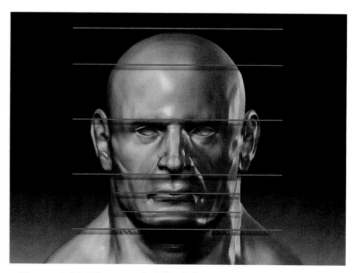

Figure 3.90 *The mouth shifted down*

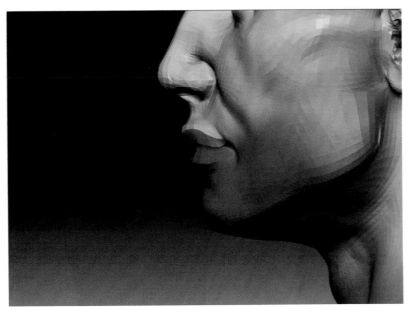

Figure 3.91 Shifting angle of the upper lip to the lower lip

Move to a side view, and check the placement of the ears. They should fall between the brow line and the bottom of the nose. Figure 3.92 shows the ears shifted back into place. Also note the ears should be at an angle just behind the midline of the side of the head.

9. From the side, check the mass under the chin. In Figure 3.93 you can see I have shifted this back, taking care to add a plane break at the Adam's apple. Now change to flat color mode to view the silhouette. Here I adjust the profiles of the head, taking care with the plane breaks at the hairline and top of the head (Figure 3.94).

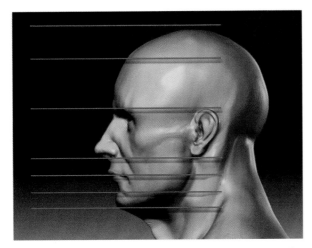

Figure 3.92 The ears fall between the brow line and the bottom of the nose.

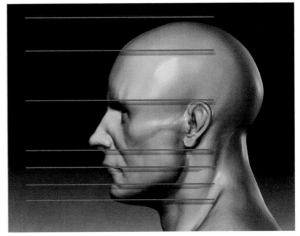

Figure 3.93 Adjusting the shapes of the underside of the chin

10. At this stage, you can sharpen the edge of the Masseter muscle at the angle of the jawbone. So mask out the angle and mass in the muscle using the Inflate brush (Figure 3.95).

At this point, you can refine and strengthen some of the muscles of the neck. They have gone a little soft in the process of working and need to be reintroduced and, in some cases, strengthened to match the heroic quality of the figure you are sculpting.

1. Mask out the clavicles, and mass them in with the Claytubes brush (Figure 3.96(a)). The collar bones or clavicles will be important in the next chapter when you work on the torso since they form the attachment for the Deltoid and Pectoralis muscles. Here you will attach the Sternomastoids (Figure 3.96(b)).

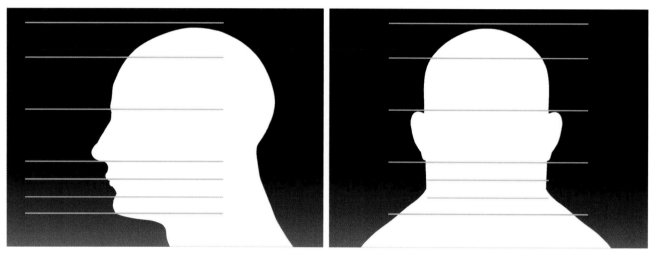

Figure 3.94 Checking the head in silhouette

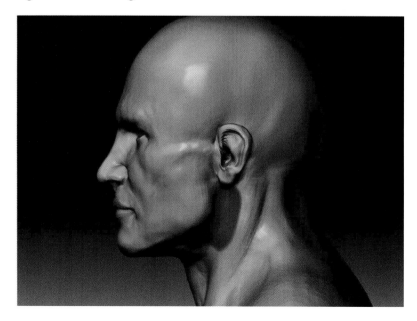

Figure 3.95 Masking the angle of the mandible to help create a sharp edge to the Masseter muscle of the jaw

Figure 3.96 *Strengthening the neck muscles: (a) reinforcing the clavicles, (b) sculpting the Sternomastoid with the Claytubes brush*

2. Using the Claytubes brush, stroke in the Trapezius muscle. You will look at this muscle in more detail in the next chapter. For now, sculpt it in from the base of the neck, as shown in Figure 3.97.

3. Use the interactive light script to move the light, and check the sculpture under different lighting conditions. Interactive light is located under ZPlugin → Misc Utilities. Click the interactive light button to move the light source with your mouse. This will work only on standard materials and not Matcap materials. Remember to check the shapes of the shadows and look for areas that are too defined or lacking form. Adjust them accordingly (Figure 3.98).

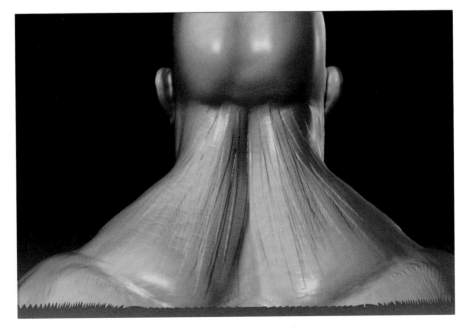

Figure 3.97 *Starting to suggest the Trapezius muscle*

You may want to load an earlier iteration of your skull sculpture as a subtool. By turning visibility on and off with transparency on, you can check to see that the general form of the skeletal understructure has remained consistent with the original skull. If not, use the Move brush to make any adjustments necessary at a lower subdivision level.

Congratulations! You have completed the sculpture of the human head. The head is by far one of the most difficult parts of the body to sculpt well, owing to the intense level of familiarity we all have with the way a human head should look. Figure 3.99 shows the finished head sculpture.

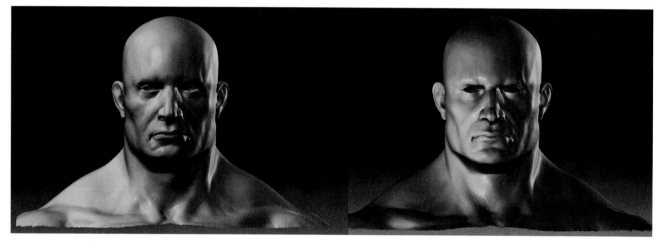

Figure 3.98 *Checking the sculpture under different lighting conditions*

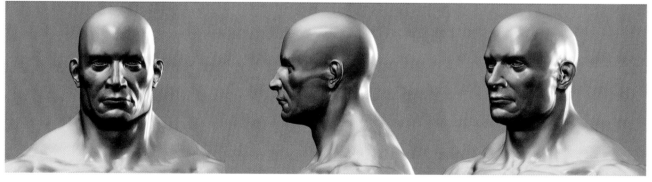

Figure 3.99 *The final head and neck sculpture*

What's Next?

In the next chapter, you will move on to the shoulders and chest, continuing your work down the figure. You will be revisiting the neck as you work to ensure the parts of the figure continue to work together as a whole.

four

The Torso

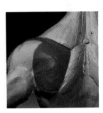

Starting with the figure *as you left it in Chapter 3, in this chapter you will address the central pillar of the human body: the torso, abdomen, and pelvis. This area includes the chest, back, shoulders, waist, and hips. The shoulders and hips are areas of transition that you will address again in later chapters on the arms and legs, where you will explore how these forms transition into the limbs. For now, you will keep these areas rough in relation to the areas of current focus.*

In Figure 4.1, you can see the torso of the finished hero with the skin and fat removed. I have created this sculpture as a reference for you while you work, and the ZTool is available on the DVD. In this chapter, you will pay attention to specific bony landmarks on the surface as well as muscle groups. Those landmarks are as follows:

> *Sternum*
> *Sterno-clavicular notch*
> *Thoracic arch*
> *Acromion process*
> *Spine of the scapula*
> *Superior anterior iliac crest*
> *Superior posterior iliac crest*

Figure 4.1 *The heroic torso in écorché view*

You will also be dealing with some specific muscle groups:

Pectoralis
Rectus abdominis
External oblique
Serratus
Trapezius
Latissimus dorsi

Rhomboids
Teres major
Infraspinatus
Deltoid
Erector spinae

Figure 4.2 identifies these groups on the hero character.

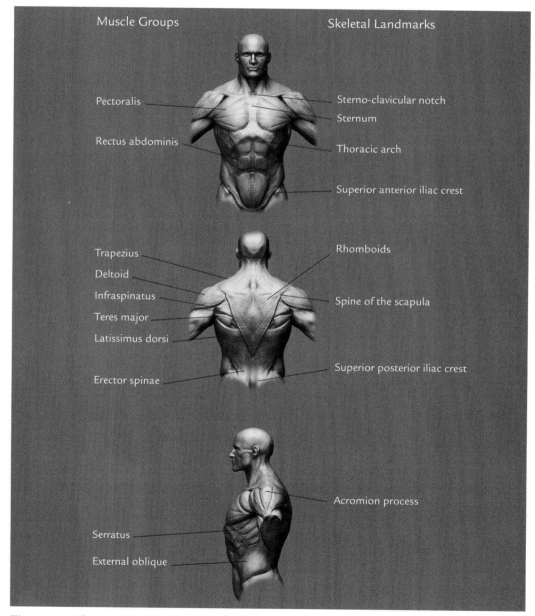

Figure 4.2 The muscles as well as bony landmarks labeled

Changing the Torso Masses

You will begin by making some general changes to the mass of the torso. The gesture sculpt you created in Chapter 2 was of a generic human male physique (Figure 4.3). In this chapter, you'll give this character more heroic proportions. You will do this by adding muscle mass to the chest and back as well as slightly changing the relation between the chest mass and pelvis mass. This creates a more arched back posture. By thrusting the chest out, you can create a heroic stance. Figure 4.4 illustrates the differences.

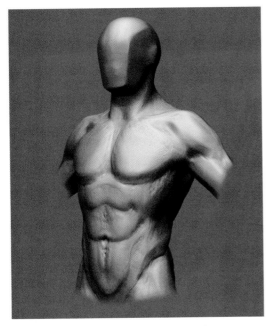

Figure 4.3 The generic male torso from Chapter 2

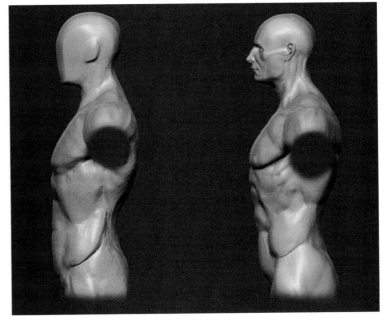

Figure 4.4 This comparison image illustrates some of the changes you will make to the torso to bring it more in line with a heroic figure.

Model Preparation: Storing a Morph Target

Before you start to sculpt, let's store a morph target of the figure in its current state. As you may recall from Chapter 3, a *morph target* is a copy of the mesh in its current state that ZBrush stores in memory. Once you've stored a morph target, you can switch between the current version and the stored target at any time by clicking the Switch button. Another useful aspect of a stored morph target is that you can use the Morph brush to blend between different versions of the sculpture.

Because you will be working on the torso independently of the arms and legs in this book, it's a good idea to keep the original mesh stored in memory as a morph target. This way, you can easily correct any problems that may arise later where the torso meets the arms or legs. For example, if you find that the shoulders have moved too far in relation to the arms, it's a simple matter to use the Morph brush to blend off the difference.

Having a stored morph target also has the added benefit that you can check the changes you have made between the original gestural sculpt and the more refined sculpt. Check the DVD for a video illustrating morph targets and how they are stored and used.

1. To store a morph target, step to the highest subdivision level of the ZTool. Under the Tool menu, open the Morph Target flyout menu, and click the Store morph target button. This will store a morph target that you can recall at any time by clicking the Switch button.

2. You will now isolate the head and torso from the rest of the figure as you work. From the front view, draw a show marquee by holding down Ctrl+Shift, click-dragging, and pulling the green marquee around the torso and head (Figure 4.5). This will isolate it from the legs and arms since you will be focused on this area.

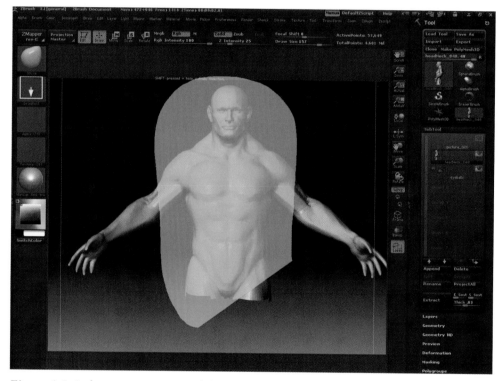

Figure 4.5 A show marquee around the figure

Adjusting the Chest Mass

In this section, you will begin by adjusting the mass of the torso into a more heroic shape. The underlying skeleton of the existing torso is consistent with what you want in the end; however, the mass of the overlying muscle needs to be greater, creating the bulky torso apparent in superheroes.

Figure 4.6 Move brush settings

1. The first change to make is increasing the mass of the chest and back. Whenever you make large form changes like this, the Move brush is the best choice, so switch to that brush. Lower the ZIntensity setting to make it easier to create subtle changes (Figure 4.6). Using the Move brush, pull the width of the shoulders and chest out to match Figure 4.7. What you are doing here is adding muscle mass more than changing the skeletal structure, so do not pull too far.

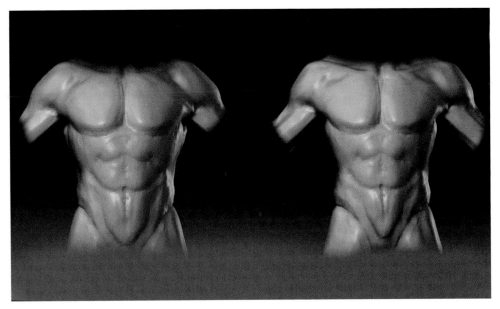

Figure 4.7 *Changing the width of the chest*

These changes may also be easier to make if you step down in subdivision levels. By making large shape changes like this at lower subdivision levels, you are moving fewer points to affect the high-resolution mesh. Remember that changes in the lower subdivision levels telegraph up in ZBrush.

2. Move to the side view, and adjust the form of the chest, as shown in Figure 4.8(a). Notice how the upper chest is pulled out and the overall egg shape is adjusted from the back as well. In Figure 4.8(b) you can see the masses of the chest and pelvis in overlay.

3. At this stage, switch to silhouette mode (the Flat Color material) to check the profile of the figure. Always remember that this is an invaluable way to see the overall shape of your work quickly and clearly (Figure 4.9).

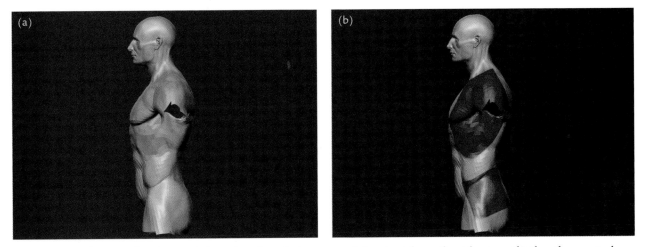

Figure 4.8 *Adjusting the chest: (a) changing the relative mass of the chest from the side view, (b) the rib cage and pelvis masses*

4. Note that you are adjusting the arch of the back, and as a result, you affect the angles between the chest and pelvis. Figure 4.10 shows the major plane breaks at the end of this stage.

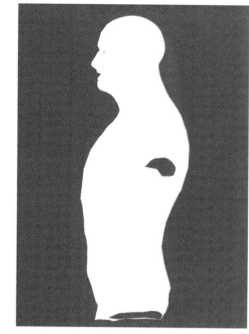

Figure 4.9 *The figure in side view with the Flat Color material applied*

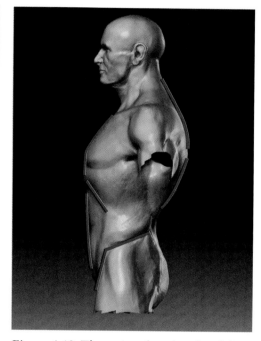

Figure 4.10 *The major plane breaks of the torso at this stage*

Sculpting the Torso

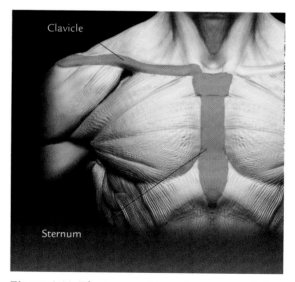

With the masses in place, you can now start addressing specific muscle groups of the figure. In this section, you will begin with the Pectoralis muscles. These are the large chest muscles that make up the upper torso (Figure 4.11). They attach at the clavicle, sternum, and humerus bones.

Pectoralis

It is important to note that these muscles originate at the sternum of the rib cage and insert on the upper arm bone or humerus. You also need to understand that this muscle is actually three separate sections or heads. This becomes

Figure 4.11 *The two most prominent parts of the Pectoralis muscle originate at the clavicle bone and the sternum.*

important in the ways they affect the surface of the fleshed figure. The first two heads are the most visible and create important highlights and shadows. These two are the *sterno-costal* head, which connects to the center of the rib cage, and the *clavicular* head, which attaches to the collar bone, or clavicle (Figure 4.12).

The Clavicles

As you work on the chest, it is important to be aware of the clavicles, or collar bones, and how they interrelate to the chest as well as the neck and shoulders. The clavicles are part of a structure known as the *shoulder girdle*. You will look at the shoulder girdle more later as you sculpt the back. The shoulder girdle is composed of the clavicles as well as the scapulas or *shoulder blades*. As you have already seen, the clavicles are curved bones that form an attachment point for muscles of the neck. They also serve as anchors for the muscles of the chest, including the Pectoralis as well as the Deltoids.

Notice how the clavicles look like handlebars from the top—they sweep back toward the center of the shoulder. You can think of the bone as being divided into thirds. The first third from the outside forms the attachment of part of the Deltoid muscle. The second third has no attachments visible, while the third section is the attachment for part of the Pectoralis muscle. This configuration is important to understand.

The division between the sternocostal and clavicular heads of the Pectoralis often makes a visible line on the chest, especially in individuals with more definition. It also serves to create a small hollow between the chest and the shoulder, known as the *infraclavicular fossa*, as shown in Figure 4.13. The Pectoralis muscle appears to radiate out from the upper arm.

1. To sculpt this muscle form, mask out the area of the Pectoralis muscle, and invert the mask so the area of interest is isolated. Select the Standard brush, lower your draw size to 10, and with ZSub etch in a line from the clavicle to the armpit, as shown in Figure 4.14.

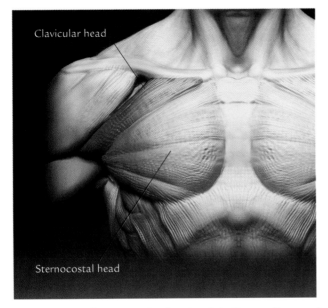

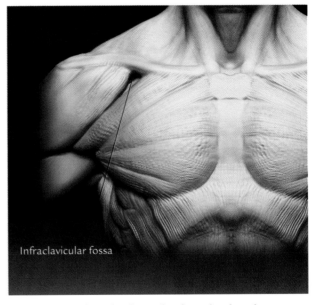

Figure 4.12 *The two major heads of the Pectoralis muscle*   ***Figure 4.13*** *The infraclavicular fossa landmark*

2. This will start to create the clavicular head of the Pectoralis muscle. Using the Standard brush, lower the draw size, and add some striations in the direction of the muscle flow. I will often sketch in directional lines like this as I work. They will often be smoothed down by the end but will remain as subtle highlights and shadows on the final figure. As you work, be careful to retain the planes sculpted in Chapter 2. You don't want to obliterate them; instead, you want to keep them as a guide since the muscle shape and placement are just as important as the crests and planes of its form. Figure 4.15 shows this process.

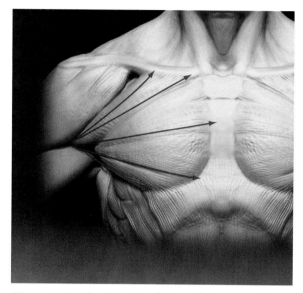

Figure 4.14 *The directional flow of the Pectoralis muscle from the arm to the center of the rib cage*

Figure 4.15 *With the area for the Pectoralis muscle isolated, start sketching in the clavicular head.*

Figure 4.16 *Adjust the smoothing curve to create a softer Smooth brush.*

3. To refine the shape you've made, you need to smooth it. Edit the smooth curve by going to Brush Smooth curve and lowering the point (Figure 4.16). This allows you to smooth with less adverse effects. Smooth the surface gently, being careful not to destroy the work so far. Remember to hold down the Shift key while changing the brush curve so it only affects the Smooth brush.

4. You will now build up the mass of the muscle. Select the Claytubes brush, and continue to sculpt in the shape of the Pectoralis. This will fill in the recesses first and generally build up the forms (Figure 4.17). Smooth back the surface, and with a mask, isolate the area for the clavicular head of the Pectoralis. Continue to refine the Pectoralis shape against the mask.

When working on the figure, always be sure to move it often so you can see every angle as the shapes develop. In particular, I find it useful to look at it from the top and bottom to make sure the shapes are turning back in space correctly. In Figure 4.18, you first see the chest from the front. It appears to be normal; however, by tilting the figure back in space, you see the chest is entirely too flat.

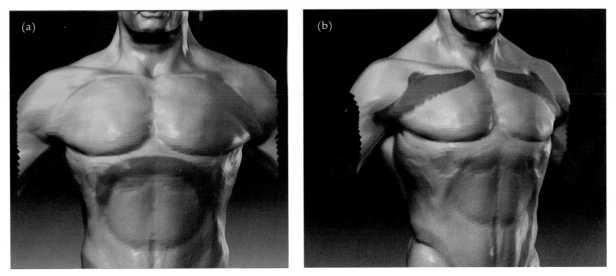

Figure 4.17 *Building up the muscle mass: (a) massing in the Pectoralis muscles with the Claytubes brush, (b) isolating the different heads*

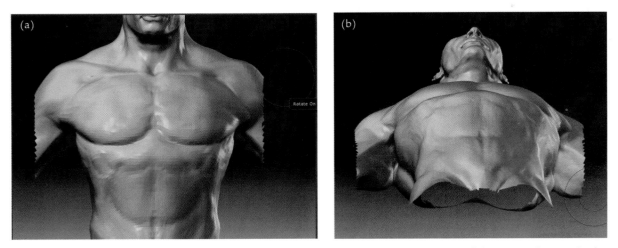

Figure 4.18 *Moving the figure to see different angles: (a) from the front, the volume of the Pectoralis may look correct, (b) from below, the muscles are flattened and do not seem to wrap around the figure*

5. Use the Move brush to accentuate the cylindrical shape of the chest form, and make sure the muscles appear to wrap naturally around this shape (Figure 4.19).

6. Here I use the Flatten brush with a ZIntensity of 10 to reintroduce the planes you worked out in Chapter 2. As I show how to sculpt throughout this book, I will reintroduce these plane changes as you add and alter volumes. By revisiting the planes, you can help keep the muscled figure from looking overly "inflated." It also helps to maintain a sense of structure to the form.

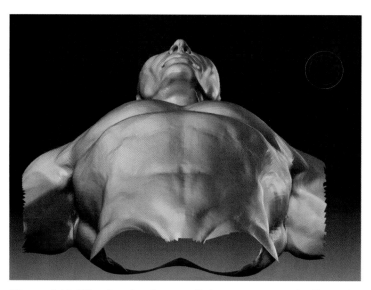

Figure 4.19 *The chest has been pulled out to correct the flattening from Figure 4.18.*

Abdominal Muscles

In this section, you'll move down the torso into the abdominal region. Here you will be looking at the Rectus abdominis (Figure 4.20). The abdominals are often called the "six-pack," but if you were to take away the skin and look at this sheath of muscle, there are actually eight units of muscle fiber instead of six. The confusion stems from the fact that the first two are rarely visible except on the fittest of individuals.

These muscles form a central pillar from the arch of the rib cage down to the pubic bone of the pelvis. To sculpt them, you will mask out the lower border of the rib cage.

Figure 4.20 *An* écorché *view of the Rectus abdominis*

1. Paint a mask over the arch of the rib cage, as shown in Figure 4.21. Make sure the abdominals flow down from the ribs but do not alter the shape of the barrel of the chest.

2. Select the Standard brush, and lower your draw size. With this brush, sketch the flow of the muscle as it feeds up into the rib cage. The striations flow diagonally off, as shown in Figure 4.22. Note the "W" shapes. Notice also that the navel remains in place; this was your third-head measure, and you want to keep it from migrating off measure.

Figure 4.21 *The lower border of the rib cage masked in preparation for sculpting the abdominal muscles*

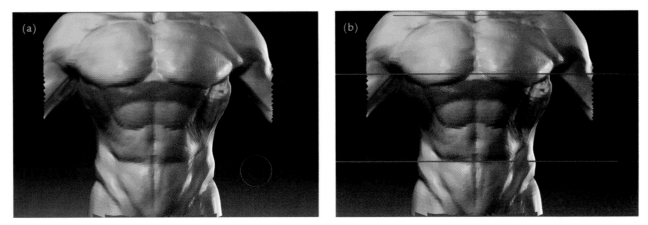

Figure 4.22 *Sculpting the abdominal region: (a) etching in the shape of the abdominals with the Standard brush, (b) checking the placement of the navel in relation to the eight-head measure*

3. Move to the side view, and select the Move brush. Notice from Figure 4.23(a) that the abdominals are out too far from the core of the figure. There is also no plane change at the waist. Move the forms back, as shown in Figure 4.23(b). Also note the plane change. The body bends at this point. You will often see the flesh bunch and fold here as the torso is in motion.

4. The abdominal muscles terminate in a rounded form at the pubic bone, as shown in Figure 4.24. Here the Rectus abdominis and the External oblique flow together and attach along the dividing line between the pelvis and legs. Use the Standard brush to sketch in this shape, and use the Claytubes brush to mass it in. You will address the oblique in the next section.

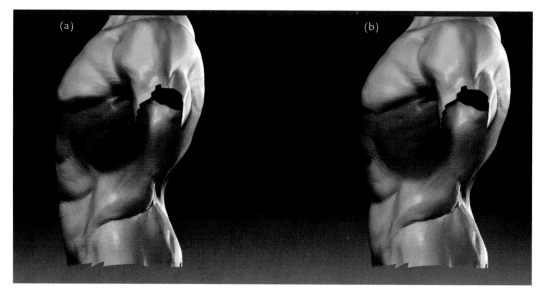

Figure 4.23 *Sculpting the abdominal region: (a) the profile of the abdominals in side view, (b) shifting the abdominals back (notice the plane break at the navel)*

Figure 4.24 *The abdominal muscles end at the pubic bone.*

Serratus and Oblique

From the side view, the torso is dominated by two muscle groups, the Serratus and the External oblique. The *Serratus* are the small fingerlike muscles that cover the sides of the ribs. Often they may be mistaken for ribs themselves, but as you can see in Figure 4.25(a), they are independent shapes. The *External oblique* is a long sheet of muscle that interweaves between the Serratus and extends down the sides of the figure, attaching to the pelvis as well as weaving into the abdominals. The character of all the muscles of the core, or *trunk*, is that they weave together in a complex web that allows the great compression and extension of the trunk.

1. From the side view, press in the hollow of the armpit using the Standard brush with ZSub (Figure 4.26). Mask out the area for the Serratus, and invert the mask as shown in Figure 4.26(b) to isolate the area for sculpting.
2. Using the Standard brush, sketch in the four fingers of the Serratus. They flow off the scapula like fingers to each rib; however, usually only four are actually visible on the fleshed figure. Unmask some more areas for the oblique. Using the Standard brush, lower your draw size, and select alpha 01 to create a fine-tipped brush. With ZSub turned on, sketch in the interweave and lines that descend over toward the abdominals (Figure 4.27).

You now need to adjust the Latissimus dorsi muscle that forms the back wall of the armpit. You will look at this muscle in more depth in the next section as I discuss the back.

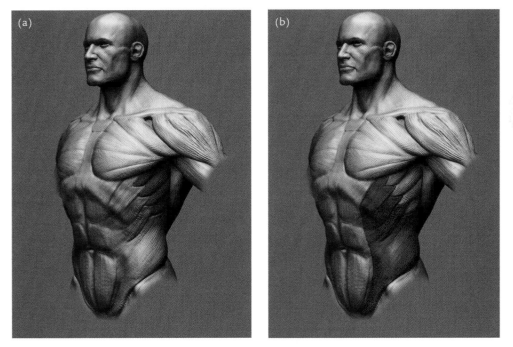

Figure 4.25 *Torso muscles: (a) the Serratus muscles, (b) the External oblique muscle*

This muscle wraps around the underside of the arms and inserts on the humerus bone of the arm. The External oblique flows diagonally down from the Serratus toward the abdominals. It creates a triangular shape into which the External oblique fits (Figure 4.28).

3. With the Standard brush and a low draw size, sketch in the Latissimus, as shown in Figure 4.29.

4. Mask the Latissimus, and add striations for a sense of directional flow (Figure 4.30). You'll smooth these back later, but for now they serve to help add visual interest to the surface and guide the eye.

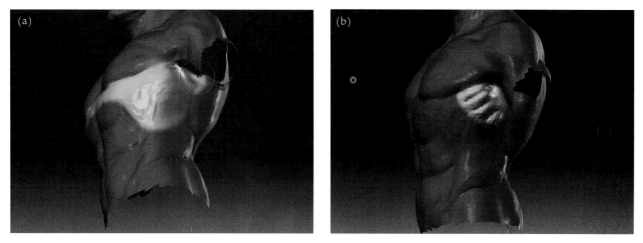

Figure 4.26 *Sculpting the torso muscles: (a) pressing in the hollow for the armpit, (b) the area for the Serratus unmasked*

Figure 4.27 *As you sculpt the Serratus muscles, note the striations of the External oblique as well.*

Figure 4.28 *The insertion of the oblique in relation to the Latissimus. The oblique is shown in red; the Latissimus dorsi is shown in blue.*

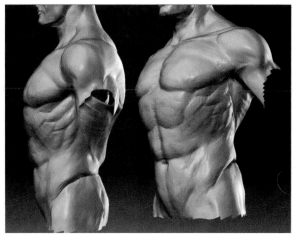

Figure 4.29 *Sketching in the Latissimus muscle from the side*

Figure 4.30 *Sculpting the striations on the Latissimus muscle*

With the Latissimus in place, you can now further refine the External oblique. The oblique also forms the Flank pad muscle shown in Figure 4.31(a). In Figure 4.31(b), you can see the muscle area isolated with masking and the striations sculpted in with the Standard brush. Notice that it flows diagonally from the top to bottom and inserts beneath the lat.

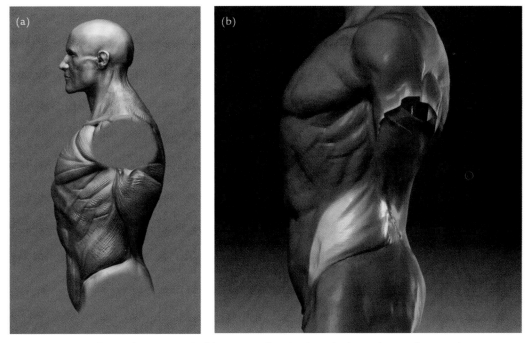

Figure 4.31 *Refining the External oblique: (a) the Flank pad, (b) sculpting the muscle*

5. From the front view, notice how the oblique flows over the bony protrusions of the iliac crests of the pelvis. These are very important bony landmarks on the figure, especially when you deal with the muscles of the anterior or frontal aspect of the leg in Chapter 6. For now note how their presence influences the direction of flow of the External oblique as it wraps around the abdomen to insert in the crotch (Figure 4.32).

At this stage, your torso should look like Figure 4.33 in the front and on the side. As always, be aware of the rhythms of both the profile curves of the form and the internal forms and how they relate. This gestural flow between parts is what makes the sculpture feel alive. These relationships are ultimately more important than anatomical accuracy.

At this point, you are ready to move to the back of the torso and examine the muscles that compose the complex surface forms visible when viewing the figure from behind.

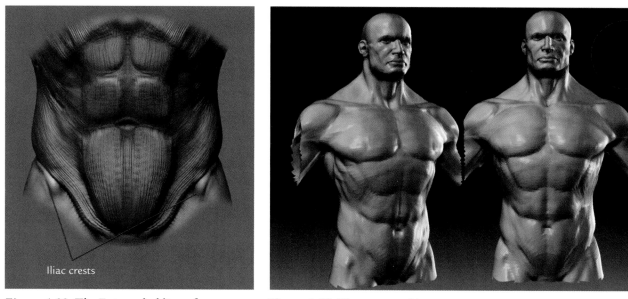

Figure 4.32 *The External oblique flows over the iliac crests of the pelvis.*

Figure 4.33 *The torso at this stage*

Muscles of the Back

The back is the most complex area of the torso. It has the greatest number of muscles visible at the surface of the figure, as well as complex movable bony landmarks. This complexity is mostly created by the mechanism of the shoulder girdle, whose muscles are most prominent on the posterior or back view of the figure.

The shoulder girdle is a mechanical system composed of the clavicle, scapula, and associated muscles. Its function is to allow the great range of motion we enjoy in our arms. Were it not for this complex machinery, the arm would never rise beyond 90 degrees from the side.

Many of the muscles in the upper back manipulate the scapula. Although it is beyond the scope of this book to examine the mechanics of this structure, I will cover the major landmarks created by the scapula and clavicle.

The shoulder girdle creates several important surface bony landmarks that I must note now to assist you in placing the muscles of the back and arm (Figure 4.34). The first landmark is the acromion process, and it is created at the join between the scapula and the clavicle at the center of the Deltoid, or *shoulder*.

From the acromion process, you can trace the line of the spine of the scapula back diagonally toward the center of the back. This is an important landmark from which many back muscles originate. The spine of the scapula is visible on the fleshed figure in most cases as a raised ridge. In the case of a more muscular person, especially a heroic body type, the increased muscle mass on either side of the bone makes it appear as a recess.

You can see all of these landmarks in Figure 4.35.

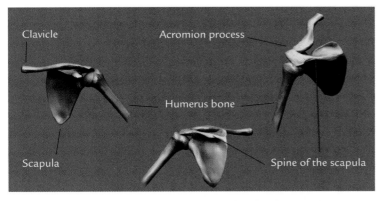

Figure 4.34 *The skeletal components of the shoulder girdle*

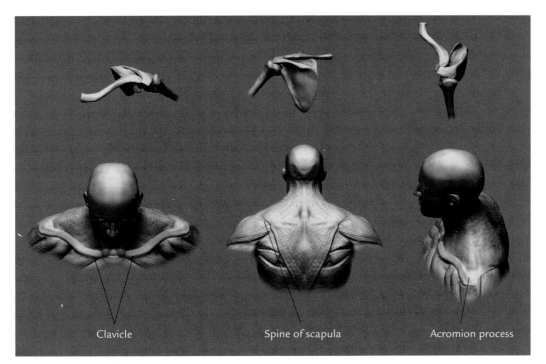

Figure 4.35 *The bony landmarks of the shoulder girdle*

Now that you have an understanding of the skeletal structure of the shoulder girdle, let's try sculpting the muscles of the back. First let's look at the overall form as a whole. Just as the chest needed to be adjusted from the bottom view to correct an unnatural flattening from the top view, notice in Figure 4.36(a) how the back has become rather flat. You need to correct this by adding the plane changes that are created by the scapula bones and back muscles, as shown in Figure 4.36(a).

Follow these steps to correct this:

1. Select the Move brush, and from the top view, pull the scapulas out from the back. Notice the "W" shape they create in outline, as shown in Figure 4.36(b). This will create an important plane change in the back and also set the stage for the inclusion of the Rhomboid muscles, which connect the scapulas to the spine.

2. Rotate to the back view, and using the Standard brush, mask out the line of the spine of the scapula (Figure 4.37). Remember this can be traced from the point at the Deltoid where the clavicle and scapula meet. Figure 4.38 shows the shape of the scapula in overlay over the figure.

3. With the spine of the scapula masked, select the Claytubes brush, and start to mass the Trapezius muscle up to the base of the skull, as shown in Figure 4.39. You will return to this muscle as the back progresses. Because it is such a thin sheet, it is defined mostly by the shapes of the muscles it lies over.

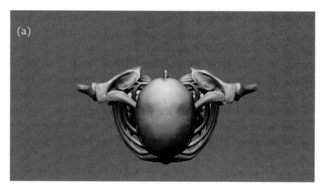

Figure 4.36 Adjusting the chest: (a) pulling the scapulas back

(b) from the top view this angle created by the scapulas is apparent

Figure 4.37 Masking the spine of the scapula

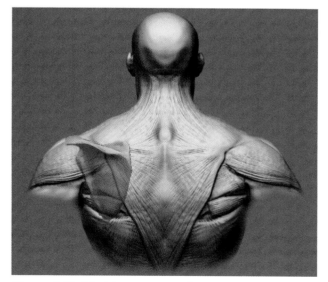

Figure 4.38 The Trapezius muscle

4. At this stage, mask out the shape of the scapula as a whole. This will allow you to add the Rhomboid muscles (Figure 4.40). The Rhomboids originate at the medial border of the scapula (the edge toward the center of the body) and insert at the spine.

5. You will now add the Latissimus dorsi muscle. The *lat* muscle, as it is also known, was addressed earlier in this chapter while you worked on the sides of the figure. Isolate the shape of the muscle, as shown in Figure 4.41. This muscle wraps around from the armpit to extend down the back and originate at the pelvis.

6. With the area for the Latissimus dorsi unmasked, select the Claytubes brush. Start to mass in the shape of the muscle. Do not make it too thick because this is a sheet of muscle that lies almost like a cape against the back (Figure 4.42).

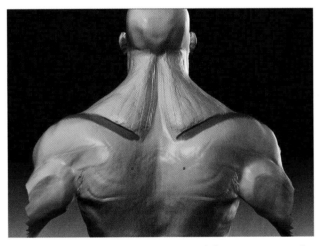

Figure 4.39 *Roughing in the start of the Trapezius with the Claytubes brush*

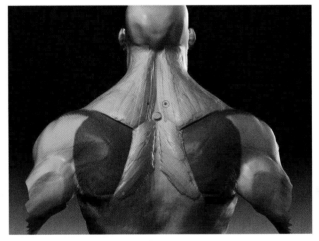

Figure 4.40 *With the scapulas masked out, mass in the Rhomboid muscles.*

Figure 4.41 *Sculpting the Latissimus dorsi muscle*

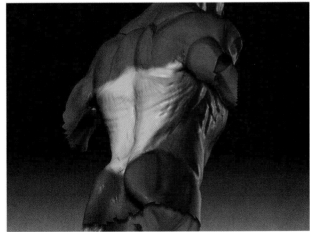

Figure 4.42 *The flow of the Latissimus muscle*

7. At this stage, you will return to the Trapezius muscle, which flows from the base of the skull to the clavicles, spine of the scapula, and spinal cord. The Trapezius muscle is very much like a cape draped over the shoulders. Isolate this area with a mask, and use the Claytubes brush to mass in the muscle form as it flows from the skull to the spine of the scapula, extending it further down the length of the back (Figure 4.43).

8. Moving again to a bottom view, you can see the scapulas still lay a little flat against the back. You need to reinstate the crest between the medial border and the Rhomboids. Select the Move brush, and pull the borders of the scapulas out (Figure 4.44). These kinds of breaks and plane changes ultimately add up to a more believable figure. It is always very important to continually evaluate your progress from every possible view. As you watch the video of this figure sculpt in progress, notice how often I move around the form. You can never move enough.

9. With the Smooth brush, smooth the noise on the back, as shown in Figure 4.45.

Figure 4.43 Continuing to sculpt the Trapezius

Figure 4.44 From the bottom view, correcting the angle of the scapulas

Figure 4.45 Smoothing the noise on the back

At this point, you will be working on the muscles that directly attach and flow off the scapulas. These are complex in that they are partially visible on the surface in some areas while elsewhere they flow deep under other muscles. I have tried to clarify this with *écorché* images at different depths to illustrate the muscle shape and placement.

10. You will now accentuate the posterior head of the Deltoid muscle where it attaches to the spine of the scapula (Figure 4.46). Mask the underside of the Deltoid, as in Figure 4.47. Using the Standard brush with a small draw size and a low intensity, stroke along the edge. Use the ReplayLast button found in the Stroke Palette. This will repeat the last stroke drawn in ZBrush.

11. You will now indicate two prominent muscles that originate on the scapula and attach to the humerus bone. These are the Infraspinatus and Teres major (Figure 4.48). Clear the masks from your figure. Select the Standard brush, and with a small draw size, etch in the division shown in Figure 4.49. These two muscles are often visible on the surface of a fleshed figure (Figure 4.50).

Figure 4.46 *The Deltoid muscle attaches to the spine of the scapula.*

Figure 4.47 *Building up the edge of the Deltoid muscle*

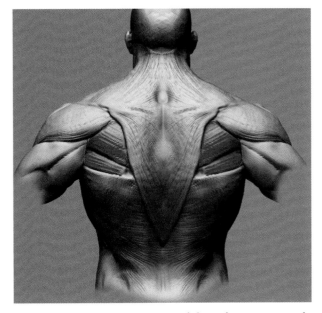

Figure 4.48 *The écorché view of the Infraspinatus and Teres major*

Figure 4.49 *Sketching the Teres major*

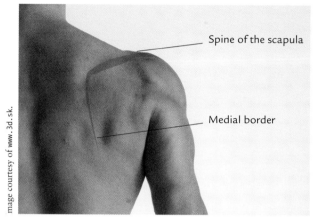

Spine of the scapula

Medial border

mage courtesy of www.3d.sk.

Figure 4.50 *Here you can see the scapula in a photo reference.*

12. You will now extend the Trapezius to the bottom of the rib cage. This is a very thin muscle and is defined more by the shapes of the muscles beneath it. Mask out the surrounding areas, and indicate the shape lightly with the Claytubes brush, as shown in Figure 4.51.

13. At the base of the back, you will find two pillars of muscle that extend from the sides of the tailbone up the back (Figure 4.52). These are the Erector spinae muscles. They manifest as two thick muscle forms on either side of the spine.

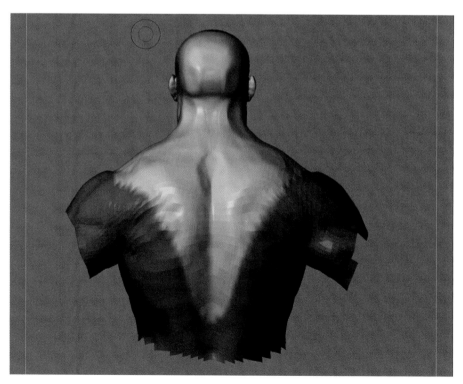

Figure 4.51 *Trapezius area masked*

At this stage, it's a good idea to zoom back from the figure and look for any areas that need to be refined. Remember to keep an eye out for the planes I have discussed as well as the silhouettes. Now use the interactive light to move the light source and check how the shadows react under different lighting conditions. Are the shadow shapes correct and consistent? If not, revisit those areas, and continue to massage them from a lower subdivision level, making subtle changes and then stepping back up to the higher levels. In Figure 4.53 you can see the final torso.

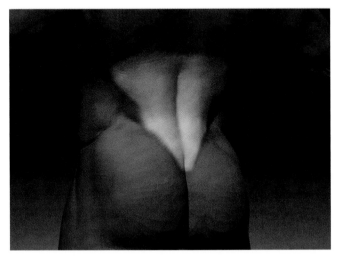

Figure 4.52 *Sculpting the pillars of the Erector spinae at the lower back*

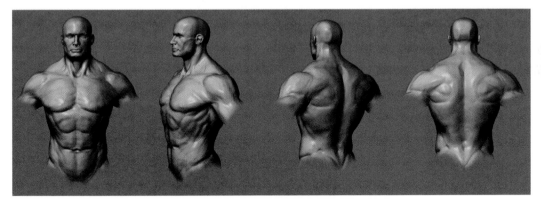

Figure 4.53 *The final torso*

What's Next

Congratulations, you have completed work on the torso! In this chapter you looked at several complex areas, including the back and shoulders. You examined the muscle groups of the core of the figure as well as some transitional areas such as the hips and shoulders that will serve you in later chapters on the legs and arms. Let's move on to sculpting the arms.

five

The Arms

In this chapter, you'll move *from the torso into the arms. In Chapter 4, I touched on the transitional areas of the shoulder into the arm. Muscles such as the Deltoid as well as the Teres major of the scapula were shown, but only in surface detail. In this chapter, you will revisit these areas and look at the manner in which they interconnect into the form of the arm. Examining the origins and insertions of these muscles will, I hope, clarify the mechanism of the shoulder area.*

Figure 5.1 shows the arm as it will appear when you've completed this chapter. This chapter's look at the arms will end at the wrist, because the intricate complexities of the hands and feet require a chapter of their own; you'll return to them in Chapter 7.

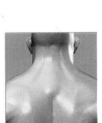

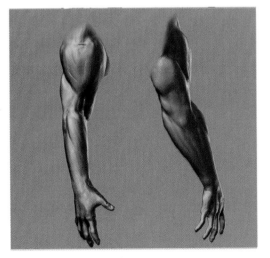

Figure 5.1 *The final arm*

Basic Forms

The arms of the figure form one of the two parts of the *appendicular* skeleton, which consists of the arms and legs; the center trunk is known as the *axial* skeleton (Figure 5.2). When artists deal with the appendicular skeleton, a common mistake is to make the proportions of the limbs too long or short compared to the figure as a whole. Luckily, there is an easy way to determine the length of the arms in relation to the body.

On an eight-head figure, the total width of the arms and shoulders—the arm span—is itself eight heads. You can see this in Figure 5.3, where the arm span has been placed in relation to the standing body. This measure is longer than people often imagine. Try standing now, and place your arms at your side; notice how far down the thigh your fingertips actually touch. Many new sculptors place the hands too high on the arm or generally misrepresent this proportion. Because this is an area of common confusion, it is important to take care that the arms fall within an acceptable measure. Other important measures include the elbow, which falls at nearly the bottom of the rib cage. You can see these two measures in Figure 5.4. (Note that the lowest ribs are deeper inside the figure and are usually not visible on the surface.) This is one of those situations where having the tool of a canon of measure is helpful. Otherwise, you would be left to guess or place the arms on sight alone.

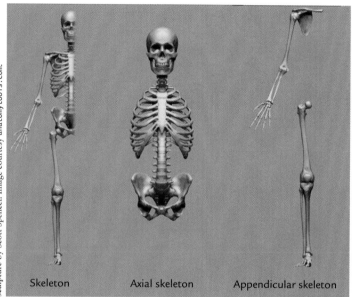

Sculpture by Scott Spencer. Image courtesy anatomytools.com.

Skeleton   Axial skeleton   Appendicular skeleton

Figure 5.2 The axial and appendicular skeletons

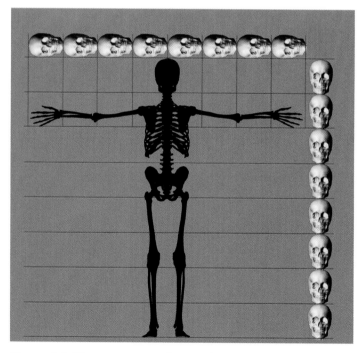

Figure 5.3 The arm span is also equal to eight heads.

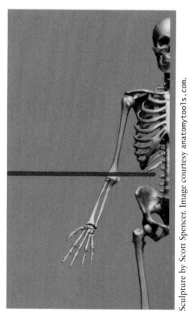

Sculpture by Scott Spencer. Image courtesy anatomytools.com.

Figure 5.4 The elbow falls at about the bottom of the rib cage.

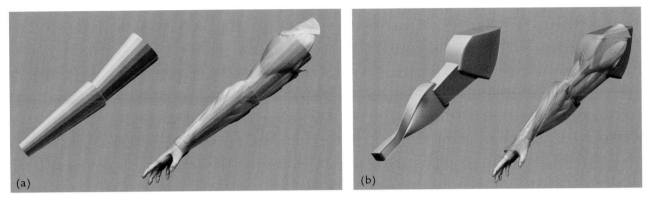

Figure 5.5 Visualizing the arm: (a) as cylinders, (b) as compound box objects

Before looking at the more specific shapes of the arm determined by its muscles and bone landmarks, let's take a look at the shape of the arm in its most simplified whole. You can see the arm overall as a cylindrical shape (Figure 5.5(a)). This is the simplest dimensional representation of the arm and the easiest to visualize. If you add another level of complexity, you can picture the arm as box forms, as shown in Figure 5.5(b). Notice the way the upper arm box wedges into the forearm box. Also note the forearm and how it tapers at the wrist. I recommend taking the time to build a model similar to this as an exercise. Although it may appear simple at first, you can learn a lot by building these block forms of the figure. I recommend loading the mid-resolution version of the figure supplied on the DVD and experimenting with building a simplified block model over it in a polygon modeling program, similar to the figures shown here.

Muscular and Skeletal Anatomy

The arm itself consists of three bones. The upper arm is the humerus bone (Figure 5.6). The lower arm consists of two bones: the radius and the ulna. The ulna bone rotates in a hinge fashion around the distal end of the humerus and creates the bony protrusion of the elbow (Figure 5.7). This protrusion is an important skeletal landmark and is called the *olecranon process* (Figure 5.8), commonly called the *elbow*.

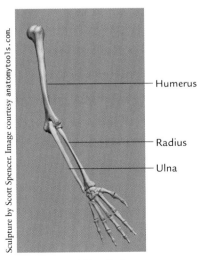

Sculpture by Scott Spencer. Image courtesy anatomytools.com.

— Humerus

— Radius

— Ulna

Figure 5.6 The skeleton of the arm

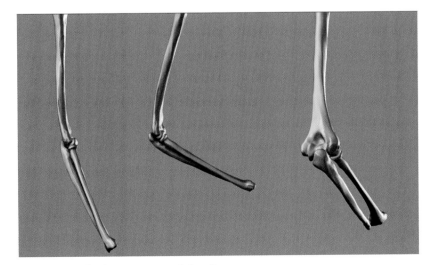

Figure 5.7 The hinge action of the elbow

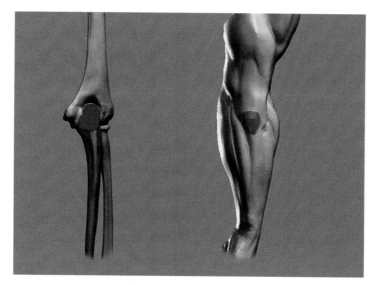

Figure 5.8 The olecranon process

The radius bone rotates with the ulna, but also has the ability to rotate around its own axis, crossing the ulna bone, into two positions known as *pronation* and *supination*, as pictured in Figure 5.9. As you may recall from Chapter 1, the default anatomical position is with the arm in supination.

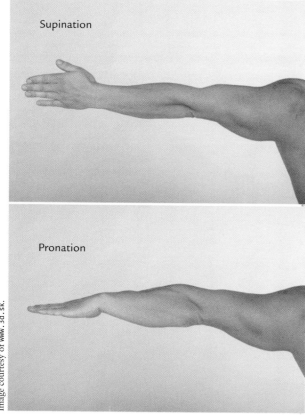

Supination

Pronation

It is also important to notice that the bones of the upper arm are not in a straight line in relation to those of the forearm. This is a result of the joint between the humerus, radius, and ulna. The ulna rides in a groove on the humerus called the trochlea (Figure 5.10). Because of the angle created by this structure, the forearm actually angles out slightly from the median line of the body. This allows the arms to swing freely without striking the pelvis or legs. This effect is known as the carrying angle and is an important subtlety to be aware of while sculpting the arm (Figure 5.11).

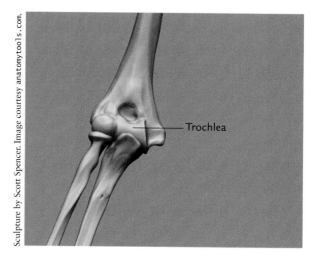

Trochlea

Image courtesy of www.3d.sk.

Sculpture by Scott Spencer. Image courtesy anatomytools.com.

Figure 5.9 The arm in pronation and supination

Figure 5.10 The ulna rides in the trochlea.

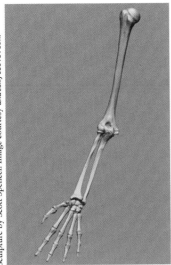

Sculpture by Scott Spencer. Image courtesy anatomytools.com.

Figure 5.11 *The carrying angle of the arm*

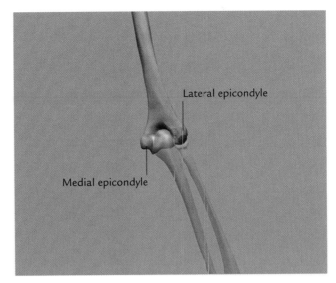

Figure 5.12 *The lateral and medial epicondyles*

While you are looking at the joint between the humerus and the radius and ulna, I'll point out two important bony landmarks on the humerus, the *lateral epicondyle* and *medial epicondyle* (Figure 5.12). These will come into particular importance when you sculpt the forearm muscles, because they represent the points of origin for many of the surface muscles in this area.

The lateral epicondyle is located toward the outside of the arm, the lateral aspect of the body. It is the location of the *unified extensor tendon*, which is the point from which the Extensor muscles originate. This landmark is visible from the posterior view of the arm (Figure 5.13). From the front view, it is covered by the *Brachioradialis* and *Extensor carpi radialis* and *Extensor longus radialis* muscles, as shown in Figure 5.14.

The medial epicondyle is located toward the body—the medial aspect. It is the location of the Flexor tendon and therefore the origin of the Flexor group of muscles on the forearm (Figure 5.15). This bony protrusion comes close to the surface and forms a plane break in the silhouette of the arm (Figure 5.16).

Figure 5.13 *The lateral epicondyle is the origin of the Extensor tendons as shown here in écorché.*

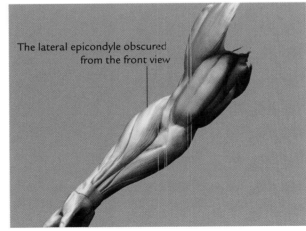

The lateral epicondyle obscured from the front view

Figure 5.14 *From the front, this landmark is hidden from view by the Brachioradialis muscle.*

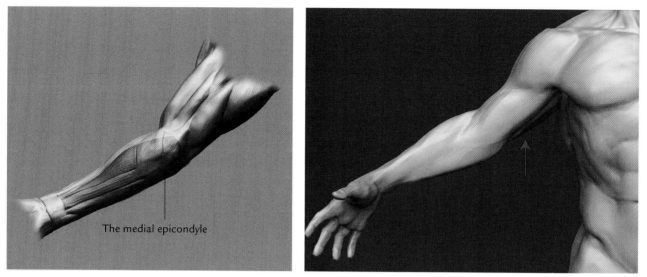

Figure 5.15 *The medial epicondyle is the origin of the Flexor tendon.*

Figure 5.16 *From the front view of the arm, you can see the medial epicondyle creates a pronounced plane break in silhouette.*

Skeletal Landmarks Addressed in This Chapter

As you continue with this chapter, you will be working on the specific skeletal and muscle landmarks illustrated in Figure 5.17.

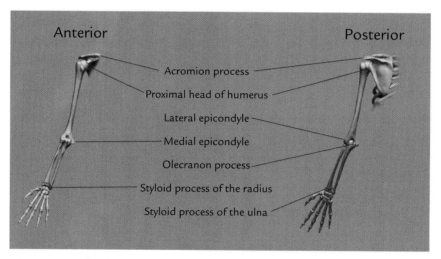

Figure 5.17 *The skeletal landmarks of the arm discussed in this chapter*

Muscles Addressed in This Chapter

When you work on the forearm, you will deal with a somewhat abbreviated number of muscles so that you can focus on those muscles that have the most direct and apparent influence on the surface anatomy. Although I highly recommend taking an in-depth look at the muscles and bones of this area, I should stress that doing so is not entirely necessary for sculpting a convincing and natural forearm.

The forearm is one of the more complex areas in terms of the interweaving of a number of muscles from a deep to a superficial layer. One of the most in-depth and educational dissections I was fortunate to do during the course of my research was of the forearm. By taking back each layer, I acquired a new appreciation of the beauty as well as intricacies of the structure.

I do not believe this level of examination is necessary, however, to learn to sculpt the forms of the forearm. In the interest of keeping this tutorial concise and clear, I have chosen to simplify this section and illustrate how to envision and represent the complex surface landmarks and forms of the forearm by focusing on the most important muscle groups, illustrated along with the associated landmarks in Figure 5.18.

These images should prove a useful reference as you move forward and start to look at the steps of sculpting the arm. Also remember to reference the *écorché* ZTool I have included on the DVD. This is the final heroic male sculpture with the major muscles sculpted in.

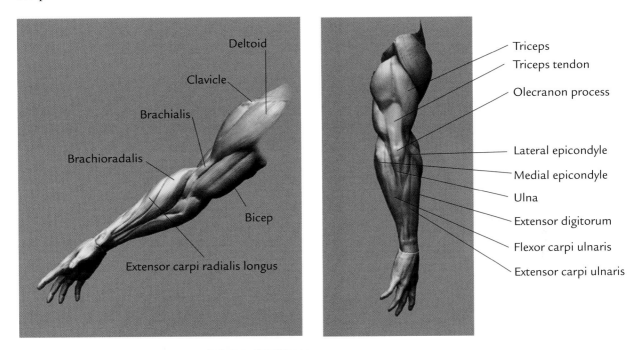

Figure 5.18 The muscles you will sculpt in this chapter

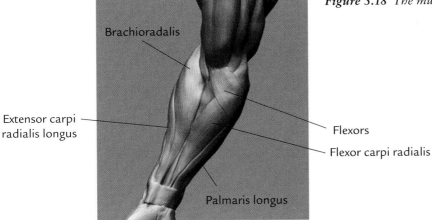

Sculpting the Arm

You are nearly ready to begin sculpting the arms. There is still quite a bit of anatomical detail you need to learn about, however, so I will pause to discuss those details at several points along the way.

To begin sculpting, you'll isolate the torso and arms from the rest of the figure using a hide marquee:

1. As before, hold down Ctrl+Shift and click-drag a marquee around the legs.
2. Release Shift to make the marquee red. When you release, the legs will be hidden. I recommend working on the arms with the torso visible because it helps relate the parts to the whole.

I have included a video on the DVD of the sculpture in progress as well as several other segment videos dealing with specific areas. In theses videos, you will see how I apply the information in the text with an overall approach to sculpting.

Shoulder and Upper Arm

You're going to begin sculpting with the anterior view of the upper arm. In order to do that, you need to understand what muscles compose the shapes you see and how these muscles relate to one another. You will begin by revisiting the Deltoid muscle. The Deltoid consists of three distinct heads (Figure 5.19), which originate on the clavicle, the acromion process, and the spine of the scapula; they are called the *clavicular head*, *acromion head*, and *scapular head*, respectively. Muscle heads are seen often as furrows on the surface of the skin. One of the most defined examples of this you have seen so far is the delineation between the clavicular and sternacostal heads of the pectoralis in Chapter 4. These divisions are important to note because even if they are simply hinted at on the surface of the figure, they can add an enormous amount of visual interest to the surface as well as a sense of anatomical veracity.

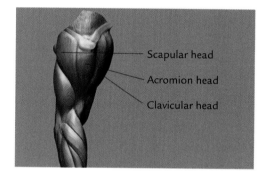

Figure 5.19 *The Deltoid muscle consists of the acromion head, the clavicular head, and the scapular head.*

Notice how the Deltoid wraps around the humerus, inserting almost halfway down the shaft. This point of insertion is equal to the second head measure down or the nipples on a fleshed human. The insertion of the Deltoid muscle can appear misleading from the outside. The Deltoid appears to flow into another muscle that lies under the Biceps. This muscle is called the Brachialis.

The Biceps does not lie against the humerus; rather, it lies over two muscles called the *Brachialis* and *Coracobrachialis*. The Brachialis is visible on the surface of the arm just beneath the Deltoid insertion as well as on the underside of the Biceps. The Coracobrachials is visible under the Biceps extending up into the armpit. Figure 5.20 shows the Biceps pulled away so the Deltoid, Brachialis, and coracobrachials are visible, as is their effect on the surface of the final arm.

The Biceps muscle lies over these two muscles. It originates at the head of the humerus and inserts on the radius. This is counterintuitive because the angle of the muscle makes it appear that it is inserting on the ulna. When sculpting, it is important to note this subtle inclination of the flow of the muscle from the lateral to the medial (Figure 5.21).

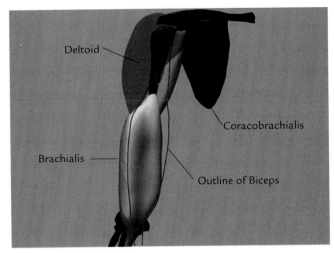

Figure 5.20 *You can see how the Coracobrachialis and Brachialis lie beneath the Biceps, and only a small portion is actually visible on the surface.*

Figure 5.21 *The apparent inclination of the Biceps*

Armed with this information concerning the underlying muscular structure of the anterior aspect of the upper arm, let's start sculpting. When you sculpt, try to stroke along the direction of the muscle flow of each muscle from origin to insertion. This is a technique I use often. I find this approach helps develop form in a fluid manner and also helps me maintain a sense of rhythm.

1. Begin by isolating the Deltoid with a mask. Select the Claytubes brush, and stroke the muscle in the direction of each head discussed earlier (Figure 5.22). Make sure the strokes emanate from the location of each origin to the shared insertion on the arm. For the front of the figure, this would be from the clavicle to the insertion point (Figure 5.23). As you sculpt, keep the profile of the figure in mind, particularly the crests of the silhouette. The Deltoid has two crests, shown in Figure 5.24. Try to avoid letting the silhouette become too soft.

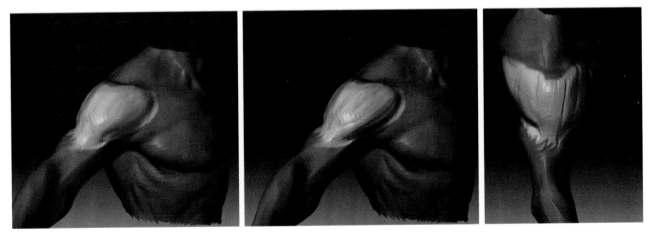

Figure 5.22 *Sculpting the Deltoid*

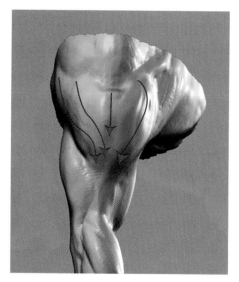

Figure 5.23 *These radiating arrows illustrate the flow of the Deltoid muscle.*

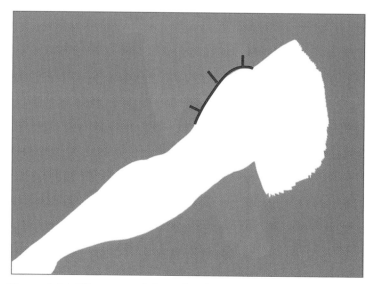

Figure 5.24 *The crests of the Deltoid in silhouette*

2. Subtract from the mask the area for the Biceps. You can do this by holding down Ctrl and Alt while painting. You will now be subtracting from the mask instead of adding as you paint. Clear the area for the Biceps, as shown in Figure 5.25.

3. Using the Claytubes brush, mass in the volume of the Biceps muscle (Figure 5.26(a)). Carry each stroke of the tool in one motion along the full length of the muscle. Making long strokes at this roughing-in stage is a good habit and, as said before, helps keep your approach loose and gestural as you work. This is analogous to gesture drawing where lines are created to communicate action and force. In this case, you are sculpting lines of action in terms of the direction or flow of the muscle form. Notice that I have continued the unmasked area on the underside of the arm, as shown in Figure 5.26(b).

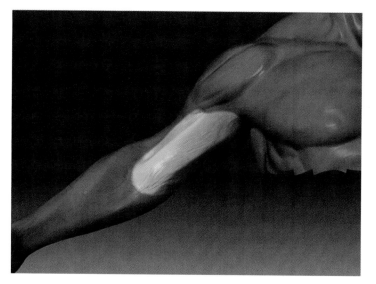

Figure 5.25 *The area for the Biceps unmasked*

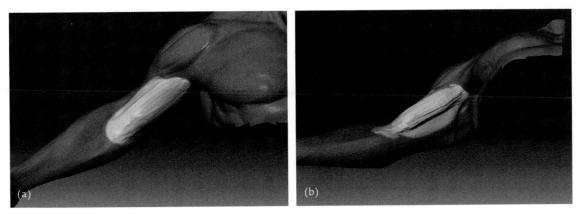

Figure 5.26 *Massing in the Biceps: (a) using one motion, (b) the underside of the arm now unmasked*

As you sculpt the Biceps (Figure 5.27), make sure to take into account the trapezoid shape in the profile of the muscle. The Biceps, like most muscles, has a defined shape. Muscles are not blobby bundles of tissue that are held together by skin. Instead, they have structural forms that define the outward appearance of the body. The Biceps is not spherical volume in its final shape; it appears as more of a trapezoid in cross section. You can see this in Figure 5.28.

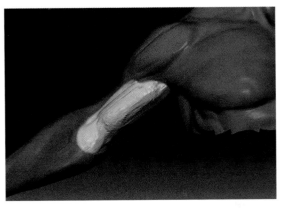

Figure 5.27 *Sculpting the Biceps with Claytubes*

4. Now move to the top view of the arm. Clear the masked area just beneath the insertion of the Deltoid by painting out the mask while holding down Ctrl+Alt. You will now sculpt the portion of the Brachialis muscle that is visible beneath the Biceps on the outside of the arm.

Figure 5.28 *The Biceps muscle has a trapezoid shape.*

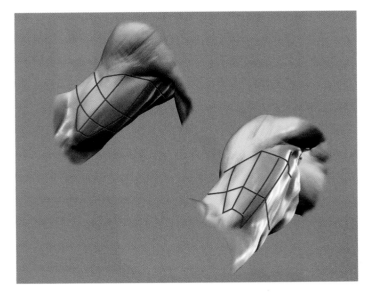

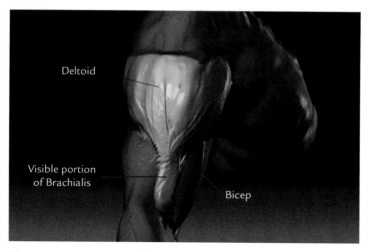

Figure 5.29 Massing in the Brachialis

5. Using the Standard brush, mass in this area, as shown in Figure 5.29. Notice here I have deepened the division between the Triceps at the back of the arm and the Deltoid for clarity. From the front view, you can see how the Brachialis is visible peeking out from beneath the Biceps.

6. Rotate to the underside of the arm. Clear the masking from the entire arm by holding down Ctrl and dragging a marquee somewhere off the model. When the mask is clear, with the Ctrl key held down, click once on the document window to mask the entire model.

7. You will now unmask just the area for the Brachialis and Coracobrachialis muscles. Holding down Alt and Ctrl, paint out the areas shown in Figure 5.30. These will be the Brachialis and the Coracobrachialis. The Brachialis muscle is seen both on the underside of the upper arm as well as on the outside just beneath the insertion of the Deltoid. The Coracobrachialis extends from the middle of the upper arm into the armpit. It connects deep inside the shoulder on the scapula. The only visible portion of the Coracobrachialis is in the armpit area just beneath the Bicep. Both of these muscles are massed in using the Inflate brush with alpha 01 (Figure 5.31).

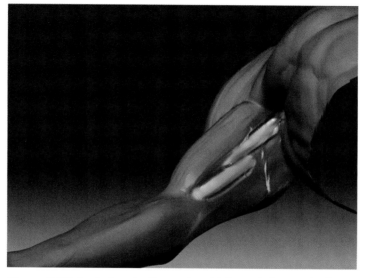

Figure 5.31 Inflate brush settings

Figure 5.30 Sculpting the Coracobrachialis and the Brachialis

As you have already seen in many cases, the naming of the muscles seems more complex at first sight than it really is. The Biceps is a good example of this; it gets its name from the fact it has two heads. Compare this to the Triceps muscle, which has three heads.

The two heads of the Biceps muscle are not often visible, but sometimes on individuals with more muscle definition, you can discern the division between the two heads of the Biceps as it extends up into the armpit. We will etch this division in using the Standard brush. It will be more pronounced in these stages, but this form will be refined and become more subtle as you work the area. Using the Standard brush with a draw size of 25 and alpha 01, etch this dividing line as in Figure 5.32.

With the muscles of the anterior aspect of the upper arm sculpted in, you can now move on to the back of the arm.

Figure 5.32 *Etching in the division between the two heads*

Triceps

From the back, the entire upper arm is encompassed by the Triceps muscle, so called because it has three heads. Each of the heads has its own origin, and they all insert into a single large, flat tendon called the *Triceps tendon*, which ends at the olecranon process or elbow. As viewed on the body, this muscle appears to originate from beneath the Deltoid and continue down the length of the back of the arm to the elbow (Figure 5.33).

The Parts of the Triceps

You will take a brief look at the various heads of the Triceps, but the focus will ultimately be on the shape as it appears on the final figure. As in many other areas of sculpting, the underling physiology, although it's helpful to understand, is not always as important as the combined shape that is created in relation to other muscles, bone, and fat.

You can see the three heads of the Triceps muscle in Figure 5.34; they are called the *long head*, the *medial head*, and the *lateral head*. The long head and the medial head are both located on the inside of the arm toward the medial line of the body. The lateral head, as can be surmised by the name, is on the outside or lateral aspect of the arm.

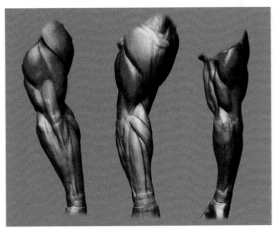

Figure 5.33 *The Triceps viewed in* écorché

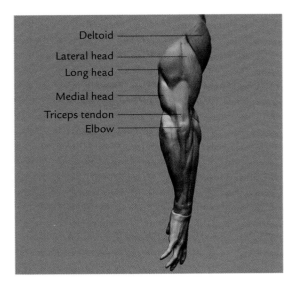

Figure 5.34 *The three heads of the Triceps, with surrounding landmarks*

The three heads of the Triceps insert into a common tendon that grabs the olecranon process of the ulna. These three heads function to extend the forearm after it has been bent at the elbow.

Sculpting the Triceps

Now you have broken down the Triceps into its individual parts and examined how they lie on the skeleton. With this information in hand, you will now sculpt this form on your model.

1. To sculpt this shape, isolate the area for the Triceps with a mask, as shown in Figure 5.35. Make sure the mask extends from the torso to the olecranon process.
2. Select the Claytubes brush, and mass in the volume of the Triceps. Don't worry about the heads yet; just get a mass in place at this time. Notice in Figure 5.36 how I am massing in as a horseshoe shape around the space for the tendon.
3. Select the Flatten brush, and use it to flatten out the length of the Triceps tendon, as shown in Figure 5.37. This tendon is pointed at the end toward the body and extends into the elbow, wrapping around the bone. As you saw earlier, this allows the muscle to act on the forearm, straightening out the arm.
4. Rotate to the underside of the arm, and mass in the medial and long heads. Notice how they extend all the way to the center of the underside of the arm. These are two large, thick muscle heads and should mass out the underside of the arm entirely (Figure 5.38).

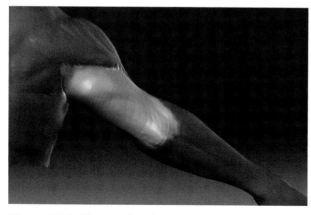

Figure 5.35 *The area for the Triceps isolated*

Figure 5.36 *Massing in the Triceps*

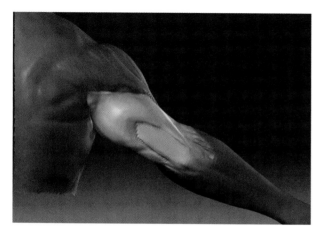

Figure 5.37 *Flattening the Triceps tendon*

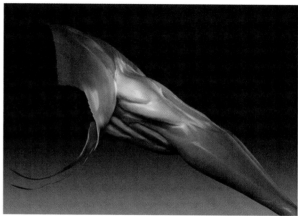

Figure 5.38 *The long and medial heads from below*

5. At this stage, you need to make some further refinements to the underside of the Triceps. With the Standard brush, accentuate the divisions between the muscles, and smooth the entire area gently with the Smooth brush at 20 intensity. Remember to make sure the Smooth curve is adjusted to help soften the effects of the brush.

6. Mask the torso, and inflate the Triceps against the masked area, as shown in Figure 5.39. This has the effect of puckering the mesh in this area and giving the impression of compressed flesh. Use this technique judiciously because it can introduce problems when remeshing a figure or generating normal maps.

7. Select the Flatten brush, and dial the ZIntensity down to 20. Gently add some planes to each head of the muscle. You don't want to create geometric shapes with the brush; rather, you are trying to create areas of plane breaks that catch shadow and add to the structural sense of the form. Figure 5.40 shows the result at this stage.

8. Moving to a top view, you can see that the Triceps muscle is too flat. Select the Move brush and pull its shape back, massing out the back of the arm, as shown in Figure 5.41. This is another good example of the importance of moving constantly around the sculpture. Problem areas may not always be readily apparent until you look at the figure from a new point of view.

Figure 5.39 Using the Inflate brush against a mask

Figure 5.40 Flattening planes

Figure 5.41 Moving the Triceps mass from the top view

At this stage, you can take an overall look at the upper arm as you have sculpted it so far. The point here is to refine the muscles and their relationships to each other. This is not a final refinement pass but more a continuing process of reexamining the sculpture as it progresses. By allowing yourself to work on areas as a whole like this and continuing to reshape them as the sculpture progresses, you can keep the work unified.

1. From the front view, use the Standard brush with a low ZIntensity to slightly accentuate the divisions between the muscles. Selecting the Claytubes brush and turning off the alpha, you can fill in the deep recesses with a simple stroke, making the divisions more subtle. Figure 5.42 shows my work at this stage.

2. Using the interactive light script or your hot key, move the light source. Check the shadows and highlights under different lighting circumstances. This will help call out areas that may need more attention.

At this stage, you are ready to move on to the lower arm. Once the figure is completed, you will make another refining pass, but this is as far as you should go with only one half of the limb completed. Notice that with the upper arm sculpted, there are two distinct triangles of space with no muscle, as shown in Figure 5.43. These areas represent where the Flexors and Extensors of the forearm originate. These two groups of muscles form the majority of the surface forms of the lower arm. Visually, the forms of the upper and lower arm are tied together by this overlapping of Flexors and Extensors. It is common for new sculptors to misunderstand this relationship. Without this interlocking of shapes, the arm would look more like a bent tube than an arm. Let's now move on to the forearm in detail.

Figure 5.42 *Refining the muscles from the front*

Figure 5.43 *The triangular area masked on the left represents the area for the Extensor muscles, while the area on the right is for the Flexors on the underside of the arm.*

Lower Arm

The forearm is one of the more daunting and complex areas for most artists. That's because there are so many muscles here, needed to manipulate the five digits of the hand. Adding to the complexity is that these muscles do not lie in a straight line along the length of the bone; they actually appear to radiate across the forearm.

It is my hope in this chapter to demystify these shapes and render them easier to recognize and reproduce. By breaking down the complex forms of the forearm into two distinct sets of muscles divided by the bone of the ulna, the form is much easier to sculpt. Let's begin by looking at the bony landmarks of the elbow and how these influence the placement of the forearm muscles.

The Parts of the Lower Arm: Elbow

The elbow is composed of several bony landmarks. There are three of these bony landmarks that will be important to you. Two are deep under the flesh but serve as central points of origin for many of the forearm muscles. The third is the elbow itself, the olecranon process of the ulna. This is the bony end of the ulna that sockets into the distal end of the humerus rotating around its head (Figure 5.44).

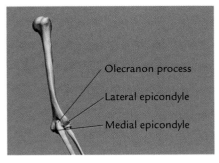

Figure 5.44 The epicondyles and the olecranon process

The other two bony landmarks are the lateral and medial epicondyles, also shown in Figure 5.44. These are the bony protrusions on either side of the elbow, and they are each apparent on a different side of the arm. The lateral epicondyle is visible from the back of the arm (Figure 5.45). This point is the central location for the Extensors of the hand.

The medial epicondyle can be felt easily just under the skin, and it serves as a point of insertion for the Flexors of the hand. By understanding these two points and the muscles that extend from them, you are well on your way to a better understanding of the forearm.

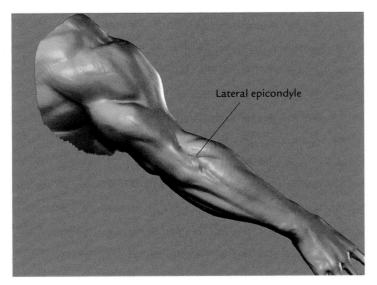

Figure 5.45 The lateral epicondyle visible on the surface

The forearm muscles can often be simplified into two triangular shapes. From the back of the arm, you can see the Extensors, as shown in Figure 5.46(a). On the anterior view of the forearm, the Flexors radiate in a similar manner, as you can see in Figure 5.46(b).

Together these two groups of muscles radiate out from their insertions and curve around the forearm. The ulna bone serves as the dividing line between these two groups, the Flexors and Extensors (Figure 5.47).

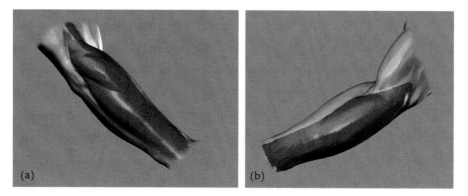

Figure 5.46 *Forearm muscles: (a) the Extensors highlighted, (b) the Flexors highlighted*

Figure 5.47 *The ulna serves as a dividing line between the Flexors and Extensors, as shown here in écorché.*

Sculpting the Lower Arm

Now that you have an understanding of the forearm as a whole, let's look at the process of sculpting these muscles:

1. Begin by masking all but the forearm, leaving the triangle of space between the Triceps and Brachialis unmasked. Here you will see that I have also smoothed the forearm.

2. You will begin by sculpting in the forearm muscles that originate on the humerus. These are the Brachioradialis and the Extensor carpi radialis longus (Figure 5.48). Select the Standard brush, lower your draw size to 20, and select alpha 01. Sketch in the division between the Triceps, Brachialis, and these two muscles. This serves to accentuate the triangle of origin here.

3. Using the same brush, sketch in the division between the Extensor carpi radialis longus and the Brachioradialis as they turn around the forearm, as shown in Figure 5.49(a). Rotate around to the front view of the arm and continue these lines, turning them to point toward the thumb, as shown in Figure 5.49(b).

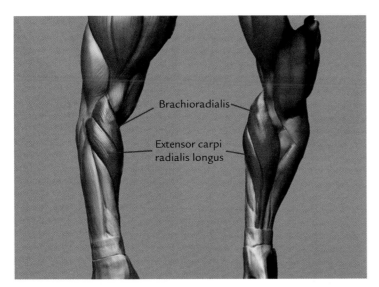

Brachioradialis

Extensor carpi
radialis longus

*Figure 5.48 The
Brachioradialis and
Extensor carpi radialis
longus seen in* écorché

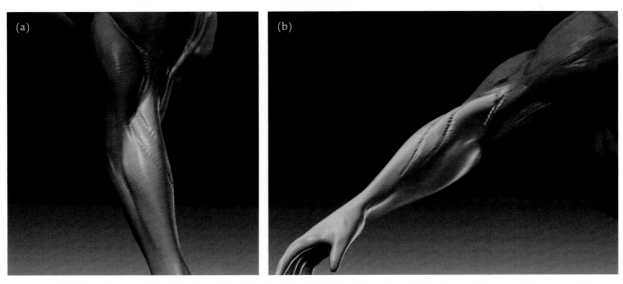

(a)

(b)

*Figure 5.49 Sketching in the division: (a) using the Standard brush to sketch the flow of the muscles around the
forearm, (b) the same lines from the front view as they turn around the form of the arm*

4. From the back of the arm, notice the triangular shape left between the elbow and the
   Extensor carpi radialis longus. Select the Standard brush again, and sketch in the outline of another muscle form here, as shown in Figure 5.50(a). This is the Extensor digitorum and represents one of the most visible Extensors, because it is a large, flat
   muscle that extends to the wrist, where it splits into several tendons for the fingers
   (Figure 5.50(b)).
5. At this stage, you need to mask out the length of the ulna bone. You can trace this by
   starting at the elbow and tracing a line to the pinky-finger side of the wrist. Notice that
   the line is not exactly straight. There is a slight jog to the length, so the elbow itself will
   appear higher than the bony landmark at the termination of the bone at the wrist. Ctrl-
   click to invert this mask, and sketch in the ulna with the Claytubes brush (Figure 5.51).
   The ulna will serve as a dividing line between the Flexors and Extensors.

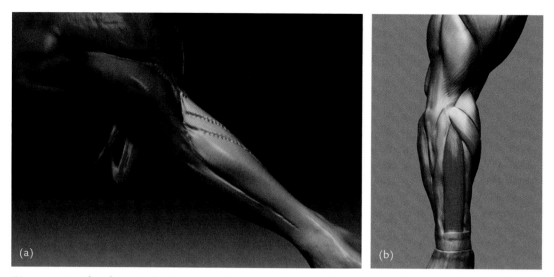

Figure 5.50 *Sketching in the Extensor digitorum: (a) one of the most visible Extensors, (b) the Extensor digitorum seen in* écorché

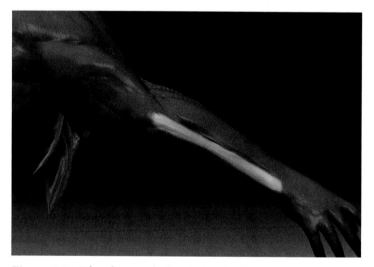

Figure 5.51 *The ulna masked and sketched in*

6. With the Claytubes brush, mass the Extensor digitorum, allowing it to overlap the ulna (Figure 5.52). This shape is actually a second narrower muscle called the Extensor carpi ulnaris, but you will treat it as one form here to simplify the shape.

7. Continue to sculpt the flow of the Extensor muscles with the Claytubes brush, as shown in Figure 5.53. Drag the brush along the length of the arm in strokes that mimic the flow of the muscles. I find that by sculpting in this manner, not only can I create the shape more easily, but it also results in stray tool marks—"happy accidents"—that find their way into the final surface and add to the realism. Experimentation will illustrate this for you in your own work.

8. Mask out the Biceps and Brachialis. By masking these muscles, you can sculpt against them, sharpening the definition in the muscle form here. From the front view, continue to refine the form and flow of the Brachioradialis muscle, as shown in Figure 5.54.

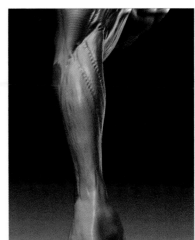

Figure 5.52 The Extensor digitorum and Extensor carpi ulnaris in more detail

Figure 5.53 Continuing to sculpt the forearm muscles with Claytubes

Figure 5.54 Sculpting the Brachioradialis muscle from the front with a mask on the Biceps

9. Mask out the Triceps muscle. Select the Move brush, and pull on the origin of the Brachioradialis and Extensor carpi radialis longus (Figure 5.55(a)). You are trying to establish the plane breaks here that are visible in the figure silhouette (Figure 5.55(b)).

10. Move to the back view, and continue to adjust the volume of these forms, as shown in Figure 5.56. Select the Inflate brush with no alpha and the ZIntensity set to 10, and brush over the muscles to increase their volume.

11. At this stage, the forms at the back of the forearm have become soft. With the Standard brush, etch the outline of the Extensor digitorum again (Figure 5.57). Create a deep sharp "V" here so the form will remain after the next step.

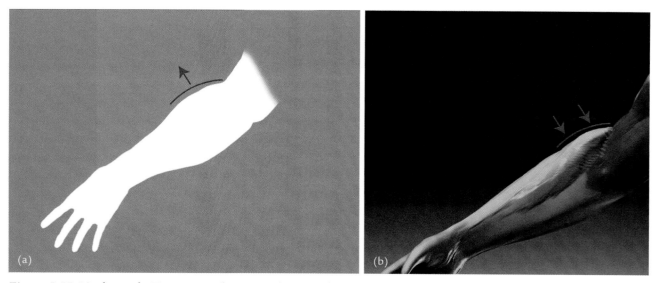

Figure 5.55 *Mask out the Triceps muscle: (a) use the Move brush to pull the Extensors up in the direction shown in the image, (b) plane breaks from the front of Radialis muscles in silhouette view*

Figure 5.56 *Inflating the volume of the muscle forms*

Figure 5.57 *Etching in the Extensor digitorum at the elbow again*

12. At this point, you need to push the forms back into the surface with a low ZIntensity pass of the Smooth brush. The intent is not to erase the shapes but to make them more subtle. Press the Shift key to access the Smooth brush settings. Lower the ZIntensity to 40 and adjust the curve under the Brush menu as shown in Figure 5.58a, and stroke along the surface. After the surface is softened a bit, you may choose to reintroduce some volume with the Claytubes brush, as shown in Figure 5.58(b).

13. From the back view, repeat this process. In Figure 5.59 I have taken the further step of etching some divisions back in with a Standard brush using alpha 01 and a ZIntensity of 10. From the top view, reinforce the flow of the Extensor carpi radialis longus and Brachialis.

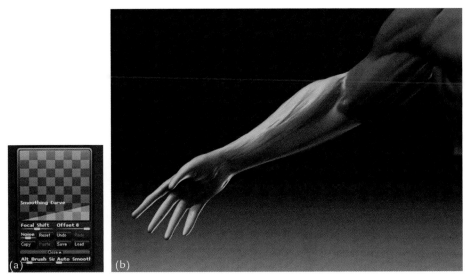

Figure 5.58 *Pushing the forms back: (a) lowered smoothing curve (midrange),
(b) the surface smoothed and further sculpted*

Figure 5.59 *The muscle definition on the back of the arm is
reinforced with the Standard brush.*

You are now ready to add the Flexors. The Flexors encompass the anterior aspect of
the arm. Rotate to the underside of the arm. From this view, you can see the area where you
will sculpt the Flexors radiating from the medial epicondyle, as shown in Figure 5.60.

1. Isolate the area for the Flexor muscles with a mask, as shown in Figure 5.61.
2. Accentuate the depression of the Lateral epicondyle, as shown in Figure 5.62(a). On
   the underside of the arm, repeat this process, adding a small protrusion for the medial
   epicondyle (Figure 5.62(b)).
3. At this stage, take an overview of the arm. From the front view in silhouette, the high
   point of the forearm Extensors should be a crest. This high point coincides with the
   crest of the Flexors on a diagonal line, as shown in Figure 5.63. Use the Standard
   brush with a draw size of 20 and alpha 01 to pick out the shadow between the muscles
   and generally refine the forms. Be sure to check your work from unusual angles, as
   shown in Figure 5.64.

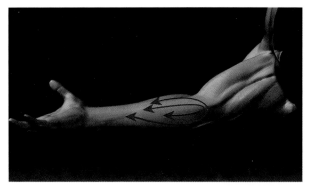

Figure 5.60 *The Flexor point on the underside of the arm*

Figure 5.61 *Isolating the underside with a mask*

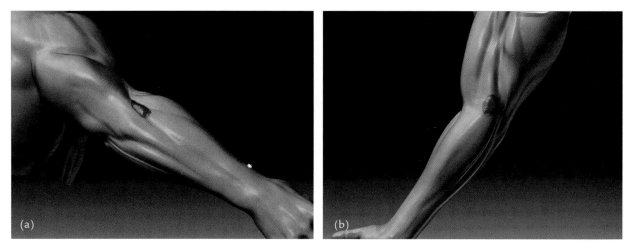

Figure 5.62 *Accentuate the depression: (a) accenting the lateral epicondyle, (b) accenting the medial epicondyle*

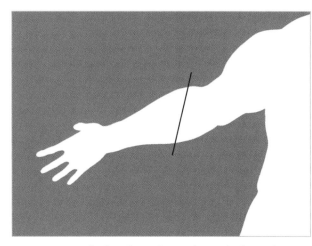

Figure 5.63 *The line here shows the angle from the highest crest in the top and bottom profiles of the arm muscles.*

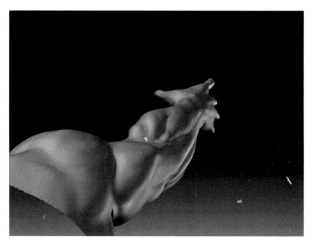

Figure 5.64 *Looking at the sculpture from unusual angles can call to attention volumes that need adjustment.*

At this stage, I think the arms need a slight rotation. This is a purely aesthetic choice on my part and can be skipped, but I'll cover the process here to show how you can accomplish it. For a video of this process, please see the DVD.

1. To rotate the forearm, you use ZBrush transpose rotation tools. To enter the transpose Rotate tool, press the R key on the keyboard, or click the Rotate button at the top of the screen.

2. Step down a few subdivision levels. Lower divisions are easier to manipulate with the transpose tools than denser meshes. In this case, my mesh is at level 4 with a total of 71,000 polys. I want to mask the body down to the point I want to rotate, in this case the lateral epicondyle.

3. To mask, you use ZBrush's topology-based mask feature. While in rotate mode, hold down the Ctrl key and click-drag down the arm. A mask will appear that seems to follow your cursor. This is topology-based masking. When the mask appears as in Figure 5.65, release the mouse button.

4. Now click and drag the mouse from the end of the mask to the tips of the fingers. Move to the top view, and move the first orange circle to center on the lateral epicondyle. You can move the circle by clicking the orange circle, not inside (Figure 5.66).

Figure 5.65 Mask to the forearm

Figure 5.66 The circle moved

5. Now click and drag inside the center circle, and the forearm will begin to twist (Figure 5.67). This may require some resculpting once it is complete, but it is a very quick way to repose a figure. You will look at transposing in more depth in Chapter 11.

Congratulations! You have completed the arm. Figure 5.68 shows the final result. You have learned about the skeletal and muscular anatomy of the arm and put this information into practice.

Figure 5.67 *The forearm rotated*

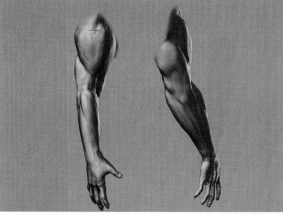

Figure 5.68
The final arm

What's Next?

You will return to the arm in Chapter 9 when you sculpt the finishing pass over the entire body, adding a sense of fat and skin as well as details such as superficial veins. At this point, you have all the information to sculpt a human arm convincingly. Let's move on to look at how to sculpt the pelvis and legs.

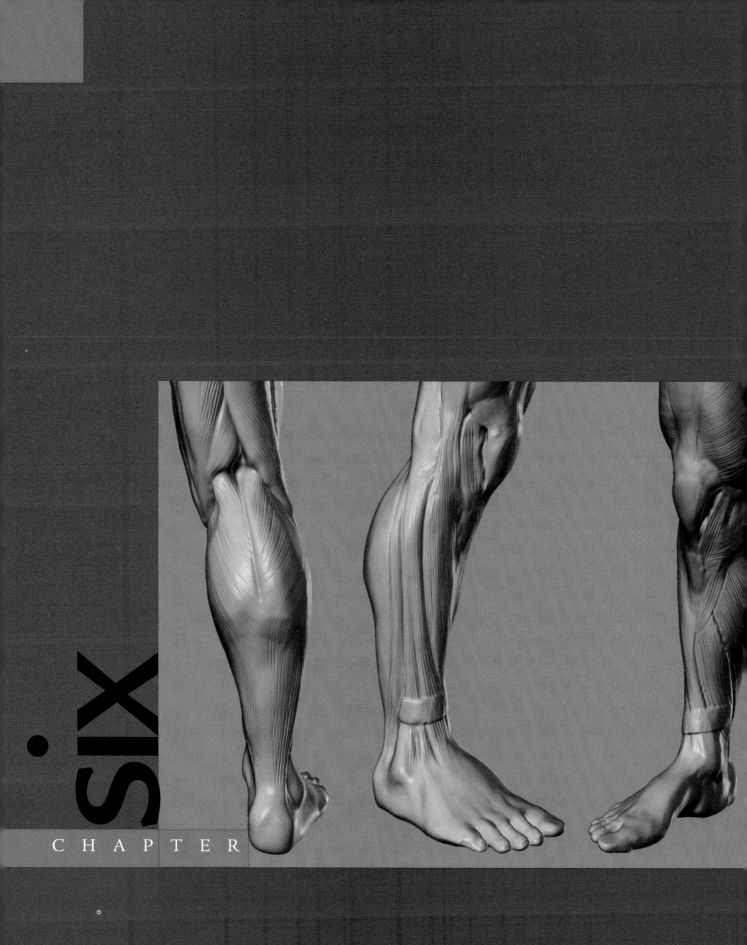

six

The Pelvis and Legs

Now that you have looked *at the arms, you will move on to the second part of the appendicular skeleton, the legs. As we did in the previous chapter, in looking at the limbs I will also talk about the transitional areas between the limbs and the trunk. In this case, you will begin by sculpting the pelvis and buttocks.*

Basic Pelvis and Leg Forms

As you saw in Chapter 5, the limbs can be reduced to their simplest shapes as boxes or cylinders. Just as you reduced the arms to basic geometric shapes, you will do the same here with the legs. By simplifying the shapes, you can better understand their more complex forms. You may also better examine how the masses of the upper and lower legs relate to each other by looking at them in more simplified terms. As I have already discussed, in many cases it is the relationship between the masses—the gesture, rhythms, and silhouette—that is more important than isolating the individual anatomical forms.

The legs can be most simply represented as two cylindrical forms, as shown in Figure 6.1. These two cylinders have a slight taper from the top to bottom.

The internal shapes of the leg are composed of several oval forms, as shown in Figure 6.2. The red areas illustrate the oval shapes, and the blue areas represent the more boxed form of the structure of the knee. The heads of the tibia and femur bones are quite close to the surface at the knee, which is why the shape maintains a more structural quality. You will look at this in more depth later in this chapter when I discuss the bony landmarks known as *condyles*.

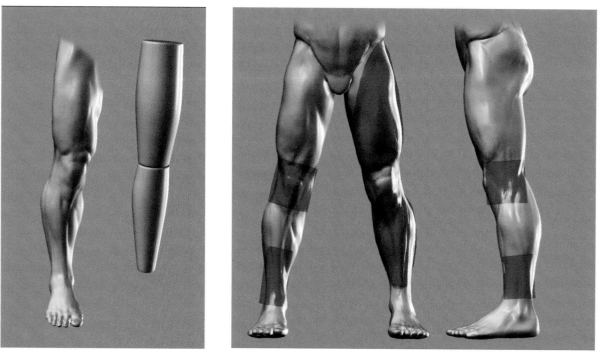

Figure 6.1 *The leg represented as cylindrical forms*

Figure 6.2 *The oval forms of the leg*

As you have seen before, the silhouette of the figure can offer many cues to accurate muscle and bone placement in the form of important plane breaks or crests in the outline. For example, Figure 6.3 shows the major breaks on the silhouette of the leg. You need to keep these in mind as you work. Try to refer back to these points of reference as you sculpt; it can become quite easy to lose sight of the overall outline when facing the complex internal forms of the sculpture.

Figure 6.3 *Crests and breaks in leg silhouette*

When you forget to introduce and maintain these breaks in the silhouette, the figure takes on a softer appearance. This is one of the main reasons some sculptures may look "soft," or undefined, even when the internal anatomic forms are in place. Figure 6.4 shows the outline created by these interlocking shapes in the leg. These are not specific anatomical forms in themselves. These are simply points on the silhouette of the figure where the outline typically is broken by a high or low point. Being aware of these points helps create an accurate profile, which in turn guides you when placing internal forms.

Another useful visual cue to bear in mind concerning the silhouette of the leg is the relationship of high to low points on the upper leg and lower leg. While working on the muscles of the leg, it is useful to keep in mind the consistent relationship between the crests on the outer and inner profiles of the leg. Figure 6.5 shows these angles and how they may be drawn on the figure. Avoid evening these out or accidentally making them too flat. The result will be a limb that appears too much like a cylinder or a sausage (Figure 6.6).

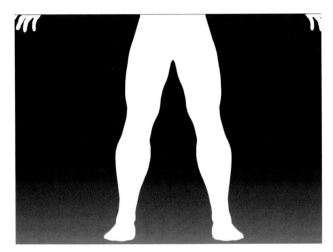

Figure 6.4 *The legs shown in silhouette*

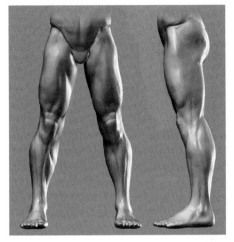

Figure 6.5 *High and low angles, with an example of a bad silhouette*

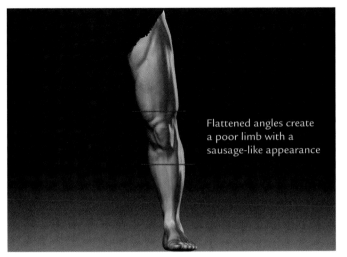

Flattened angles create a poor limb with a sausage-like appearance

Figure 6.6 *When the angles and crests of the limb are flattened, it takes on an unnatural sausage-like appearance.*

As you sculpt, try to keep these visual cues in mind. Step back from the sculpture often, and try to reintroduce the rhythms and crests that may have been lost in the process of working the surface. I find when I sculpt there is a constant interplay between working on internal shapes and then relating those shapes to the expected profiles of the figure as a whole (Figure 6.7). Before you move into sculpting, let's take a moment to look at the skeleton and musculature in more detail.

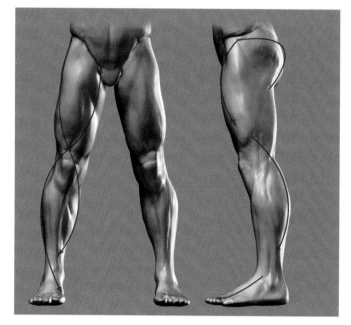

Figure 6.7 Leg lines and rhythms

Skeletal and Muscular Anatomy

In this section, you'll survey the major bones and muscles of the lower limbs. Note that you'll learn more about many of these features during the sculpting process. Figure 6.8 illustrates the bones of the hip and leg. They consist of the pelvis, femur, patella, tibia, and fibula. The pelvis consists of the two hip bones joined at the sacrum, or *tailbone*. The upper leg consists of the long and very strong femur bone. The lower leg is composed of two bones, the tibia and fibula. These are similar to the radius and ulna of the lower arm bones, but they lack the rotational abilities of the forearm. The joint between the femur and tibia is protected by the kneecap, or *patella* bone.

Figure 6.9 illustrates the major skeletal landmarks. These consist of the great trochanter, the iliac crest, the patella, the condyles of the tibia and femur, and the malleolus (or anklebones). The great trochanter, illustrated in Figure 6.10, is the bony protrusion at the side of the femur. It lies approximately at the midpoint of the figure and is often used as a starting measure, since it can be considered the midline. You will look at this landmark as it relates to the Gluteus muscles later in this chapter.

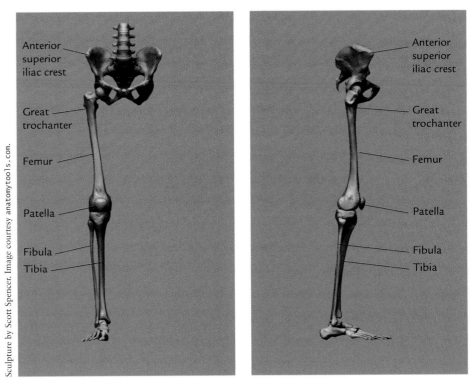

Figure 6.8 *The bones of the hip and leg*

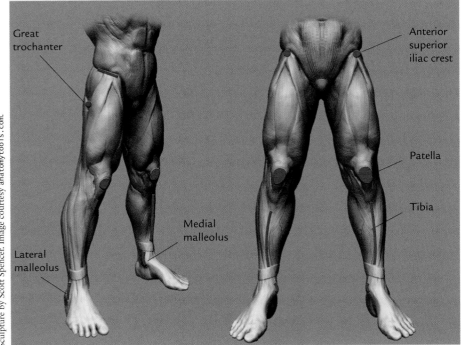

Figure 6.9 *Bony landmarks marked on an* écorché *view*

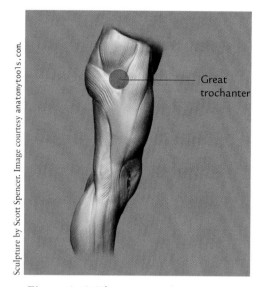

Sculpture by Scott Spencer. Image courtesy anatomytools.com.

Great trochanter

Figure 6.10 The great trochanter as shown in écorché

The iliac crest is the bony spine of the top of the hip bone. It is mainly visible at the front of the figure and serves an important anchor point for the muscles of the upper leg, as illustrated in Figure 6.11.

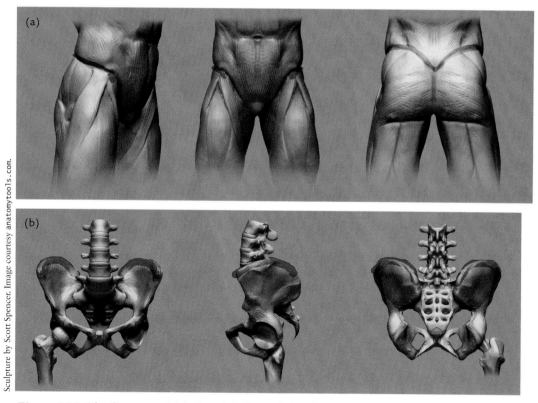

Sculpture by Scott Spencer. Image courtesy anatomytools.com.

Figure 6.11 The iliac crest: (a) in écorché, *(b) in skeletal views*

The patella is also known as the *kneecap*. It serves to protect the space between the femur and tibia when the leg bends and the area within the joint may be exposed. When the knee bends, the patella slides over the joint, protecting the exposed space between the bones.

Figure 6.12 shows the distal head of the femur and the proximal head of the tibia. When you start sculpting the knee, it will be important to recognize these landmarks. The head of each bone has what are called *condyles*. There are two condyles per bone: the lateral condyles (found at the sides) and medial condyles (found toward the middle). Figure 6.12 also shows these forms labeled. They will become important when you begin sculpting the knee, along with the muscles of the lower leg.

The anklebones are actually protrusions from two separate bones. The inside anklebone is called the *medial malleolus* of the tibia. The outside anklebone is the *lateral malleolus* of the fibula. Figure 6.13 identifies these landmarks. Notice how the naming helps show the placement. The lateral malleolus of the fibula is on the outside, or lateral aspect, of the leg, while the medial malleolus of the tibia is on the inside.

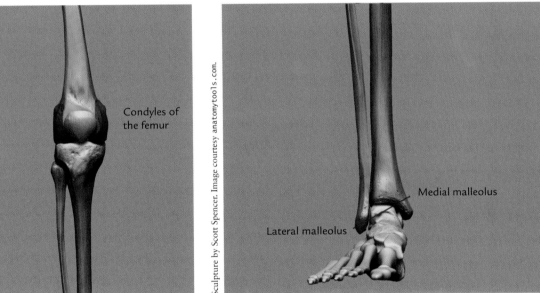

Sculpture by Scott Spencer. Image courtesy anatomytools.com.

Sculpture by Scott Spencer. Image courtesy anatomytools.com.

Condyles of the femur

Medial malleolus

Lateral malleolus

Figure 6.12 The condyles of the femur

Figure 6.13 The malleoli of the anklebones. Notice the angle from high to low between the bones.

Muscles of the Pelvis and Leg Addressed in This Chapter

The pelvis and legs are composed of several important muscles. You will look at some of the major ones in this chapter that have a direct influence over surface form. Figure 6.14 shows these muscles labeled on the *écorché* of the figure.

In many cases, two muscles may lie so close together they seem more like one form on the surface of the figure. As you sculpt, you will mass in shapes like this together. One example of this is the combination of the Soleus and Gastrocnemius, the two muscles that together form the mass of the back of the calf. These two muscles are most easily addressed as a single form. You will also see this effect with the Gluteus medius and maximus muscles.

Although there are in fact two glute muscles visible on the surface form of the sculpture, you will address them as one shape when sculpting. The following list covers the muscles of the leg you will be looking at in this chapter. There are other muscles, but these are the ones that have the most pronounced effect on the surface forms of the sculpture:

The Muscles of the Buttocks
Gluteus maximus
Gluteus medius

The Muscles of the Upper Leg
Tensor fasciae lata
Sartorius
Gracilis
Great trochanter
Iliotibial band
Vastus lateralis
Vastus medialis

Rectus femoris
Bicep femoris
Semitendinosus
Semimembranosus

The Muscles of the Lower Leg
Extensor digitorum longus
Gastrocnemius
Peroneus longus
Tibialis anterior
Soleus

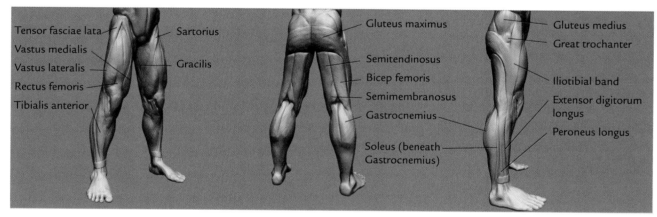

Figure 6.14 The muscles of the pelvis and leg

Sculpting the Pelvis and Legs

You will now begin to sculpt the legs using the information presented so far. The first step will involve using the transpose tools to shift the pose of the legs into a more dynamic position. You will open the stance and shift the legs back slightly so the figure's weight appears to thrust forward, adding a more heroic appearance.

Adjusting the Leg Position

Before you start sculpting this area, I'll show how to adjust the pose. Although you want to keep the figure somewhat neutral for ease of remeshing and rigging, you also want it to have a sense of life. To do this, you will use the transpose move tools to shift the legs back and spread the figure's stance wider. By moving the legs back, you make the figure appear to lead more with his chest. By opening the legs wider, you give his stance a more solid and heroic feel (Figure 6.15). This process is shown in a video on the DVD; take the following steps to try it yourself.

Figure 6.15 Leg positions before and after

1. To move the legs, step down to subdivision level 3. You want to be at a lower subdivision level to make working with the transpose tools easier. Higher subdivision levels have too many polygons and tend to be harder to manipulate. Press the R key to enter transpose rotate mode, or use the Rotate button at the top of the screen (Figure 6.16).

Figure 6.16 The Rotate button

2. Hold down the Ctrl key, and click-drag from the torso to the leg. This activates topology masking and will allow you to mask the figure down to the legs. Make sure that X symmetry is on for this process by pressing the X key on the keyboard. At this point, the legs should be unmasked (Figure 6.17).

> You can also find the X symmetry option, along with Y symmetry and Z symmetry, on the Transform palette, which is accessible by clicking the Transform menu at the top of the screen. Click the Activate Symmetry button and the X modifier to engage the X symmetry option. You can also press the X hot key.

3. Click and drag the mouse to draw a transpose line along the front of the leg from the center to the bottom of the foot (Figure 6.18(a)). Rotate to a side view of the figure, and move the transpose line back into the center of the hip (Figure 6.18(b)). Now rotate back to the front view.

4. Click in the center of the lowest circle, the one at the foot. Drag out to the side to rotate the leg out (Figure 6.19(a)). Move to the side view and repeat the process, but this time, rotate the leg back, as shown in Figure 6.19(b). You will now want to adjust the ankles so the feet appear to rest on the ground plane.

Figure 6.17 The legs unmasked

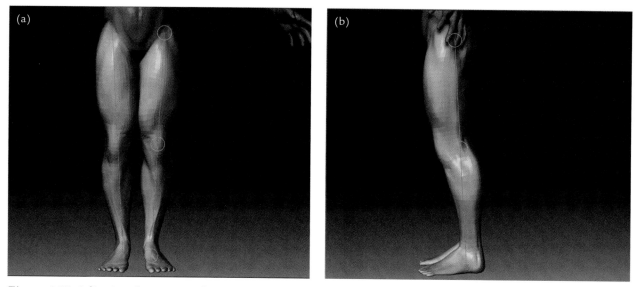

Figure 6.18 *Adjusting the pose: (a) drawing a transpose line along the front, (b) the transpose line moved from the side*

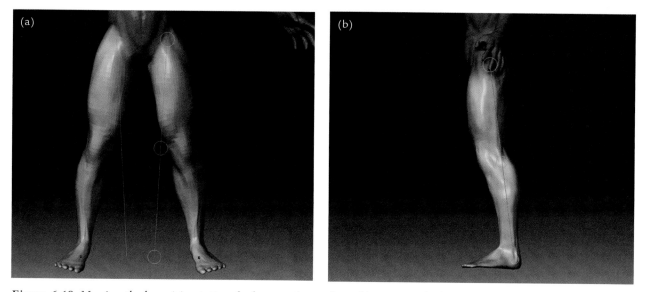

Figure 6.19 *Moving the legs: (a) rotating the leg out, front view, (b) rotating the leg back, side view*

5. Click and drag again on the leg from the front view to draw a new transpose line. This time, end at the ankle (Figure 6.20). Hold down Alt, and click-drag in the last circle to rotate the ankle so the foot lies on the ground plane. When pressing Alt in transpose mode, the effect changes to what is called *bone posing*. Bone posing rotates from the last circle of the transpose line and allows you to bend limbs as though they were rigged with a skeleton. The algorithm contains a skinning process that helps prevent the mesh from collapsing at the point of rotation.

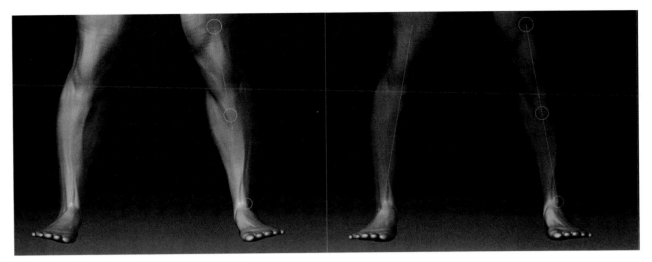

Figure 6.20 *Drawing a transpose line to the ankle*

6. At this point, turn on guide marks, and check the proportions (see Figure 6.21). You need to move the pubic bone down as well as the feet based on the figure position in relation to the measure lines shown here. You'll do that in the next stage.

Figure 6.21
Measure
lines on

Sculpting the Pelvis and Buttocks

At this stage, you are ready to begin sculpting the transition from the trunk into the pelvis. You will start by etching in the general flow of the major muscles of the buttocks as well as the pelvis.

1. Select the Standard brush. Set your draw size to 8, and select alpha 01 to help create a smaller etched line. From the front view, sketch in the inverted "V" shown in Figure 6.22. This will represent the hollow just under the iliac crest created by the origin of several muscles. Also carve the furrow where the lateral Oblique flows over the iliac crest and down toward the pubic region. Notice in Figure 6.23 how the Oblique muscle breaks its flow at the iliac crest.

2. Select the Move brush, and pull the groin down to account for the genitals, as shown in Figure 6.24(a). This region lies beneath the fourth head measure, which corresponds to the pubic bone and great trochanter. Leaving it off can seriously affect your ability to judge proportions and the general flow of muscle and skin in the groin. Using the Move brush, adjust the shape of the furrow at the waist, as shown in Figure 6.24(b).

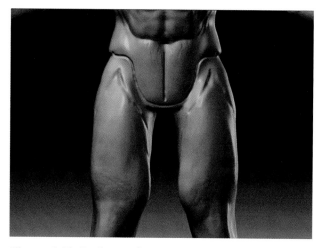

Figure 6.22 Sculpting the "V" and the inguinal ligament

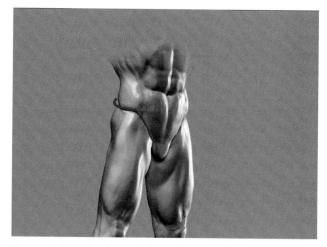

Figure 6.23 The flow of the Oblique is broken at the iliac crest.

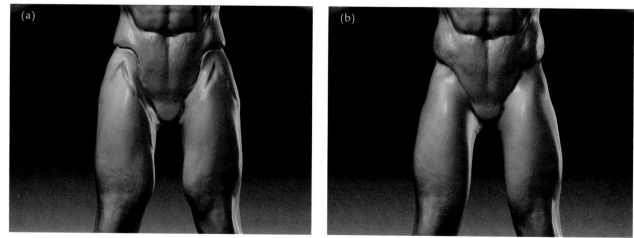

Figure 6.24 Working on the furrow: (a) pulling the groin down, (b) adjusting the furrow shape

3. Move to the side view so you can address the muscles and shape of the buttocks. As you can see in Figure 6.25(a), it is too shallow at this time and lacks any real definition. Turn on the measure guides, and use the Move brush to pull the buttocks back. The cleft between the buttock and the leg is created by a fatty deposit. This point should lie just beneath the fourth head measure line (Figure 6.25(b)).

4. Turn off the measure guides, and select the Claytubes brush. Mass in the Oblique muscle, as shown in Figure 6.26(a). Move to the back view, and use the Claytubes brush to continue to mass in the glute muscles, as shown in Figure 6.26(b). There are two glute muscles, the Gluteus maximus and Gluteus medius. You can see these muscles in *écorché* in Figure 6.27. I usually consider them as one shape, and they are often referred to as the *glutes* when addressed together as a group.

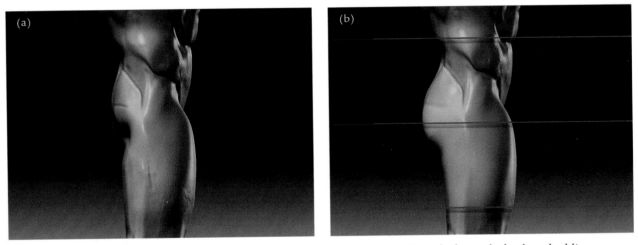

Figure 6.25 *Working on the buttocks: (a) side view of the buttocks, (b) pulling the buttocks back and adding a furrow from the side with measure lines on*

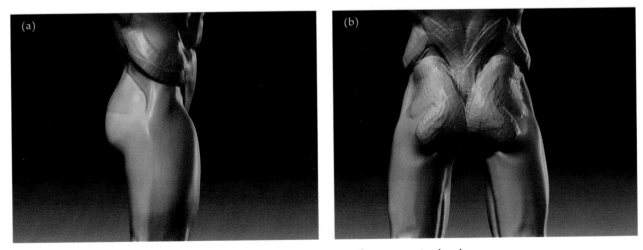

Figure 6.26 *Working on the glutes: (a) massing in the Oblique, (b) massing in the glutes*

5. Notice that I am sculpting the flow of the muscles as I work even when using the Claytubes brush. The glute muscles can be seen to radiate out from around the great trochanter (Figure 6.28).

6. Move to the side view. Here you can see that the upper thigh is far too thick; the silhouette is off. Selecting the Move brush, shift the front profile back in place, as shown in Figure 6.29.

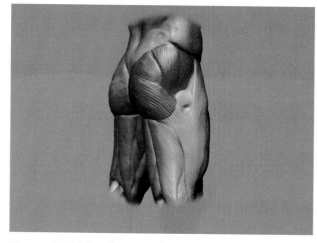

Figure 6.27 The glute muscles shown in écorché

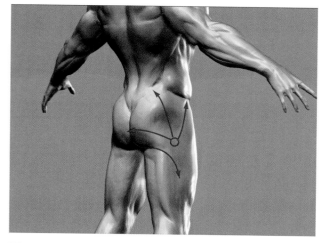

Figure 6.28 The radiating flow of the glute muscles

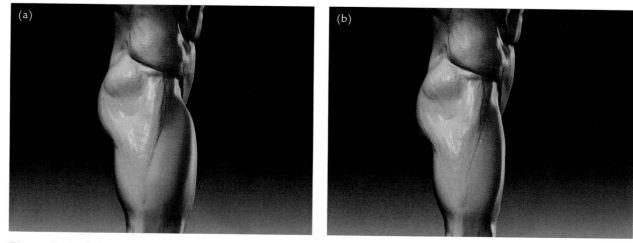

Figure 6.29 Shifting the front profile of the thigh back

Sculpting the Upper Leg

You will now address the forms of the upper leg. In this section, you will look at how the leg transitions from the pelvis into the limb.

1. Return to the front view. You will now etch in the major muscles of the upper leg, starting from the inverted "V" you created earlier (Figure 6.30(a)). This "V" represents the origin of the Tensor fasciae lata (TFL), as well as the Sartorius and

the Rectus femoris muscles (Figure 6.30(b)). This makes it an ideal point to start sketching in the muscles.

2. With the Standard brush, make sure your draw size is around 10 and you have alpha 01 selected. Start by extending the medial leg of the "V" down to the inner thigh, as shown in Figure 6.31(a). Notice how this line hooks around a teardrop shape near the inside of the knee. This is where the Sartorius muscle curves around the Vastus medialis muscle, which you will address shortly. Figure 6.31(b) shows these muscles in *écorché*.

3. Moving to the front view, etch in the Rectus femoris muscle, as shown in Figure 6.32(a). This long muscle attaches to the kneecap and extends up into the furrow just beneath the iliac crest, as you can see in Figure 6.32(b).

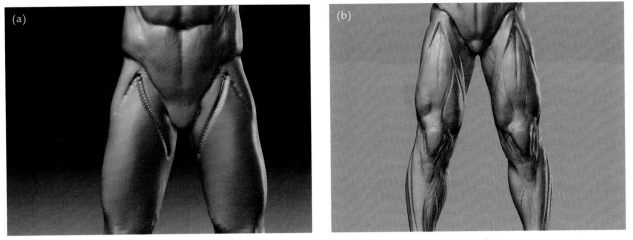

Figure 6.30 *Sculpting the upper leg: (a) sketching in the V-shaped hollow where the Tensor fasciae lata and Rectus femoris muscles attach to the pelvis, (b) the hollow shown in* écorché

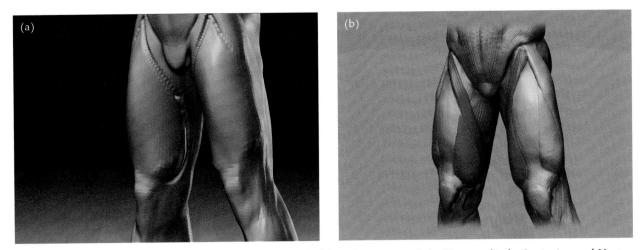

Figure 6.31 *The muscles in* écorché: *(a) extending medial line down around the Vastus, (b) the Sartorius and Vastus medialis in* écorché

4. Now move to the side of the leg, and etch in another teardrop shape; this is the Vastus medialis muscle. In Figure 6.33 you can also see the shape of the Vastus medialis on the inside of the left leg.

   When taken together, these muscles are called the *quadriceps* group. You may notice I've mentioned only three muscles, but *quad* would indicate there must be four. There is a deeper muscle beneath the Rectus femoris called the *Vastus intermedius*. Because it is not visible on the surface of the figure, you will consider only the shape of the surface muscles it influences. You can see the group as a whole in Figure 6.34.

5. Move to the front view. Now that you have the outlines of the muscles etched in, you will select the Claytubes brush to mass in their forms. Figure 6.35(a) shows the Rectus femoris massed in using the Claytubes brush. Be careful not to add too much here because it will disturb the silhouette of the leg. You simply want to give some form to the outline you have created. Figure 6.35(b) shows the Vastus medialis massed in with the same technique. Now move to a side view, and mass in the Vastus lateralis with the same brush, as shown in Figure 6.35(c).

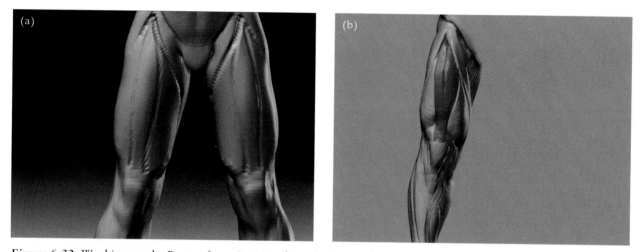

Figure 6.32 *Working on the Rectus femoris: (a) etching the Rectus femoris, (b) the Rectus femoris in écorché*

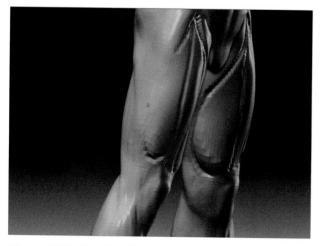

Figure 6.33 *Carving the Vastus medialis*

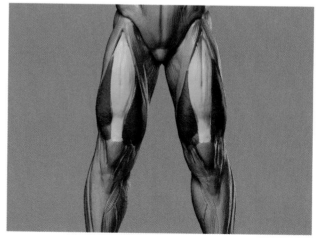

Figure 6.34 *The* écorché *view of the quadriceps group*

6. At this stage, turn on the measure guides. Using the Claytubes brush, indicate the knee-cap. Notice in Figure 6.36 that I've placed it just above the sixth head line. Remember that the head measure falls not on the knee but on the bony protrusion of the tibia.

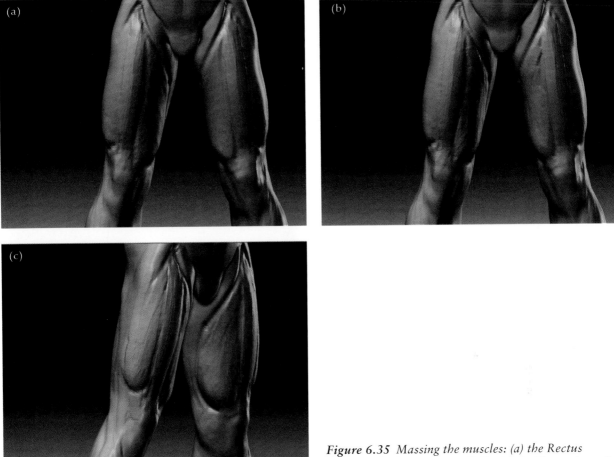

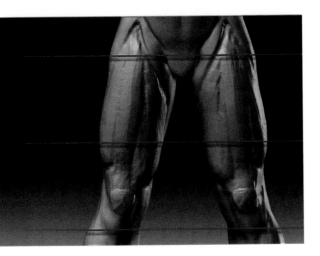

Figure 6.35 Massing the muscles: (a) the Rectus femoris, (b) the Vastus medialis, (c) the Vastus lateralis

Figure 6.36 Roughing in the knee

7. Turn off the measure guides, and select the Standard brush. Etch in the divisions again where they may be getting lost, as shown in Figure 6.37(a). At this point you are less concerned with the surface finish and the appearance of flesh than with the placement of muscles and the rhythms between them. You will take the surface to a finer finish later when the muscles are placed. Also note on this image the angle between the Vastus lateralis and Vastus medialis. In Figure 6.37(b), notice how the lateral head is higher.

8. Smooth back with a softened Smooth brush to achieve the results shown in Figure 6.38.

9. Move to the side view, and isolate the area for the TFL and the iliotibial band (ITB) with a mask (Figure 6.39). With the Claytubes brush, stroke down this unmasked area lightly. The ITB is actually a thin strong tendon sheath that wraps around the Vastus lateralis. It gets its shape from the underlying muscle it encases.

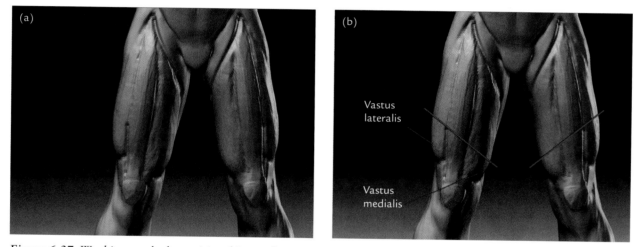

Figure 6.37 *Working on the knee: (a) etching in divisions again, (b) the angle of the Vastus lateralis to the Vastus medialis*

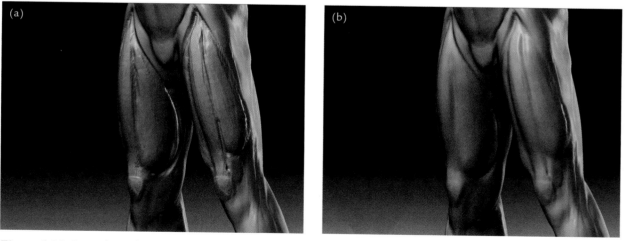

Figure 6.38 *Smoothing the forms back*

The important thing to note is that it sticks out from the side of the leg and is actually visible from the back. You can see this in *écorché* in Figure 6.40(a). Moving to a back view, you can see how this step starts to take form after massing in the unmasked area with the Claytubes brush (Figure 6.40(b)).

10. From the back view, continue to mass in the shape of the glute muscles, as shown in Figure 6.41. Use the Claytubes brush with no alpha and a ZIntensity of 10 to mass in this area. By removing the alpha, you give the Claytubes brush a much smoother surface effect.

11. Move down to the back of the thighs. The backs of the thighs are covered by three large muscles: the Bicep femoris, the Semitendinosus, and the Semimembranosus. The last two sit directly on top of each other, and for these purposes you will consider them as a single shape (Figure 6.42). Together these muscles are sometimes called the *hamstring* group.

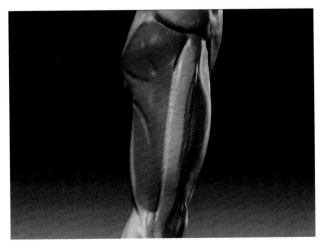

Figure 6.39 Iliotibial band masked

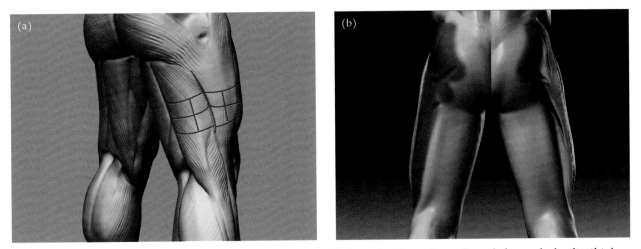

Figure 6.40 Isolate the TFL and ITB: (a) a discernable shelf where the Vastus lateralis ends beneath the iliotibial band and steps in to the Bicep femoris, (b) this step shown from back

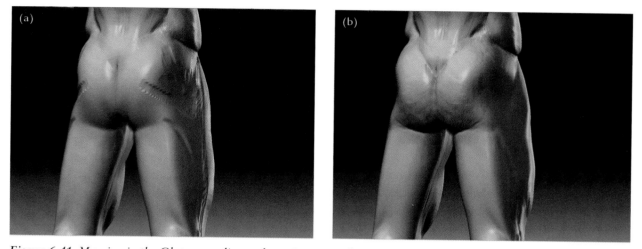

Figure 6.41 Massing in the Gluteus medius and maximus muscles

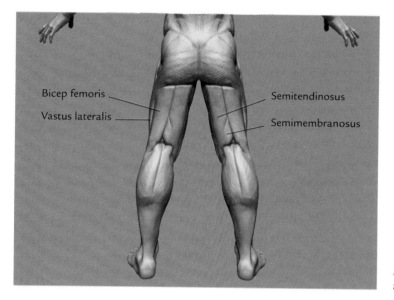

Bicep femoris

Vastus lateralis

Semitendinosus

Semimembranosus

Figure 6.42 The hamstring group in écorché with the Vastus lateralis visible from behind

12. Select the Standard brush, lower the draw size, and select alpha 01. Etch in the division between the two muscles, as shown in Figure 6.43. Select the Claytubes brush with alpha 28, and mass in the shape of the Semitendinosus muscle, as shown in Figure 6.44. Notice how it wraps around the heads of the tibia and femur, bulging toward the midline of the body.

13. Repeat this process for the Bicep femoris, as shown in Figure 6.45(a). Notice how these two muscles together form a kind of tongs shape that seems to grip the calf muscles (Figure 6.45(b)).

14. At this stage, you can reevaluate the silhouette of the legs. Switch to the Flat Color shader, and move to the side view. Here you can see that the profiles of the upper leg are off. The leg appears too straight in silhouette and lacks any of the gestural curves. Using the Move brush, shift them back into place (Figure 6.46).

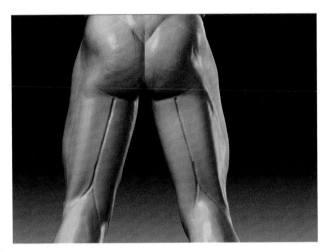

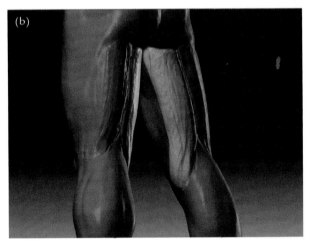

Figure 6.43 *Etching in the division at the back of the thigh*

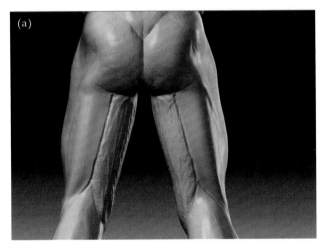

Figure 6.44 *Using Claytubes to mass in the Semitendinosus callout bulge*

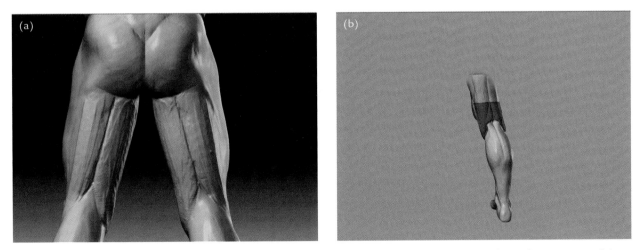

Figure 6.45 *Working on the Bicep femoris: (a) massing in the Bicep femoris, (b) the tong shape shown in* écorché

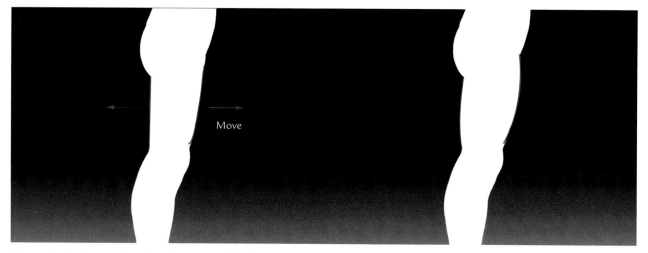

Figure 6.46 *Correcting the silhouette of the leg*

Sculpting the Knee

In this section, you will address the knee. The knee will require some examination in *écorché* before you move into sculpting. Like the ear, the knee is an apparently complex form that is easily demystified by understanding its individual parts. Figure 6.47 shows the knee in *écorché*.

Notice that the patella sits above the division between the head of the tibia and the head of the femur. The boxlike shape of the knee is formed by these two bone heads meeting. The majority of the bone surface is covered here by tendons only.

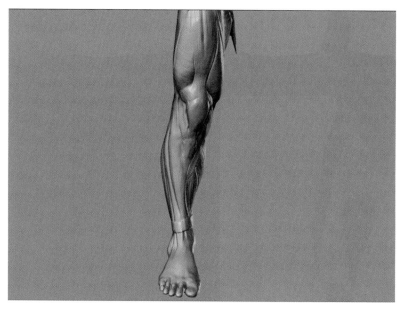

Figure 6.47 *The knee in* écorché

Note as well that the quadriceps group grasps the patella from the top by a tendon, while the bottom of the patella is attached to the tibial tuberosity, which is also the sixth head measure landmark.

1. From the front view, attach the patella via three tendons to the Vastus medialis and lateralis and via the Rectus femoris (Figure 6.48).
2. The box of the knee can be defined by the bony landmarks of the corners of the femur head and tibia head. Using the Claytubes brush, mark in bony landmarks of bone heads, as shown in Figure 6.49(a). You can see these in detail on the skeleton in Figure 6.49(b).

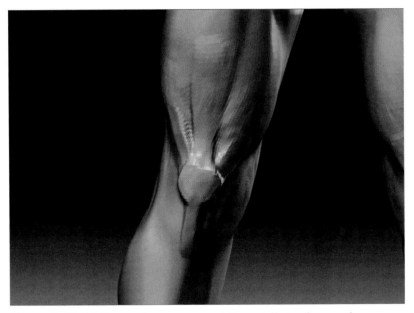

Figure 6.48 Adding tendons to connect the patella to the muscles

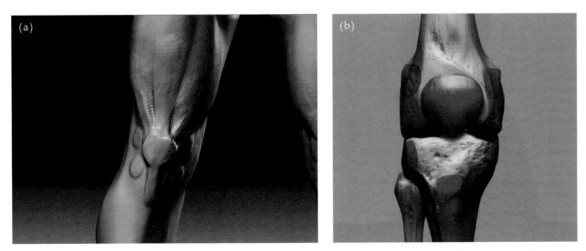

Figure 6.49 Working on the knee: (a) marking bone landmarks of heads, (b) skeletal reference of bone landmarks

3. Select the Claytubes brush, and turn off the alpha. Sketch in the tendons of the knee, as shown in Figure 6.50.

4. Continue the tendon of the Bicep femoris to the head of the fibula, as shown in Figure 6.51. There is a small bump here on the surface where this tendon attaches. Just in front of this, extend the tendon of the ITB down to the tibia. This will join with a muscle on the shin later in this chapter.

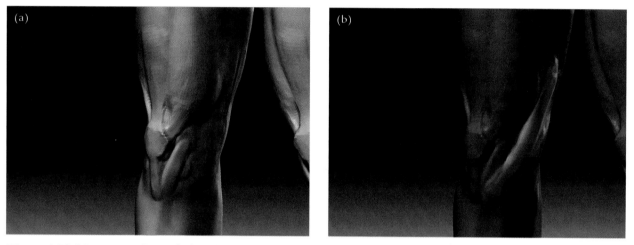

Figure 6.50 *Massing in the medial tendons of the knee: (a) front, (b) back*

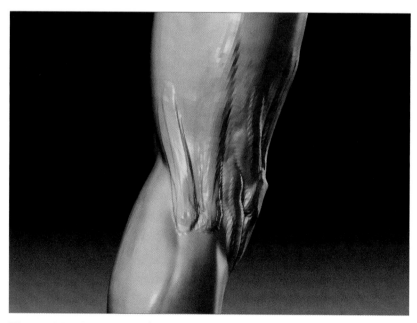

Figure 6.51 *Connecting the Bicep femoris to the fibula head and the tendon of the iliotibial band*

5. Now is a good time to smooth back what you have etched in so far. By applying what I call a *soft smooth pass* over the work, you can push it back into the surface and start creating a more subtle surface form. You can do this by editing the smoothing curve. Hold down the Shift key and open Brush → Curve. Match the curve in Figure 6.52(a). When you edit this curve while holding the Shift key it only applies to the Smooth brush. Step down a subdivision level, and, as shown in Figure 6.52(b), smooth the areas just enough to soften them, being careful not to destroy detail.

6. At this stage, I turn on the measure guides again to check the placement of the tibia based on the head measures, as shown in Figure 6.53(a). Use the Flatten brush to flatten the tendons shown in Figure 6.53(b). Also be sure to check the knee from the side view (Figure 6.54).

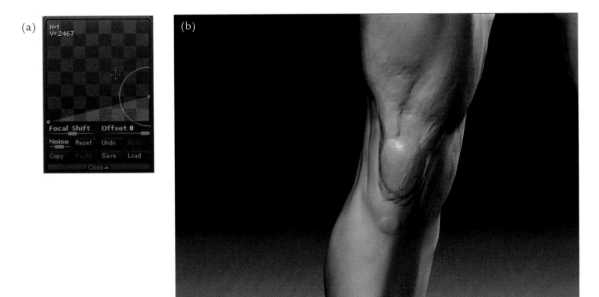

Figure 6.52 Smoothing the knee: (a) adjusting the smoothing curve under the Brush menu to create a less destructive Smooth brush, (b) gently smoothing the forms of the knee

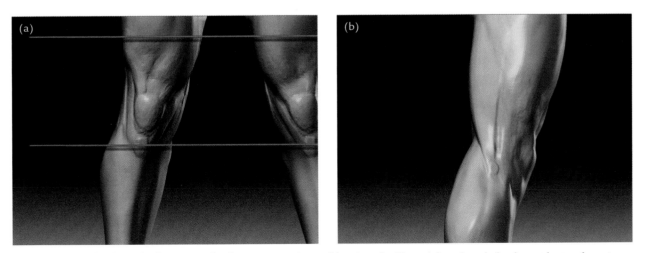

Figure 6.53 Checking the knee: (a) checking proportions, (b) using the Flatten brush to help shape the tendons in this area

7. Using the Inflate brush, mass in the inner thighs. This area is composed of the Adductor muscles in the deep layer of the figure. There is also a pad of fatty tissue here that helps fill in this area. Figure 6.55 shows this area massed in with the Inflate brush at a lower subdivision level. Working at lower levels for more general forms keeps the surface from becoming "lumpy."

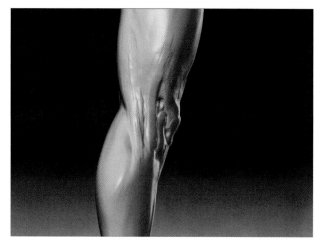

Figure 6.54 The knee shown from the side

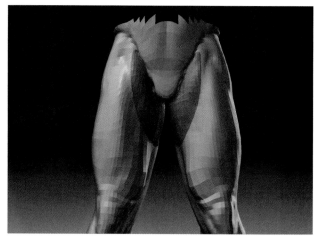

Figure 6.55 Massing in the inner thighs with the Inflate brush at a lower subdivision level

Sculpting the Lower Leg

The lower leg is similar in many ways to the lower arm; however, thanks to the limited mobility of the toes compared to the fingers, the muscles are far simpler on the lower leg. In this section, you will look at some of the major muscle forms visible on the surface of the fleshed figure. Figure 6.56 shows the lower leg in *écorché* view.

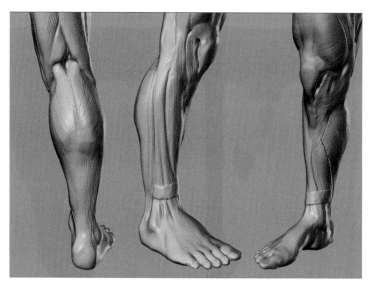

Figure 6.56 The lower leg in écorché *view*

1. You will begin by etching in the front edge of the tibia, as shown in Figure 6.57. This is called the *anterior crest of the tibia*, and it feels like a sharp ridge of bone just beneath the surface of the skin on the shin. An interesting note is this bone is in fact straight, but it has the appearance of being curved because of the way the muscles of the lower leg lie against it, as you will see shortly.

2. Using the Standard brush, add the anklebones. These are the medial and lateral malleolus bones shown in Figure 6.58. In the *écorché* view of Figure 6.59, notice the line between these two bones. It is important to maintain this angle because the inner anklebone is always higher than the outer anklebone.

3. From the side view, adjust the calf as shown in Figure 6.60(a). Make sure it comes far enough back to where the crest of the silhouette breaks. Move to the front view, and check the silhouette and angles, as shown in Figure 6.60(b). The *écorché* view in Figure 6.61 shows the profile of the calf from the side view.

(a)
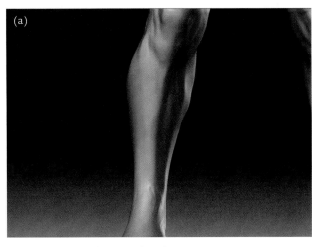
(b)
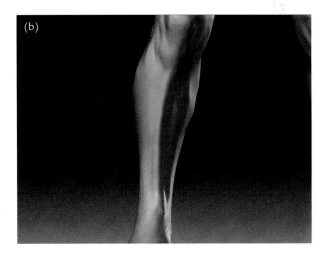

Figure 6.57 Etching in the tibia

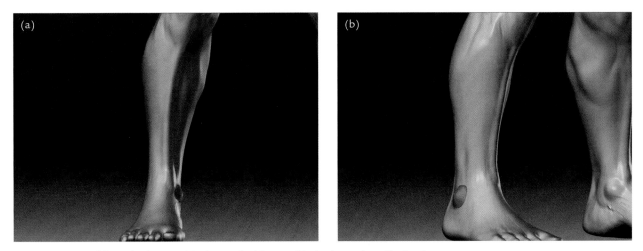

Figure 6.58 Adding the bones: (a) the medial bone, (b) the lateral malleolus bone

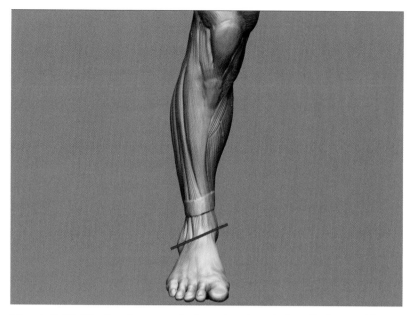

Figure 6.59 *The line between the lateral and medial malleolus visible in* écorché

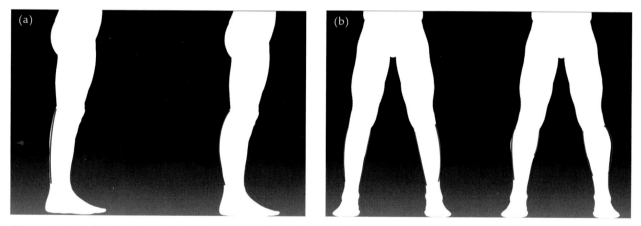

Figure 6.60 *Adjusting the calf: (a) sizing the calf in silhouette, (b) fixing the silhouette from the front*

4. You will now add one of the most prominent muscles of the lower leg. The Tibialis anterior muscle originates on the lateral condyle of the tibia just beneath the insertion of the tendon of the iliotibial band (they sometimes appear to flow into one another) and inserts into the medial arch of the foot. What is important to note is that this muscle crosses over the tibia and gives the shaft of the bone the appearance of a curve, as shown in Figure 6.62. Isolate the area for the Tibialis muscle with a mask, and mass it in with the Claytubes brush.

5. Next to the Tibialis anterior, you will mass in the form of two muscles, the Peroneus longus and the Extensor digitorum longus (EDL). These manifest as furrows on the outer side of the lower leg on the fleshed figure, as pictured in Figure 6.63. Isolate the area with a mask, and mass in the form. Figure 6.64 shows the area for these two muscles unmasked. The shapes have been massed in with the Claytubes brush.

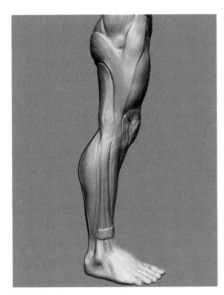

Figure 6.61 *The calf shown in* écorché. *The calf is usually the point furthest back on the figure when viewed from the side.*

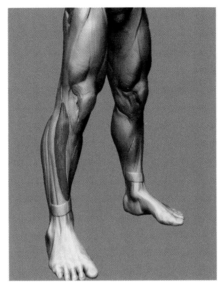

Figure 6.62 *The Tibialis anterior muscle in* écorché

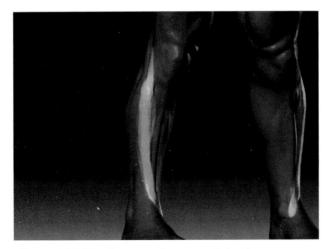

Figure 6.63 *The Peroneus longus and the Extensor digitorum longus*

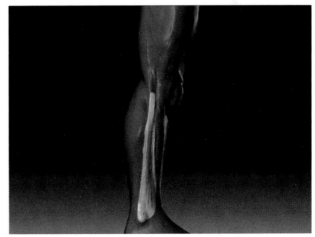

Figure 6.64 *Massing in the Extensor digitorum longus and Peroneus longus*

6. Rotate to the back view, and with the Standard brush, etch a dividing line down the center of the calf, as shown in Figure 6.65(a). This will be the bifurcation between the lateral and medial heads of the Gastrocnemius. The majority of the back of the calf is composed of the Gastrocnemius muscle, which lies over the Soleus muscle. You will treat them here as one shape. Mass in the form with the Claytubes brush (Figure 6.65(b)). Figure 6.66 shows an *écorché* view of the Gastrocnemius.

7. Rotate to the front view. Using the Claytubes brush, mass in the Gastrocnemius and Soleus muscles as they wrap around to attach to the tibia, as shown in Figure 6.67.

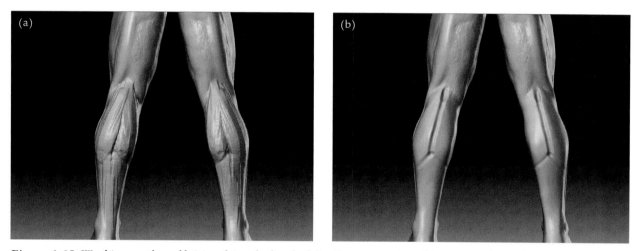

Figure 6.65 *Working on the calf: (a) etching the head of the Gastrocnemius, (b) massing the calf with the Claytubes brush*

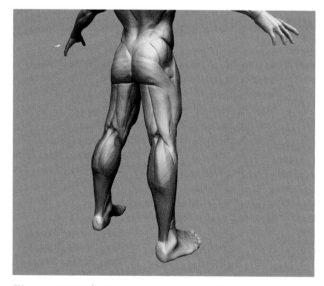

Figure 6.66 *The Gastrocnemius muscle shown in* écorché

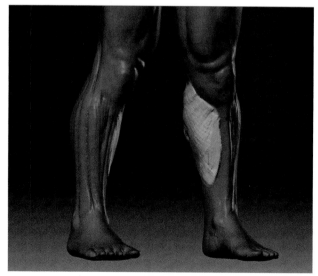

Figure 6.67 *Massing in the Gastrocnemius from the front view with Claytubes*

8. Rotate to the side view. Here you can see that the flow of the muscles down the side of the calf is uneven. Using the Move tool, shift these back into a more even sweep, as shown in Figure 6.68.

9. Now you want to add the division where the Soleus is visible beneath the Gastrocnemius from the side view. Select the Standard brush with alpha 01, and etch this form as shown in Figure 6.69. The lower leg muscles appear as long furrows on the side of the leg, and knowing which muscles are here and the direction of their flow helps you sketch them in on the surface of the sculpture.

10. From this view you can also see that the shape of the heel is awkward. Rotate to a back view, and isolate this tendon with a mask. Using the Inflate brush, I mass this area in and, moving back to the side view, correct the shape with the Move brush, as shown in Figure 6.70.

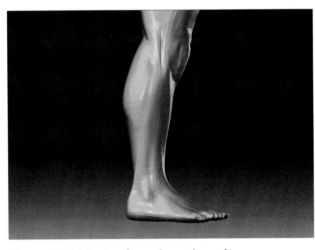
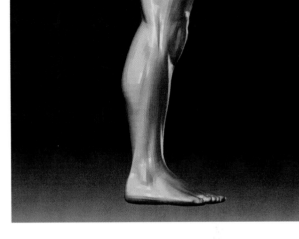

Figure 6.68 *Moving flow of muscles to be more even*

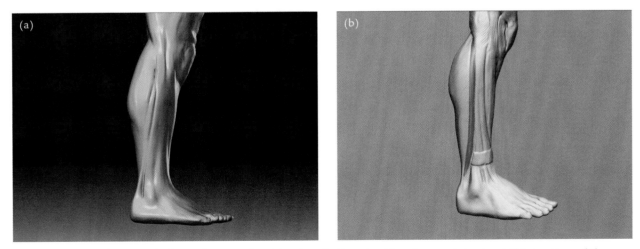

Figure 6.69 *Working on the lower leg muscles: (a) using the Standard brush to etch in the visible portion of the Soleus muscle, (b) the same area shown in écorché*

11. The heel has two distinct hollows between the tendon of the heel and the malleolus bones of the ankle. Use the Standard brush to etch in these hollow areas, as shown in Figure 6.71; this will catch shadow and help accentuate the anatomy of the ankle and heel.

12. At this stage, I decide to accentuate the tendon on the side of the knee. In Figure 6.72 you can see the area isolated with a mask. I use the Claytubes brush with no mask to work this area.

Figure 6.70 Fixing the heel

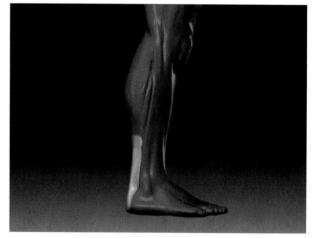

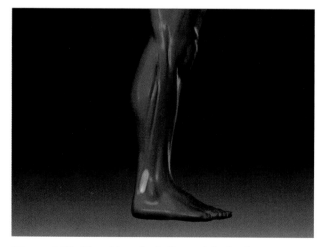

Figure 6.71 Sketching the hollow of the heel

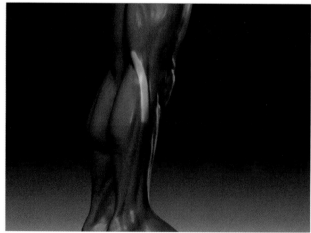

Figure 6.72 Massing in tendon at the side of the knee

13. Moving to the front view, you can see that the Soleus and Gastrocnemius should be slightly visible, peeking out from the outside of the shin. Isolate them with a mask, and pull them out until they form the outermost silhouette of the lower leg, as shown in Figure 6.73. Figure 6.74 shows the results viewed from the front.

14. Using a Visibility mask, hide one of the legs. You can do this by holding down Ctrl+Shift and click-dragging a green marquee over the leg. Figure 6.75 shows the result. With the other leg hidden, you can now more easily adjust the forms on the inside of the leg. You will mirror any changes across to the other leg later when using Smart Resym.

    Once the edits to the isolated leg are complete, you need to copy the changes to the leg that was hidden. Hidden geometry will not be edited.

15. Unhide the hidden leg and mask the leg you just edited.

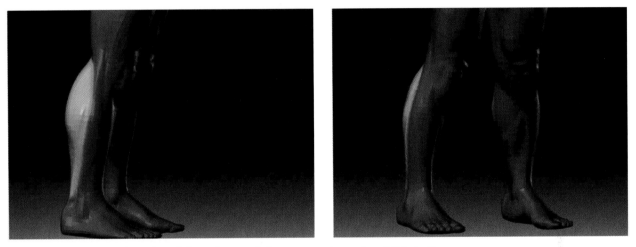

Figure 6.73 Pulling the sides of the Soleus and Gastrocnemius to be visible in front

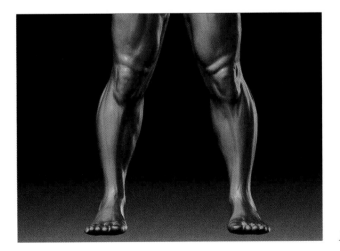

Figure 6.74 Visible from front

16. Click Tool → Deformation → Smart Resym to copy the shapes from the masked side to the unmasked side, as shown in Figure 6.76. You may find this process is more accurate if you start from a lower subdivision level and work up, clicking Smart Resym each time as you step up to a higher subdivision level. This is because by running a resym at lower levels, you reduce the total number of points ZBrush has to examine as you step up.

Figure 6.75 *One leg is hidden to make working the inside of the leg easier.*

Figure 6.76 *The result of a Smart Resym*

Sculpting the Finishing Pass

At this stage, you need to move back from the figure to look at the leg as a whole. It is easy to become distracted from the overall form when you are spending so long looking at individual aggregate parts. Rotate the leg, and move the interactive light so you can see how the forms react under different views and lighting conditions. Figure 6.77 illustrates some of the changes I make to the legs at this point to make them more attractive.

Figure 6.77 *Final tweaks*

What's Next?

Next you will start sculpting hands and feet. You will address the skeletal structure of the hands and feet as well as the basic forms of the palm, fingers, and toes with special attention given to the way in which the shapes interlock to create the complex and expressive forms of the hands and feet.

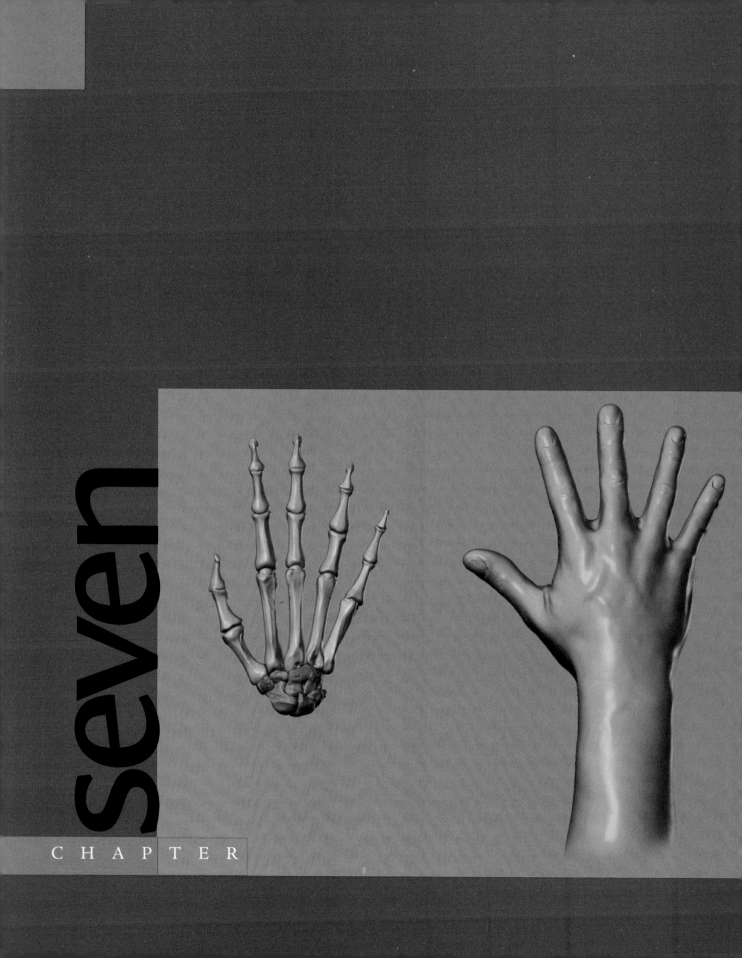

seven

Hands, Feet, and Figure Finish

In this chapter, you will look *at sculpting the hands and feet of the figure as well as do an overall finishing pass to add the impression of skin and fat over the highly developed muscled figure. Hands and feet are among the most challenging elements to draw and sculpt on the body. The hands, for example, are highly complex machines with which we are all intimately familiar. They have the ability to express a vast array of emotion and actions. The feet as well are complicated compound forms, and both can be simplified by working with them at their most basic levels.*

I'll also cover some of the more common mistakes when developing these appendages. You will look at the underlying structure of the hands and feet as well as an approach to sculpting these forms by roughing in basic shapes and refining them into a final form.

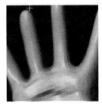

Finally, I'll cover where the fat deposits are found on the figure and how to mass in the areas between the muscles to give the impression the figure is covered in flesh and is a living being. Often when you sculpt a figure from the inside out, as you have done in this book, you find the sculpture takes on an exceedingly "cut" physique. Although this may be appropriate for some character work, I want to show you how to add another level of realism by losing some of the muscle definition under a layer of skin and fatty tissue.

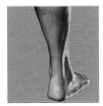

Anatomy of the Hands and Feet

In this section, you will see the underlying muscular and skeletal anatomy of the hands and feet. You will also spend some time looking at the basic forms that make up these parts. I find hands and feet easier to understand in terms of basic geometric forms rather than bones and muscles.

As with any sculpting project, a real-world reference is always needed. Try to acquire some casts of hands and feet or learn to make your own. Many books and DVDs cover life-casting procedures. I recommend the *Movie FX Magazine* (http://moviefxmag.com) DVD tutorials on life-casting body parts as well as *Mark Alfreys Ultimate Lifecasting Video*, available from www.markalfrey.com. Figure 7.1 shows some of my own reference casts. You can also purchase models from art-supply stores or eBay.

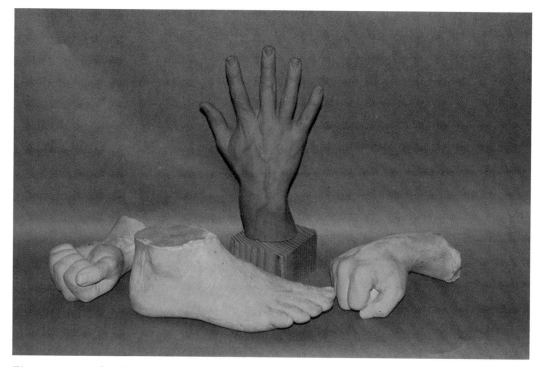

Figure 7.1 *Hand and foot reference casts*

Relative Proportions

When sizing the hands and feet, you should keep a few helpful guides in mind. You will look at some of these measures here.

The hand is roughly equal to the distance from the hairline to the bottom of the chin (Figure 7.2). Place your own hands on your face to see these measures in action. As with any proportional cannon, although there is some variance in hand and face sizing, these rules can help keep your work within the realm of believability.

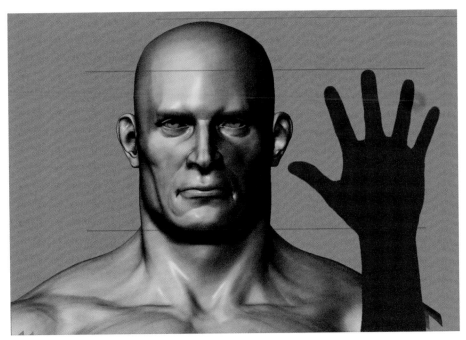

Figure 7.2 *The hand compared to the face*

The palm and fingers each represent roughly half the overall length of the hand. When considering the fingers, remember that the middle finger is the longest. The knuckles of the fingers follow an arc (Figure 7.3).

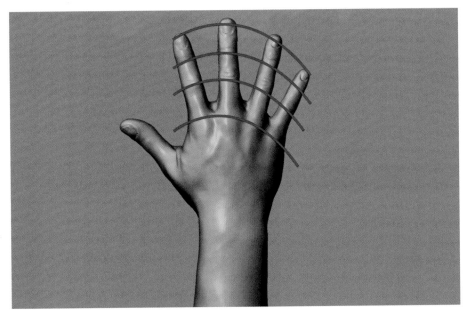

Figure 7.3 *Finger length and arc of knuckles*

The foot, when measured from heel to great toe, is roughly one head length. From the front view, the foot is roughly one-third of a head high on an eight-head figure (Figure 7.4).

Sometimes I choose to make the hands slightly larger than anatomically accurate. This depends on the figure and the pose, but I have found that when the hands are larger, it usually reads as a stylistic choice. When the hands are too small, however, it always tends to look like a mistake.

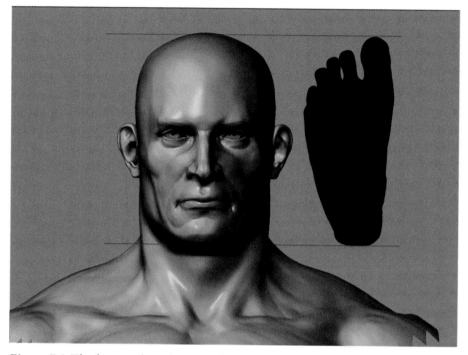

Figure 7.4 The foot can be at least one head length long.

Skeletal Structure

The hands and feet are extremely similar in their skeletal structure. Each is composed of three types of bone. The hand consists of the *carpals*, or wrist bones; the *metacarpals*, or bones of the palm; and the *phalanges*, which are the finger bones (Figure 7.5).

The foot, on the other hand, consists of the *tarsals*, or heel bones; the *metatarsals*, which form the broad length of the foot; and the *phalanges*, which are the toe bones (Figure 7.6).

In both the hands and feet, notice that there are three phalanges per finger or toe but only two for the thumb and great toe. Also notice that the carpal bones and tarsal bones are similar in number and function. Both serve to absorb shock, and there is merely one extra carpal bone when compared to the tarsals. This extra bone is a result of the higher mobility of the fingers compared to the toes.

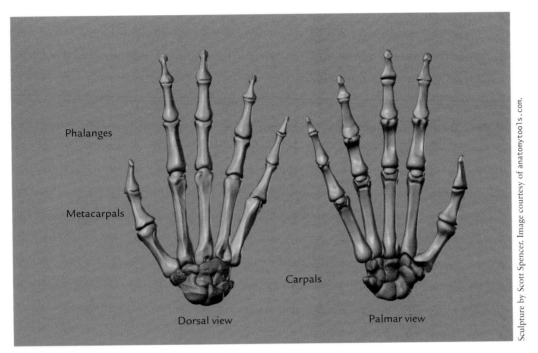

Sculpture by Scott Spencer. Image courtesy of anatomytools.com.

Figure 7.5 *The bones of the hand*

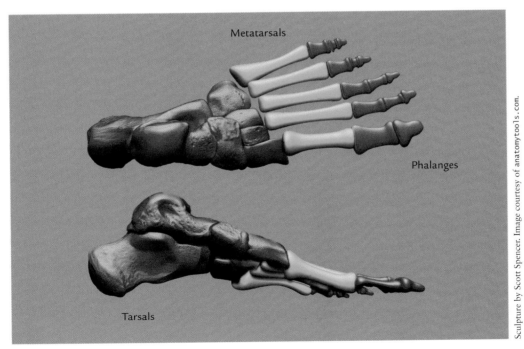

Sculpture by Scott Spencer. Image courtesy of anatomytools.com.

Figure 7.6 *The bones of the foot*

Anatomical Direction

When I refer to the surfaces of the hands and feet, I will sometimes use anatomical directions. Remember, the default position of the hand is supinated with the palm facing outward. In this case, I will refer to the palm side of the hand as *palmar* and the back of the hand as *dorsal*. When I refer to sides, the *medial* is the pinky finger side, and the *lateral* is the thumb side.

For the foot, the *medial* refers to the inside edge, or the big toe side, and the *lateral* is the outer border of the foot. The underside of the foot is sometimes called the *plantar* view, while the top of the foot is sometimes called the *dorsal* (Figure 7.7).

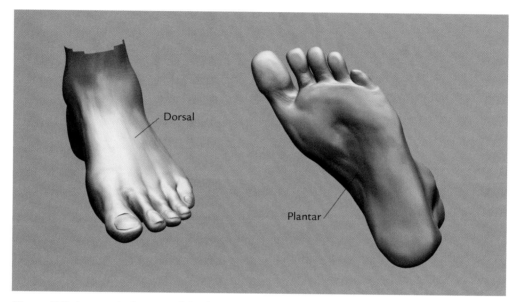

Figure 7.7 *Anatomical views of the foot*

The Surface Anatomy of the Hand

The surface anatomy of the hand is defined more by the skeletal structure on the back and by fat and muscle on the palmar side. Looking at the palm of the hand (Figure 7.8), three distinct masses are visible:

- The Thenar group
- The Hypothenar group
- The pads for the bases of the fingers

These three teardrop-shaped masses form the body of the palm.

The Surface Anatomy of the Foot

The foot consists of three arches, as shown in Figure 7.9. These are called the *medial longitudinal arch*, the *lateral longitudinal arch*, and the *transverse arch*. These are important to keep in mind when you are sculpting the planes of the basic form of the foot. These arches serve as shock absorbers for the foot, just like the springs in a car suspension.

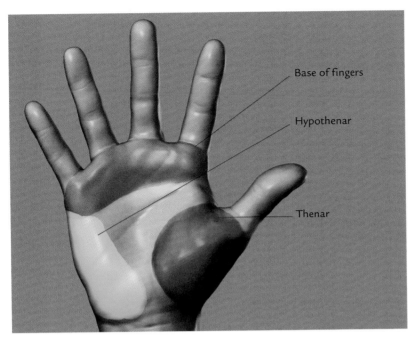

Figure 7.8 *The three teardrop shapes of the palm*

Sculpture by Scott Spencer. Image courtesy of anatomytools.com.

Figure 7.9 *The three arches of the foot: (a) lateral longitudinal arch, (b) medial longitudinal arch, (c) transverse arch*

The underside of the foot is defined by groups of fleshy pads that protect the bones of the foot from contact with the ground (Figure 7.10). These pads are as follows:

- Big toe pad, which appears as a heart shape
- Oval or triangular pads on lesser toes
- Oval for ball of foot
- Teardrop for lateral border
- Round heel

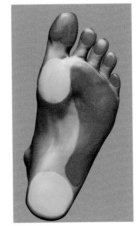

Figure 7.10 *The foot pads*

Block Forms and Planes

Just like the other parts of the body, the hands and feet are best understood by breaking them down into their individual parts. Figure 7.11 shows the block forms of the hand and foot. These figures are intended to express the largest, most basic shape relationships and are valuable exercises when learning to sculpt. Just like you did in Chapter 2 with the planed figure, I recommend trying to recreate the hands and feet in these very simplified terms to help you master the way the forms interlock and create more complex forms.

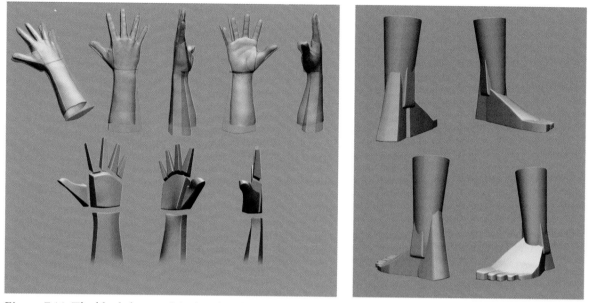

Figure 7.11 *The block forms of the hand and foot*

Take note that the palm has a decided step down from the wrist. It appears that the majority of the mass is on the palm side, while the back or dorsal side of the hand is more prominently bony, with the skeletal structure more visible. The mass of the palm is composed of the palmar muscles and the fatty pads that cushion and protect the undersides of the fingers.

Notice that the fingers attach to the palm on a bias (Figure 7.12). A common mistake is to attach the fingers directly to the palm in a straight line when they in fact taper back. This manifests as the webbing between each finger as well as the manner in which the first joint of the finger articulates, as you will see later in this chapter.

The profiles of the hand include many important crests and breaks. Figure 7.13 illustrates these lines. When sculpting, strive to include these profile lines as early as possible to help maintain a convincing structure. Notice in this image how the space between the fingers flattens into short, straight lines; also note the sharp breaks at the wrist bone and base of the thumb. By including these defined breaks in the silhouette, you can give the sculpture more definition and avoid creating a soft, ill-defined form.

The foot likewise can be broken into block forms as you saw earlier. When working with the foot, you need to also be sensitive to the crests and breaks in the gesture of the profiles. Figure 7.14 shows the foot in silhouette with the angles in question highlighted.

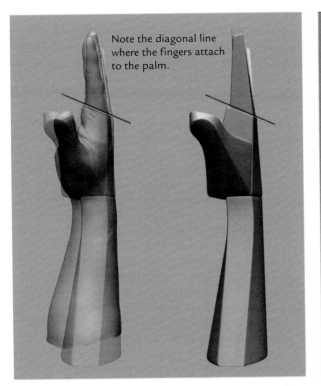

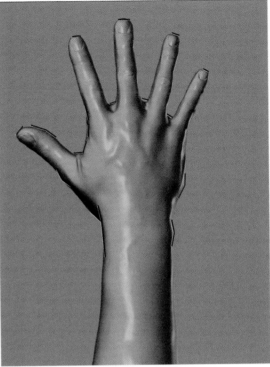

Figure 7.12 *The attachment of the fingers. (Note the diagonal line where the fingers attach to the palm.)*

Figure 7.13 *The hand crests and breaks*

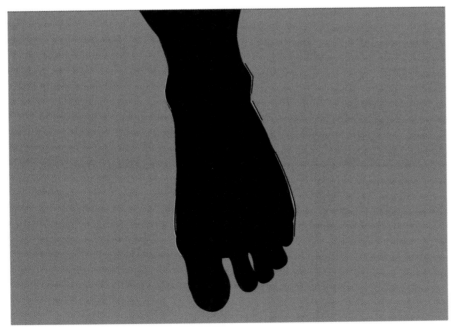

Figure 7.14 *The foot crests and breaks*

Sculpting the Hand

In this section, you will begin to sculpt a hand.

For this demonstration, you will work on an isolated base mesh of the hand and forearm. This is the same mesh used for the rest of the figure. By isolating the hand into its own model, it's easier to focus on this one part. Please see the DVD for a video of the hand of the figure being sculpted as well as the hand example in this chapter.

1. Load the `basemesh.obj` file from the DVD into ZBrush (Figure 7.15). Switch to frame mode so you can see the underlying edges. You will use the Move brush to shift the base form into shape before you add a subdivision level. Remember, you should work on the biggest shapes first, and it's always easier to remember that if you avoid the higher subdivision levels at the start.

2. Using the Move brush, adjust the arc where the fingers meet the hand. Note how they follow an arc and not a straight line (Figure 7.16). While I work, I thicken the fingers a bit by moving the individual points. You may also use the Inflate brush with a very low ZIntensity setting to increase the volume of the mesh in this area.

   The thumb in the base mesh just looks like a long finger extending from the palm. You need to adjust the wedge at the base of the thumb where it transitions into the hand. This triangular shape is created by the first Interosseous muscle and the Adductor pollicis on the dorsal or back of the hand. These two muscles bridge the gap between the bones of the thumb and the metacarpals of the palm.

3. From the back view, adjust the thumb as shown in Figure 7.17. Also note the curvature of the thumb mesh. You can see the gesture of the profiles starting to take shape already. Be aware of the overall shape you want to achieve, including any crests and breaks in the silhouette. Try to introduce these as early in the sculpting process as possible.

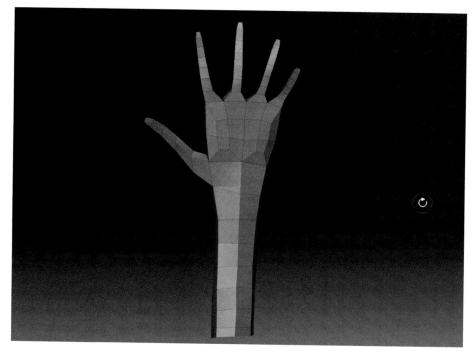

Figure 7.15 The hand base mesh loaded into ZBrush

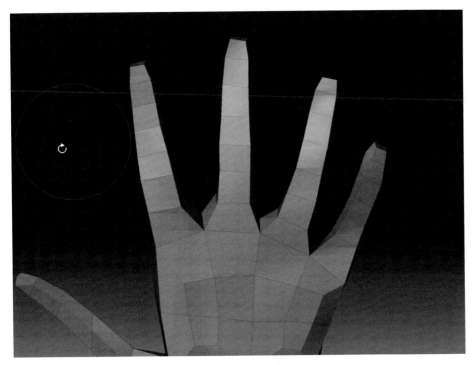

Figure 7.16 *The arc of the fingers in the base mesh*

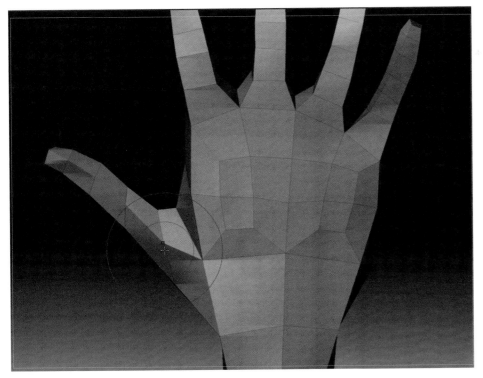

Figure 7.17 *Adjusting the base of the thumb*

4. Rotate to the thumb side (lateral aspect) of the arm. The mesh here is very thin. You need to mass in the shape of the arm as it extends up from the hand. Use the Move tool to widen this form (Figure 7.18).

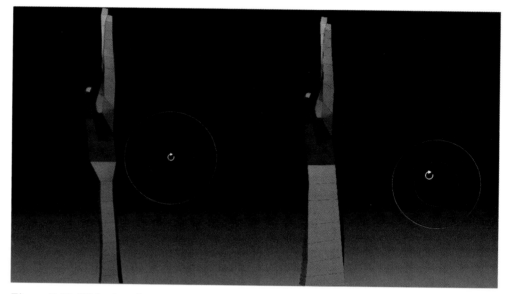

Figure 7.18 Widening the arm

5. Move to the medial or pinky finger side of the arm, and widen the taper here as well. You will now add the thickness of the forearm where the bellies of the Flexor muscles are found. This creates the taper on the palmar side of the forearm from thick at the base to thinner toward the hand (Figure 7.19).

6. Rotate to the palmar view of the hand. Use the Move brush to create the mass at the palmar base of the thumb (Figure 7.20). This mass is one of the triangular muscle groups of the hand. These are called the Thenar group. These muscles originate at the carpal bones and insert at the base of the first phalanx of the thumb.

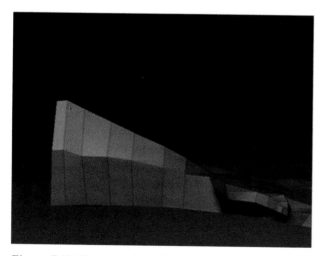

Figure 7.19 Tapering the width of the arm

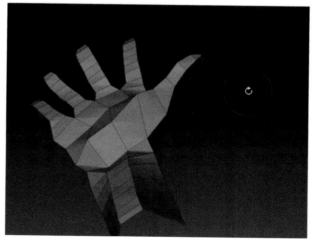

Figure 7.20 Massing in the base of the thumb

7. On the medial side of the palm, start to create the muscle mass that fills out this area. This will be the mass of the Hypothenar group of muscles. These are the counterparts to the Thenar group on the thumb. Among other functions, these muscles allow you to oppose your thumb and pinky to grasp objects. Start to suggest this mass as shown in Figure 7.21.

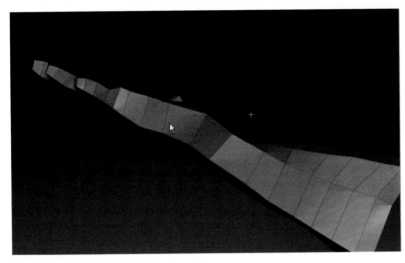

***Figure 7.21** Massing in the Hypothenar group*

8. Rotate to the dorsal view of the hand, and use the Move brush to create a convex curve (Figure 7.22). There should be a slight arc to the back of the hand, and you will start to suggest it here at the lowest subdivision level.

***Figure 7.22** Creating an arc on the back of the hand*

9. At this stage, you need to spread the fingers a bit. Using transpose masking, mask the hand, leaving the index finger unmasked. Move the finger out slightly, and then rotate it so it is oriented as shown in Figure 7.23.

10. At this stage, you are ready to add a subdivision level to the hand. Divide once, and note how the base forms you took care to create at level 1 are still present in the higher subdivision level and help to create the overall shape of the hand (Figure 7.24).

11. Now thicken the fingers using the Inflate brush. Keep the ZIntensity slider low to avoid inflating the digits too much. I have my brush set to ZIntensity 10 for this step (Figure 7.25).

12. Rotate back to the palmar view of the hand. Mask out the wrist, and use the Inflate brush to start to mass in more of the palmar muscle groups. I have massed in the shapes of the Thenar, Hypothenar, and the fleshy pads at the base of the fingers. I also inflate the thumb slightly to add mass to the tip or second phalanx. From the side and three-quarter views, thicken the base of the fingers just above the fleshy base where they join with the metacarpals. This is where the flesh and fat are thickest on the fingers (Figure 7.26).

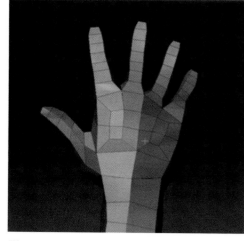

Figure 7.23 *Orienting the index finger*

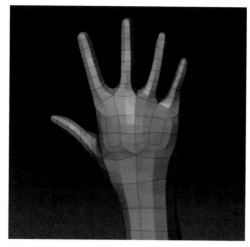

Figure 7.24 *Adding a subdivision level*

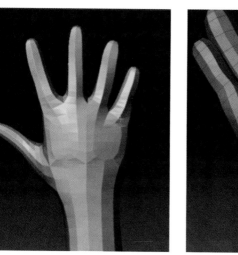

Figure 7.25 *Inflating the fingers*

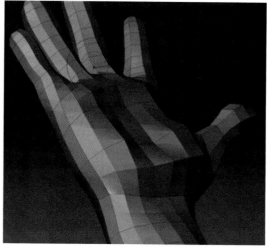

Figure 7.26 *Thickening the base of the fingers*

At this stage you are ready to add another subdivision level to the hand. The major forms are in place, and the general silhouette of the hand is working. Now you will use brushes such as Claytubes to further refine the surface as well as create a sense of bone under skin and flesh and folds on the hand.

13. Divide the hand by pressing Ctrl+D. Because you have been gradually building form as you work, the shape remains convincing as you add subdivision levels. Select the Inflate brush, and continue to thicken the fingers as well as the three masses of the palm (Figure 7.27).

14. At this stage, check the silhouette of the hand by switching to the Flat Color shader. With the hand in flat color, you can easily spot the overall profile shapes, and obvious problems will become more apparent. In Figure 7.28, I have noted the breaks in the silhouette, which I find to be important for the hand. Notice how the long curve on the outside edge of the hand actually contains three distinct breaks. I adjust the space between the fingers as well as the mass of the palm.

15. Use the Standard brush to mass in the knuckles of the four fingers. Select the Claytubes brush, and build up the back of the hand slightly. Adding just a bit of "clay" here will allow you to suggest the bones and veins of the back of the hand later (Figure 7.29).

16. Rotate to the palmar side of the hand, and using Claytubes, further define the three masses of the palm. In Figure 7.30, you can see the three masses—the Thenar, Hypothenar, and base of the knuckles—accentuated with this brush. Mask the wrist to help maintain the step between the fleshiness of the palm and the tendons of the wrist (Figure 7.31). I used the Inflate brush with a ZIntensity of 10 along the edge of the mask to start suggesting the compressing of flesh into a fold in this area.

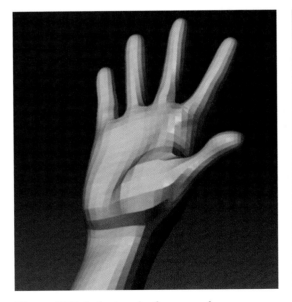

***Figure 7.27** Inflating the fingers and masses of the palm*

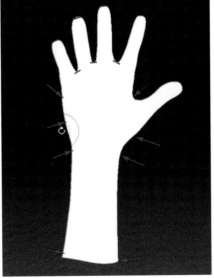

***Figure 7.28** Checking the hand in flat shade view, with outline breaks noted*

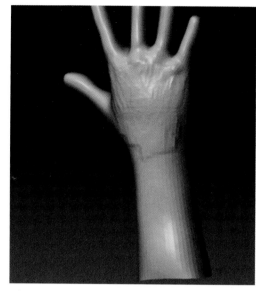

Figure 7.29 *Massing the back of the hand with Claytubes*

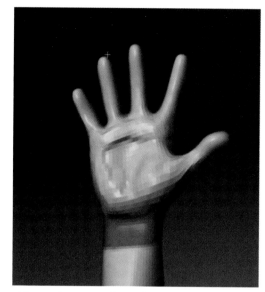

Figure 7.30 *Working the palm with Claytubes*

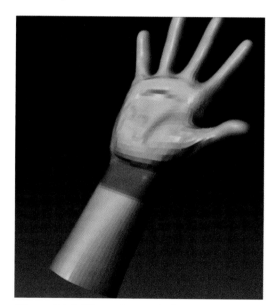

Figure 7.31 *The wrist masked*

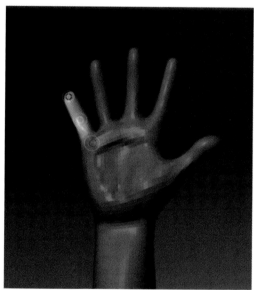

Figure 7.32 *Spreading the fingers using transpose*

17. Use transpose masking to isolate each finger, and with the Transpose Rotate tool, make sure they are evenly spread. Try to avoid making the hand look strained as if every finger were spread out. You are trying for a somewhat relaxed pose with the fingers extended (Figure 7.32).

18. Switch to the Move brush, and adjust any parts of the silhouette that are not working for you. In Figure 7.33, I worked the shape of the tip of the thumb, giving the characteristic "arrowhead" look. Switch to the Flatten brush, and set your ZIntensity to 16. Gently flatten the backs of the fingers as shown in Figure 7.34. You want to give the fingers a more rectangular shape to represent the bone structure beneath them as opposed to having them look like little sausages. This structure will be subtle once the sculpture is completed, but by introducing it now, you can avoid creating fingers that lack form and are too soft.

19. You are ready to add another subdivision level. Divide the mesh once by pressing Ctrl+D, and switch to the Claytubes brush. Start to sketch in the metacarpal bones and knuckles as shown in Figure 7.35. These are overstated now, but they serve to help you sculpt the anatomy of the hand. You will smooth them back later so they become more a part of the hand.

20. Return to the palmar view, and mask the fingers down to the fleshy base. Use the Claytubes brush to build up this flesh pad against the mask. This will help create a fleshy crease at the point where the fingers join the palm. Invert the mask, and use the Inflate brush with a ZIntensity of 16 to gently inflate the edge where the fingers meet the mask. This helps pucker the two shapes together and create a fleshy fold (Figure 7.36).

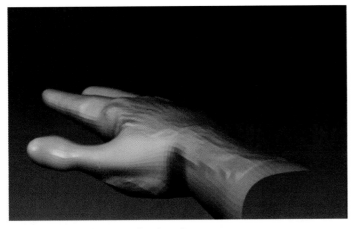

Figure 7.33 Adjusting the thumb tip

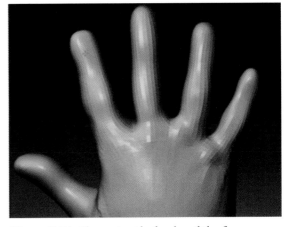

Figure 7.34 Flattening the backs of the fingers

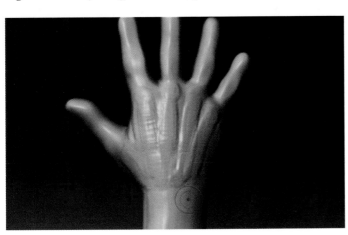

Figure 7.35 Sketching in the metacarpals with Claytubes

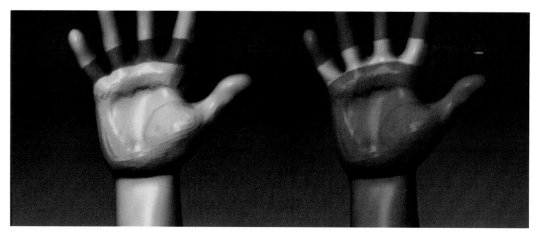

Figure 7.36 Using masking to help create the fleshy folds at the base of the fingers

21. Rotate to the medial aspect of the hand. Use Claytubes to further refine the mass of the Hypothenar muscle group and the fatty pad that sits over it. This form is a specific fleshy mass that terminates against the bony line of the pinky metacarpal, creating a nice opportunity to sculpt a transition between bone and fat as the sculpture progresses (Figure 7.37).

22. Rotate to the lateral side of the hand. Use the Claytubes brush to adjust the transition between the thumb and the wrist. In Figure 7.38, I have started to suggest the two tendons of the Abductor pollicis longus and the Extensor pollicis longus. In some books, this area is referred to as as the *anatomical snuffbox* or *radial fossa*. This is a hollow just beneath the base of the thumb when the thumb is pulled back (Figure 7.39). At this stage, use the Move brush to pull out a point to represent the bony landmark of the styloid process of the ulna. This is the "wrist bone" that is prominently visible on the medial side of the wrist.

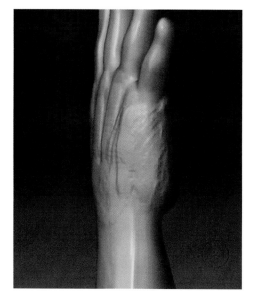

Figure 7.37 The Hypothenar group

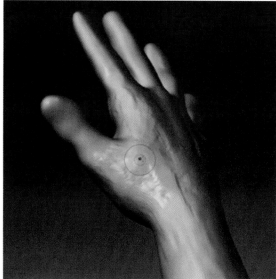

Figure 7.38 Starting to suggest the anatomical snuffbox

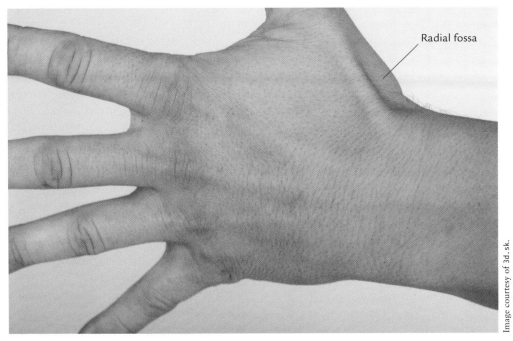

Radial fossa

Image courtesy of 3d.sk.

Figure 7.39 The radial fossa noted on a photo of the wrist

23. Rotate the palmar view, and continue to refine the form of the arm using the Claytubes brush. Figure 7.40 shows the forearm built up using this brush. Use the Move brush to adjust the shape of the fingers (Figure 7.41). Make sure to suggest bulges for each knuckle. Remember, the knuckles follow an arc and are not straight across the fingers.

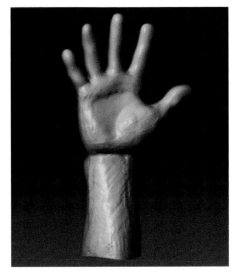

Figure 7.40 Building up forearm

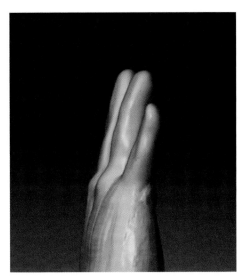

Figure 7.41 Using the Move brush to adjust the shape of the fingers

24. Use the Flatten brush with a low ZIntensity setting to plane in the back of the hand. In this case, my brush is set to ZIntensity 9. In Figure 7.42, you can see the defined plane break between the triangle wedge of the thumb and the dorsal plane of the hand.

25. Rotate to the medial aspect of the hand. Continue to use the Flatten brush to define the ramp of tendons down the back of the hand. In Figure 7.43, you can see this as well as a line etched with the Standard brush to suggest the plane change between the bone of the fifth metacarpal bone and the fleshiness of the Hypothenar group of the palm. Use the Flatten brush and the Smooth brush to refine this area further.

26. With the Claytubes brush, redefine the metacarpals, knuckles, and joints of each finger (Figure 7.44). Rotate to the palm view. You will use Claytubes here to mass in the fleshiness between each finger joint on the palmar side of the hand. On this side, the flesh puckers and bunches together where each finger bends. Isolate the area of the first phalanx with a mask, and use the Claytubes brush to build up the area (Figure 7.45).

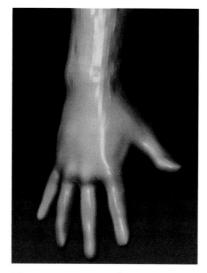

Figure 7.42 Using the Flatten brush to define the planes of the back of the hand

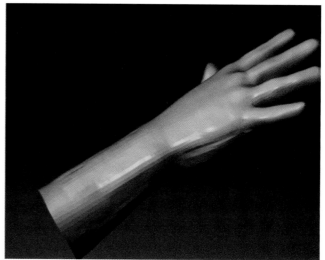

Figure 7.43 Etching a line for the break between the fifth metacarpal and the Hypothenar group

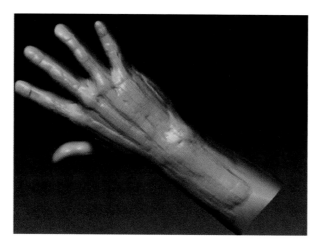

Figure 7.44 Defining the bone structure of the back of the hand

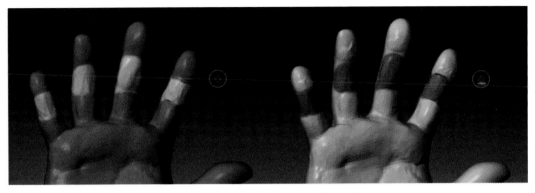

Figure 7.45 *Building up the underside of the fingers with Claytubes*

27. Step down to a lower subdivision level, and select the Move brush. Take this opportunity to adjust the shape of the fingers. From the side view, flatten the tips of the fingers slightly, and give a curved taper to the underside where the fleshy pad of the fingertips will be. This characteristic shape will help you later when you start adding fingernails, and it helps you avoid giving a nondescript sausage appearance to the fingers (Figure 7.46). You can accomplish the same effect by applying the Flatten brush with a very low ZIntensity to the back of each fingertip.

28. Use the Smooth brush to take down the noise of the Claytubes brush. To do this, you will want to smooth the high points while retaining the low so as not to destroy the form you sculpted. Select the PeakSmooth brush. This brush is a modified Smooth brush, which will only smooth the high points of the form, preserving the low. It is perfect for taking down surface noise while retaining form. Give the hand a general smoothing to remove any noise and tooling marks (Figure 7.47).

29. Switch to the Flatten brush. Continue to refine plane breaks between the different forms. In Figure 7.48, you can see how the Flatten brush has been used to define a plane change between the thumb and hand. This form is created by the first metacarpal bone of the thumb and the Interosseous muscles that fill the space between the thumbs and the metacarpal bones of the hand.

30. At this stage, don't be afraid to step down subdivision levels and make changes at the lower resolution. In Figure 7.49, I have returned to level 1 to alter the thickness of the wrist and forearm.

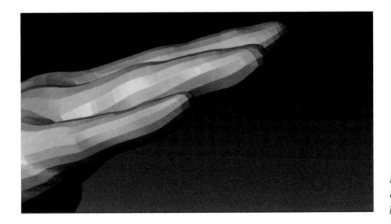

Figure 7.46 *Adjusting the shape of the fingertips*

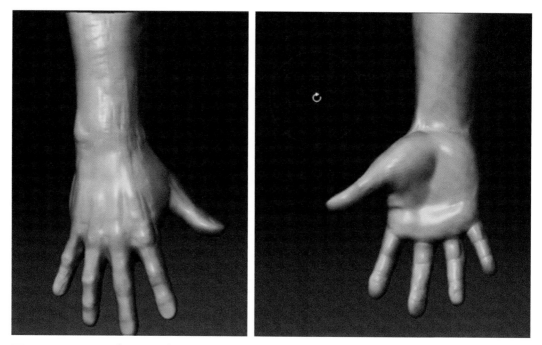

Figure 7.47 *Using the Smooth brush with BrushMod set to -100 to smooth the fine marks from the sculpt*

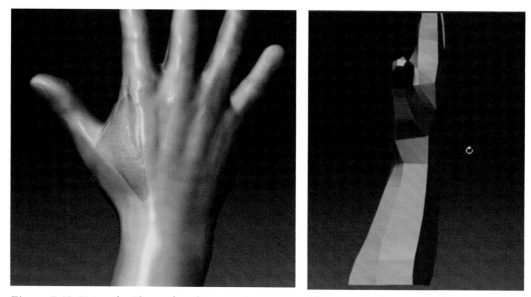

Figure 7.48 *Using the Flatten brush to continue refining the forms*

Figure 7.49 *Correcting the wrist at level 1*

Adding Flesh Folds and Details

So far, I have introduced the primary and secondary forms of the hand. You can clearly see the bone structure and muscle masses. You now will add the next layer of realism by creating the folds of fat and skin where the fingers and joints bend.

1. Return to the Move tool, and adjust the shapes of the fingers again. It is most important to give the impression of the bones of the fingers on the dorsal side of the hand and the fleshy aspect of the fingers on the palmar side. The best way to make sure the fingers look like they have a bone structure is to be sensitive to the rhythms in each finger and try to recreate them on the digital sculpture (Figure 7.50).

2. You will now revisit the pads under each finger joint. To further refine the area, you will customize the Inflate brush so it adds form in a manner similar to the Claytubes brush. Select the Inflate brush, and open its menu. Open the Brush → Curve menu. Alter the curve so it looks like Figure 7.51. This will allow you to inflate in a flattened manner instead of creating a bulbous surface when you sculpt. I have saved this brush on the DVD as `flatInflate` if you would like to import it to your brush set.

3. Use the flatInflate brush to further define the fatty pads between each phalanx (Figure 7.52). Try to maintain a line between each joint because you will create creases where the fingers bend.

4. In Figure 7.53, I have used the custom Inflate brush to build up the segments of the thumb. In this figure you can also see where I have started to suggest the creases at each joint. To do this, use the Standard brush with Alpha 01. Lower your draw size and ZIntensity. Etch in the creases lightly, and by pressing the ReplayLast button under the Stroke Palette, ZBrush will repeat the last stroke drawn. The figure illustrates the same creasing applied to the fingers as well.

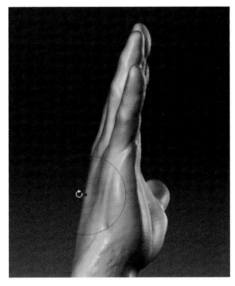

***Figure 7.50** Adjusting the fingers*

***Figure 7.51** The altered Edit Curve submenu*

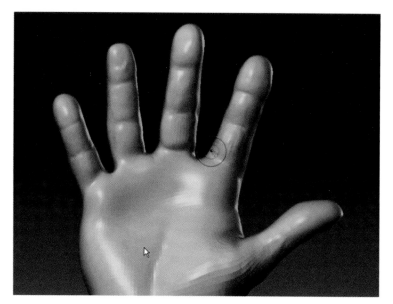

Figure 7.52 Using the flatInflate brush

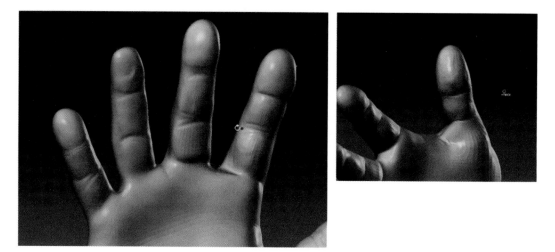

Figure 7.53 Working the thumb and creasing between the finger joints

5. Moving to the back of the hand, use the same Standard brush to make small C-shaped lines at each of the knuckles (Figure 7.54). These will eventually be the folds of skin at the knuckles.

6. While at the back of the hand, use the flatInflate brush to very subtly increase the mass of the first knuckles of the fingers. This is a small change, but it will help define the form as you finish the sculpture. In Figure 7.55, you can see this addition. I also started to suggest veins on the back of the hand using the same flatInflate brush.

7. Using the Standard brush, hollow out the palm a bit more. Use the Smooth brush and the Standard brush to further refine the creases in the finger joints (Figure 7.56).

8. Rotate to the back of the hand, and continue to suggest the wrinkles at each joint. A very subtle hollow is now added to accentuate the anatomical snuffbox. At this stage, I etch in the general shape of the fingernails very lightly (Figure 7.57). You will return to these shortly.

9. Take a moment to add some more details to the veins on the back of the hand and to add wrinkles to the knuckles (Figure 7.58). Also use the Standard brush to etch in some of the creases of the palm (Figure 7.59).

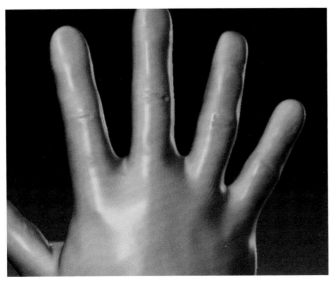

Figure 7.54 Suggesting the folds of skin at the knuckles

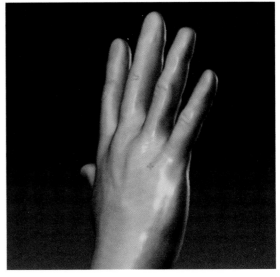

Figure 7.55 Working the back of the hand

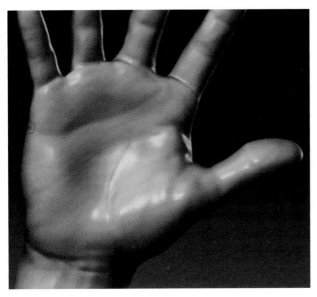

Figure 7.56 Refining the creases by sharpening them

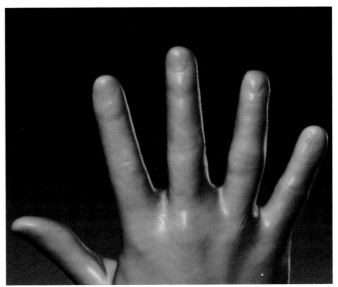

Figure 7.57 Starting to suggest fingernails

10. Refine the form of the fingers by using the Flatten brush on the sides (Figure 7.60). This helps reduce the rounded shape of the finger and hint at the bony structure beneath. Use the Standard brush to carve in the webbing between each finger. Remember, the fingers attach on a bias, not in a straight line (Figure 7.61).

11. Use the Move brush to add a taper between each knuckle. This will help create the impression of the joints beneath the skin (Figure 7.62). With the Inflate brush, add some creases to the wrist, and start suggesting veins down the arm (Figure 7.63).

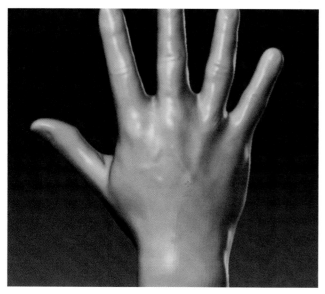

Figure 7.58 Suggesting details on the back of the hand

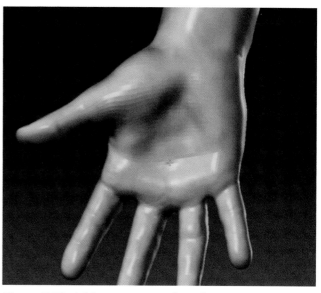

Figure 7.59 Adding creases to the palm

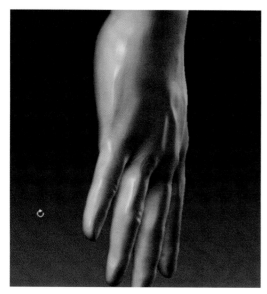

Figure 7.60 Using Flatten on the sides of the fingers

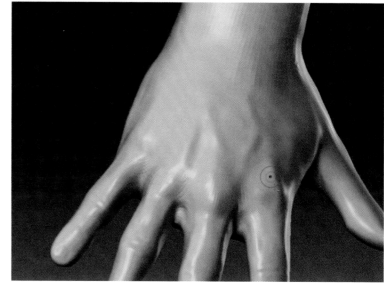

Figure 7.61 Adding the webbing between each finger

12. You can create folds in the flesh by masking out an area and inflating against the mask. This helps make one form overlap another in a more realistic way (Figure 7.64). This technique also works on the creases of the palm (Figure 7.65).

13. Add another subdivision level. You can etch more lines into the palm using the Standard brush with Alpha 02 (Figure 7.66). Folds at the knuckles are suggested using short C-shaped strokes (Figure 7.67).

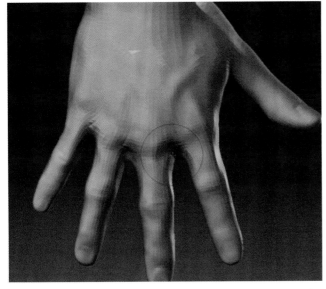

Figure 7.62 Using the Move brush to taper between each knuckle

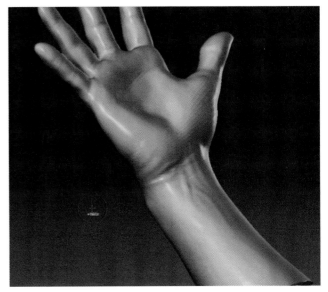

Figure 7.63 Using the Inflate brush to detail the wrist

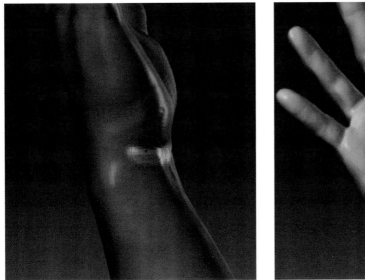

Figure 7.64 Creating folds of flesh using a mask

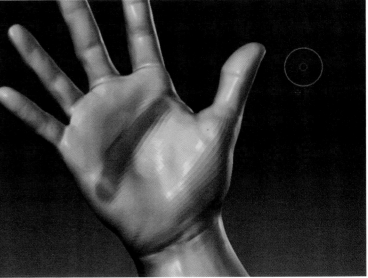

Figure 7.65 The palm creases are accentuated using a mask.

14. Return to the palmar side of the hand. Using the Standard brush and Alpha 01, etch in some light wrinkles on the underside of the finger joints (Figure 7.68).
By adding wrinkles like this at each sublevel, you build up a subtle network of surface wrinkles. The ones added lower are softer than the newer ones, making a more interesting surface visually. This also helps avoid the perfectly carved-in planned look of some sculpted folds.

15. Return to the wrist, and sharpen the wrinkles here selectively (Figure 7.69).

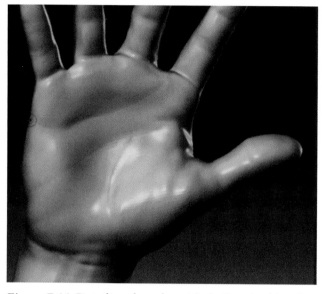

Figure 7.66 Detailing the palm with the Standard brush

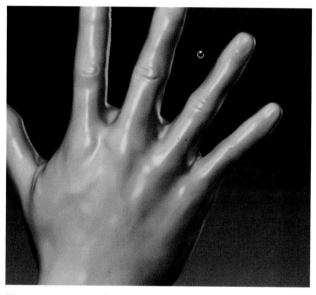

Figure 7.67 Detailing the knuckles

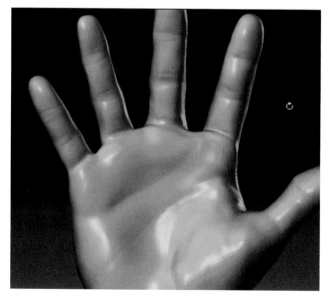

Figure 7.68 Underside wrinkles

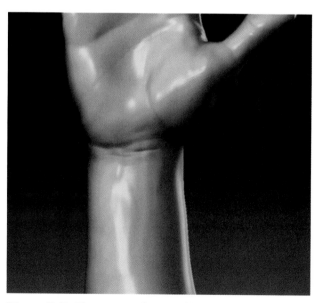

Figure 7.69 Sharpening the wrinkles at the wrist

16. Use the Inflate and the Standard brush to deepen and sharpen the puckered skin where the thumb bends back (Figure 7.70). Use the Standard brush to deepen the folds at the base of the fingers (Figure 7.71).

17. Use the Standard brush to mask in the shape of the fingernails (Figure 7.72). Note how they look like little shovel heads.

18. Invert the mask and use the flatInflate brush to mass in the fingernails (Figure 7.73). Stroke down the direction of the nail, and then smooth to remove the noise. Any remaining stroke marks will take on the natural appearance of striations in the fingernail.

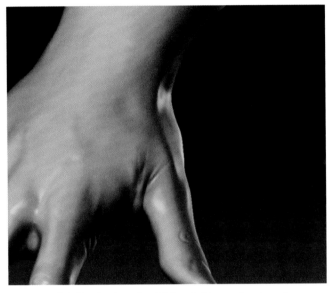

Figure 7.70 Puckering the folds of skin at the thumb

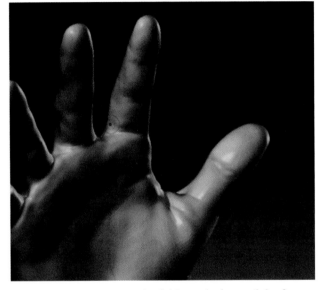

Figure 7.71 Deepening the folds at the base of the fingers

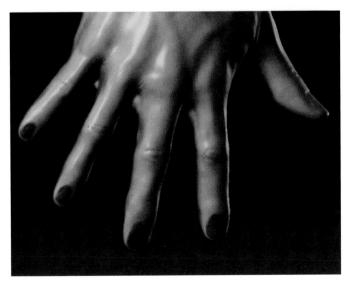

Figure 7.72 Masking in fingernails

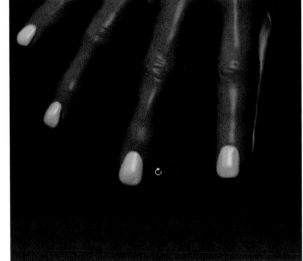

Figure 7.73 Inflating the nails

19. Invert the mask again, and use the Standard brush with a low ZIntensity setting to build up the cuticle around the nail (Figure 7.74). The nail should feel buried in the skin, not stuck on top of it.
20. To sharpen the line between the cuticle and the nail, invert the mask again for the nails that are unmasked. Use the Move brush to very gently push the base of the nail down and into the finger so the cuticle actually overlaps slightly (Figure 7.75).
21. As a final touch, use the Move tool to adjust the shape of the fingertips, blunting them slightly (Figure 7.76).
22. Add further details using the Standard brush. In Figure 7.77, veins and tendons are being suggested.

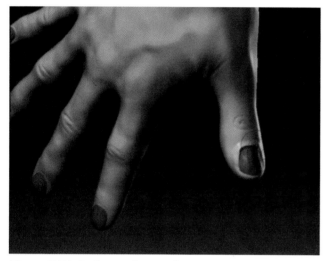

Figure 7.74 Sculpting the cuticle

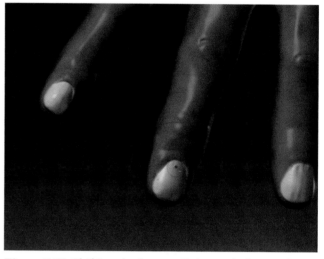

Figure 7.75 Shifting the fingernails beneath the cuticle

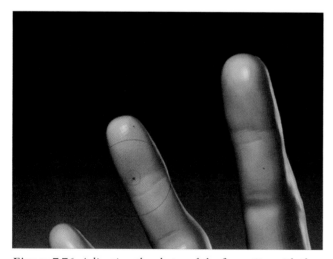

Figure 7.76 Adjusting the shape of the fingertips with the Move brush

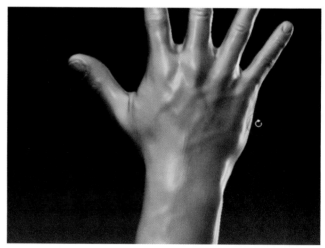

Figure 7.77 Adding further details to the back of the hand with the Standard brush

Congratulations, the hand is complete! Figure 7.78 shows the final result.

If you would like to bend the fingers slightly to give the hand a more relaxed pose, here are a couple things to keep in mind. Mask the finger with transpose; before you bend the finger, though, unmask the first knuckle. When the finger bends, it bends from the first knuckle on the back of the hand, but it folds at the base of the finger on the palmar side (Figure 7.79).

Use Transpose to bend the finger, but be sure the deformation occurs as shown in Figure 7.80, with the bend occurring at the back of the hand and a crease forming on the palmar side.

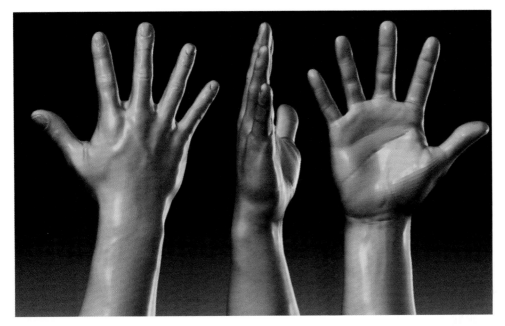

Figure 7.78 *Final hand images*

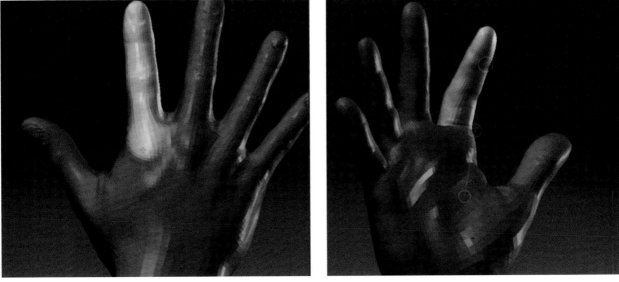

Figure 7.79 *Adjusting the mask on the dorsal side of the hand*

Figure 7.80 *Creating an accurate bend to the finger*

Sculpting the Feet

In this section, you will sculpt the foot. Although its structure is very similar to that of the hand, there are obvious differences and several nuances to the form of the foot that I will address. When it comes to detailing the skin and folds of the toes, the process is identical to that of the hand. Simply find a good photo reference or use your own foot and reproduce the detail you see.

I have included a separate foot mesh on the DVD so you can follow this lesson on an isolated base mesh of the figure foot. You can load this as `footbasemesh.obj`.

1. Load the foot base mesh into ZBrush. Select the Move brush, and adjust the side view so the heel makes contact with the ground and the top of the foot carries an arch back to the ankle (Figure 7.81).

2. Mask the mesh down to the ankle, and move to the plantar, or underside view, of the foot. Use Transpose Rotate to rotate the foot around its y-axis so the toes are no longer facing straight ahead. Adjust the base of the toes so they follow an arc in a manner similar to what you did with the fingers (Figure 7.82). Make sure to increase the size of the big toe relative to the other toes.

3. When moving the points of the base mesh, be sure to remember the profile curves addressed earlier in this chapter. Add a subdivision level with the Ctrl+D hotkey (Figure 7.83). Note that with the net division level applied, the attention you gave to the silhouette is reflected in the denser mesh. You can especially see this at the base of the medial arch of the foot.

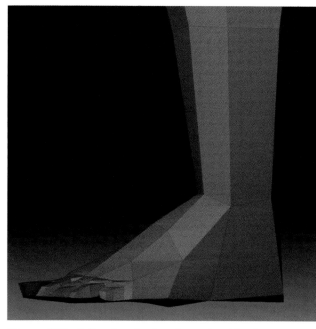

Figure 7.81 Adjusting the foot from the side view

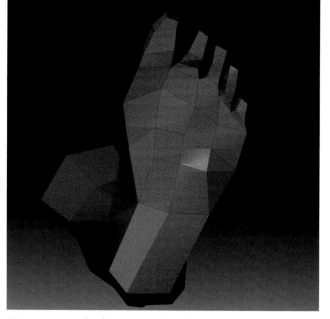

Figure 7.82 The foot rotated and toes adjusted

4. Use the Move brush to pull out the medial malleous and lateral malleous you learned about in the previous chapter. Remember, the ankle descends from the higher medial alveolus to the lower lateral one. In Figure 7.84, I have added the medial malleous with the Move brush as well as started to suggest the medial arch of the foot. This will create an important plane change as the sculpture progresses.

5. Rotate to the side view, and with the Move brush adjust the profile of the Achilles tendon (Figure 7.85). Make sure the back of the heel is not a straight line up into the calf.

6. Rotate to the back view, and continue to adjust the taper of the tendon of the Gastrocnemius and Soleus (Achilles tendon). You will recall this insertion from the previous chapter. In Figure 7.86 you can see the taper added. This also helps define the lateral and medial malleoli further.

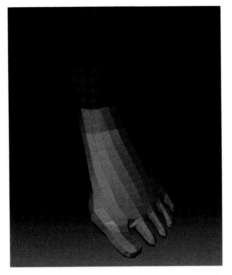

Figure 7.83 *Adding a subdivision level*

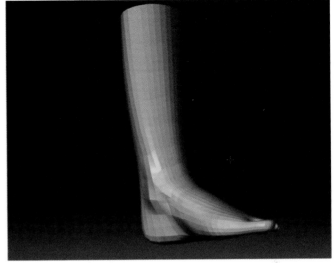

Figure 7.84 *Adding the medial malleous and medial arch with the Move brush*

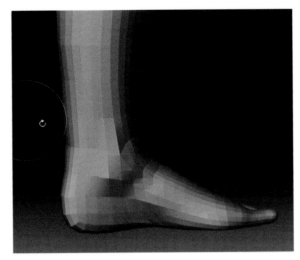

Figure 7.85 *Adjusting the profile of the heel*

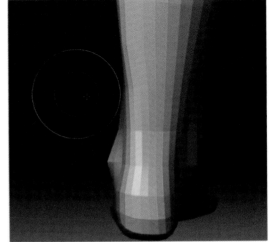

Figure 7.86 *Adjusting the tendon of the heel*

7. As a visual guide and landmark, as you continue to work the foot, sketch in the tibia with the Claytubes brush. Also accentuate the medial malleous as well as the upper border of the medial arch (Figure 7.87).

8. Rotate to the dorsal view of the foot. From here use the Claytubes brush to indicate the direction and number of metatarsal bones. This is only the initial indication, and these strokes may be lost as you continue to establish planes and form, but you will revisit them later, so the dorsal surface of the foot will have the slight indication of these bones as a secondary form (Figure 7.88).

9. Rotating to the lateral view, use the Claytubes brush with ZSub on by holding down the Alt key to subtract some form from beneath the lateral malleous. Also start to suggest the plane break where the lateral arch meets the transverse arch (Figure 7.89).

10. Return to the back view, and with the Move brush further define the plane change between the Achilles heel and the medial malleous (Figure 7.90).

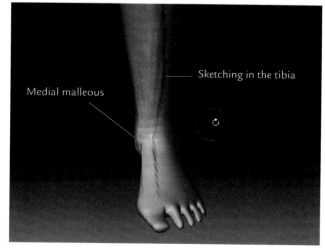

Figure 7.87 *Adjusting the shin*

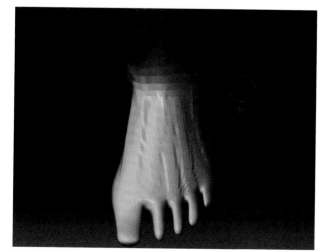

Figure 7.88 *Indicating the metatarsals*

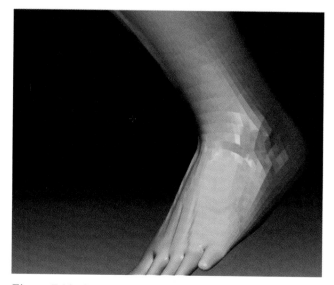

Figure 7.89 *Continuing to work the surface with the Claytubes brush and adding labels for features*

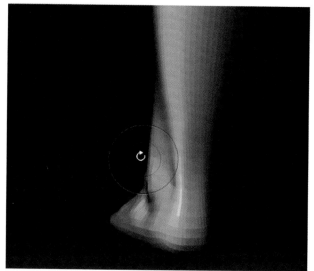

Figure 7.90 *Further defining the plane change between the lateral malleous and the Achilles heel*

11. Rotate to the medial view again, and further define the medial arch as well as the hollow between the Achilles tendon and the medial malleous (Figure 7.91).

12. Use the Flatten brush to refine the plane change between the medial arch and the transverse arch (Figure 7.92).

13. Rotate to the underside of the foot or the plantar view, and start to indicate the three surfaces of the bottom of the foot. You will address the pads of the toes later. Here I have used the Claytubes brush to build up the shapes and then Flatten to knock them back (Figure 7.93).

14. You will now start to refine the shape of the toes. Use the Inflate brush with a very low ZIntensity setting to increase the volume of the toes (Figure 7.94). Use the Move brush to adjust the shape of the toes from the top and side views. In Figure 7.95, I am adjusting the curve of the toes, starting to suggest the knuckles.

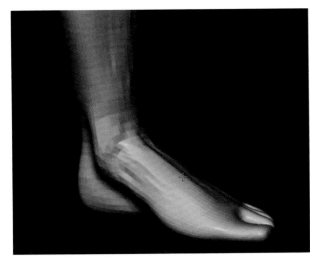

Figure 7.91 Further defining the medial arch

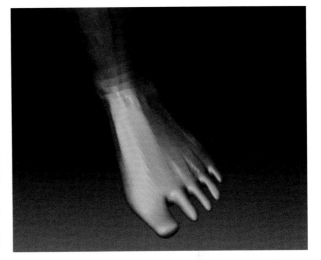

Figure 7.92 Adding the planes to the foot using the Flatten brush

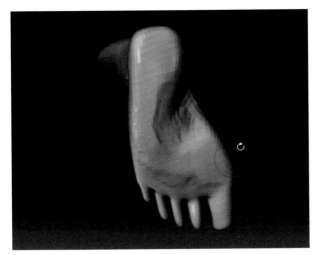

Figure 7.93 Working the plantar view of the foot

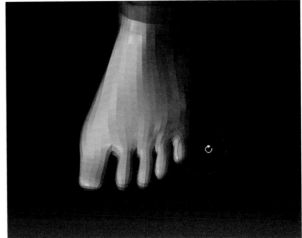

Figure 7.94 Increasing the volume of toes with the Inflate brush

15. Rotate to the side view, and use the Inflate brush with a very low ZIntensity setting to create the fleshy mass at the side of the little toe. This flesh mass rides against the metatarsal of the little toe and creates an important plane break (Figure 7.96). As I rotate around the foot, I also take this opportunity to reinforce the metatarsals that have been lost in the process so far. I reinforce the shape lightly with the Claytubes brush (Figure 7.97).

16. Rotate to the plantar view of the foot. You will now start to define the fatty pads for the toes and the compression of flesh where they meet the foot. Use the Lasso tool to mask the toes. Build up the oval-shaped pad for the ball of the foot as well as the mass of the lateral foot pad. Use the Flatten brush to press these forms down once they have been established. This helps create the sense of pressure, as if the foot is under the weight of the body (Figure 7.98).

17. Step down to the lowest subdivision level, and use the Move brush to adjust the silhouette of the foot. Remember the curves and crests from earlier in this chapter, and try to make sure they are represented in your sculpture (Figure 7.99).

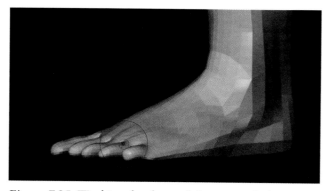

Figure 7.95 Working the shape of the toes with the Move brush

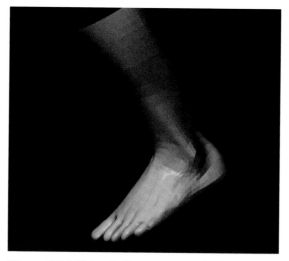

Figure 7.96 Using Inflate to create the fleshy mass at the side of the little toe

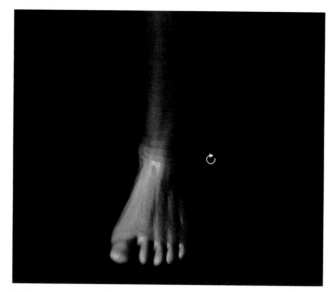

Figure 7.97 Reinforcing the metatarsals

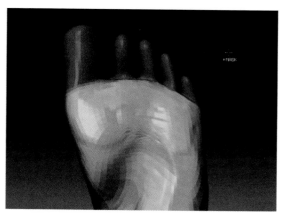

Figure 7.98 Roughing in the foot pads with Claytubes and Flatten

18. Use the Standard brush to further indicate the knuckles of the toes. In Figure 7.100, you can see the knuckles added, as well as the lateral fleshy mass of the foot that has been defined from the bones of the metatarsals. Use the Move brush to curl the little toe and compress it against the other digits.

19. Use transpose masking to isolate each toe, and use the Move brush to adjust the shape. Figure 7.101 shows a toe isolated so I can adjust the shape of the tip of the toe from the top view, as well as the shape of the toe from the side, without disturbing the nearby forms. Figure 7.102 shows the underside of the lesser toes. I have masked the toes individually and worked the fleshy tip of each. Also note the indication of creasing in the skin, which was added with the Standard brush and Alpha 01.

20. Return to the top view, and use the Inflate brush to further define the bone structure of the metatarsals. When this is complete, use the Flatten brush to plane the shapes down and make them appear less inflated (Figure 7.103). Also, I have used the Flatten brush to note where each toenail will ultimately be.

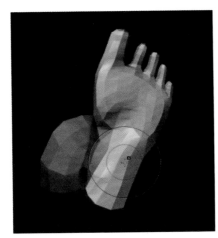

Figure 7.99 *Working the silhouette of the foot from below*

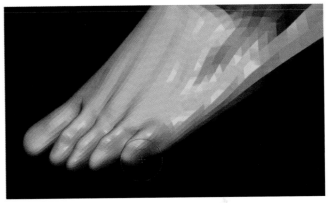

Figure 7.100 *Toe knuckles and fleshy side*

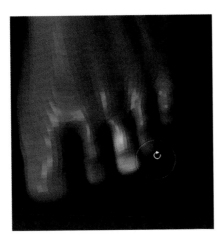

Figure 7.101 *Using transpose masking to isolate each toe*

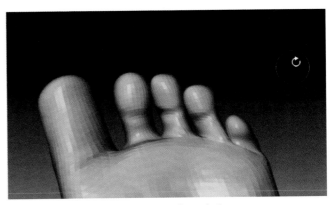

Figure 7.102 *Working the toes from below*

21. Use transpose masking to isolate the big toe. With the Move brush, create the heart-shaped pad on the underside of this toe (Figure 7.104). While the toe is masked, rotate to the top view, and continue to adjust the shape of the digit (Figure 7.105).
22. Because the little toe has a characteristic inclination toward the medial, to the point that it almost appears mashed, you will isolate it with transpose masking and use Rotate to change the angle so it moves in toward the other toes (Figure 7.106).
23. Use the Inflate brush to mass out the fleshy mass at the lateral order of the foot, just beneath the lateral arch (Figure 7.107).

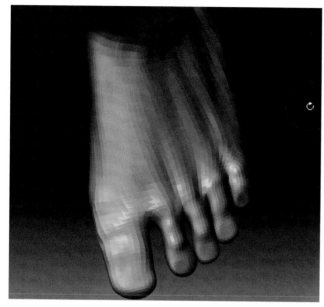

Figure 7.103 Flattening the form

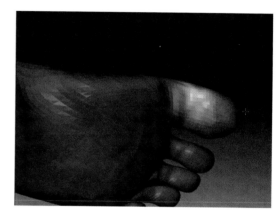

Figure 7.104 Working the bottom of the big toe

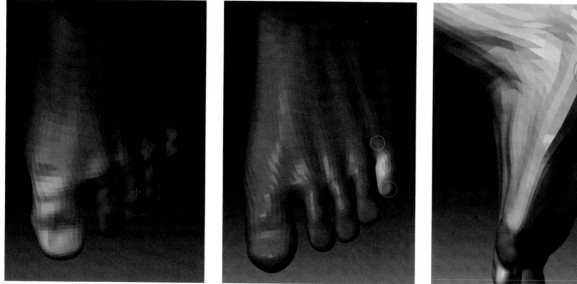

Figure 7.105 Working the top of the big toe

Figure 7.106 Changing the angle of the pinky toe

Figure 7.107 Note the mass and angle of lateral arch.

Congratulations! You have completed sculpting the foot (Figure 7.108) and the hand of the figure. These are two of the most complex and rewarding parts of the body to sculpt. You will now move on to the final stage of sculpting the figure—adding a layer of fat and flesh over the muscled form to help create a higher sense of realism. Let's get started.

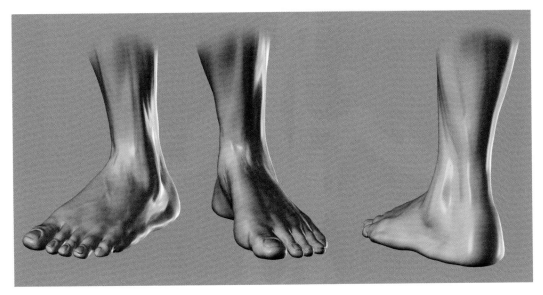

Figure 7.108 The final foot

Finishing the Figure

In this section, you will look at the figure as a whole and refine the relationships between the parts. You will also address the distribution of skin and fat across the figure. When you work a sculpture from the inside out, it's easy to arrive at an extremely defined athletic figure. This may be appropriate for some types of characters, but it's often desirable to lose some of this definition under a realistic layer of skin and fat. I'll cover where the major fat deposits are on the figure and how to sculpt between the muscles to add a sense of an encompassing layer of skin.

Beneath your skin, the entire body is encased in a fibrous layer called the *fascia*. The fascia binds the muscles together in a tight wrapping. Over this layer you find the fat, which will vary in amount and placement depending on how obese the figure is. There are major fat deposits that are present in all bodies.

You will also look at where the skin wrinkles and folds, especially in the areas of the knees, buttocks, and chest. Adding folds of flesh in the right areas will create a convincing sense of flesh.

Overall Form Changes

In this section, I'll cover the relationships between the different parts of the figure as a single unit. Using the Move brush, you will reshape the masses so they form a more unified whole, and you will ensure the rhythms between the masses stay intact.

Open the last saved ZTool of your figure. This should be the completed sculpture with the head, torso, arms, legs, hands, and feet sculpted. Step down a few subdivision levels, and select the move Brush (Figure 7.109).

Figure 7.109 *Loading the last saved ZTool of the figure*

You want to reduce the masses of the chest, pelvis, and knees to help bring the overall form of the figure into a more realistic light. The physique pictured here is fine for a fantasy barbarian or some action figures or superheroes, but I want to make a few changes to bring it closer to a sense of reality. These are simple changes using the Move brush. Begin by reducing the size of the chest using the Move brush from the front and side views. Remember the oval form of the rib cage, and make sure as you make this change to keep that underlying form intact. In many ways, I am reducing the muscle mass here more than the shape of the underlying skeleton (Figure 7.110).

At this point, I lengthen the midsection by raising the navel and tucking in the waist. Note that the thoracic arch has been narrowed slightly, helping to create the impression of a longer torso (Figure 7.111). Moving down to the legs, I narrow the knees with the Move brush. The overall gesture of the silhouettes of the legs is readdressed to create the landmark crests and valleys along the inner and outer borders of the legs. Figure 7.112 illustrates these changes as well as the lines and hits I am striving to accentuate in the legs.

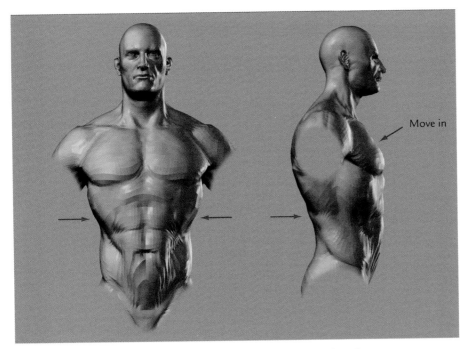

Figure 7.110 Using the Move brush to reduce the mass of the rib cage

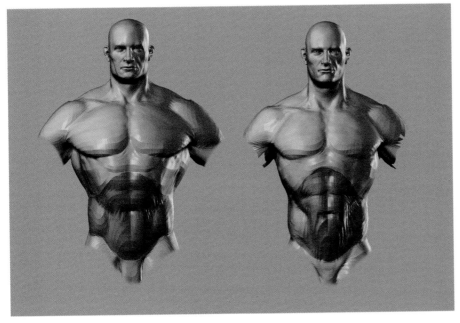

Figure 7.111 Lengthening the torso

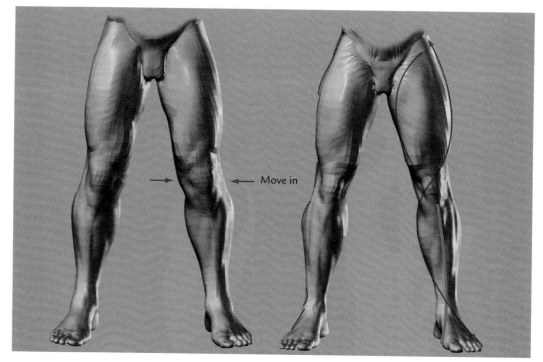

Figure 7.112 Readdressing the legs

Adding Flesh and Fat

In this section, you will use the Claytubes, Clay, Inflate, and Move brushes to create a sense of flesh and fat on the figure. So far, you have been sculpting with an aim to define every muscle orientation and insertion as well as each bony landmark. Subtlety in sculpting comes from knowing what to show and what to lose. Sometimes it's best not to show every line and furrow because this helps create visual interest in the surface, and it also makes for a more realistic figure since it implies the presence of skin and fat.

In this section, you will be working to push back some of the forms you have sculpted to make them more understated on the figure. Remember to move your light often. In many cases, a shape is at the right level of subtlety when it is visible only under certain lighting conditions. Figure 7.113 illustrates this on the surface of the figure with the divisions between the heads of the Pectoralis muscles. Note in the first image that the striations of the Pectoralis are not visible, but when the light is moved, the surface shows the subtle influence of these muscles beneath the skin. It is only possible to evaluate the forms for this level of subtlety if you constantly move the light while sculpting this finishing pass.

Remember, the light can be moved only when using a Startup Standard material like the Basic Material. I am using the hotkey I set up in Chapter 2 for the Interactive Light utility found under ZPlugin → MiscUtilities.

Figure 7.113 Moving the light helps illustrate the subtlety of some of the surface forms

Some forms can be almost entirely lost in the process of sculpting this finishing pass. These lost forms are desirable because they can create implied lines in the surface of the figure. For example, see Figure 7.114. At the back of the thigh, the furrow between the Bicep femoris and Semitendenosis muscles has been all but filled in. Under a side light, the furrow is lightly visible, implying this line that extends down to the side of the knee. You can also see this effect on the Gastronemicus muscle in Figure 7.114. This is where your own artistic choices come into play as you decide what areas of the body to accentuate and which to "lose." By choosing what to show and what to allow to sink back into the surface of the figure, you can create a beautiful surface that has the appearance of flesh and bone.

When I sculpt flesh and fat on the surface of the figure, I tend to use the Clay brush, the Claytubes brush, and the Inflate brush. The Clay brushes have the benefit of adding form into the recessed areas first. This is a value when you are trying to fill in furrows between two existing forms. In ZBrush 3.5, there is the added benefit of the Depth Control tool under the Brush menu. By manipulating the depth at which your brushes affect the surface, you can influence the way in which the spaces between the muscles are filled in. For the Claytubes brush, set the Brush Imbed slider to 0, and turn off the Alpha to create a good brush for filling in between forms.

Before I demonstrate how to sculpt fat on the figure, let's look at where the typical fat pads are found on the average male body. Figure 7.115 shows the fat pads in color for the front and back of the figure. Note that the whole

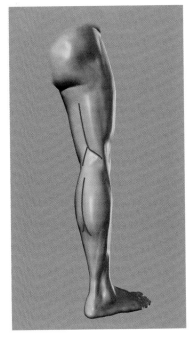

Figure 7.114 When sculpting, don't be afraid to lose some areas of detail to help unify the surface with a sense of flesh and fat. The lines in this image show the furrows in the leg that have been sublimated to help create a sense of skin and fat over the muscles.

figure is covered in a layer of fat and fascia, but these pads represent the usual areas that fat deposits are clustered on the average human. These fat deposits differ in size and placement between the sexes. Almost all real people have more fat than what is pictured here.

This image was created based on a famous image in one of Eliot Goldfinger's anatomy books.

Using what you know about muscular and skeletal anatomy, now you can observe photo references and determine where the fatty tissue is on the person in question as well as its relative depth. In the following lesson, you will add these fat pads as well as further fatty tissues at the abdomen and arms.

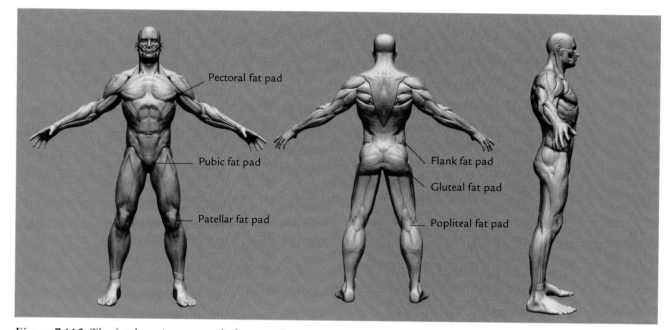

Figure 7.115 *The fat deposits on a male figure. (This image was created based on a similar illustration from Eliot Goldfinger's Human Anatomy for Artists.)*

New Brushes for Figure Finishing

When finishing the figure, I recommend using the Claytubes brush with no Alpha, the FormSoft brush, ClayFinish, and Noise02. The Claytubes brush will add form into the recessed areas first, allowing you to fill in the space between two muscles while not disturbing the overall form. When using the Claytubes brush, make sure that the Brush Embed slider under the Brush menu is set to 0 and Samples is set to 0.75. You may also choose to turn on Brush Depth and set the Outer Depth to 0. This will help the brush preserve high points and only fill into the cavities.

These settings may require some experimentation to find how to make the brush work best for you. These settings should serve as a guide to help you change the brush to your liking. It is important to remember to turn off the Alpha so the stroke is soft-edged and subtle. The FormSoft brush is similar to the Clay brushes in that it adds form in a gentle falloff. This is well suited to reinforcing muscle shapes that may have become too soft or lost in the finishing pass. The Noise02 brush creates a nice soft plane and is perfect for reinforcing planes that may have become soft without creating a hard edge on the surface of the sculpture. The ClayFinish brush is a new addition to version 3.5, which combines the behaviors of the Clay brush and the Flatten brush in new ways. This brush is quite well suited for adding subtle plane breaks to the surface and refining the shapes of the body that may have become soft while working.

Please see the accompanying DVD for videos of these brushes in action.

Using Brushes to Add Fat

Select the Claytubes brush from the Brush palette, and set the depth values as described in the sidebar. Rotate to the underside of the figure's arm. Using the modified Claytubes brush, stroke the surface of the figure. The brush will add into the recessed forms, first helping to soften the transitions in this area (Figure 7.116). Try to start and end your stroke on two peaks with a valley between them. The brush will fill in the valley and preserve the peaks.

You will also want to stroke lightly along the furrow where the Deltoid rides against the Bicep to soften the shadow in this area. Remember that you are trying to manipulate the way the surface catches highlights and casts shadows to change the manner in which the surface is perceived.

Moving to the knee, use the same brush to soften the forms of the patella. As you saw earlier, there are fatty pads that surround the underside of the kneecap and help soften the shape here. I also create a fold of fat and skin just above the kneecap. This area of compressed flesh lies between the Quadriceps muscle group on the front of the thigh and the kneecap (Figure 7.117).

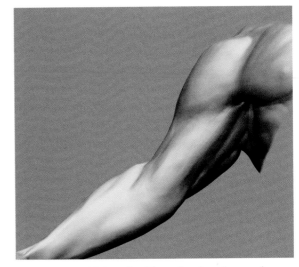

Figure 7.116 Using the Claytubes brush to soften the muscle definition of the arm

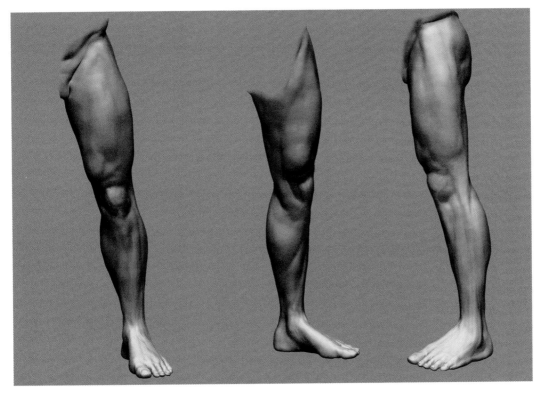

Figure 7.117 Adding fat deposits to the knee

Move to the inner thigh. Using the Claytubes brush, fill in a fatty deposit that covers the triangle between the Sartorius, Gracilis, and pubic bone. Smooth often to soften the form (Figure 7.118).

When working on flesh and fat, it is important to take gravity into account. Gravity is acting on every aspect of the figure at all times. The pull of the weight of the fat will create folds in the skin, especially in areas like the glutes. By combining masking with the Gravity brush modifier, this effect is simple to recreate.

Rotate to the back of the figure. Mask out the area on the back of the thigh just beneath the buttocks. Select the Inflate brush, go to the Brush menu, and turn the Gravity slider up to 90. Keep the arrow pointing downward to specify the direction of pull. This modifier will cause your brush to add form as well as drag it in the direction of the arrow. Stroke along the buttocks to build up the shape of the fat pads here (Figure 7.119). Because of the mask, a sharp shadow will result where one form folds over another. Clear the mask, and further refine the area with the Claytubes brush. Make sure to turn off Gravity.

You can also apply this effect to the flank pads. The External obliques are covered by a pad of fat called the *flank pad*. This pad actually overhangs the illiac crest, obscuring it from view. Depending on how much fat is in this area, a furrow may sometimes form. You will use the Inflate brush with Gravity on to create a soft overhang here, but not enough to make the figure look overweight (Figure 7.120).

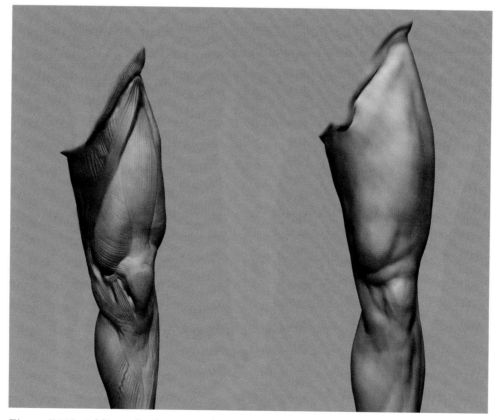

Figure 7.118 Adding a fat deposit to the inner thigh

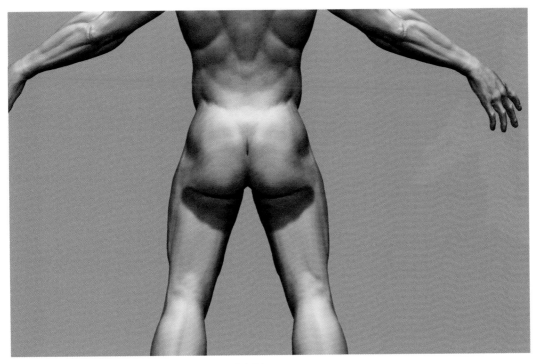

Figure 7.119 Adding gravity to the gluteal fold

At this stage, I turn off X symmetry and start to break the mirrored forms, especially in the abdominals. The abs are never perfect mirrors of one another, and breaking symmetry in this area will help create more of a sense of realism in the figure.

Select the Move brush, and turn off X symmetry. Gently shift the forms slightly to create a sense of randomness between them. I also use the Claytubes brush to fill in the furrows between the abs and create a sense of belly fat filling in the muscle definition here. Move the light as you work to ensure the definition is not entirely lost. Continue to work around the figure for one more pass with symmetry off. Even the slightest little changes between the halves will help create a sense of realism by breaking the perfectly symmetrical look (Figure 7.121).

As a final pass of detail, I like to add superficial veins to the figure. I create these using the Standard brush with Alpha 01. Select the Standard brush, and make sure your figure is at the highest subdivision level. Turn the brush's ZIntensity down to 20.

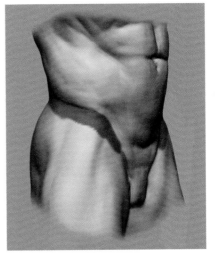

Figure 7.120 Creating the flank fat pad using the Inflate brush with the Gravity modifier on

Figure 7.121 *Breaking symmetry in the abdominals*

Begin by creating a loose sketchy line for the first vein starting at the abdomen and extending down the leg. Make sure symmetry is not on when you do this step since perfectly symmetrical veins will be more of a distraction than a valuable detail to the figure. Since the ZIntensity is low, the stroke may need to be repeated to build up the vein. Repeat the stroke by pressing Ctrl+1 on the keyboard. Continue to sketch in loose lines as shown in Figure 7.122, creating a network of veins down the leg. Remember, you can lose parts of the vein by smoothing down, creating the impression the vein descends deeper under the skin before surfacing again. Repeat this process for the upper arm as well. You can find good references for the location and direction of subcutaneous veins in the anatomy books listed in the introduction of this book.

That completes the detailing pass of this figure. Figure 7.123 shows the final sculpture as it appears now.

Congratulations! You have completed the sculpting of the human figure section of this book. So far you have learned about anatomical terminology, skeletal structure bony landmarks, and muscle groups for the whole figure. I have talked about creating a sense of gesture and weight in the sculpture as well as adding flesh and fat to the final sculpt. You are now ready to move on to creating costume elements and textures for this character.

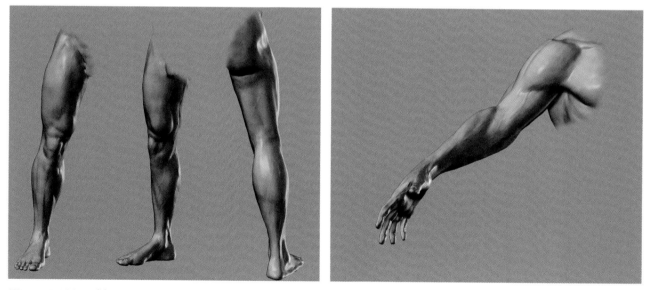

Figure 7.122 *Adding veins to the figure*

Figure 7.123 *The final figure*

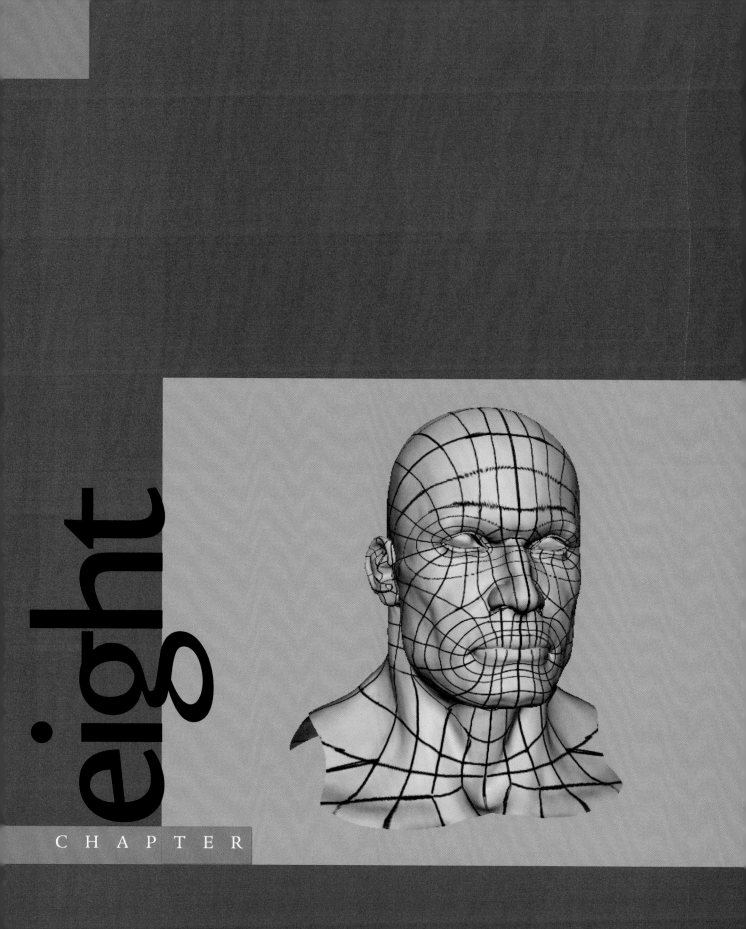

eight

Remeshing

Now that the sculpting phase *is complete,* *you may decide your model needs to become part of an animation pipeline for film or video games. The base mesh you created in Chapter 1 is ideal for the process of sculpting the character, but it is not suited for rigging and texture mapping. In this chapter, you will learn how to rebuild the underlying topology to be suitable for such applications.* Remeshing, *also known as* retopology, *is the process of creating a new underlying base topology for a model while retaining the high-resolution detail of the original sculpture. This can involve creating a new ZTool that retains the multiple levels of subdivision; or it can involve simply creating a "cage mesh" that contains the volume of your high-resolution image and then uses Create a Normal Map or another map-generating method to create a normal or displacement map that captures the high-resolution details of the sculpture and is ready to apply to the low-resolution model. The latter approach is often used in game pipelines for normal mapping.*

Figure 8.1 shows the hero figure being remeshed.

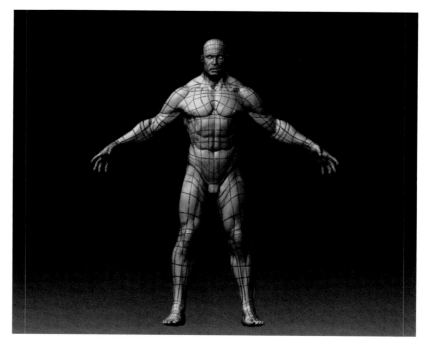

Figure 8.1 The hero being remeshed in ZBrush

What Is Remeshing?

Remeshing refers to the process of rebuilding the underlying base mesh of a sculpture while retaining the higher subdivision's details. In theory, you could begin with an ordered animation-ready mesh in ZBrush and avoid remeshing entirely. Many people prefer to work this way, but I find it has drawbacks. Often a model with topology laid out for specific forms can be less malleable in ZBrush, and you may actually find yourself fighting against the existing edge layout to create the forms you want. By starting with a simple mesh, you can get the maximum number of subdivision levels and total freedom to sculpt the forms you want. Once the design/sculpting phase of the figure is complete, you can remesh the model into an animation-ready topology that lends itself to rigging; such a mesh also makes it easier to create efficient texture coordinates to facilitate creating texture maps. This allows the artist to tailor the edge flow to the specific shapes that were defined in the sculpting phase instead of trying to sculpt shapes into an existing topology.

Problems can manifest in areas like the head or shoulder region, or anywhere else major forms have been looped into the mesh. Figure 8.2 shows the base mesh of the hero's legs compared to the high-resolution sculpt. Notice how much I was able to sculpt from very little underlying topology. This was a benefit of using a very simple sculpt to start.

Often in interactive applications such as video games, the topology will have to define not only the muscle forms of the character, but also costume elements. This allows the normal mapping to perform more efficiently, because there will be a polygon edge where a hard edge should appear on the model. The result will be that the figure will look correct from all angles. These topology edges also help define the silhouette of the figure, which is very important in game models. Since you are limited to your poly count, making the best use of your edges to define the profiles is imperative. To do that, you need to understand and apply topology theory.

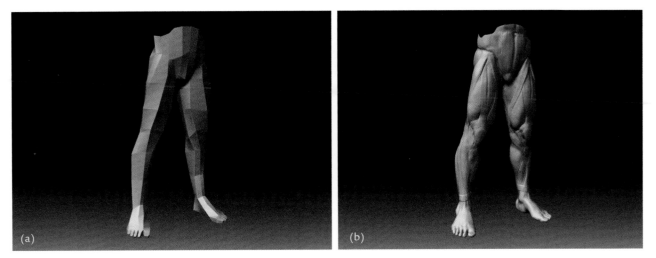

Figure 8.2 *The hero's legs: (a) in the base mesh, (b) in the high-resolution sculpt*

Why Remesh?

The model you built in Chapter 1 was specifically designed to facilitate ease of sculpting. The underlying edges were placed evenly down the model to make for a very simple block man. This kind of model allows for the most flexibility when sculpting in ZBrush. When you want to texture and animate a model, you will do better with a more elaborate underlying topology. By having edges that conform to the areas of high deformation, a setup artist can rig the character so it deforms realistically when animated. Figure 8.3 shows the character's knee bending in the sculpt mesh compared to the remesh. Notice how the edge loops help you maintain the volume as the limb deforms.

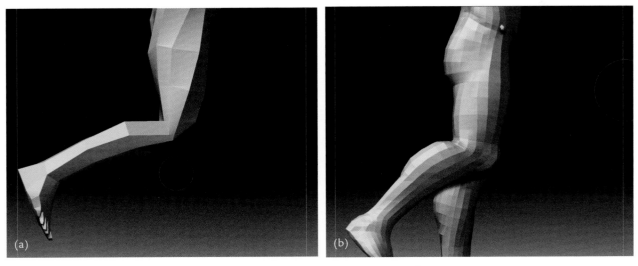

Figure 8.3 *Bending the knee: (a) in the original sculpt mesh, (b) in the remesh*

These same loops are helpful to a texture artist who needs to isolate parts of the body and generate texture coordinates (UVs). The process of laying out topology can be involved and technical, and it is often best approached after the sculpting phase. This allows design aspects to be worked out ahead of time without the limitations that may be introduced by topology.

Figure 8.4 shows the original topology of our figure's head compared to the remeshed animation model. Both retain the same high-resolution details, but the remeshed head will be far more suitable to an animation pipeline because of the logical flow of faces around the eyes and mouth. For an exhaustive look at edge flow for animation, I highly recommend Jason Osipa's book *Stop Staring: Facial Modeling and Animation Done Right* (Sybex, second edition: 2007).

Figure 8.5 shows how a properly edge-looped face can assist the modeler in sculpting realistic blend shape targets. Notice how the edge loops allow you to pull a realistic nasolabial fold from the existing geometry at the lowest subdivision level.

In addition to its benefits for animation, an ordered mesh also accommodates the process of texture mapping. By having the limbs looped in a sensible manner, the artist can cut UV edges and unwrap the model more efficiently. Figure 8.6, for example, shows how an ordered mesh of a character from the waist down can be efficiently peeled open for UV mapping.

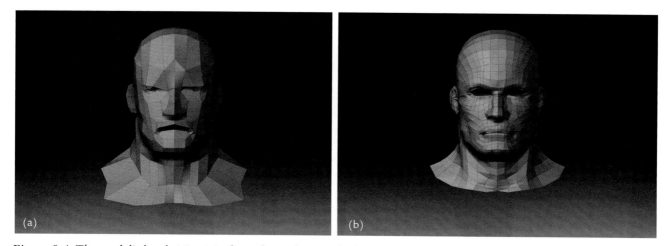

Figure 8.4 *The model's head: (a) original topology, (b) remeshed. Note the flow of loops around the eyes and mouth.*

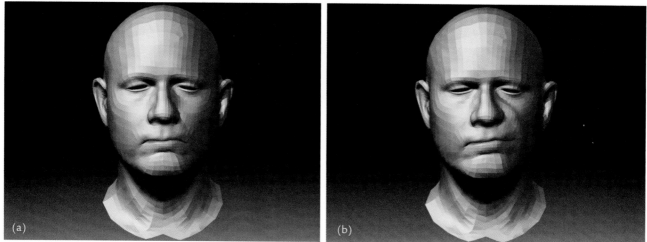

Figure 8.5 *A properly edge-looped face makes it easy to create realistic expressions.*

Model courtesy of Kyle Mulqueen

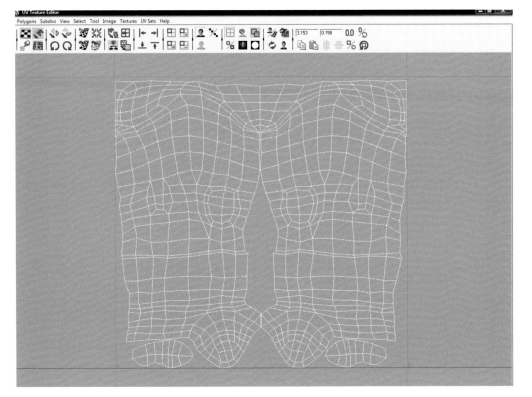

Figure 8.6 UV peeled open leg

These benefits are difficult to appreciate unless you have experienced the challenges of trying to UV and animate a mesh that was not designed for such a purpose. After even one attempt at this, the benefits of an ordered mesh will become clear. By taking a few hours to create a standard topology for your figure, you will open up many more applications for the model as well as have far fewer problems down the pipeline.

In a professional environment, an ordered mesh is mandatory. In both film and games, the pipeline depends on having a model that is not only a good sculpture, but is properly UVed and usable for the setup artists to rig and bind. Even if you don't plan to animate the model, a standard topology will allow you to more easily pose the mesh in ZBrush as well as have more freedom and flexibility when generating UVs and painting textures.

In this chapter, you will learn about two methods of remeshing the sculpture into an animation-ready topology. You will first examine how to use ZBrush's built-in topology tools. This is a powerful set of tools you can use to quickly generate models directly inside ZBrush. Later in this chapter, you will look at an alternate approach to generating an animation mesh, a Maya plug-in by Digital Raster called NEX.

Introducing the ZBrush Topology Tools

In this section, you will work with the ZBrush topology tools, which are located under the Tool menu when you are working with ZSpheres. My special thanks to this book's technical editor, Paul Gaboury from Pixologic, who cowrote this section and created the example demonstrating the strengths of the ZBrush topology tools.

Laying out topology for an animation mesh can be very daunting. ZBrush simplifies the process and makes creating new topology easier than ever before.

Polypainting

Before constructing your topology with the retopology tools, you will lay out your topology by polypainting your topology lines right onto the mesh. *Polypainting* is the process of painting RGB color directly onto your mesh in ZBrush. This topology map will help guide you as you start laying in edges and will generally help keep the process simple and easy to complete.

1. Load the hero ZTool into ZBrush. Draw it on the canvas, and enter edit mode with the T hotkey.

2. You will need to fill the character with the color white as a base on which to paint. Make sure MRGB is on at the top of the screen, white is the selected color, and the fast shader is the active material. Select Color → Fill Object to flood the mesh with white.

3. Since you will be using polypainting to color the mesh, you need to make sure there are enough subdivisions to display the lines crisply. Divide your mesh up enough to capture the polypaint; in most cases, a few million polygons will be enough. When complete, your mesh should look like Figure 8.7.

4. Select the Standard brush with a Freehand Stroke setting. To help draw smoother lines as you draw, turn on Lazy Mouse in the Stroke menu. Set LazyRadius to 10.

Figure 8.7 The mesh filled with the material and color

Remeshing the Head

You will start by remeshing the head. This is the focal point of the character, and it contains many of the most specific loops for animation. Those are the loops around the mouth and eyes that allow for natural facial expressions. Notice how these loops mirror the flow of the underlying facial anatomy, discussed in Chapter 3. When you are building a mesh for animation, always try to run the major loops of edges so they encircle the areas of greatest muscular deformation on the face. These take the shape of a bandit's mask around the eyes and what I call a clown mouth around the lips. You will see both formations shortly.

1. Begin by narrowing your work area by holding Shift+Ctrl while you drag out your selection area, which will be a green square. Everything that is in the green square will be selected, and the rest of the mesh will be hidden. Select just the head, as shown in Figure 8.8.

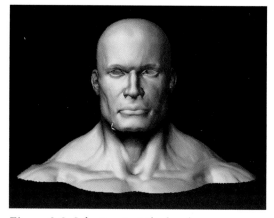

Figure 8.8 Selecting just the head

2. When creating an animation mesh, edge loops control the expressions that you will apply to a mesh. The first edge loops on a face are crucial for animation, as shown in Figure 8.9. They will establish the base for all expressions. Here you can see the bandit mask and clown mouth. Draw the loops around the eyes and mouth. To create a centerline, turn on the X symmetry by clicking X. You can also find this in the Transform palette. You will see two red dots on either side of your mesh. Drag until both dots touch, and hold the Shift key to draw a straight line down the middle of your mesh.

3. You will want to add loops inside the first major edge loops to further define the eyes and mouth. Notice in Figure 8.10 how the last two loops inside the eye don't loop all the way around both eyes, but rather form the "eyeholes" in the bandit mask.

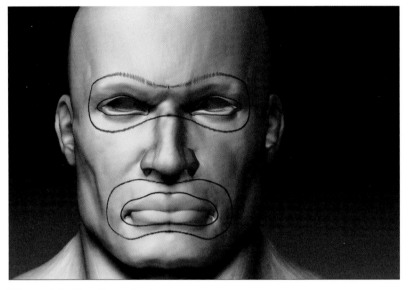

Figure 8.9 First face edge loops

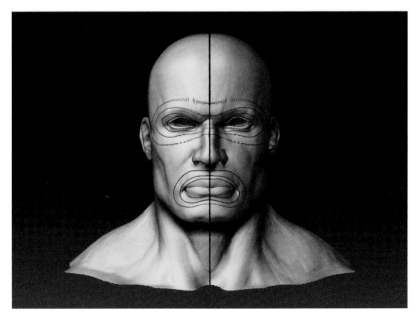

Figure 8.10 Drawing the eye rings

4. Continue to draw in your edge loops on the face, as shown in Figure 8.11, in order to create topology to capture the various expressions of the human face.

5. Finish off the topology of the head, as shown in Figure 8.12. Maintain the edge loops of the eyes and mouth. Maintain the basic shape of the ears to capture the detail for the projection that will be applied to the new topology.

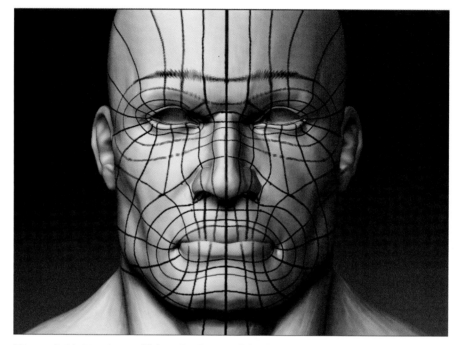

Figure 8.11 *Finishing off the edge loops of the face*

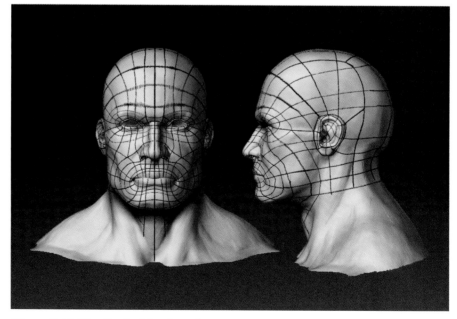

Figure 8.12 *The finished head mesh*

Drawing the Shoulder Topology

The shoulder is another region of high deformation that requires some specific loops to allow for realistic movement in animation. In Chapter 5, I discussed the shoulder girdle and the range of motion it is capable of doing. To accommodate this general deformation, you need to loop the shoulders in a way that allows the most flexibility in animation. Here you will use the "cape" loop popularized by Jeff Unay in *Maya Hyper-Realistic Creature Creation: A hands-on introduction to key tools and techniques in Autodesk Maya* (Autodesk Maya Press, 2008).

Establishing the shoulders in an animation mesh is key to creating a fluid animation. The perfect shoulder topology will take on a cape form, as shown in Figure 8.13.

1. Once the cape is established, be sure to create topology that follows the Deltoids into the Pectoralis major, as shown in Figure 8.14. The cape is key to the rotation of the shoulder, so make sure that the topology establishes the form of the Deltoid.

2. As you move down the arm to the elbow, make sure to create at least a minimum of three to four edge loops for the elbow to allow a natural bend, as shown in Figure 8.15.

3. The wrist will have a great deal of movement in the ulna and radius, so be sure to create enough edge loops to capture the full range of the wrist, as shown in Figure 8.16.

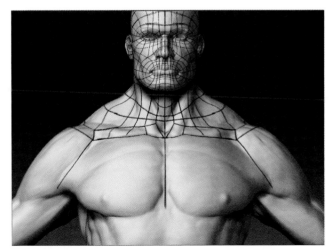

Figure 8.13 Establishing the cape of the shoulders

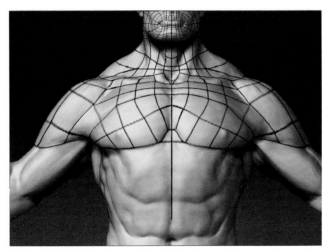

Figure 8.14 Topology of the Deltoid and Pectoralis major

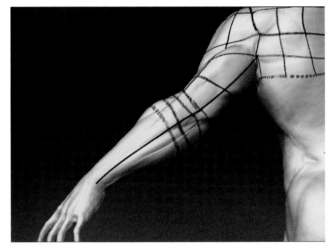

Figure 8.15 Edge loops of the elbow

Figure 8.16 Edge loops of the wrist

Drawing the Hand Topology

The hand has several planes, which makes it difficult to maintain a quad poly mesh, as shown in Figure 8.17. Be sure to draw the topology to fit an animation, but also keep the form of the hand, avoiding creating triangles or *ngons* (faces with more than four points). Although triangles are acceptable if hidden in unobtrusive areas and kept to a minimum, ngons should never be left in the mesh.

Ngons and triangles can produce a pinch or unfavorable result during animation. The first lines to establish on the hand are the edge loops around knuckles, as shown in Figure 8.18. Be sure to have at least five total faces wrapping around each finger, as shown in Figure 8.19. If you have just four faces, ZBrush will often interpret it incorrectly during projection.

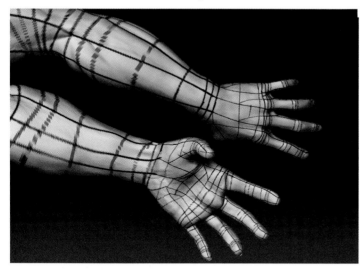

Figure 8.17 The hand with the topology lines drawn out

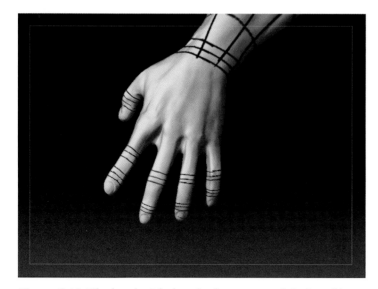

Figure 8.18 The hand with the edge loops around the knuckles

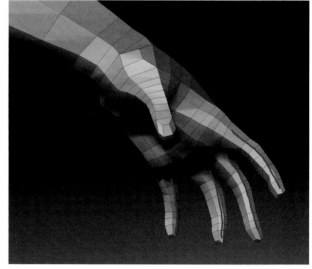

Figure 8.19 Make sure there are at least five faces around each finger.

Drawing the Core, Legs, and Feet

You will now move on to the torso of the figure. You will lay out the edge loops to define the core of the body as well as the legs and feet of the figure. As you work, you should be sensitive to areas of high deformation so you can place your edge flows to allow for maximum range of motion when the figure is animated. Be sure to follow the form of the core and add edge loops at key pivot points of the mesh. The knees, ankles, and toes are key for creating a mesh that will animate well. These are the key pivot points of a mesh for animation; be sure to add edge loops here.

1. Much movement will happen for a figure at the core. This is where the topology flow must follow the form of your sculpt. You will notice in Figure 8.20 that the topology will follow the Gluteus maximus and the iliac crest.

2. As you move down the leg to the patella, there will need to be a minimum of four to five edge loops around the knee. There will be severe pinching in the Biceps femoris if there is not enough topology in the area. As you can see from Figure 8.21, the edge loops start at the base of the Vastus medialis, and the last loop ends at the tibial tuberosity.

3. Down the tibia bone, you continue to the ankle, where the next set of edge loops must be applied. In Figure 8.22 you will notice that I have drawn lines that take on the shape of the ankle and calf.

Figure 8.20 *The topology form of the core*

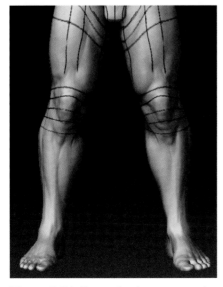

Figure 8.21 *Four edge loops around the knee*

Figure 8.22 *The ankle and calf edge loops*

4. As you move down the foot to the toes, the best solution for drawing your topology is to use ZBrush's topology masking. First make sure that X symmetry is on so that the topology lines are drawn on both big toes. Switch from draw mode into move mode at the top of the interface. Once you are in the move mode, you can create a topology mask by holding Ctrl. Place your brush at the first joint of the big toe, and draw your topology mask just like Figure 8.23.

5. Once you have the mask, press Ctrl, and click the canvas to inverse the mask. Alternatively, you can go to the Tool palette, select Masking, and click Inverse. Then, once the mask is inverted so that only the big toe is masked (Figure 8.24), go back into the Masking menu and select HidePt. This will hide anything that is not masked. Now you will be able to draw the perfect topology lines.

6. Repeat steps 4 and 5 for every toe.

With all the topology lines being worked out ahead of time, creating the new topology will be an extremely easy process. It will be a simple matter of tracing the lines you have just taken the time to plan.

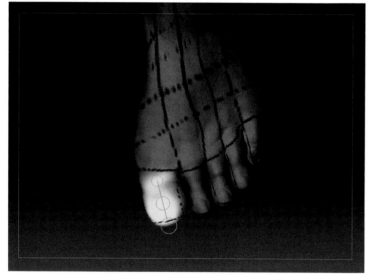

Figure 8.23 Masking out the big toe

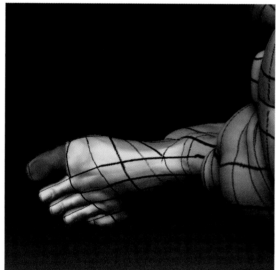

Figure 8.24 The inverse of the big toe mask

Opening the Mouth

At this point, there is one thing you need to take care of—you need to open the mouth in order to create topology for both lips without intersecting the upper lip with the bottom. You will use the Masking, Transpose, and Polygroups menus to open the mouth. With the mouth open, you'll be able to continue your edge loops down into the inner lip area instead of having the mouth mesh end abruptly at the line of the lips.

1. First you need to drop the mesh to its lowest subdivision level and use a Lasso to select the lower mandible. Remember to select a piece of your mesh, hold down Shift+Ctrl, and click the canvas to drag out your selection. However, this time you will let go of Shift, and the box will turn red. This is telling ZBrush to hide what is in the red. It should look like Figure 8.25. Once you have the mandible hidden, turn on PolyFrame mode by pressing Shift+F or selecting from the menu on the right side of the screen. Then click Group Visible in the Polygroup menu, which you can find by going to the

Tool palette and selecting Polygroups. Your mesh will change color. This has just made the rest of the head its own polygroup.

2. Show your entire mesh again by holding Shift+Ctrl and clicking inside the canvas. Go to the midsubdivision level of the body. We don't want too many faces here to work with, so level 3 should be fine. Select the head polygroup by holding Shift+Ctrl, and click the head polygroup that you just made. This will hide the mandible. Under Masking in the Tool palette, click the Mask All option. This will mask the head. Now bring the mandible back by holding Shift+Ctrl, and click the canvas. Now your mandible will not be masked. You should have a masking like Figure 8.26 that is ready to move the bottom part of the mouth. Click Rotate at the top of the interface, and draw out your action line. Now grab the middle of the last circle that is in front of the jaw and pull down. You'll end up with an open mouth much like Figure 8.27.

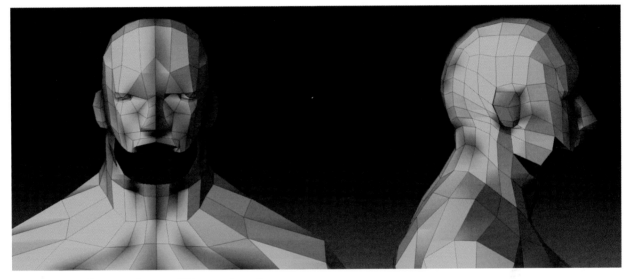

Figure 8.25 Showing the mandible unselected

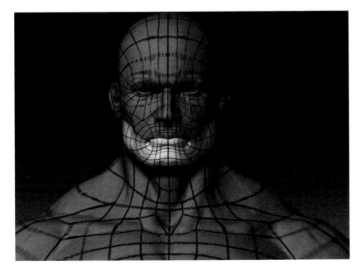

Figure 8.26 The masking of the head

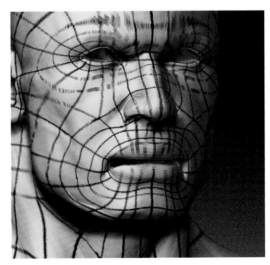

Figure 8.27 The open mouth

Using the ZBrush Topology Tools

Now that you have laid out your topology lines, you can construct the new topology. This will be a quick and easy process, thanks to the polypainting you did first. Keep in mind that it is OK not to follow these polypainting lines exactly. Sometimes there are changes that become apparent as you start laying in the edge loops. Don't consider the map to be absolutely necessary—it is there to assist you.

1. To create new topology in ZBrush, you will be using a ZSphere. Make sure that your ZTool sculpt is loaded. Go to Tool, and select the ZSphere. Drag a ZSphere onto the canvas (Figure 8.28), and put it in edit mode. Move down the Tool palette until you come across the Rigging menu, and click Select Mesh.

2. A pop-up window will open for you to select your sculpted mesh. Once you have selected your sculpt (Figure 8.29), move to the Topology menu, and select Edit Topology. You are now able to create new animation-ready topology. Before you begin to lay down the topology, click in the empty canvas a few times to unselect the ZSphere.

Figure 8.28 A ZSphere on the canvas

Figure 8.29 The sculpt selected in the ZSphere

Remeshing the Face

Let's begin with the head of your sculpt. ZBrush's retopology tools are a basic click-one-vertex-at-a-time system. Before you begin building the topology, drop your brush size to 1.

When you click your mesh, you will see a red circle. Continue to click three other circles to form a poly face. You will notice that when you close a poly face off, the red circle will have two white triangles, as you can see in Figure 8.30. This is letting you know that the starting point of your next vertex will begin from the red circle, as you can clearly see in Figure 8.31.

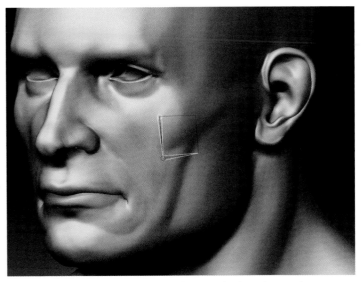

1. To begin with the face, the first step is to establish the edge loops around the eye. In Figure 8.32 you can see the edge loop of the eye, and in Figure 8.33 you can see the resulting mesh from the topology. To view your mesh, go to the Tool palette, select the Adaptive Skin menu, and click the Preview button. The shortcut to this is the A key. This will display your mesh at a density level of 2. If you adjust the density level, ZBrush will subdivide your mesh by that number. When you finish the topology, this number will dictate the number of subdivision levels your mesh will have. Continue adding the edge loops for the eyes so that you get to the result of Figure 8.34.

Figure 8.30 The very first poly face applied to the mesh

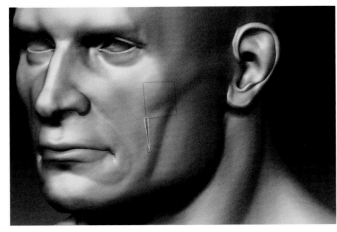

Figure 8.31 The next vert that is laid down

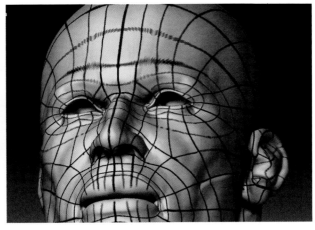

Figure 8.32 The first edge loop topology of the eye

Figure 8.33 The resulting mesh from the topology

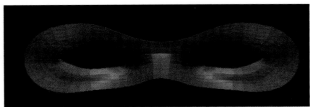

Figure 8.34 The adaptive skin of the eye edge loops

2. Continue to build the topology down to the nose. As you can see in Figure 8.35, I had to change my edges a little from the original polypaint. I did not factor in the loop at the end of the nose. Once you complete the nose, you should get something like Figure 8.36.

3. Now move to the mouth, where you must have several edge loops to capture the extreme movements outward that mouths can make. Figure 8.37 will show the topology edge loops for the mouth.

4. Once the mouth has been completed, you can finish the rest of the head off except the ears, as shown in Figure 8.38. It is a good idea to keep previewing your mesh as you build by using the A key. Once you have completed the ears, as shown in Figure 8.39, you can move on to the Deltoids.

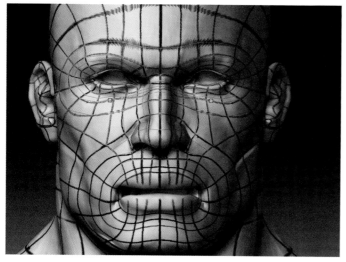

Figure 8.35 The topology of the nose

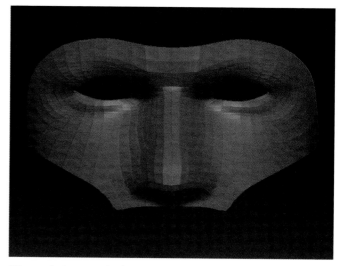

Figure 8.36 Finished nose with adaptive skin

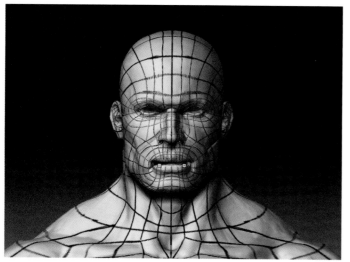

Figure 8.37 The edge loops of the mouth

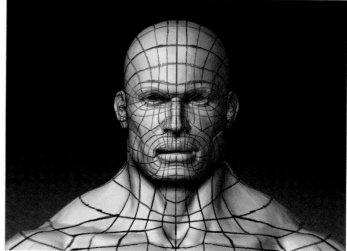

Figure 8.38 The rebuilt head topology

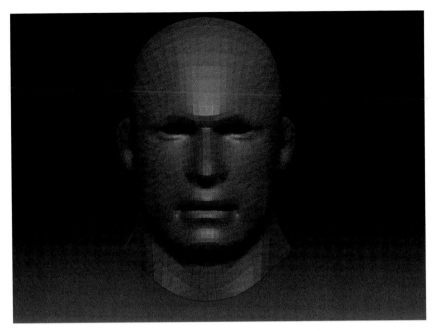

Figure 8.39 The finished head

Remeshing the Shoulders

The shoulders seem to be the easiest features to create; however, often people do not create accurate animation topology for this area of the anatomy. You must be sure to create geometry that resembles a cape over the shoulders, as you can see in Figure 8.40. This will give the mesh result shown in Figure 8.41; the finished shoulders with the armpits will look like Figure 8.42.

1. Make sure to draw out the arms as basic cylinders with several edge loops around the joint, as you can see in Figure 8.43.

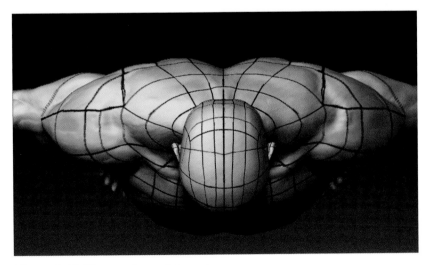

Figure 8.40 The topology of the cape

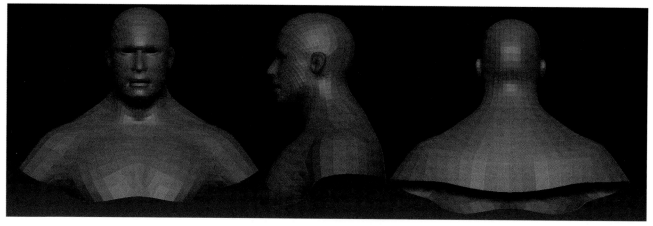

Figure 8.41 *The adaptive skin of the Deltoids*

Figure 8.42 *The shoulders finished with the armpits*

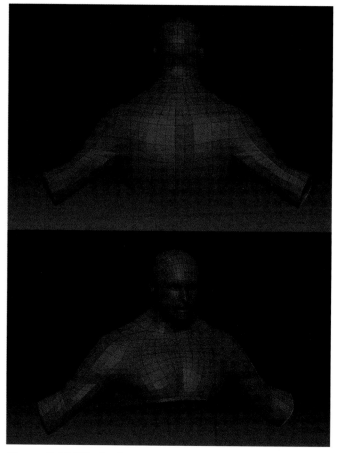

Figure 8.43 *The basic arm geometry*

2. As you build the topology down the arm to the wrist, make sure to have enough edge loops at the wrist to capture the range of motion that this part of the anatomy has, as you can see in Figure 8.44.

3. The hand is the area that could change the most from your polypaint. As you can see in Figure 8.45, at first I stayed with the painted lines. However, by the time I was done, I had added many faces to create a more animation-ready hand, which is shown in Figure 8.46.

4. The torso is as basic as it gets, except when you build up the iliac crest or at the bend of the waist. Usually you will be able to determine whether more edge loops are required. As you can see in Figure 8.47, I stayed consistent with the polypaint. The torso was followed exactly to the polypaint. In Figure 8.48, you can see that I continued to work down the torso into the genitals and Gluteus maximus.

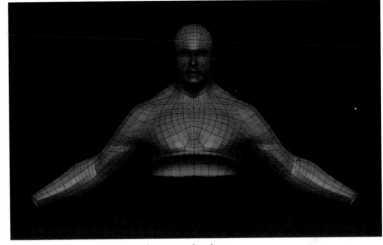

Figure 8.44 The arm and wrist edge loops

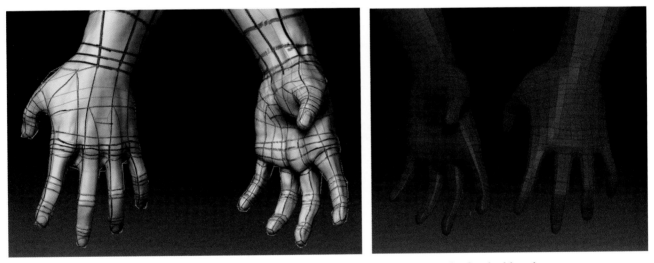

Figure 8.45 The topology laid out on the hand following the polypaint

Figure 8.46 The finished hand

5. The leg is much like the arm in that it takes on a cylinder shape but must have at least four edge loops around the knee and the ankle. You can see in Figure 8.49 how basic the mesh is with just a few tweaks. The ankle's topology does take on some of the characteristics of the sculpture as you build the topology in the general shape of the ankle; see Figure 8.50.

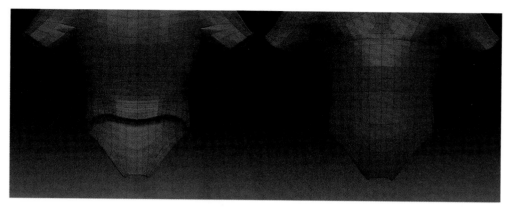

Figure 8.47 *The torso in adaptive mode*

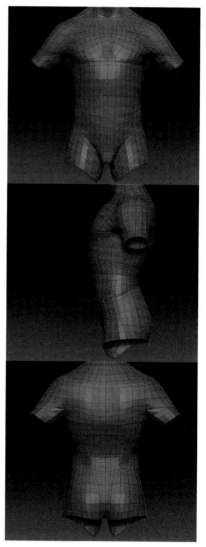

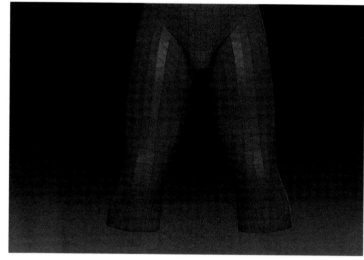

Figure 8.49 *The leg finished in adaptive mode*

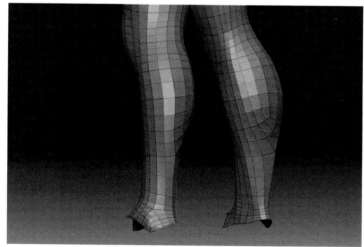

Figure 8.48 *The torso completely finished*

Figure 8.50 *The start of the ankle*

6. Once you get past the ankle, you are in the home stretch on your way to the feet. The feet are much like the hands in that there will be a little tweaking needed to have a quality flow of quads, and as you can see in Figure 8.51, you will need several edge loops to establish a foot that can be animated.

Now you have constructed a complete animation-ready mesh with ZBrush's topology tools. Your finished mesh should look something like Figure 8.52, depending on your topology flow.

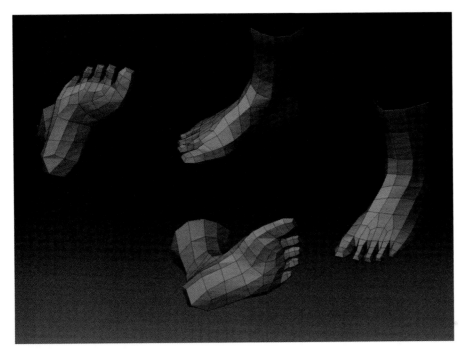

Figure 8.51 *The foot finished*

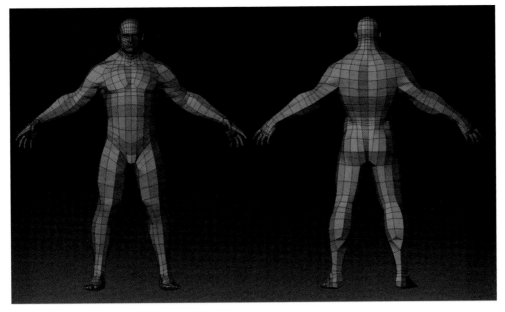

Figure 8.52 *The finished mesh*

7. To create a new ZTool, simply click the Make Adaptive Skin button under the Adaptive Skin menu. If you wish to project the sculpt into your new animated-ready mesh, make sure that projection is on in the Tool → Projection menu, and set the density in Tool → Adaptive Skin to a level high enough to capture the sculpt. In most cases, having the Density slider set to 4 or 5 will capture all of the mesh. However, this is a setting that will be adjusted on a per-mesh basis. This will project the sculpted detail into the new topology and create a new ZTool in your Tool palette. You may notice that the poly-paint also transfers. This can be useful if you need to transfer both sculpture as well as texture detail from one mesh to another.

Remeshing a Head with NEX

Now that you have seen how to use the topology tools, let's look at an entirely different approach to remeshing. In this section, I'll show how to use a third-party Maya plug-in called NEX.

Once NEX is installed, you'll begin with a topology map drawn in ZBrush using poly-painting just as you did earlier in this chapter. Although a topology map is not necessary, it is a useful tool to help you plan the edge flow ahead of time and give yourself a guide for at least the starting loops. I find it useful to begin a mesh, although often the end topology will deviate somewhat from the original plan.

Creating the Initial Mesh with NEX

NEX is included as a demo on this book's DVD. You can download it and several instructional videos at draster.com. After running the installer, you will need to activate NEX in Maya. NEX has many extremely valuable modeling tools, and in this section I will only scratch the surface by covering one called Quad Draw. I encourage you to look at the videos of other NEX tools and see how it can be further incorporated into your workflow. Take the following steps to configure NEX as a Maya plug-in:

1. Run the NEX installer. When this is complete, start Maya.
2. In the Maya interface, select Windows → Settings And Preferences → Plug-In Manager.
3. Make sure to select Loaded and Auto Load on the line marked dRasterMaya.mll (Figure 8.53). This ensures that NEX will load every time Maya starts and is always available.

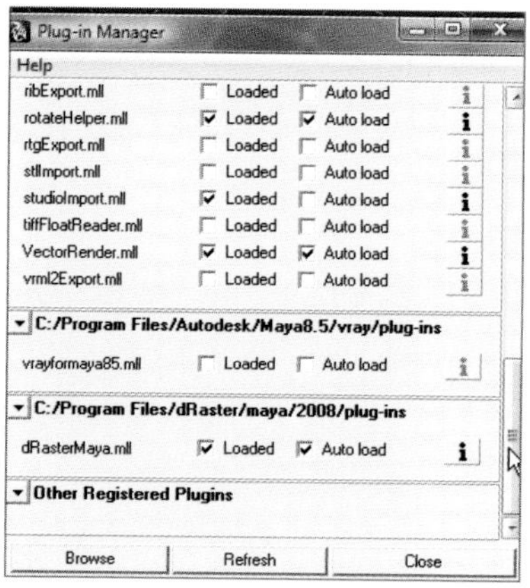

Figure 8.53 Setting NEX to Auto Load with Maya

NEX is now loaded and ready for use. You can access the NEX panel in the user interface in one of two ways. The first is clicking the NEX icon in the upper-right corner of the screen, shown in Figure 8.54(a). You can also invoke the NEX panel by clicking the NEX menu in Polygon menu and selecting NEX Panel (Figure 8.54(b)).

1. You will begin by loading the head model into Maya. This model is included on the DVD as basehead.obj. This is an export of the midsubdivision level from ZBrush. When I exported, I made sure the polygon count was less than 1 million, since I know my system cannot handle that many polygons in Maya. It is only important to have

enough faces to represent the major forms of the high-resolution mesh. Import the model by selecting File → Import in Maya.

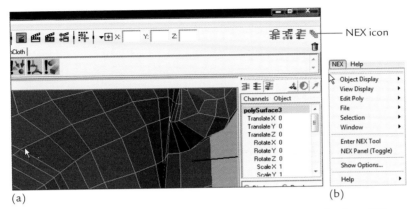

(a)   (b)

Figure 8.54 *Two ways to access NEX: (a) its panel icon, (b) the NEX menu*

2. When you load the model into ZBrush, you will want to add the topology guide map. This map is also included as a TIFF file on the DVD as topoMap_head.tif. To add it to the mesh session, add a new Blinn shader to the head geometry. Open the Attribute Editor for the shader, and in the Color channel, attach the topology guide map (Figure 8.55).

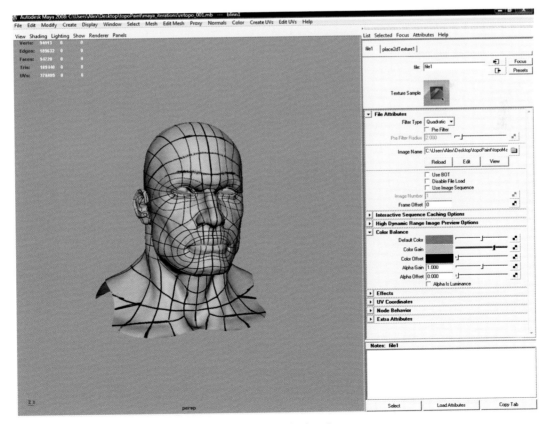

Figure 8.55 *The topology guide map assigned to the head*

3. To help isolate the base model so that you don't accidentally select it while you are working, create a new layer for it called *base head*. Add the head model, and set the layer to Reference. This way, you can see and draw topology on the head, but you cannot accidentally select the geometry.

4. At this stage, also turn on X-ray shading mode. Because you will be building new faces that often will appear just inside the surface of the base model, you need some way to see both the base model and the new faces. If you don't activate X-ray shading mode, you won't be able to see the topology as you work. X-ray shading is accessed via the viewport Shading menu option (Figure 8.56). Figure 8.57 shows the head loaded into the basehead layer and X-ray shading on.

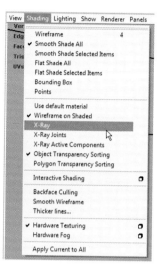

Figure 8.56 X-ray shading mode

Because you have a map on the base head and X-ray shading turned on, some of these illustrations may look a little strange. I assure you that when you are rotating the model around it is much easier to see what you are doing while you work. You can always toggle off X-ray as well as the basehead layer's visibility if you find you are getting lost.

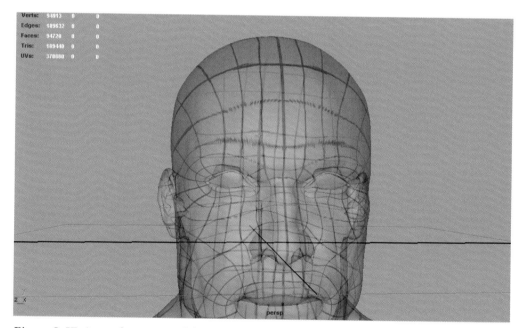

Figure 8.57 A new layer created for the head and X-ray shading on

5. Make sure nothing is selected, and activate the NEX menu by clicking the icon in the upper right of the screen. Click the Quad Draw button, and from its option menu, select the base head. This tells NEX you will be drawing new polygons on the surface of the basehead object. Figure 8.58 shows the screen with Quad Draw activated.

6. Draw the first face by placing four dots where the vertices should be. You will place these dots by clicking each point intersection on the topology guide map, as shown in Figure 8.59. Although Quad Draw is activated, these dots appear as green points on the model. If you make a mistake and need to move a point, simply drag it with the middle mouse button to where you want it to be. If you need to delete a point, hold down Ctrl. Notice that your pointer now has an X on it. Drag across any points or faces you want to remove, and they will disappear when you release the mouse.

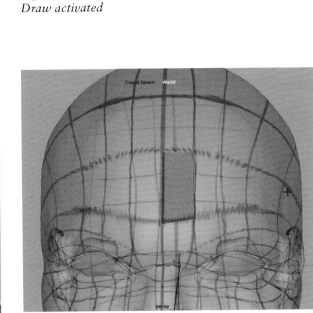

Figure 8.58 Quad Draw activated

Figure 8.59 Drawing the first face

7. To generate a polygon face from these points, hold down the Shift key, and click in the middle of these four points; a face will be generated. Before you continue to work, you'll want to set this up so that the new faces are shaded differently from the originals, and you'll also want to activate mirror mode. Exit quad draw mode by clicking the quad draw button again. Press F8 to enter object mode, and select the new face. With the face selected, add a Blinn shader, and set the color to a light red, as shown in Figure 8.60. This will help you clearly see the new topology as it is built.

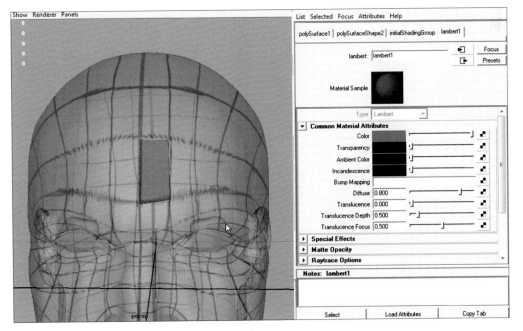

Figure 8.60 Adding a red Blinn to the new faces

8. You want to mirror this as an instance to the other side of the head so you can see the mesh grow on both sides. With the face selected, select Edit → Duplicate Special. In the Duplicate Special Options dialog box, select Instance as the geometry type, and enter **–1** in the X scale field (Figure 8.61). Click OK, and the face will now mirror to the other side.

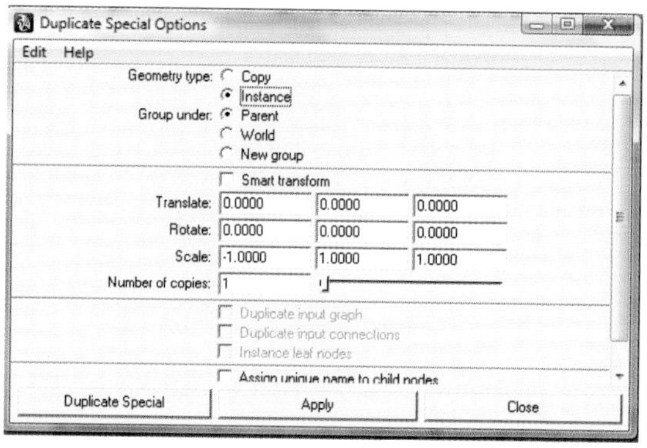

Figure 8.61 *The Duplicate Special Options dialog box*

The next stage of creating the initial mesh is to draw new faces.

9. With the new face selected, enter Quad Draw again. NEX will understand that you want to add to the selected topology. Draw more points based on the guide map, as shown in Figure 8.62. Remember that to build faces for each set of four points, hold down Shift and click inside each of the four new faces to generate the polygon (Figure 8.63).

10. Figure 8.64 shows the eye area generated in this manner. Notice the empty triangle area on the side of the nose. You will correct this later using the standard Maya polygon tools. Often you will need to finesse the topology beyond what you originally planned in the guide map.

11. At this point, it is a matter of tracing the guide topology of the face and drawing new topology as you go (Figure 8.65).

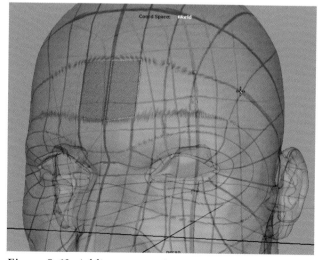

Figure 8.62 *Adding more points*

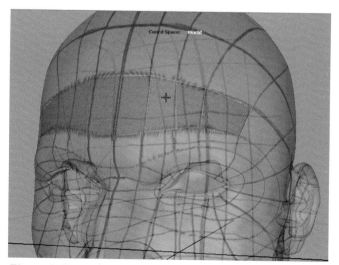

Figure 8.63 *Making the new faces*

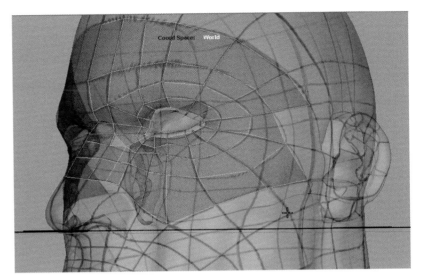

Figure 8.64 *Remeshing the eye area*

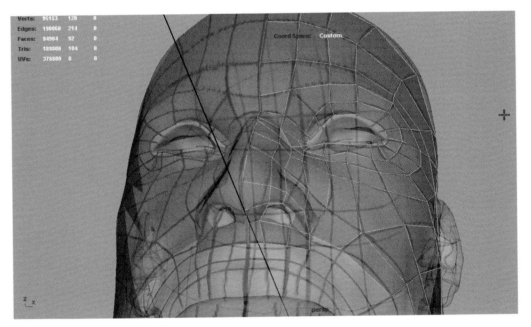

Figure 8.65 *Drawing topology*

12. In the nose area, continue the loop under the nostrils (Figure 8.66). As I mentioned, the guide map is only a guide, and the topology may change. Exit Quad Draw, and select the Cut Polygon tool. In Figure 8.67 you can see me redirect these edges so the loop continues down under the nose.

13. Continue around the mouth, as shown in Figure 8.68.

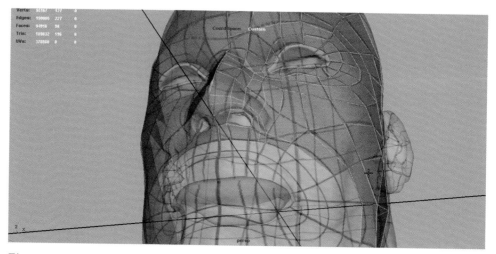

Figure 8.66 *Drawing the faces under the nose*

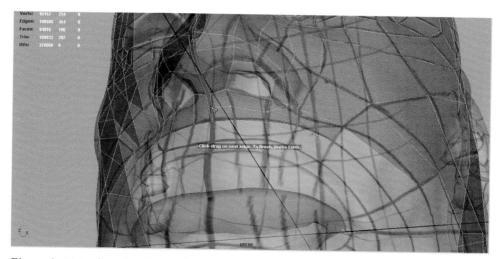

Figure 8.67 *Redirecting faces using the Split Polygon tool*

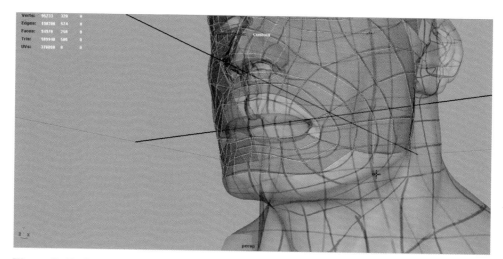

Figure 8.68 *Continuing the faces around the mouth*

14. In Quad Draw, you can move components like edges and points. In Figure 8.69 I have moved the edges around the mouth to the very center of the lips. To move a component, hover over a point or edge, and then drag with the middle mouse button to move it. As it moves, it will remain "stuck" to the basehead surface.

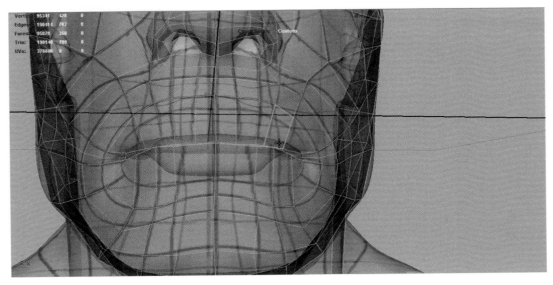

Figure 8.69 *Lip edges moved in*

15. You will now cut a new loop in these long faces. Hold down Shift, and a dotted line will appear, previewing the new edge loop. Move the mouse while holding down Shift, and you will see how interactive placement of the loop is possible. Click to execute this loop.

Figure 8.70 shows the face topology as it stands so far. I have turned off visibility on the head layer to make it easier to see in the image. At this point, you will build the remainder of the topology to the neck and back of head, leaving the ears for last.

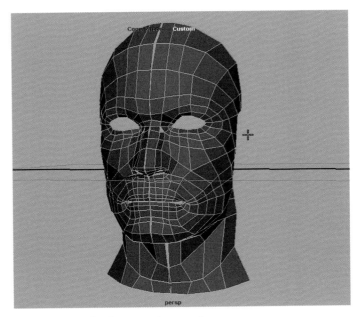

Figure 8.70 *The face topology so far*

16. Continue to build the faces surrounding the ear area (Figure 8.71). I like to leave the ears for last, since often I will need to add more loops from the ears to define their shapes. Having the rest of the head in place makes it easier to determine where these loops will ultimately flow.

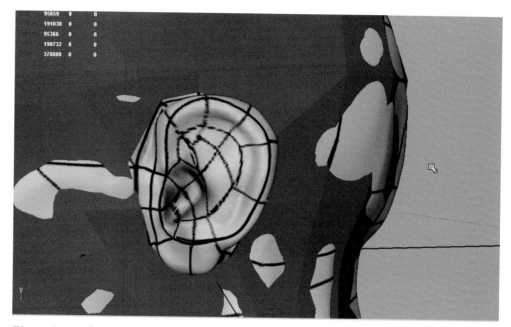

Figure 8.71 *The topology has been drawn to the ear area.*

17. Zoom into the ear area, and start building faces based on the guide map (Figure 8.72). This is a tight area, and it can be easy to get lost here. I usually take it slow and aim to create as many quads as possible. Usually ears need to be reworked a bit manually by cutting new edges and adding new faces before they are perfect. The process of adding these faces with NEX will save you a lot of time (Figure 8.73).

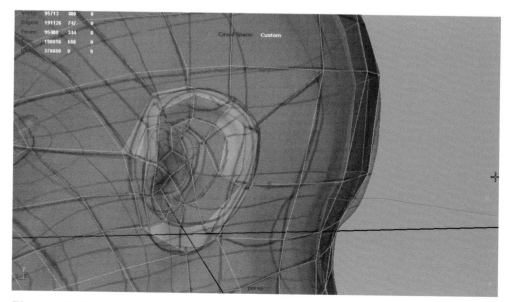

Figure 8.72 *Drawing the ear faces*

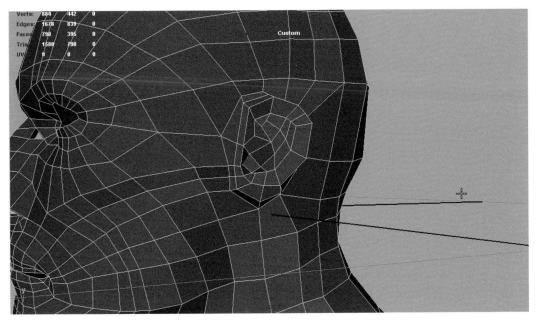

Figure 8.73 The rough ear topology

At this point, you have built your base mesh using NEX. Now you will leave NEX and use the Maya polygon tools to refine the flow of the ears and the eye and mouth areas.

1. First you will want to snap the midline and duplicate the model as a copy instead of an instance. Delete the copied side of the model, as shown in Figure 8.74. Select the edges that run down the centerline of the face. This can be done by selecting an edge and then pressing the right arrow key. Make sure to deselect any extra edges in the shoulders or mouth area.

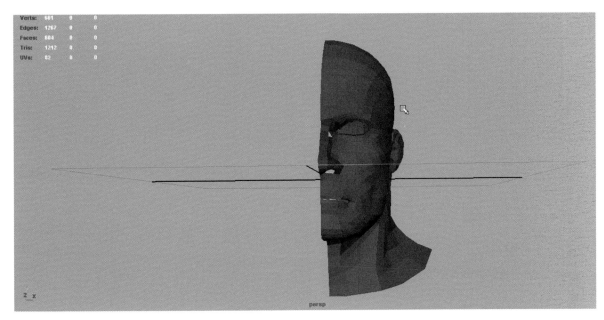

Figure 8.74 Delete the instance side of the geometry.

2. Convert this edge selection to points by pressing Ctrl+F9. With the vertices of the midline selected, press the W key to enter move mode. Hold down the X key, and move the vertices toward the centerline. They will snap along this line, closing any gaps. If this does not work, then you need to turn off Keep Spacing on the Move tool. Hold down the W key and the left mouse button to see the Move marking menu; make sure Keep Spacing is deselected (Figure 8.75).

3. With the mesh selected, click Edit → Duplicate Special, and in the option box, set From Instance to Copy. Click the Duplicate Special button, which will make a new copy of the mesh mirrored on the opposite side.

4. Select both sides, and click Mesh → Combine to merge them into one model. Now, to merge the vertices down the centerline, go into vertex mode, and select the center verts of the head (Figure 8.76). Click Edit Mesh → Merge Options. In the option box, set the threshold to .05, and click Merge to merge the points of the centerline.

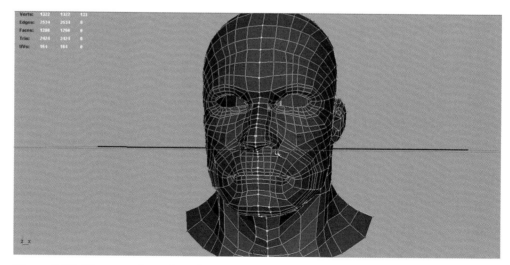

Figure 8.75 *The Move Marking menu*

Figure 8.76 *The centerline selected*

5. You may want to check to make sure the points have merged by turning on Border Edge view. Go to Display → Polygons → Custom Polygon Display, and make sure Border Edges is on. Click Apply and Close, and now the edges between unmerged verts will be highlighted in green.

6. Check the model to be sure all the center vertices are merged. Figure 8.77 shows the topology at this stage.

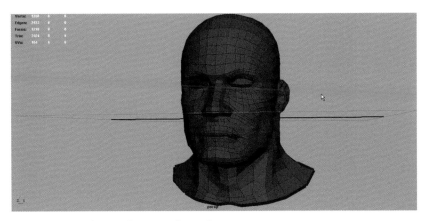

Figure 8.77 The newly merged topology

Adding the Eye and Mouth Bags

In this section, you will add the internal structure of the character's mouth as well as the thickness of the eyelids. The inside of the mouth is called the *mouth bag*, and it is there to prevent you from seeing into the character's skull when he opens his mouth. The video for this process is included on the DVD.

At this point, you will extrude the eyelids inward and create a mouth bag. The eyelid extrusion is to help add thickness to the lids, and the mouth bag exists to keep the head from appearing empty when the mouth is opened.

1. To extrude the eyelids, select one edge from both eyeholes. Select Mesh → Fill Hole to create a polygon face in the hole, as shown in Figure 8.78.

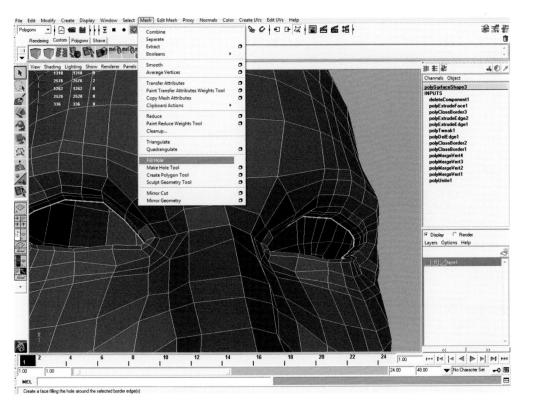

Figure 8.78 Using the Fill Hole tool

2. Click Edit Mesh, and make sure Keep Faces Together is on. Now click Extrude (Figure 8.79). Use the Move Manipulator to extrude the face back into the head, giving thickness to the eyelid. You can repeat this extrusion multiple times to add edge loops by pressing the G hotkey. This will repeat the last command in Maya.

3. To generate the mouth bag, fill the mouth hole by selecting an edge and then selecting Mesh → Fill Hole. Extrude this face into the head (Figure 8.80).

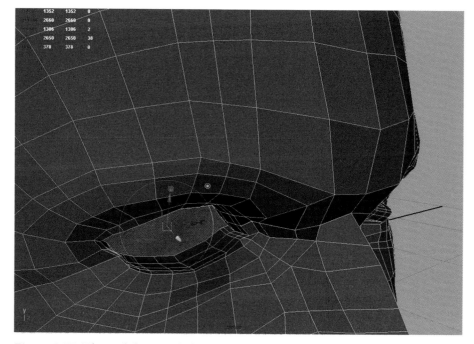

Figure 8.79 The eyelids extruded in

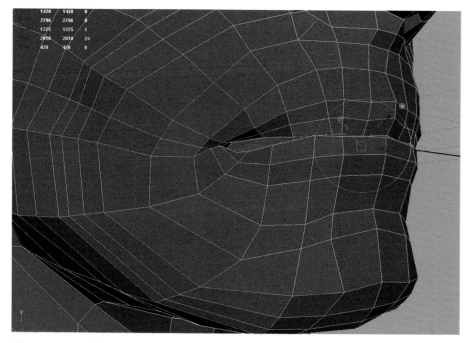

Figure 8.80 Filling the mouth hole

4. Rotate to the inside of the head, select the points of the mouth face, and spread them out into the shape of the mouth cavity. Once you have a suitable space created, select the mouth face, and extrude it back again into the head (Figure 8.81). Once you are halfway in, rotate the faces (Figure 8.82), and extrude them down the throat, scaling them down. Now you can delete the mouth face.

5. Finally, remove the triangle at the bridge of the nose by selecting one edge and using the To Edge Ring And Collapse function in the Edit Mesh marking menu. You can find this by selecting an edge, holding down Ctrl, and clicking the edge. From the Marking menu, select Edge Ring and then To Edge Ring And Collapse.

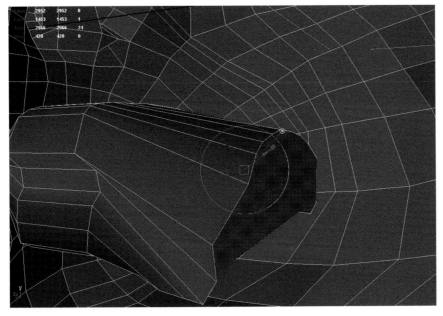

Figure 8.81 *The mouth extruded in*

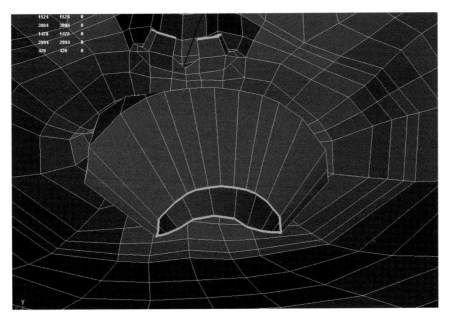

Figure 8.82 *Rotating the mouth bag faces*

The base mesh is now complete. At this stage, I will show you how to take this new ordered base mesh and apply it to your ZTool, creating a new ZTool that retains all your sculpted work but uses the new low-resolution topology.

This process is shown on video that is available on the DVD. Please refer to this video for more information.

The ZTool of this demo is also available on the DVD. In it you will find the high-resolution head as well as the remeshed low-resolution base appended as a subtool. The two heads sit on top of each other in 3D space. In this section, you'll learn two ways to use this remeshed base. The first technique will create a new ZTool with the new topology.

1. Select the Base Mesh subtool. Turn on double-sided view by selecting Tool → Display Properties → Double.

2. Load the headZtool.ztl model from the DVD. Draw it on the canvas, and go into edit mode with the T key. You will notice there are two subtools: the high-resolution head and the new low-resolution topology. Select the remeshed head, and make sure it is the active subtool. Hide the high-resolution head by turning off its visibility icon in the SubTool menu. With the low-resolution head selected, use a show marquee to hide the back of the head so you can see the mouth bag (Figure 8.83).

3. Press the W key to enter transpose mode. You will use topology masking to mask the outside of the head down to the lips, leaving the mouth bag unmasked. Hold down Ctrl and drag toward the mouth to mask the face (Figure 8.84).

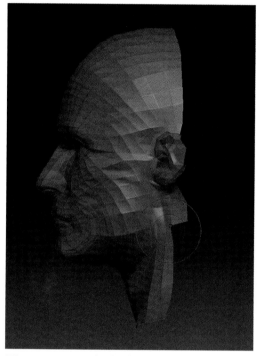

Figure 8.83 Hide the back half of the head.

4. Now, rotating to the back of the head, you can see inside that the mouth bag is unmasked. Ctrl-click the background to invert the mask for the mouth bag, which is now masked (Figure 8.85). You want to now polygroup the mouth bag separately from the head. To do this, select Tool → Masking → Hide Pt. This hides any unmasked faces.

5. The mouth bag will now be isolated on-screen. Select Tool → Polygroups → Group Visible to polygroup the mouth bag faces.
   You may want to also polygroup the faces of the inner eye with the same technique. This is shown in detail on the DVD video for this tutorial.

6. At this stage, with all the new geometry polygrouped, divide the head to four subdivision levels, and store a morph target by selecting Tool → Morph Target → Store MT.

7. Turn on the visibility of the high-resolution head by clicking into the eyeball icon in the SubTool menu.

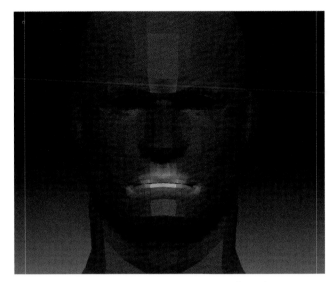

Figure 8.84 *Use topology masking to isolate the inner mouth.*

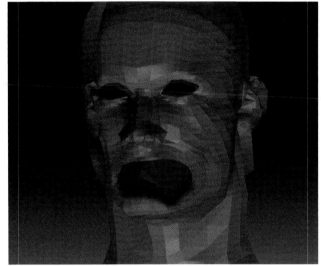

Figure 8.85 *Rotate to the back of the head, and invert the mask so the inner mouth is masked.*

8. With both tools visible and the remeshed head still selected, click the Project All button in the SubTool menu. This will project the remeshed head onto the original head. Notice that this will create strange spikes in the geometry (Figure 8.86). This is a result of the mouth bag trying to project as well. That is why you polygrouped it and stored a morph target. You can also reduce issues like this using the PA Dist and PA Blur sliders discussed in the following sidebar.

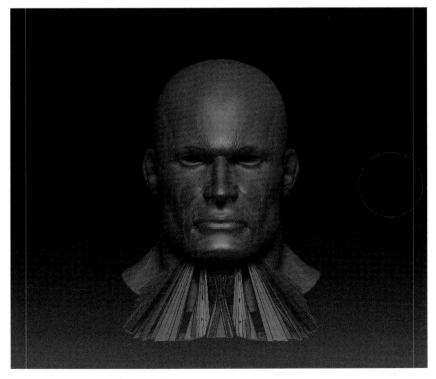

Figure 8.86 *Projection problems*

Under ProjectAll in the Subtool menu, you will find two sliders called PA Dist and PA Blur. These stand for Project All Distance and Project All Blur. Using these sliders can help prevent the mouth bag from projecting into the mesh. I included this process since it will always work in those cases where the sliders may not be able to stop all the points from projecting. PA Distance adjusts the project distance of the mesh and is useful for tweaking tight areas like between fingers and toes. PA Blur smoothes the mesh while projecting, giving you further control when areas are problematic. These sliders are best used by hiding parts of the mesh, applying your PA Dist and PA Blur settings, and using Project All on isolated areas of the model. These settings will differ for every model, so it is important to experiment with them to find what works best in each scenario.

9. Hide the high-resolution head again, and click Switch under Tool → Morph Target. Hold down Ctrl+Shift and click the head so only the polygrouped mouth bag is visible; mask this, and show the head again. From the Brush menu, select the Morph brush (Figure 8.87). Turn up ZIntensity to 100, and turn on X symmetry. Brush around the surface to restore the detail while keeping the mouth bag isolated (Figure 8.88).

You have now successfully restored the detail to the head without the problem of the mouth bag trying to project as well. Often this process will require some resculpting at the lip and eye seams, but it is a huge time-saver compared to resculpting an entire model.

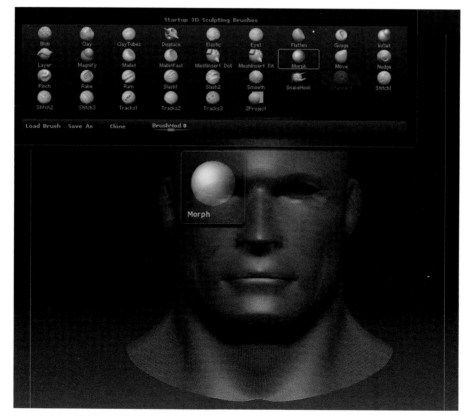

Figure 8.87 The Morph brush

Figure 8.88 The newly restored details

What's Next?

In this chapter, you saw how logical edge flow is beneficial in that it allows for more natural deformations in animation. It also supports the texture artist by giving logical places to split the UV seams as well as helping to keep textures from stretching during animation. You have seen two different approaches to remeshing a model as well as some tricks to adding geometry to a ZTool without disturbing the high-resolution levels.

nine

Texturing

In this chapter, you'll learn *techniques for creating a realistic skin texture for the male figure model using polypainting and reference imagery.* Polypainting *refers to the process of applying RGB values to the polygons of the model using the sculpting brushes. In essence, you are painting colors directly onto the geometry of the model. The colors you paint on the model can be converted into 2D texture maps, which are exported from ZBrush and can then be combined for rendering in a shader network and rendered in mental ray for Maya 2009. You can use these same texture maps in shader networks in similar 3D programs as well.*

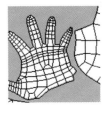

UV Texture Coordinates

3D modeling and animation programs use X, Y, and Z coordinates to describe the position of a point in 3D space. Likewise, U and V coordinates are used to describe the position of a point on a 3D surface. Textures applied to a 3D model are actually 2D images wrapped across the surface of the model. By defining the U and V coordinates, you enable the software to determine how the 2D texture should be positioned on the 3D surface.

If you can imagine drawing a dot on a cardboard box and then unfolding the box and laying it out flat on the ground, you can see how the position of the dot on the unfolded box relates to the dot on the box when it is assembled into a cube (see Figure 9.1).

The first step in preparing a model for texture mapping is defining its U and V coordinates. You can then use the coordinates as a guide in a paint program to help you paint the textures so that they appear correct on the surface of the model.

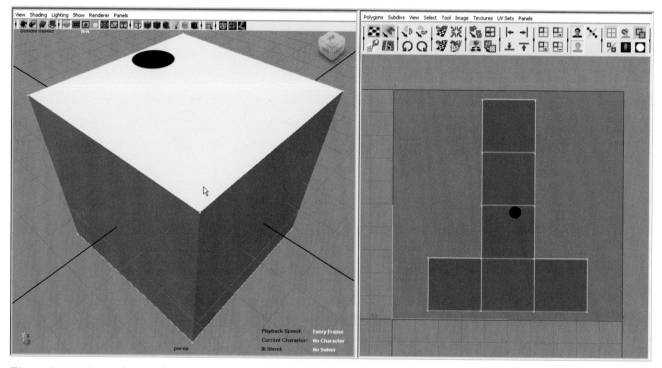

Figure 9.1 *UV coordinates describe the position of a point on the surface of a 3D object.*

U and V coordinates must be explicitly mapped for polygon and subdivision surface models; by contrast, NURBS surfaces have implicit UVs that are part of the parameterization of the surface itself. This book is concerned with polygon mesh-based characters, so we won't discuss NURBS UV coordinates. UV coordinates not only affect how textures are placed on the surface, but also determine how fur and hair behave, along with other texture-based effects such as bump and displacement maps.

The 2D arrangement of U and V texture coordinates is referred to as the *UV layout*. Keep several points in mind when creating a UV layout for any 3D model, including characters:

- You have the choice of either letting the computer generate UV coordinates, using any of several methods of automatic UV mapping, or defining the coordinates by hand so that they are "human readable" (meaning that the shapes of the UV coordinates and the way they relate to 3D forms can easily be recognized by human artists). Human-readable coordinates are usually preferable in most situations because they allow for easy texture editing by artists using 2D paint programs. This is very important when working in a production pipeline where teams of specialized artists divide the work of creating characters (see Figure 9.2).

- Overlapping UV coordinates must be avoided at all costs; they can cause serious artifacts on the surface of the rendered model and even crash the rendering software.

- Stretching, pinching, and warping of the coordinates should be kept to a minimum as much as possible.

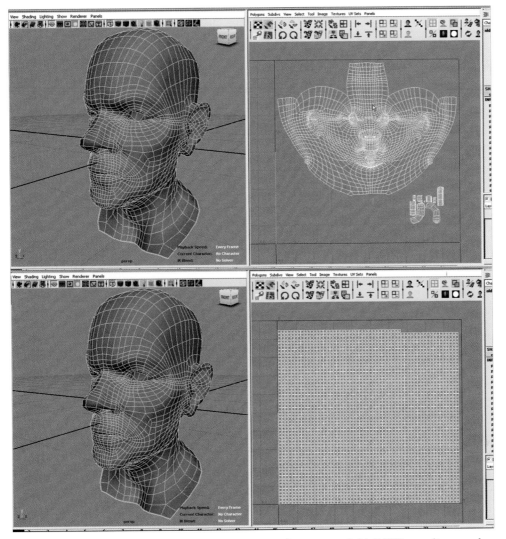

Figure 9.2 *The head model in the top image uses "human-readable" UV coordinates; the head model in the bottom image uses automatic UV mapping generated in ZBrush.*

- The seams where the edges of any two sections of the layout (known as *UV shells*) meet should be strategically placed in areas that are less visible or follow the contours of the geometry. The seams can be noticeable in a render, and are even more so when hair and fur are applied.
- There are many ways UV coordinates can be mapped for characters. Most of the time, you want to prioritize the space in your UV layout for areas of the model that will receive more detail. So the face and hands may need to use more space than the rest of the body. Typically, 25 percent of the layout is devoted to the head and hands, and the remaining 75 percent is devoted to the body; however, these proportions may differ depending on what you are trying to achieve.

Mapping UV Texture Coordinates

Most 3D modeling and animation programs have tools that allow you to map the UV coordinates of a model. For the most part, these tools are fairly similar from one package to the next. In addition, there are stand-alone UV mapping programs, such as UVLayout by Headus, devoted to mapping UV texture coordinates quickly and easily. Pixologic's ZBrush has automatic UV mapping tools that are fairly basic but not necessarily ideal for creating UV coordinates for professional-quality models.

This chapter demonstrates how to create UV texture coordinates for the male figure model using Headus UVLayout. This chapter uses the Professional version of the program. This has a few features that are not available in the demo version, such as symmetry mode and copy-and-paste UVs; however, you should still be able to follow along using the demo version. UVLayout is fast and easy to use. Even the demo version is, in many ways, superior to the UV texture-editing tools that are part of larger 3D packages such as Autodesk's Maya. You can download UVLayout from www.uvlayout.com.

UVLayout Demo Modes

The demo version will allow you to export an OBJ file with UV coordinates at the end of the session; however, if you reopen the same model in UVLayout, the UV coordinates are deleted, so you'll have to recreate your work. You'll also find versions of the model on the accompanying DVD that have UV coordinates created in UVLayout, so you can continue working through the exercises using these examples.

You can run the demo version of UVLayout in one of three modes:

- When you're working in the default demo mode, only the very basic tools are available.
- When you're working in hobbyist trial mode, all the hobbyist/student-level tools are available, but you will not be able to save your work. Select About UVLayout → Try Hobbyist Version to activate this mode.
- When you're working in professional trial mode, all tools are available, but again you will not be able to save. Select About UVLayout → Try Professional Version to activate this mode.

For more information about the various modes and restrictions of the modes, visit the following site:

www.uvlayout.com/index.php?option=com_wrapper&Itemid=76

Preparing the Model for UV Texture Mapping

You can map the UV texture coordinates at any stage of the modeling process. You can even use polypainting techniques in ZBrush (covered later in the chapter) to paint colors on the model before creating UV coordinates. ZBrush allows you to import UV coordinates created in other programs into your model at any time, which means you have the freedom to change UV texture coordinates or even create alternate versions of the UV layout if needed.

For the sake of instruction, this chapter introduces UV layout techniques before texture painting, but keep in mind that, in practice, the order of the workflow is actually much more flexible.

When you are ready to create UV texture coordinates for your ZBrush sculpt, follow these steps:

1. In ZBrush, load the `textureStart.ztl` ZTool found in the Chapter 9 folder of the DVD. Draw the tool on the canvas, and switch to edit mode (T).

2. Set the SDiv slider to the lowest subdivision level.

3. In the Tool palette, scroll down, and expand the Export subpalette.

4. Make sure the Qud button is on. Turn the Txr and Grp buttons off (see Figure 9.3).

   When you enable the Txr button, ZBrush will include the UV coordinates as part of the exported OBJ file for the current subdivision level. Since you're going to create new UVs, you don't need this button to be on now. The Grp button splits the object into sections. Always turn this button off.

5. The values for the Scale, X Offset, Y Offset, and Z Offset sliders have been determined so that the size and position of the model are consistent when the model is exported to another 3D program such as Maya. For the most part, you can leave these values the way they are.

6. Save the model as `maleFigureUVs_v01.obj` to a folder on your local disk. This model is also available on the DVD that accompanies this book.

7. Close ZBrush.

Figure 9.3 *The Export options are set before the tool is exported as an OBJ file.*

UV Mapping with headus UVLayout

In this section, you'll create the UV coordinates using UVLayout by headus. To download a version of UVLayout, visit `www.uvlayout.com`, and click the link that says Try. Install the program on your computer. The UVLayout demo expires after about one month, at which time you need to download and install a new version.

The standard workflow for mapping UVs in UVLayout begins by defining the shells. You do this by selecting edge paths along the surface of the object and cutting these sections off of the model. It looks as though you're breaking the model into pieces, but in reality you are just splitting the object into UV shells. As you'll see, the 3D display gives you a more intuitive sense of how the shells are defined.

Once you have split a shell from the body, you can then flatten the shell and use interactive tools to unfold the UVs and fix any warping, stretching, or overlapping that may occur.

1. Start UVLayout. Click the Load button, and use the file browser to find the `maleFigureUVs_v01.obj` file you exported from ZBrush. Once it is loaded, the figure appears in the UVLayout editor window as a 3D object. Click the Display button to expand the display options. Make sure the view mode is set to Ed (edit mode), as shown in Figure 9.4.

2. Zoom in to the object by right-clicking and dragging in a blank part of the view. Rotate the view by dragging with the left mouse button. Zoom in to the character's left shoulder.

3. To define the UV shell for the left arm, you'll want to cut along the edge. To do this, hold the mouse over an edge, and press the C key. This highlights an edge path.

UVLayout automatically defines the edge path. The path stops when the software is not able to determine how to continue the path. The edge path may not follow exactly where you want to create the cut, but that's OK; it's very easy to edit the edge path. Use the W key to weld stray edges back together. Once you get the hang of it, you can precisely define the edges of the shell as you see fit. Sometimes it takes a little back-and-forth between cutting and welding.

4. Continue creating edge paths around the left arm and under the armpit until you've defined a loop all the way around the arm.

5. To remove the edge paths that stray from the edge you want to cut, press the W key while holding the mouse over the stray edge paths.

6. Once you have defined the cutting edge, hold the mouse over the left arm, and press Enter. The arm will separate from the body (Figure 9.5).

7. To move the arm away from the body, hold the spacebar and middle-mouse-drag over the left arm. If the arm will not move away from the body, double-check and make sure all the edges around the arm have been cut properly using the C key.

Remember, you're not actually breaking the model apart; this is just a 3D representation of the UV shells.

Symmetry Mode

The Professional version of UVLayout has a symmetry mode, which mirrors actions from one side of the figure to the other. To activate symmetry mode, click the Find button, and then select an edge that runs along the centerline of the model. Tap the spacebar. One half of the model will turn dark gray to show that symmetry mode is enabled. Selecting, cutting, and welding edges on the brighter side will be mirrored to this dark side, and vice versa.

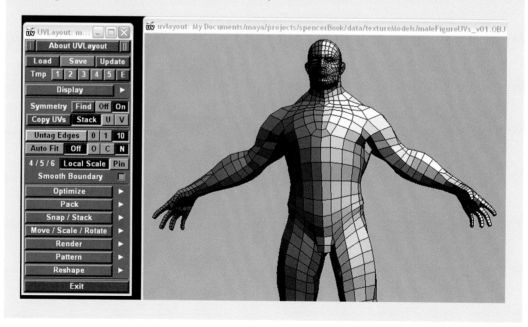

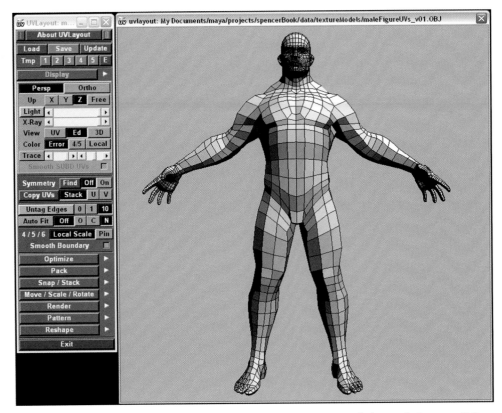

Figure 9.4 *The male figure model is loaded into UVLayout, and the mode is set to Edit.*

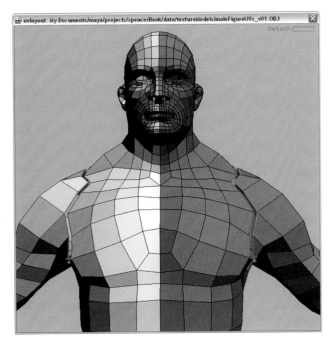

Figure 9.5 *The UV shell for the arm is defined by cutting selected edges. When a complete path has been created, pressing the Enter key separates the arm shell from the rest of the figure.*

8. Use the same process to separate the hand from the arm.

9. Move the hand away from the arm. Use the C key to cut a line of edges along the front of the arm. Press Enter when you have selected a complete line of edges from the inside of the arm down to the wrist.

10. Use the same process to separate the top of the hand from the bottom of the hand. This will require a little more care as you define the line of edges around the perimeter of the hand.

11. When you are finished, you should have one shell for the arm and two for the hand (Figure 9.6). At this point, you are ready to drop these shells so that they can be edited in UV mode. Hold the mouse over each shell, and press D. The shells will disappear from the 3D view. That's OK; they are just being dropped to UV mode.

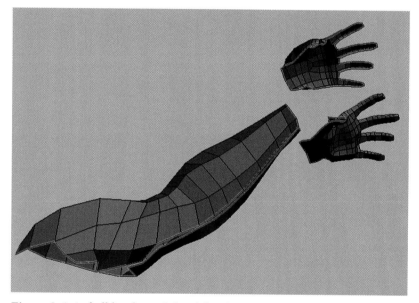

Figure 9.6 *A shell has been defined for the arm; two shells are created for the hand.*

Creating Shells

Here are some tips for creating shells:

- Separate the top of the foot from the bottom. Be careful of edges on the insides of the toes that may be hard to see; you may want to zoom inside the model to find these.
- Separate the ears from the head.
- Split a seam along the inside of the leg so that the tubular structure can be flattened by the software properly. You can also do this for the neck.
- Each shell that you create will be flattened out. Keep this in mind as you define the shells; you want to make it as easy as possible for the software to figure out how to flatten the shell.

12. Continue the process to create shells for the other arm, each leg, each foot, the front of the torso, the back of the torso, the neck, the face, and the back of the head, as shown in Figure 9.7.

13. Drop each piece by pressing D while holding the cursor over each shell. When all shells are dropped, the software will automatically switch to UV edit mode.

14. You'll see the figure again with green lines outlining the shells. To switch to UV edit mode, click UV under the display settings.

Editing UVs

Editing UVs involves flattening each shell, moving UV points to prevent overlapping, and arranging the shells in such a way as to optimize texture space.

To flatten a shell, hold the cursor over the shell, and hold the F hotkey. The shell will start to distort as the software attempts to flatten the 3D geometry into 2D texture coordinates. As the shell is flattened, you'll see the polygons change color. The color feedback indicates stretching or warping that will appear in the UVs. You want the shells to be as light green as possible. Blue and red areas indicate overlapping or warped UVs (see Figure 9.8). Try to reduce these colored areas as much as possible.

In the UV editor, you can use the following mouse and keyboard actions:

- Select a shell by clicking it.
- Move the shell by holding the spacebar and middle-mouse-dragging.
- Rotate the shell by holding the spacebar while left-clicking and dragging.
- Scale the shell by holding the spacebar, right-clicking, and dragging.
- To move an individual UV, select the shell, hold the Ctrl key, and middle-mouse-drag the UV.
- Cut an edge using the C hotkey.
- Weld an edge using the W hotkey.

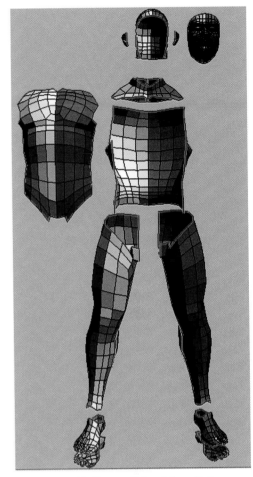

Figure 9.7 *Shells are defined for all the major parts of the model.*

Many more functions are described in the help files. Click About UVLayout in the UVLayout control panel to open the documentation.

Once you have flattened your UV shells, in the Professional version of UVLayout, you can use the Optimize menu's Overlap option to finalize the flattening of the shells. The Overlap feature will find and highlight any overlapping UVs in the layout. To run it, expand the Optimize menu, and click Overlap. When you discover overlapping UVs, you can fix them by holding the Ctrl key while middle-mouse-dragging individual UV points so that they no longer overlap. Parts of the mesh such as the toes and ears are prone to overlapping UVs (see Figure 9.9).

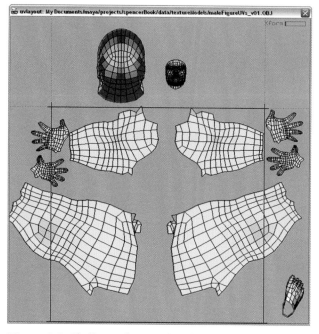

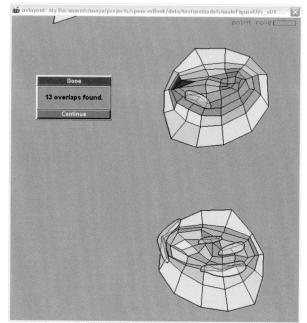

Figure 9.8 *Shells are flattened in the UV editor. The color feedback tells you whether the coordinates are warped or stretched. Ideally you want the shells to all be light green.*

Figure 9.9 *The Professional version of UVLayout can find and highlight overlapping UVs. Some of the overlaps are found in the ear.*

If you are using the demo version of UVLayout, the Overlap feature is not available. In this case, take the time to inspect your UV coordinates carefully for any overlaps. Taking the time to do this now will save you the trouble of having to re-create the UV texture coordinates later. The demo version allows you to export UV coordinates with the model when you are done; but if you import the model again to make adjustments, the coordinates are deleted, and you'll need to go through the entire process again.

The final step in the process is arranging the UVs within the square space of the UV. UVLayout will automatically pack the UV shells for you using the controls in the Pack menu. You can choose to allow UVLayout to automatically rotate the shells to optimize the texture space. Figure 9.10 shows one such arrangement. Before packing the shells, I scaled the head and hands up somewhat so that more texture space is devoted to these parts of the body.

Click the Save button, and save the model as `maleFigureUVs_v02.OBJ`. You can find a version of the model in the Chapter 9 folder of the DVD.

The Save feature on the demo version exports the model with UVs. This means you can actually import the UVs created in the demo version in ZBrush. However, if you try to reopen the model in UVLayout, the UV coordinates will be automatically removed. This is to encourage you to buy the Student, Hobbyist, or Professional versions of the software. In either case, you can also use the `maleFigureUVs_v02.OBJ` file in the Chapter 9 folder of the DVD to continue the exercise.

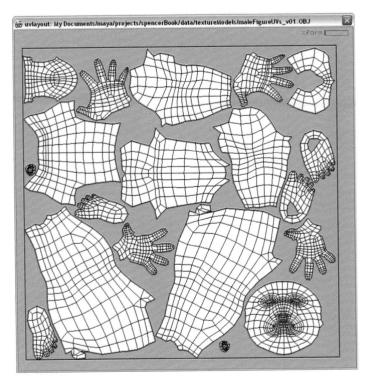

Figure 9.10 *The UV shells are packed within the square area of the texture space.*

Importing UVs into the Tool

The UV coordinates created in UVLayout (or any other 3D application) can be imported into the ZBrush tool at any time. To do this, take the following steps:

1. Open ZBrush. Load the `textureStart.ztl` tool found in the Chapter 9 folder of the DVD into ZBrush. Draw the tool on the canvas, and switch to edit mode.

2. Set the SDiv level in the Geometry subpalette of the tool palette to level 1.

3. Expand the Morph target subpalette. Delete any existing morph targets, and store a new morph target.

4. Click the Import button at the top of the Tool palette. Find the `maleFigureUVs_v02.OBJ` file created in the previous section (there is a version in the Chapter 9 folder of the DVD as well), and load it into ZBrush.

   You will not notice any immediate change to the model.

5. To verify that the UVs were imported into the model, expand the Texture Map section, and click New From UV Map or New From UV Check, as shown in Figure 9.11. These buttons will create texture maps based on the imported UVs. You can see the arrangement of UVs by hovering the cursor over the texture swatch; note that ZBrush UV coordinates are upside down relative to UVLayout (and Maya's coordinates). This is not a problem and is easily corrected when the final texture maps are exported from ZBrush.

UV Check

The New From UV Check button creates a texture map that diagnoses any potential problems with the UV coordinates such as overlapping. If the texture is completely gray, there are no problems with the UVs. If there are areas that appear bright red, as shown here, you'll need to fix and reimport the UVs. If your model does not have any UV coordinates, it may disappear from the canvas when you use the New From UV Check button.

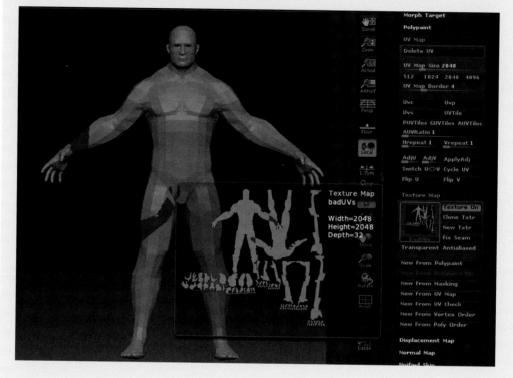

6. After checking the UV map, it's a good idea to switch to one of the higher SDiv levels to make sure the import process was successful and the model has retained the proper detail at the higher SDiv levels.

   The colors in the texture map give you a visual indication of how the UVs are laid out on the model. You can compare the colors of the texture with the colors on the 3D tool to get an idea of how one relates to the other.

7. Save the tool as maleFigureUVs.ztl. You can find a version of the tool in the Chapter 9 folder on the DVD.

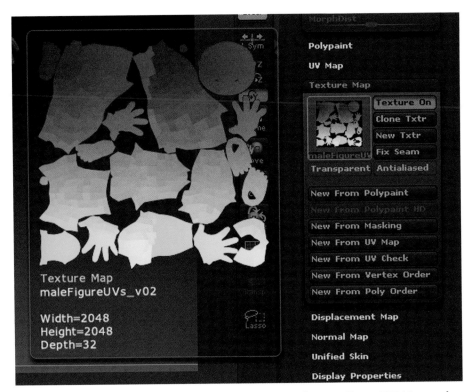

Figure 9.11 *The imported UVs can be verified using the New From UV Map and New From UV Check buttons in the Texture Map subpalette.*

Creating Texture Maps for Skin

To achieve truly realistic-looking skin in a render, it is important to think in terms of layers. Human skin is made up of layers of tissue that cover muscle, bone, blood vessels, and organs. The way in which light interacts with these layers of skin is what gives skin its unique appearance. Light is both absorbed and reflected by skin in a special way.

In general terms, when photons of light come in contact with skin, they penetrate the outermost layers of the skin, bounce around within the structure of the tissue, and are then reflected back into the environment. Warm colors such as red and orange are absorbed more deeply into the skin because their wavelengths are longer. Cooler colors such as blue and green have shorter wavelengths and are reflected back into the environment for the most part. *Subsurface scattering* is a term used to describe the effect created when light bounces around within a material such as skin. This subsurface-scattering phenomenon is what gives skin its translucent quality.

An obvious example of this phenomenon is the way in which the skin on the ear appears to glow reddish orange when there is a bright light behind it. Subsurface scattering is actually present under all lighting conditions and can be quite subtle.

Creating Textures for Subsurface-Scattering Shaders

If your goal is to render a realistic skin texture for a character in a 3D package such as Maya (using mental ray), it is important to create texture maps that work well with the special subsurface-scattering shaders used by mental ray.

Using mental ray and Other Renderers

mental ray is available as a render option in Maya, 3ds Max, and Softimage XSI. Many other renderers use shaders similar to mental ray's subsurface-scattering shader, so you should be able to adapt your ZBrush workflow for whatever software package you are using.

This chapter is not about rendering with mental ray per se, but it's important to understand a little bit about how a typical subsurface-scattering shader works when you paint texture maps in ZBrush. You'll create three texture maps to create the color of the skin. These maps can be exported and used as layers in a shader in your 3D package of choice. Over the course of painting these maps, you'll explore a few of the amazing texturing tools ZBrush has to offer. You are by no means limited to these techniques, of course; you can combine techniques and tools to create your own particular workflow.

Subsurface-Scattering Shaders

Rendering realistic skin has become much easier in recent years with the development of subsurface-scattering shader techniques in most major 3D software packages. Each software package has its own way of producing the effect using physically accurate algorithms as well as convincing "cheats" that simulate subsurface scattering. When rendering with mental ray, you can take advantage of the simple skin shader that uses lightmaps to simulate the effect of subsurface scattering. In Maya, there is a specific mental ray shader you can use for skin, labeled misss_fast_skin_maya (misss stands for Mental Images Subsurface Scattering Shader).

You don't need to be an expert in writing mental ray shaders to create realistic skin for your character, but when you are preparing to paint a realistic skin texture map for a figure, it's important to understand a little about how the misss_fast_skin_maya shader works. Rather than just paint a single texture that has a skin color, moles, freckles, veins, and so on, as if it were a single coat of paint, you'll actually be painting three color maps, which will be combined in the shader to create the look of skin and its behavior when it reacts to light. In the misss_fast_skin_maya shader, the three color maps are connected to the epidermal, subdermal, and back scatter color channels (see Figure 9.12).

By default the shader uses colors for each channel to simulate the skin. To achieve truly realistic skin, you connect texture maps to each channel. The texture maps you paint on the model in ZBrush are connected to the subsurface-scattering layers of the shader. Figure 9.13 shows a simple sphere, rendered in Maya using mental ray. Three color maps have been painted and connected to the misss_fast_skin_maya shader, which is applied to the sphere. Specular and bump maps are also used to simulate the texture of the skin. By themselves, the color maps do not look like skin, but when they are combined and carefully lit in Maya, the result can be very realistic.

The deepest layer in the skin shader is the back-scattering layer. This is where the skin meets muscle, fat, and bone. The colors applied to this layer are most apparent when an intense light is shining from the side of the character opposite the rendering camera.

The next layer up is the subdermal layer, where you'll find capillaries, scar tissue, and veins. If a character has a tattoo, some of the dark ink of the tattoo may be visible in this layer.

The top scattering layer is the epidermal layer. This is where you'll find moles, freckles, pores, some capillaries, embedded hairs and stubble, and the overall color of the skin. It is fairly common practice to use the same texture map for both the diffuse channel of the shader and the epidermal layer. Some artists also prefer to use a much lighter and less saturated version of the epidermal texture in the diffuse channel of the shader.

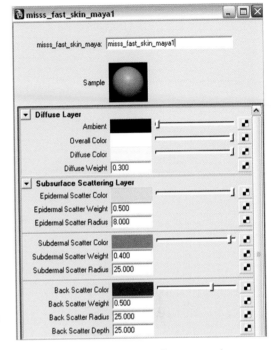

Figure 9.12 *In mental ray for Maya, the misss_fast_skin shader uses three color channels to simulate the translucent quality of skin.*

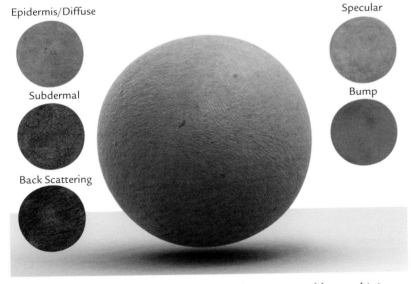

Figure 9.13 *The color of the skin on the sphere is created by combining three texture maps in the fast skin shader. Bump and specular maps also help sell the look of the skin.*

In addition to the three color maps used in the shader, you'll also want to paint a specular layer to control how the texture of the skin reflects the light source. The intensity of the specular map will allow the rendered skin to look wet or dry, oily or clean.

In ZBrush you'll paint a separate version of the texture map for each of the subsurface-scattering layers in the shader. Although this seems like a lot of work, the maps are similar enough that one map can serve as a starting point for the others. What may seem strange at first is that you'll be painting very colorful maps that will not look like skin until they are combined in the final shader.

Painting the Back-Scattering Layer in ZBrush

The back-scattering map is the deepest layer of the skin shader. It adds a quality to the skin that is subtle but missed when absent. The colors of the layer are not part of the skin but actually the color of what lies beneath the skin. The map itself does not need to be overly detailed; mostly you want to paint the model to show the muscle and fat; some hint of bone, especially on the skull; and some of the major veins and arteries.

1. Open ZBrush, and load the `maleFigureUVs.ztl` model on the canvas. Switch to edit mode, and set the SDiv slider to the highest level, which should be 6. In the Polypaint subpalette of the Tool palette, make sure Colorize is on so that you can paint on the model (Figure 9.14). When polypainting a model, you apply color information to each vertex of the model. The color values are blended across the polygons that share the vertices. This means that in order to create a detailed map that looks good in a final render, you need more polygons/vertices. The more you have, the better your texture's quality.

2. Start by filling the model with a reddish orange color. Choose something close to 196, 69, 54 in the Color Chooser. In the Color palette, click the Fill Object button (make sure a gray material is applied to the model before you start painting, such as the MatCap Gray material). If white spots appear on the model when you fill it with a color, make sure no masks have been applied to the model. Expand the Masking subpalette of the Tool palette, and click Clear.

3. Set the current sculpting brush to Standard. You want to make sure that the brush only applies color to the model and makes no change in the geometry. To do this, make sure the Rgb button on the top shelf is on and the Zadd, ZSub, M, and Mrgb buttons are off.

4. Set the RGB Intensity slider to 25. Use the Standard brush to paint the model. Use a deep, dark red for areas where there are thick muscles. Use a pale yellow for areas of bone. You can paint a light pink at the tendons. At this point, you're just blocking in color. Activate Symmetry along the x-axis in the Transform palette to make the process faster.

5. Once you are happy with the back-scattering pass, save the tool as `maleModel_BS.ztl`. You can see a version of the tool in the Chapter 9 folder on the DVD.

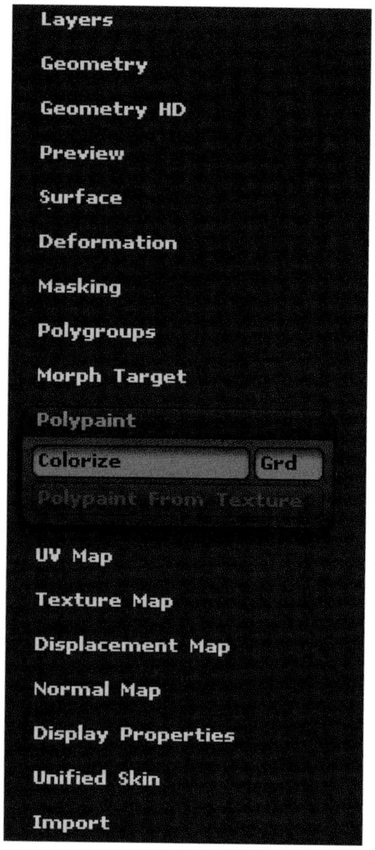

Figure 9.14 Colorize is enabled in the Polypaint subpalette of the Tool palette.

Creating the Back-Scattering Layer

Here are some tips to help you create the back-scattering layer:

- A color anatomical chart or reference model will help you determine where to paint the colors on the model to indicate thick muscle or bone.
- Use alphas and different stroke types to create variation in the colors on the model. This detail, although subtle, can add depth to the final rendered texture.
- Create striated patterns in the muscle that suggest the direction of the muscle. To do this, you can choose an Alpha setting for the brush such as 59, 60, or 61.
- Think in terms of building up layers of color in successive passes with a low RGB Intensity value as opposed to painting each area of the model completely in isolation. There's no need to get overly detailed at this point. You can paint in some of the larger veins and arteries, but make sure you consult a reference for their proper placement.

Figure 9.15 shows the model in the Flat render style so you can see just the colors of the final back scattering.

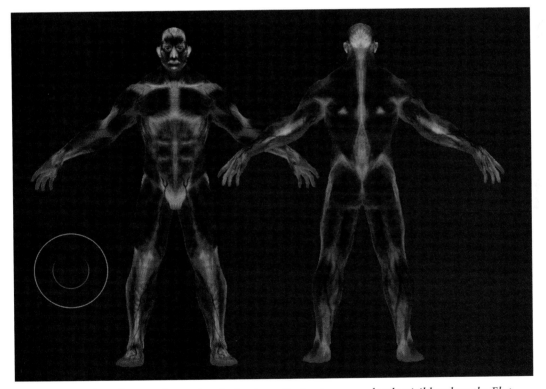

Figure 9.15 *The colors used to paint the back-scattering pass are clearly visible when the Flat material is used.*

Painting the Subdermal Layer in ZBrush

The subdermal layer lies beneath the surface of the skin. You can see a wider variety of color and detail in this layer because shorter wavelengths of light are able to penetrate to this depth. This means you can start applying cool colors such as blue and purple in some areas.

To begin the subdermal layer, you can start by painting on top of the back-scattering layer:

1. Load the `maleModel_BS.ztl` tool into ZBrush. Draw it on the canvas, and switch to edit mode.
2. Save the model immediately as `maleModel_SD1.ztl`.
3. Set the color picker to a dull pinkish color such as 188, 109, 100. Choose the Standard brush, and set the RGB Intensity slider to 10. Make sure ZAdd, ZSub, M, and MRGB are off. Only RGB should be on.
4. Choose the Spray Stroke style. In the Stroke palette, set Color to 0 to eliminate the color variation in the stroke.
5. From the alpha library, choose Alpha 36.
6. Paint lightly over the model to even out the color, but try not to completely obscure the back-scattering color.
7. Once you have a light pink painted over the model, as shown in Figure 9.16, save the model. This light pink color will serve as the base coat for the subdermal layer.

At this point, it can be useful to start referring to a photographic reference. One of the most useful sources for photographic reference is the 3D.sk website. It was not difficult to find a reference that matched the male figure used in this chapter. Images from the Oldrich set of photographs work quite well.

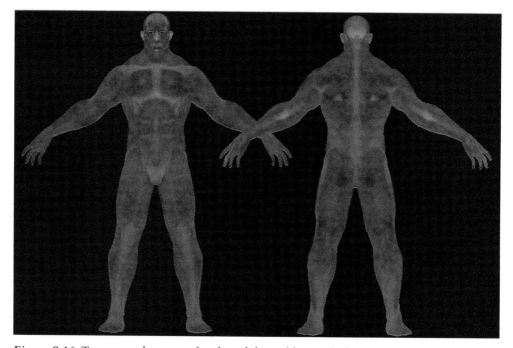

Figure 9.16 To create a base coat for the subdermal layer, the back-scattering layer is lightly painted over with a pink color.

Let's start by taking a look at the torso. Figure 9.17 shows a cropped image of the torso taken from the Oldrich set from 3D.sk. You can see that the color of the skin is not completely uniform. Areas closer to the bones of the sternum are white with very subtle bluish and cool hues. Areas around the major muscle masses are warmer colors, with slight orange, yellow, and brown tints.

When you start to paint colors into the subdermal layer, make them appear exaggerated and saturated at first. This colorful layer will eventually be masked beneath additional color passes, but its presence will add variation to the skin tones that will add to the realism in the final render.

8. Using the Spray stroke, paint a dark reddish orange on the tops of the Pectoral muscles. Use Figure 9.18 as a rough guide. Use a variety of saturated hues to break up the uniform color of the flesh.

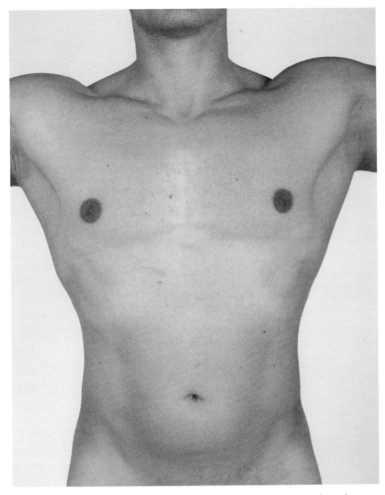

Figure 9.17 *A reference image of the torso from the 3D.sk website*

3D.sk

3D.sk (www.3D.sk) is a family of sites devoted to offering artists a wide variety of photographic reference images. You pay a one-time fee that covers all future uses of the image. The most popular site is Human and Animal Photo References for 3D Artists and Game Developers. It's easy to see why this website is a foundation for most types of fantasy illustration of 3D artwork and a basic source for game developers.

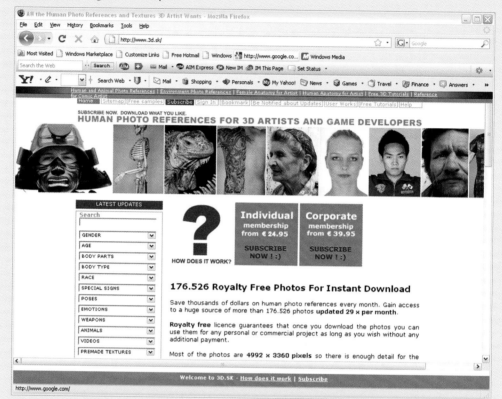

The categories of images they provide are Modeling Photo Reference, Animation Reference Photos and Movies, Details of Eyes, and Faces.

For their regular photo sessions, they typically shoot full-body images of models in various categories of poses, including classical figure drawing, action fighting, and movement, as well as specifically requested poses. For modeling poses and details, they use diffuse lighting; for figure drawing and action poses, they prefer hard shadows.

3D.sk also offers the following specialty sites:

- Female Anatomy (http://female-anatomy-for-artist.com)
- Human Anatomy (http://human-anatomy-for-artist.com)
- Environment Textures (http://environment-textures.com)
- Reference for Comic Artists (http://photo-reference-for-comic-artists.com)
- 3D Tutorials (http://free3dtutorials.com)

Painting Colors into the Subdermal Layer

Here are some tips to keep in mind while painting colors into the subdermal layer:

- On bony areas such as the sternum and in areas that are recessed or appear in shadow, paint cooler colors such as blue and purple.
- Use warm colors such as orange and red over the major muscle masses.
- Overall, red, purple, blue, and orange colors work well. Use yellow and green sparingly. Overuse of green and yellow can lead to a sickly look, but small amounts can add to subtle variation in the skin. Remember that this layer is below the surface of the skin. The ethnicity of your character can be augmented by shifting the specific hues that you paint in these areas; however, for the most part, since this layer is below the actual pigmentation of the skin, these guidelines can be applied to all ethnicities.
- You can mix colors by painting overlapping areas of color with a low RGB Intensity setting.
- It can be helpful to take reference photographs into Photoshop and examine the color channels in isolation to see how red, green, and blue colors are distributed and where they are mixed together.

As you work over the other parts of the body, keep in mind that the goal here is to create variations of hue in different parts of the body. You want to end up with a very colorful paint job; this will go a long way toward adding visual interest to the look of the skin in the final shader (see Figure 9.18).

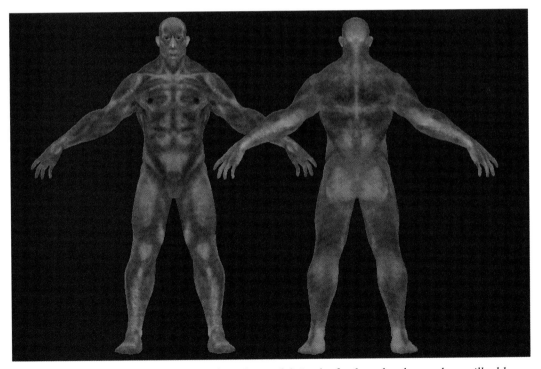

Figure 9.18 Vibrant colors are painted on the model. In the final render these colors will add subtle variations in hue.

The face is where you'll find the greatest range of color. You can group the colors generally so that cooler colors follow the jawline, reds and oranges are grouped at the center of the face, and yellows are found in the upper part of the head and cranium. Within these regions you'll find pockets of other colors (see Figure 9.19). For instance, the area around the eyes may have some blues and purples, and the bony protrusions of the chin and zygomatic bones may add pale yellow.

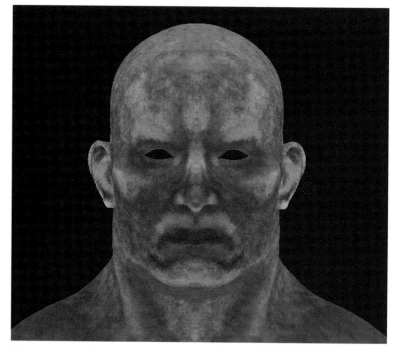

Figure 9.19 *The face is segregated loosely into color regions.*

Save the tool as maleFigure_SD2.ztl. To see a version of the model so far, open the maleFigure_SD2.ztl tool from the Chapter 9 folder on the DVD.

Mottling the Skin

Once you have the color regions defined for the figure, you can break up the look of the skin and simulate the subcutaneous texture of the skin using a mottling pass.

1. Open the maleFigure_SD1.ztl tool. Draw it on the canvas, and switch to edit mode.
2. Choose the Standard sculpting brush. Make sure that only the Rgb button on the top shelf is active. The Mrgb, M, Zadd, and ZSub buttons should be off.
3. Set the RGB Intensity to 8. Set the color to white. Choose Alpha 01 from the library. Zoom into the model, and set the draw size to around 3 or 4.
4. Use the Standard brush to draw a squiggly pattern all over the surface of the model. Use looping figure-eight strokes, and vary the width and size of the strokes somewhat as you go (see Figure 9.20).
5. For large regions of the model, use the Drag Rect stroke style with Alpha 22. Increase the Rgb Intensity to 16.

6. When working along the centerline of the model, turn Symmetry off to avoid creating a white stripe of overlapping strokes running down the middle of the figure.

7. Once the mottling pass is complete, you can paint in dark blue and red veins similar to what was created in the back-scattering pass (see Figure 9.21). Other areas of detail such as the tiny red blood vessels in the ears, the dark area of the hairline (if the character has dark hair), and the dark purple color of the lips can be painted in this pass.

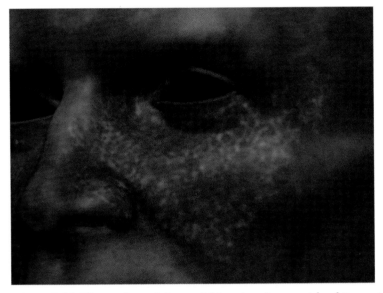

Figure 9.20 *The surface of the model is painted over with white squiggling lines to break up the look of the color.*

Figure 9.21 *Blood vessels are painted back onto the subdermal pass.*

8. Finally, to tie the colors together, set the color to a light pink such as 184, 105, 115. Set the RGB Intensity to 4, and use the Spray stroke to lightly coat the body.

Figure 9.22 shows the finished subdermal pass using the Flat-render-style material.

9. Save the tool as maleFigure_SD3.ztl. To see a finished version of this tool, open the maleFigure_SD3.ztl tool from the Chapter 9 folder on the DVD.

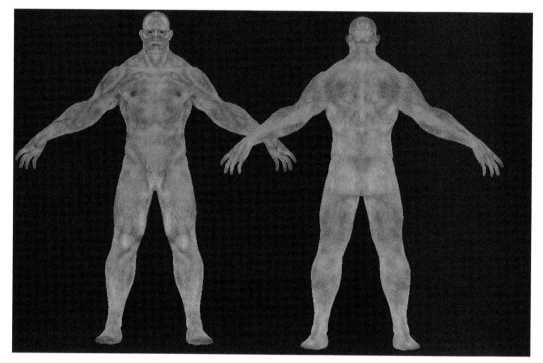

Figure 9.22 The completed subdermal pass shown using the Flat-render-style material

Painting the Epidermal Layer

The colors of the epidermal pass most closely resemble what you see on the skin surface. To paint this pass, you can lightly cover the model with a flesh tone and then add details such as moles and freckles. This section uses a European man as an example. Other ethnicities will obviously use different hues. This layer is where the pigmentation of the skin will have the most influence on the color of the skin surface.

1. Load the maleFigureSD3.ztl tool into ZBrush, draw it on the canvas, and switch to edit mode.
2. Fill the model using the MatCap_Skin04 material found in the Material Library. In the Modifiers section under the Materials palette, set Opacity to 60.
3. Set the color to a flesh tone such as 230, 176, 135.

4. Use the Standard brush with a Spray stroke and a low RGB Intensity such as 2. Make sure the Zadd, ZSub, M, and Mrgb buttons are off; only RGB should be on.

5. Paint over the surface of the model without completely obscuring the underlying colors.

6. After the model is colored with a light pink, you can dust areas with red and orange hues to help define the muscles. Use Figure 9.17, shown earlier, as a guide.

7. On the face, use the Spray stroke with Alpha 40 to add detail to the skin texture. Use a dark blue color around the beard area and reddish colors around the nose and eyes. By allowing the colors of the subdermal pass to show through, you already have a fair amount of subtle coloration in the skin tone.

8. Use a pale purplish red for the lips; try not to make the color too strong.

9. Finally, you can add details such as moles and freckles to increase the realism of the skin. Use a brownish color with the Spray stroke and Alpha 51 to add freckles. Moles can be drawn in by hand using the Dots stroke style and a dark brown (Figure 9.23).

Figure 9.24 shows the final epidermal color using the Flat render style. Figure 9.25 shows the model using Preview render.

10. Save the model as `maleFigureED.ztl`. To see a finished version of the model, load the `maleFigureED.ztl` tool from the Chapter 9 folder of the DVD.

Figure 9.23 *The final skin tone is painted on top of the colors applied earlier. Details such as moles and freckles are added as well.*

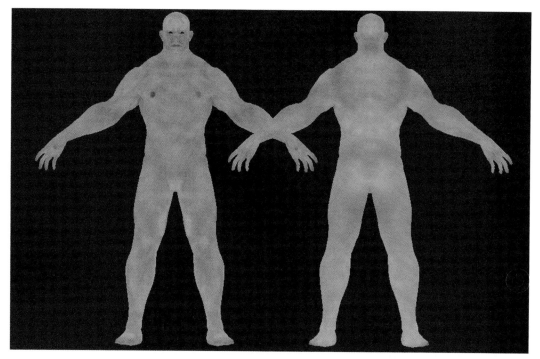

Figure 9.24 The epidermal layer in the Flat render style

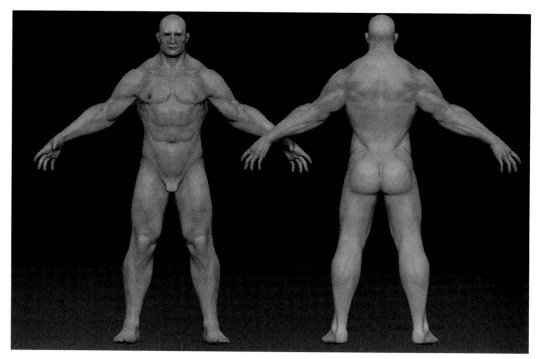

Figure 9.25 The epidermal layer in the Preview render

Exporting Textures from ZBrush

At this point, you'll need to convert the polypainting that you've created on the various versions of your model into textures that can be loaded into a 3D program such as Maya so they can be rendered.

1. Load the maleFigureBS.ztl tool into ZBrush. Draw it on the canvas, and make sure you are in edit mode. This model should have UV coordinates already. Make sure the model is at SDiv level 6.

2. Expand the UV Map section, and click the 2048 button. This sets the size of the texture you will create from the colors painted on the model.

3. Make sure the RGB slider is set to 100. Expand the Texture Map section, and click the New From Polypaint button. This converts the colors into a texture map (see Figure 9.26). You'll see the texture as long as the Texture On button is active.

4. To export the texture, click the Clone button. This places the newly created texture in the texture inventory. You can then use the Export button in the texture inventory to save the texture to your local disk. Save the texture as a TIFF file. Name it maleFigureBS.tif.

5. Repeat this process for the maleFigureSD3.ztl tool and the maleFigureED.ztl tool so that you end up with three texture maps for the back-scattering, subdermal, and epidermal layers.

The exported textures can be brought into Maya and connected to the channels of a shader network. Figure 9.27 shows a render created in Maya using the misss_fast_skin_maya shader and mental ray. This image was created using the textures painted in this chapter. To see how the shader was set up, open the maleFigureRender.mb scene in the Chapter 9 folder of the DVD.

Figure 9.26 To create a texture from the colors on the model, use the controls in the UV Map and Texture Map section of the Tool palette.

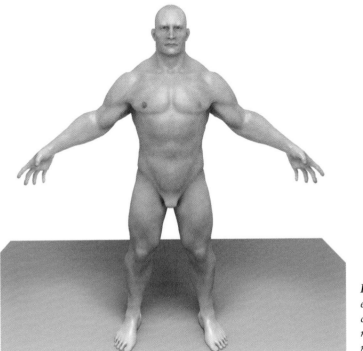

Figure 9.27 The exported textures are connected to a shader network and rendered in mental ray for Maya.

Surface Noise

Surface noise is a new feature that adds a procedural noise to the surface of a 3D polymesh tool. You can use it as a quick way to add a bumpy quality to the skin, which can then be further enhanced with the sculpting brushes.

Activating Surface Noise

Take the following steps to activate the surface noise feature in your figure model:

Figure 9.28 The controls for surface noise

1. In ZBrush, load the `maleFigureED.ztl` tool from the Chapter 9 folder on the DVD, or continue with the model from the previous section. Make sure the SDiv slider in the Geometry palette is at the highest level.
2. In the Morph Target subpalette, delete any existing morph targets using the DelMT button. Store a new morph target using the StoreMT button.
3. In the Tool palette, expand the Surface subpalette. Turn on the Noise button. The Noise button adds a procedural noise to the entire surface of the model. When you turn on the button, the bumpiness you see on the model is a preview; it actually has not changed the surface yet. Before applying the noise, you'll want to make some adjustments using the controls (see Figure 9.28).
4. Set the scale to 1 to make the size of the noise as small as possible.
5. Set the strength to –.001 to make the bumps appear as slight depressions.
6. The ColorBlend slider adds color to the noise. Set this value to 0. You can fine-tune the way the noise is applied using the Edit Curve setting in the Surface section.
7. Once you are happy with the look of the noise, click the Apply To Mesh button to transfer the preview to the geometry of the tool (see Figure 9.29).
8. Use the Smooth Peaks, Morph, and Noise brushes to selectively smooth the bumpiness of the model.

You can add other details using other sculpting brushes.

Figure 9.29 The surface noise feature adds a slight bumpy quality to the skin.

Converting Bumps to a Normal Map

The details created in the surface of the model can be converted into a normal map and exported as a texture. You can then add this to the shader network in Maya to create a more realistic skin surface.

Normal maps are a special type of bump map that use red, green, and blue colors to alter the surface normal at render time. This gives a very realistic type of bump to the surface, which renders very quickly. Creating normal maps in ZBrush 3.5 is very easy. Normal maps are calculated by comparing the lowest subdivision level with the highest subdivision level and then recording the difference as an RGB value in a texture map.

1. In the Geometry subpalette of the Tool palette, set the SDiv slider to 1.
2. Expand the Normal Map subpalette on the Tool palette. Turn on the Tangent Adaptive and SmoothUV buttons.

   The Tangent button creates a *tangent space* normal map, which is ideal for deforming objects such as characters. In reality, many artists use tangent space maps for everything. Turn on the Adaptive and SmoothUV buttons to help optimize the quality of the map.
3. Click the Create Normal Map button to create the map. It will take a few minutes to generate.
4. To export the map, click the Clone NM button. This places a copy of the map in the texture library. From there you can click Export and save the map as `maleFigureNormal.tif`.

   In Maya this map can be plugged into the bump map channel of the misss_fast_skin_ maya shader. Make sure to set the Use As setting in the Bump2D node to Tangent Space Normals, as shown in Figure 9.30. As with all texture maps exported from ZBrush, the UV coordinates are flipped vertically, and you need to correct this in Maya.
5. Select the place2DTexture node connected to the Bump2D node in the Hypershade. In the Repeat UV fields, set the second field to −1, as shown in Figure 9.31.
6. To see an example of the completed shading network, open the `figureRender.mb` file in the Chapter 9 folder of the DVD.

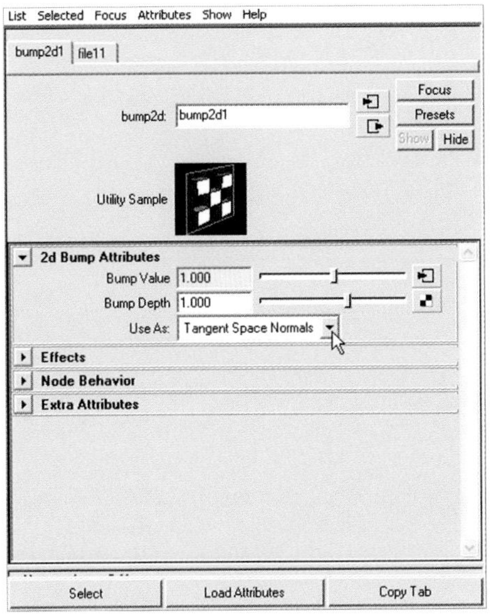

Figure 9.30 The settings for the bump2Dtexture node

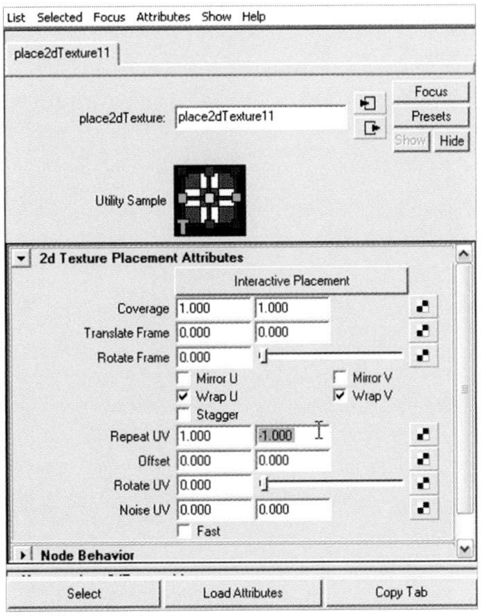

Figure 9.31 The settings for the place2DTexture node

Creating a Costume

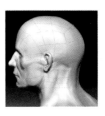

In this chapter you will *make costume elements for the character you have sculpted. You will be making a formfitting superhero costume as well as some accessories to complete the look. To do this, you will use the ZBrush retopology tools introduced in Chapter 8, as well as an external polygon modeler, in this case Maya, a tool that's familiar to most 3D modelers. You will also use Photoshop, the industry-standard image-editing program. You can use the techniques in this chapter to create any kind of costume from superhero to solider to barbarian warrior, or even a regular guy in a shirt and pants. The choice is yours. What is important is to understand how to combine ZBrush with Maya to create costumes built directly from the base sculpture.*

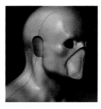

Be sure to check the DVD for a video of the full costume process to assist in your understanding of this workflow, which includes some stages that aren't demonstrated in the book. Some of the techniques in this chapter will require an understanding of how to lay out very simple UV coordinates. For more information on this process, please see the preceding chapter in this book on texture mapping or Eric Keller's excellent Mastering Maya 2009 *(Sybex, 2009). I also show alternate approaches to creating the same effects, so if you prefer not to lay out UVs, you can still use many of the techniques in this chapter.*

Figure 10.1 shows the final figure you'll complete in this chapter.

Figure 10.1 The costumed figure

A Costume Workflow

The approach you will take in this chapter is to use the ZBrush retopology tools to create a costume piece such as a shirt. You will generate a mesh that conforms to the surface of the sculpture and then give it a thickness so it is more than a two-dimensional shell. Once you have created this model, you will import it as a subtool and begin to sculpt the appropriate drapery and folds that would occur on that part of the body. By starting with a projected mesh, you will retain the anatomical form you sculpted so that you are creating only the sense of fabric over these forms. It's a huge time-saver and keeps you from having to resculpt muscle form to show through the clothing.

Creating the Mask

You will start by making the classic superhero mask. This is a cowl that drapes over the shoulders with openings for the eyes, mouth, and ears.

Preparing the ZBrush Topology Tools

You will create the hood base mesh using the ZBrush topology tools much in the same way you used them to remesh the figure in Chapter 8. Prepare your mesh as discussed in that chapter. You will begin by drawing topology over the head of the figure. I have hidden the body in this chapter's images to simplify this process.

Making a Base Mesh

With the mesh linked to a ZSphere and ready for remeshing, you will start drawing the actual edges of the new mesh. The approach will be similar to the way you created an animation mesh in Chapter 8. The difference is that here you have less emphasis on animation topology. However, if your model is intended for animation, you may want to consider your edge layout for the costume as carefully as for the body. For more information on edge layout and topology, see Chapter 8.

1. Start by creating a loop of edges around the eyes, as shown in Figure 10.2. Consider this a kind of "bandit mask" shape. Make sure X symmetry is on by pressing the X hotkey, and start from the center of the head working out.

2. As you work, you will want to check the resulting mesh often. To do this, press the A key to preview the adaptive skin. You may remember this same hotkey from Chapter 1 where you used it to preview a ZSphere model. With the topology tools, pressing A displays the polygon mesh that will result from your current network of faces (Figure 10.3). Since you will want to capture the surface detail of the sculpture, turn on Projection under Tool → Projection. You will also want to raise the Adaptive Skin resolution, under Tool → Adaptive

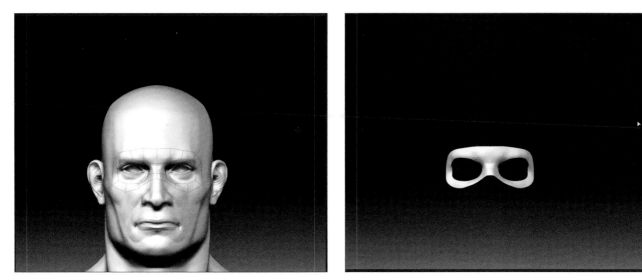

Figure 10.2 *Begin the mask by making a "bandit mask" loop around the eye area.*

Figure 10.3 *Press the A key to preview the mesh projection based on your drawn topology.*

Skin, to 5 (Figure 10.4). This will ensure that the projected mesh is dense enough to capture the surface forms. Remember to check the mesh often as you work by pressing the A key. This will save time and effort by helping you catch any errors in the mesh as they occur.

Figure 10.4 *To capture the sculpted surface form of the underlying model, turn on Projection, and raise the Adaptive Skin setting's Density slider to 5.*

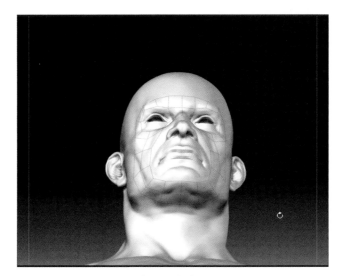

Figure 10.5 *Continue the mesh down the cheeks, connecting at the centerline under the chin.*

3. Continue the edges down the cheek and under the chin, as shown in Figure 10.5. Next, continue to expand the loops from the underside of the chin around the sides of the face to the top of the head (Figure 10.6). This will create a row of long rectangular faces. Subdivide these long faces by cutting a new edge through them (Figure 10.7). To do this, simply click an edge to start the cut, and move to the next edge; you will see

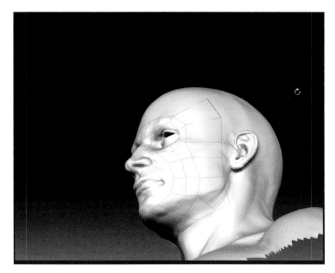

***Figure 10.6** Continue the mesh up the sides of the face to meet at the center of the top of the forehead.*

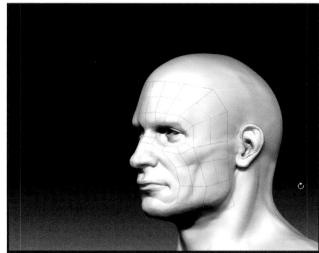

***Figure 10.7** Subdivide the long faces by cutting a new edge through them.*

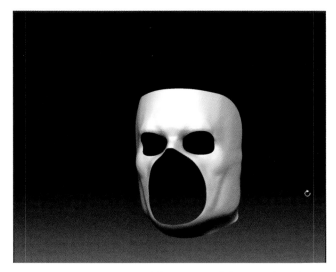

***Figure 10.8** A preview of the projected face mask so far*

a short yellow line. This is a visual cue that you can place an edge here. Cut a new edge down the length from the top of the head to the underside of the chin. Press the A key to check the mesh so far (Figure 10.8).

When you're cutting new edges and you get to the centerline of the figure, it's often easier to cut the edge from the center out instead of to the edge.

---

4. Cut a new edge from the corner of the eye to the top of the ear, as shown in Figure 10.9. Continue two more faces, which extend back over the ear. Press the W key to switch to move mode. You can now drag points on the surface. Pull the points around the perimeter of the ear. Continue a row of faces up to the top of the head (Figure 10.10).

5. Continue a network of faces around the ear. You want to maintain a hole for the ear. Move the points apart to keep them from sealing over. You may also add an odd point on the edge to prevent the mesh from sealing in this area. The Max Strip Distance slider controls how many polygon edges will define a hole in the mesh. This slider is located under the Tool → Topology menu. With this number set to 4, the hole here will not be closed automatically by ZBrush.

6. Continue the mesh up the sides of the head, as shown in Figure 10.11. Remember to check your progress often by pressing the A key (Figure 10.12).

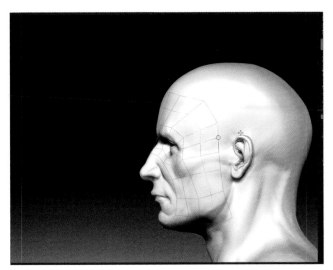

Figure 10.9 *Cut a new edge from the corner of the eye to the top of the ear.*

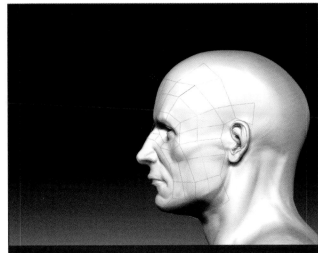

Figure 10.10 *Continue the new faces from the top of the ear to the top of the head.*

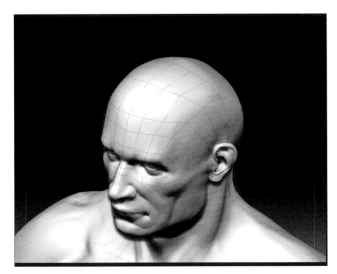

Figure 10.11 *Continue the mesh up the sides of the head to the back.*

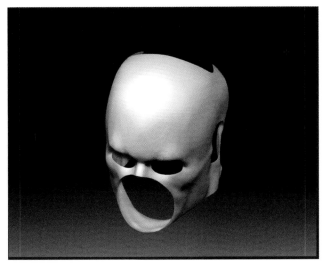

Figure 10.12 *Press the A key, and check your progress.*

7. Move to the back of the head, and continue the mesh down, as shown in Figure 10.13.
8. At this point, the head is complete (Figure 10.14). Check your projection with the A key to make sure there are no problem areas (Figure 10.15). You will now continue the mask down over the shoulders. Figure 10.16 shows the mesh extended down to the collarbones. Remember that you want to drape the mask over the shoulders, so be sure to extend it down far enough to look natural.

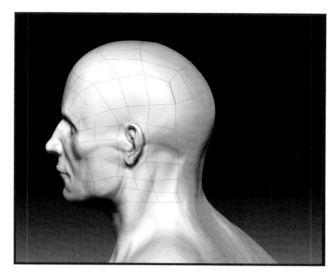

Figure 10.13 *Continue the edges down the back of the head.*

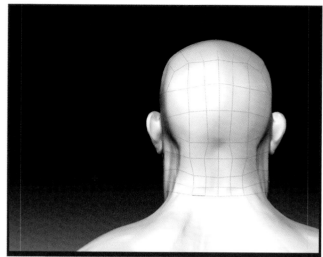

Figure 10.14 *The mesh has been completed down the back of the head.*

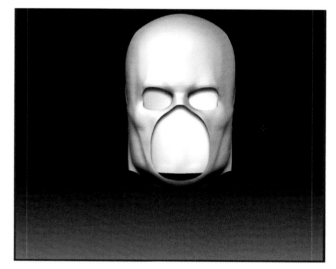

Figure 10.15 *Check the projection with the A key before moving on to the shoulders.*

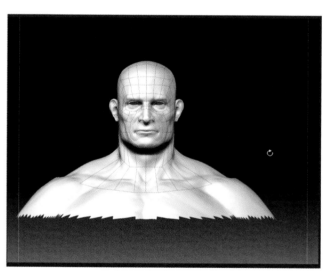

Figure 10.16 *Extend a new row of faces from the neck down to the collarbones.*

9. Cut a new edge along this string of long faces to help increase the detail in the shoulder area (Figure 10.17). Figure 10.18 shows the final projection of the mask. Save your work at this time. Notice that it captures the sculpted form of the parts of the head that it covers but has no thickness. You will correct this in the following stage.

When saving a file in which you are building topology, save it like any other ZTool. When you load it later, to continue working after drawing it on the canvas and entering edit mode, select Tool → Topology, deselect Edit Topology, and then select it again to activate topology editing.

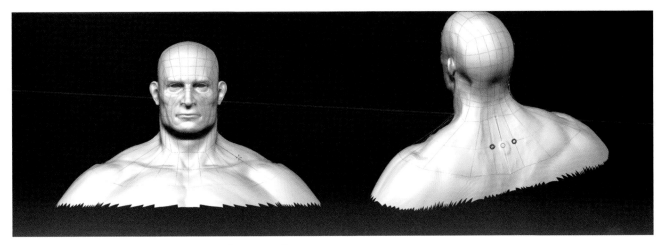

Figure 10.17 The long faces divided with a new edge

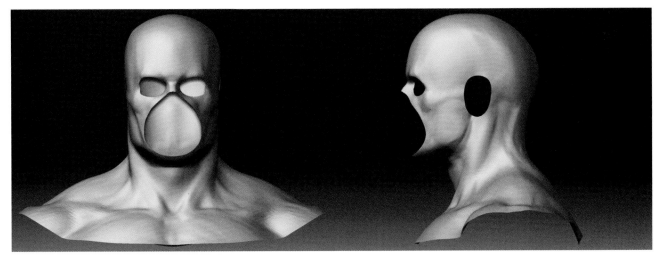

Figure 10.18 The mask projection

Generating a Hero Mask from the Topology

The topology lines are complete, and when you preview the mesh, it looks good. The next step is to create a model of the mask from this edge layout that can be loaded as a subtool and sculpted. Although it is possible to generate a mesh with thickness using the ZBrush Topology tool, you cannot have thickness and also capture the surface forms of the sculpt. The following tutorial is a useful trick for having the best of both worlds:

1. At this stage, you could generate a mask mesh with thickness by turning off Projection and setting Skin Thickness on the Topology menu to a value greater than 0. If you enter these settings and preview the mesh, you will see it does create a new skin with thickness, but does not capture any of the surface form. Since the mask is a formfitting costume element, you will want to capture the surface form as well as have a thickness.

Select a resolution that maintains as much of the surface form as possible without being too dense. In this case, I set the skin density to 3 since it maintains the form while also being a low-enough polygon count to make dividing and sculpting the mesh possible (Figure 10.19). The density you set here will be the lowest subdivision level of your resulting mesh, so try to strike a balance between surface detail and workability.

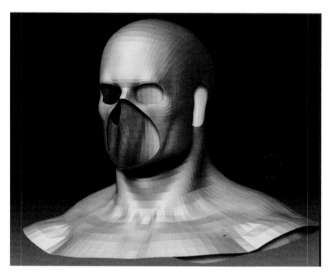

Figure 10.19 The Projection set to a mesh density of 3

Figure 10.20 The skin generated from your topology will appear in the Tool menu with Skin_ *prefixed on the file name.*

2. Select Tool → Adaptive Skin → Make Adaptive Skin. This will create a new tool in the Tool menu prefixed with *Skin_* (Figure 10.20). This will be the polygon mesh generated from your topology network. Select this ZTool, and save it separately.
   You will notice that this tool has no thickness. It is a paper-thin mask. You will want to give the mask some thickness for a more realistic appearance. By adding a thickness to the mask, you will get nicer shadows and highlights at the edge where it meets the skin.

3. To create a thickness, you will use a tool under the Morph Target menu called MorphDiff. You may recall that a morph target stores a copy of the current mesh in memory. MorphDiff creates a new mesh based on the difference between a model and its stored morph target. Select Tool → MorphTarget → Store MT. You may need to click Del MT to delete any stored data first.

4. You now want to offset the mesh from its original volume. To do this, open the Tool → Deformation menu, and increase the Inflate slider by 7 (Figure 10.21). A useful trick to help see how much the mesh is offset is to store a snapshot on the canvas by pressing Shift+S before inflating. You will then be able to see the original position as well as the new position and judge whether the thickness is acceptable (Figure 10.22). When you are done, clear the snapshot by pressing Ctrl+N.

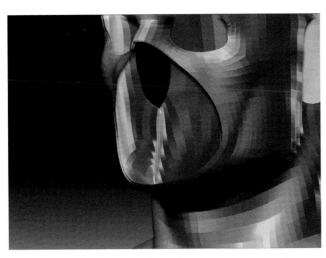

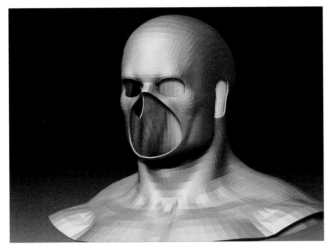

Figure 10.21 *Use the Inflate slider under the Deformation menu to inflate the entire mask by 7.*

Figure 10.22 *Use a snapshot of the canvas to visualize the thickness generated by the Inflate operation. The inner shell in this image is the snapshot, while the outer is the mask ZTool after inflating.*

5. You have now inflated the entire mask just enough to offset the shell from its original position stored in the morph target. Select Tool → Morph Target → CreateDiff to generate a new ZTool based on the difference between the stored morph target and the inflated shell. You will now have a new tool listed in the Tool palette, whose name begins with *MorphDiff_*. Figure 10.23 shows the MorphDiff_mask, which retains surface detail and also has a thickness. This mesh is also polygrouped so that the inner shell, the thickness, and the outer surface are all easily isolated by pressing Shift+Ctrl-click (Figure 10.24). This will make sculpting and manipulating the mask much easier as you move into the detailing phase.

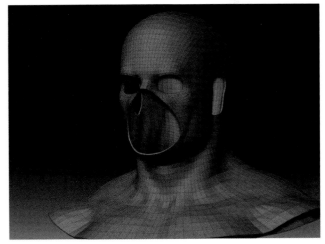

Figure 10.23 *The mask with thickness*

Figure 10.24 *The mask polygrouped*

You have now seen how to use the ZBrush topology tools to create a costume element. The shirt and pants are created in much the same way using the topology tools directly on the sculpture. You can see this process in action in videos included on the DVD. Also on the DVD you will find videos showing how to use Maya to generate accessories like the gloves and belt illustrated in Figure 10.25.

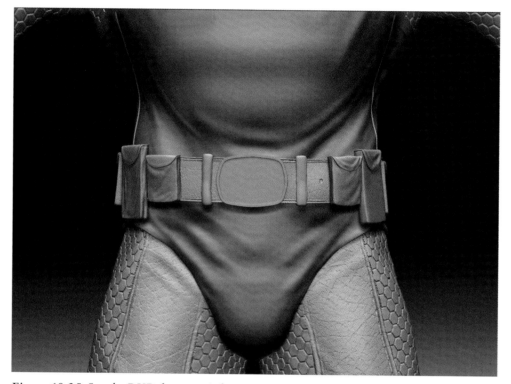

Figure 10.25 *See the DVD for more information on creating accessories like the utility belt shown here.*

The Shirt, Pants, and Other Elements

In the interest of focusing on procedures and minimizing repetition, this chapter does not demonstrate how to create each element of the costume. For the elements I'm not walking through, consult the video in the associated chapter folder to see how these parts were created. The general process is the same for each, but you may find the video helpful. The ZTools for these articles are also included on the DVD. Some general notes on these elements follow.

The Shirt

Just as you did with the mask, the shirt is built directly over the sculpture using the Projection options, so you can maintain the care and form you sculpted in the chest and arms. Since it is a tight-fitting article, you want many of those shapes to show through. If this were a more loose-fitting article, you could bypass the projection steps.

continued

The Pants

The pants are built in the same manner as the shirt. Please see the DVD for a full video demo of both costume elements.

Gloves and Boots

On the DVD you will find a video walk-through of the gloves, boots, and belt.

Sculpting the Costume Details

Once you have finished making the meshes for your costume elements, it's time to focus on sculpting them. Most of these articles of clothing are formfitting, so the idea will be to create stress wrinkles where the cloth is compressing or stretched across forms. You will begin by looking at the mask.

Sculpting the Mask

To begin, you will load the costume meshes into the ZTool. The easiest way to do this is to use Subtool Master, whose option Multi Append will load multiple ZTools and obj files from the disk into your current ZTool as subtools. This function is an incredible time-saver when you need to combine multiple models into a single subtool stack. For this tutorial, you can follow along with your own ZTools or load the parts directly from the DVD. I have also included a ZTool with all costume meshes preloaded called 000_HeroWithCostumeMeshes.Zztl.

1. Begin by loading the hero body ZTool. Draw the model on the canvas, and enter edit mode. Select ZPlugin → Subtool Master to load Subtool Master.

2. From the Subtool Master menu, click the Multi Append button (Figure 10.26). This will open a file browser. Go to the location where you saved your costume meshes, or load the sample ones off the DVD. You can select multiple files by Ctrl-clicking them in the menu. Click OK to import the selected files as subtools (Figure 10.27). You can mirror parts such as the gloves and boots later.

3. Select the Mask subtool, making it active. You can also choose to hide the other tools at this time. I have kept the head and eyes visible to assist in sculpting the mask (Figure 10.28).

4. The first detail you will add is a seam running the length of the mask. This trick involves a creative use of an undocumented ZBrush feature, which was first demonstrated to me by Brandon Lawless at Gentle Giant Studios.

   When the model is in PolyFrame mode and you have the Lasso tool selected, Ctrl+Shift-clicking an edge will hide a ring of edges. By using this technique you can isolate a ring of edges running the entire midsection of the mask ZTool. Mask this ring, and then inflate it to create what appears to be a seam in the fabric.

   This can be a tricky approach as you start to get into the higher subdivision levels because of the difficulty of clicking an edge between two points. It may take some patience. See the associated video on the DVD for the process in action. You will also start from the lower subdivision levels and work your way up to simplify the process.

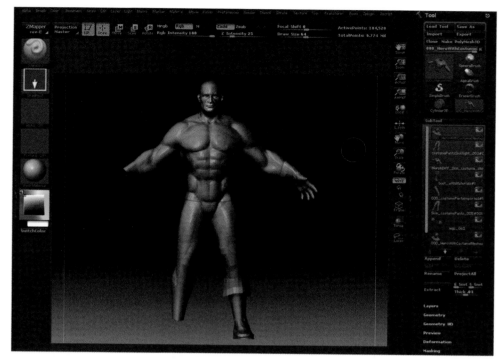

Figure 10.26
The Multi Append button

Figure 10.27 *The costume elements loaded as subtools*

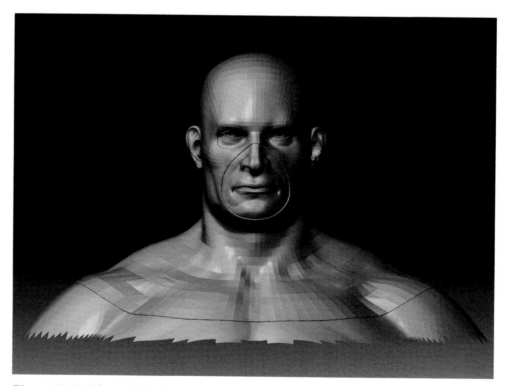

Figure 10.28 *The mask loaded as a subtool in the hero ZTool*

5. Hide all other subtools but the mask. At subdivision level 1, turn on frame mode with Shift+F, and make sure that lasso selection mode is on by clicking the Lasso icon on the right-side dock. You may also find it useful to polygroup the entire head by selecting Tools → Polygroups → Group Visible. If the head belongs to multiple polygroups, it is possible that clicking will simply select groups rather than the edge ring. This will clean up the polygroups; because you will be adding more as you progress, starting with just one can simplify the process.

6. Lastly, you will want to turn on double-sided render by selecting Tool → Display Properties and clicking the Double button. This will allow you to see any internal polygons that might be facing away from the camera view.

7. Ctrl+Shift-click an edge between two points above the ear, as shown in Figure 10.29. Notice in the image that the crosshair of the cursor lies between the points when the button is clicked. This will hide the edge ring. Repeat the process for a ring of faces beneath the ear extending to the shoulder, as shown in Figure 10.30.

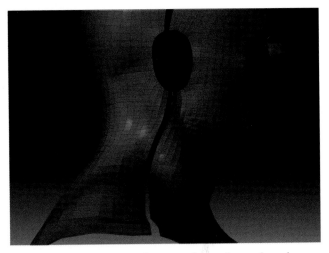

Figure 10.30 *Continue the seam down the neck and shoulder.*

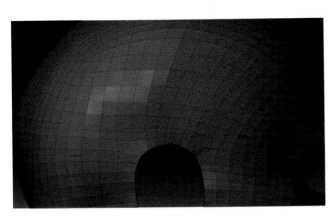

Figure 10.29 *Ctrl+Shift-click between the two points shown here to hide the edge ring. You will see the crosshair is between the points, not on them.*

8. Now invert the selection so that only the edge rings are visible by Ctrl+Shift-dragging the background. This will invert the visible selection, as shown in Figure 10.31. Polygroup these separately from the rest of the head by selecting Tool → Polygroups → Group Visible. They will now display a different color. Ctrl+Shift-click the background to show the entire head again. You will now add a subdivision level with Ctrl+D.

9. At the next subdivision level, the edge ring you selected will have two strips of poly edges (Figure 10.32). Isolate the polygroup by pressing Ctrl+Shift-click, and then use the same process to hide one of the poly strips. Be sure to do this for the strip at the top of the head as well as the

Figure 10.31 *The selection inverted, so only the selected edge rings are visible.*

shoulder. Once the strip is isolated, polygroup it, and show the entire mesh again. You will now see three separate polygroup colors on the mesh. There is the head (in green in this image) and two colored strips for the edge rings (here, yellow and purple), as shown in Figure 10.33. To simplify the process, hide one of the edge rings for the seam, and polygroup the remaining two polygroups by selecting Tool → Polygroups → Group Visible. This will reduce the number of polygroups to 2.

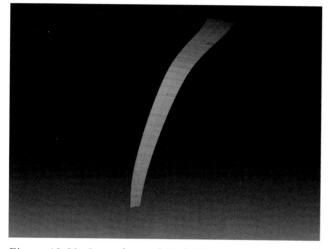

Figure 10.32 Once the mesh is divided, the edge ring will now have two strips of polygons.

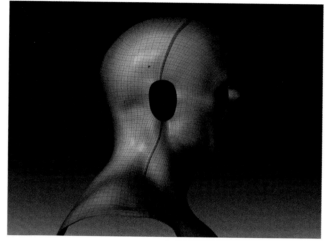

Figure 10.33 The whole mask visible with three separate polygroups displayed

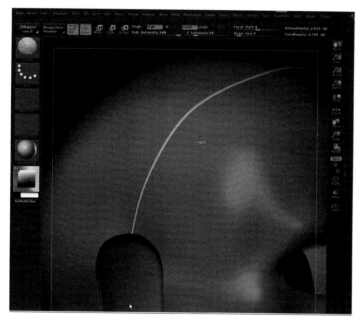

Figure 10.34 The seam isolated with a mask

10. The process is repeated for the next subdivision level. Divide the mesh with Ctrl+D, and isolate the strip polygroup. Again, it is now two strips of faces instead of one. Hide one strip, and polygroup the remaining faces. Repeat this process until level 4 or 5. This will allow you to polygroup the finest possible line of polygons to use as a seam. The higher the subdivision levels, the thinner and more realistic this seam line will appear. At some point, you will run out of subdivision levels, or the mesh will become so fine you can no longer hide rings with this technique.

11. To create the seam, select and mask the edge ring at the highest subdivision level. Reveal all of the mesh, and invert the mask so only the single strip of polygons is unmasked (Figure 10.34). Select Tool → Deformation → Inflate, and set the slider to -4 to inflate the seam into the head.

12. Clear the mask, and save your work. Figure 10.35 shows the completed seam.

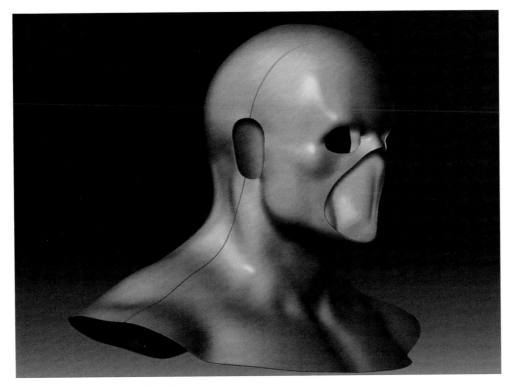

Figure 10.35 The completed seam

At this stage, you are ready to start sculpting the wrinkles and buckles of the mask fabric. You will do this using the Standard brush with Lazy Mouse turned on and the Morph brush as a blender.

1. Before you do this, you will store a morph target at the highest subdivision level. This will allow you to use the Morph brush as a blender or eraser on the detail you are about to sculpt. Store a morph target by selecting Tool → Morph Target → Store MT. At this stage, save your ZTool.

2. Select the Standard brush and Alpha 01. Turn on Lazy Mouse in the Stroke menu, or use the L hotkey. Stroke along the surface, creating striations in the fabric in areas of stretching or compression. In Figure 10.36 you can see I have added stretch marks to the shoulders as well as the chest. Feel free to go overboard at this point. You will use the Morph brush to reduce the number of marks and blend them into the surface. Rotate to the back of the head, and add compression wrinkles to the base of the skull (Figure 10.37). Another area that is prime for these kinds of wrinkles is under the chin (Figure 10.38). Use the Standard brush with ZSub to cut wrinkles here.

3. Make sure to create small hash marks along the seam from the front to back. These will help give the impression of the fabric bunched where it is joined (Figure 10.39).

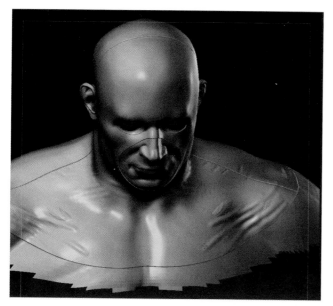

Figure 10.36 Adding stretch wrinkles with the Standard brush

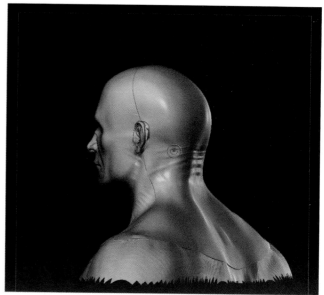

Figure 10.37 Add strokes to the base of the skull to make it appear the fabric is bucking there.

Figure 10.38 Adding folds beneath the chin

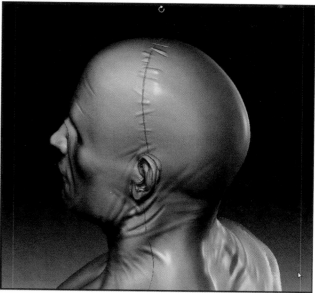

Figure 10.39 Creating hash marks along the seam

4. Select the Morph brush, and set the intensity to 8. Stroke along the surface to blend back the previous marks made by the Standard brush. You will see how the Morph brush acts as a blender when set to a lower intensity. If you need to erase a mark completely, set the ZIntensity to 100. This is superior to using Smooth, since the Smooth brush would destroy the seam detail. Because you stored the morph target after

making the seam, the Morph brush will not disturb this element at all. Figure 10.40 shows the Morph brush used to erase details at the neck and jawline. Notice that the seam remains intact.

Figure 10.40 *Using the Morph brush to blend off the sculpted details*

5. Use the Move brush to create a furrowed brow on the mask. Use the Standard brush to add forehead wrinkles so an expression is apparent beneath the mask (Figure 10.41). Make sure to work this area with X symmetry off; otherwise, the forehead will look perfectly symmetrical and highly unnatural.

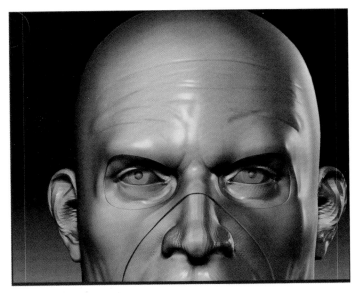

Figure 10.41 *Forehead wrinkles and brow furrow*

6. Add cheek striations; also add bunched-up fabric in areas of high movement, such as beneath the chin, the jaw, the back of the skull, and the shoulders. Figure 10.42 shows the final mask.

Figure 10.42 The final mask sculpt

Sculpting the Shirt

You will now work on the shirt. The process will involve many of the same techniques we used to create the mask, especially for isolating edge rings to help create surface details.

    1. Select the Shirt subtool. You will isolate a seam line the same way on the shirt as you did for the hood. Figure 10.43 shows the loops isolated for the shirt panels. I want to give the impression the sleeves are separate material from the shirt. You will use Inflate to add a raised border instead of a recessed seam line.

Figure 10.43 Polygroup the loops shown here for the shirt.

2. Divide the shirt to level 5 or 6 depending on the limitations of your machine. Hide everything but the polygrouped loops. Mask them by Ctrl-clicking the background. Ctrl+Shift and drag a marquee off the model to reveal all geometry again, and invert the mask so the polygroup strips are unmasked (Figure 10.44).

Figure 10.44 Isolate the polygroups with a mask.

3. You will now inflate the strips using Tool → Deformation → Inflate. Set the slider to 5 to create the raised borders. The strips will now be offset from the surface, as shown in Figure 10.45. Clear the mask, and save your ZTool.

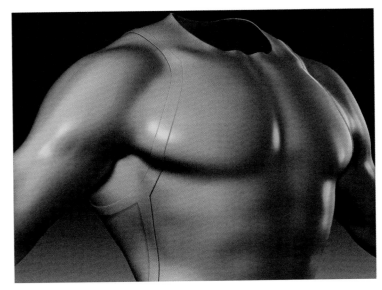

Figure 10.45 The inflated strips

You will now move on to sculpting the stretching and compression of the fabric. Make sure to store a morph target as you did on the mask before you begin.

1. Use the Standard brush with Alpha 01 to sketch in stretch marks across the raised forms of the chest. Be sure to alternate between ZAdd and ZSub as you work (Figure 10.46).

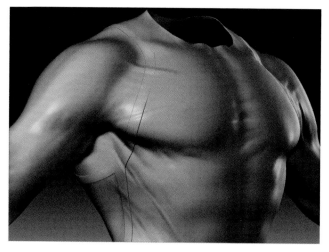

Figure 10.46 Adding folds with the Standard brush

2. Rotate to the back and add a web of compression wrinkles radiating from the back of the armpit, as shown in Figure 10.47. You will also want to create a sense of fabric stretched across the muscles of the back. In Figure 10.48 I have used a zigzag pattern of strokes to create the sense of fabric settling against the muscles of the lower back and compressing toward the waist.

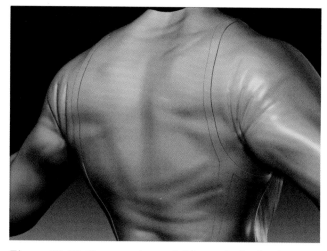

Figure 10.47 Compression wrinkles at the back of the armpit

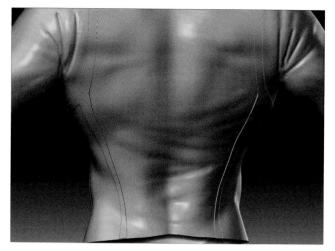

Figure 10.48 Adding wrinkles in a zigzag pattern toward the waist

3. From the front view, use the same brush to create wrinkles that flow from the shoulders down the front of the shirt. Notice how the definition of the muscle forms is filled in by the fabric stretched between them. I also add tension lines beneath the Pectoralis muscles (Figure 10.49).

Figure 10.49 *Adding more stretched wrinkles and folds to the chest*

Adding a Repeating Pattern to the Sleeves

You have created some wrinkles and folds in the fabric of the shirt. You will now add a different kind of surface detail. I want to give the sleeves the impression of being made of a different material with a fine repeating texture. In this case, you will make a honeycomb texture that stretches over the sleeves. To do this, you will need to make use of the UV coordinates of the mesh.

UVs on the shirt have been laid out flat in Maya. The shirt is available on the DVD as an obj file as well as a ZTool. For more information on UVs, please see Chapter 9 as well as Eric Keller's exceptional guide to Maya, *Mastering Maya 2009* (Sybex, 2009). I have imported the UVs into the shirt ZTool on the DVD so you won't have to manually lay them out for this tutorial.

1. You will now import the new UVs into the model. Go to Preferences ImportExport, and turn on Import Mat As Groups (Figure 10.50). Step down to level 1. Import the shirtUV.obj file into the current shirt ZTool by selecting Tool → Import and browsing to the file on the DVD. This will import the new UVs into the model but leave the higher subdivision levels and sculpted details intact.

2. Enter frame mode by pressing Shift+F. You will notice there are new polygroups now (Figure 10.51). These groups correspond to the sleeves; the front, back, and side panes of the shirt; and the raised borders. This is because I assigned different materials to the mesh in Maya for areas I wanted to polygroup separately. See the boot video on the DVD for a demonstration of this process. These new polygroups will assist you in isolating the different parts of the shirt to detail them.

Figure 10.50
Turn on Import Mat As Groups in the Preferences ImportExport menu.

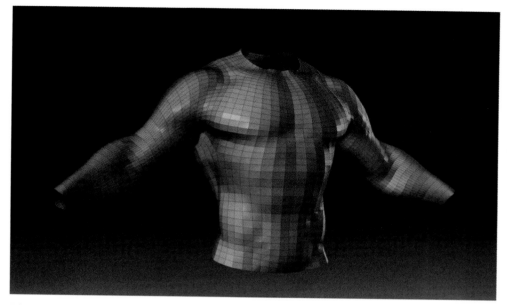

Figure 10.51 *The new polygroups*

3. Step up to the highest subdivision level, and hide all parts of the mesh except for the sleeves (Figure 10.52).

Figure 10.52 *At the highest subdivision level, hide all but the sleeves.*

4. Since the UVs are laid out flat, you can view a texture that can be tiled on the surface of the model. You will create a honeycomb texture for the shirtsleeves using a single PSD that can be tiled.

5. Select Texture → Import, and browse to honeycomb.psd on the DVD. Load this texture into the Texture Map palette under the Tool menu. The honeycomb texture will

now appear on the sleeves (Figure 10.53). You will now mask the geometry based on this color texture.

The honeycomb texture is a free alpha that was made available on ZBrushCentral.com by the user Polaris. ZBrushCentral is a great source for user-generated content like this. Also be sure to check ZBrush.com for an extensive library of alphas, texture, and materials!

Figure 10.53 The honeycomb texture applied to the sleeves

6. To mask the sleeves, select Tool → Masking, and click Mask By Intensity. This will create a mask on the surface of the ZTool based on the color intensity of the texture. Turn off the texture by selecting the Texture Off in the Texture Map sub-palette. (Figure 10.54). The mask will remain on the surface of the ZTool.

Figure 10.54 Turn off the color texture by selecting Texture Off in the sub-palette.

You will now inflate the honeycomb texture on the surface of the shirt mesh.

7. Select Tool → Deformation → Inflate, and set the slider to 4. The honeycomb pattern will now appear as etched into the surface of the arms. Ctrl+Shift-click the

background to show the hidden parts of the shirt (Figure 10.55). Figure 10.56 shows the complete set of costume elements so far.

Figure 10.55 *The shirt with the honeycomb pattern etched into the sleeves*

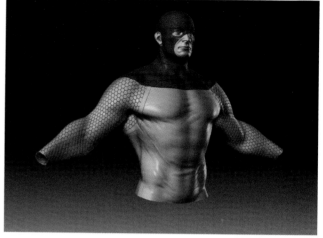

Figure 10.56 *The costume elements so far*

Sculpting the Pants

In this section you will sculpt the formfitting pants. You will be looking at ways of editing the ZTool to make it easier to work with by removing inside faces. You will also look at how to create the impression of tight-fitting leather material combined with other patterned material types. You will also look at sculpting seams with the Stitch brush.

1. You will begin by deleting the inner shell of the pants. You only need to retain the thickness, and you do not need the duplicate inner shell. Ctrl+Shift-click the inner shell polygroup to hide it, as shown in Figure 10.57.

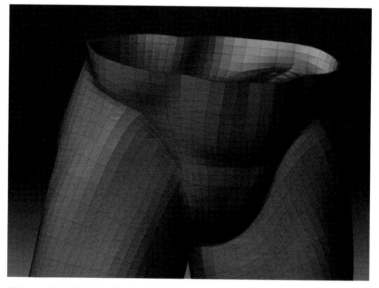

Figure 10.57 *Ctrl+Shift-click the inner shell polygroup to isolate it.*

If you are working along with the tutorial using the ZTool provided on the DVD, you can skip this step. The inner shell of faces has already been removed on your ZTool.

2. Once the inner shell is hidden, step up to the highest subdivision level, and mask everything by Ctrl-clicking the background (Figure 10.58). This mask will prevent you from losing details when you delete the hidden faces. This mask must be applied at the highest subdivision level.

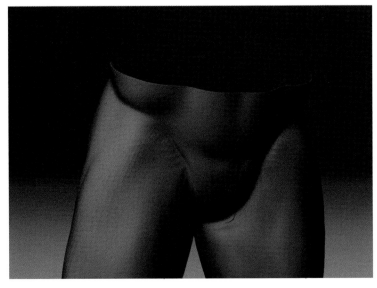

Figure 10.58 *Mask the highest subdivision level.*

3. Step back down to level 1. Under Tool → Geometry, click Delete Hidden to remove the inner shell faces. The outer shell remains, along with the faces of the width of the pants (Figure 10.59).

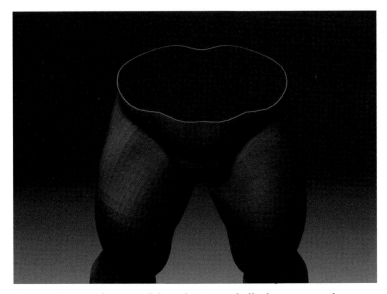

Figure 10.59 *After you delete the inner shell, the outer surface as well as the thickness of the pants remain.*

4. At this stage, create a seam polygroup for the outer and inner sides of the leg, just as you did previously. Figure 10.60(a) shows the polygroup for the outer leg seam, while Figure 10.60(b) shows the inner thigh seam. Isolate these seams with a mask, and using the Inflate slider, inflate them by −5. This will create a seam in the pants, as shown in Figure 10.61.

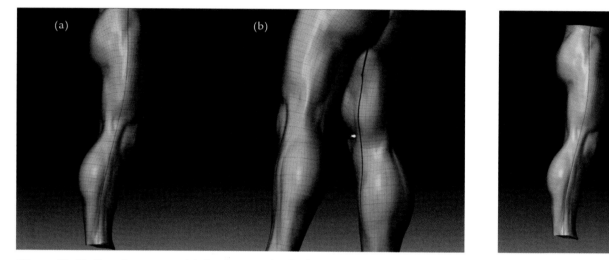

Figure 10.60 *Creating a seam: (a) for the outside, (b) for the inside of the leg*

Figure 10.61 *The leg seam*

Many classic superhero costumes have the outer shorts placed over the tights. You want to create the appearance of fabric lain over fabric here in a technique similar to the one used on the borders of the shirt. You will create this outer layer of cloth for the shorts by creating a polygroup selection based on the topology and inflating it to create an offset from the rest of the legs.

1. To begin, use the Claytubes brush to fill in the furrow between the glutes (Figure 10.62). This area is covered by cloth, so you wouldn't want this level of definition between the buttocks.

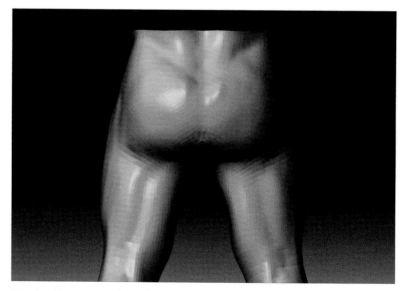

Figure 10.62 *Use Claytubes to fill in the buttocks.*

You will use topology masking to isolate the area for the shorts. Recall that when you laid out the topology for the pants, you were sure to lay edge loops in a loop around the legs. Topology masking will follow this edge loop pattern and allow you to define a perfect area for the shorts.

2. Step down a subdivision level, because topology masking is easier at the midlevels of resolution than at the highest. Press the W key to enter move mode. Hold down Ctrl, and drag from the pelvis toward the leg. You will see the mask grow along the leg. Stop when the mask lies approximately where the leg meets the pelvis (Figure 10.63).

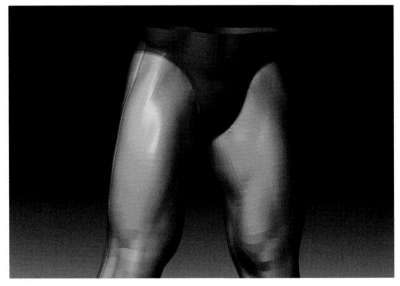

Figure 10.63 Use topology masking to isolate the area for the shorts.

3. Ctrl-click in the document window to invert the mask. Use the Smooth brush to remove the seam from the side of the leg where it overlaps the shorts. Since these will be sitting on top of the tighter pants, you wouldn't want the seam to continue across them (Figure 10.64).

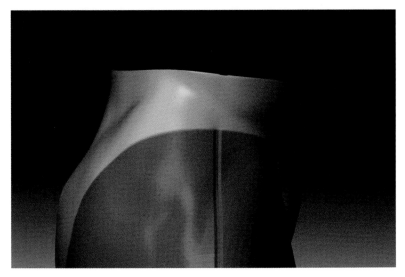

Figure 10.64 Smooth away the seam on the shorts area.

4. Step up to the highest subdivision level. Select Tool → Masking → Invert to invert the mask so the legs are now unmasked. Alternately, you could Ctrl-click the document window off the model to invert the mask. Once the legs are unmasked and the shorts are masked, select Tool → Masking → HidePt to hide the legs (Figure 10.65). When these faces are isolated, polygroup them by selecting Tool → Polygroups → Group Visible.

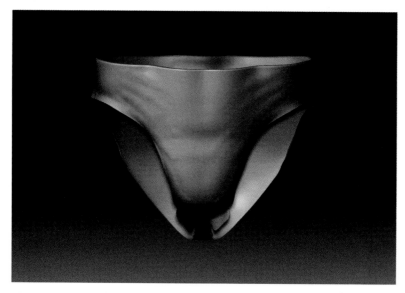

Figure 10.65 Isolate the shorts.

5. Now Ctrl+Shift-click the polygroups to mask the legs, leaving the shorts unmasked. Inflate the shorts by selecting Tool → Deformation → Inflate and setting the slider to 5. This will offset the shorts, as shown in Figure 10.66.

Figure 10.66 Inflating an offset for the shorts

Now that all the seams and offsets are inflated, store a morph target. Save your work before moving on. The next step is to add some bunching of fabric at the buttocks and knees, as well as some stretching lines at the thighs.

1. Select the Standard brush with Alpha 01. Turn on Lazy Mouse with the L hotkey. Make sure to turn off X symmetry. When you are creating these folds and wrinkles, a perfectly symmetrical object will appear very unnatural. You will achieve much better results working with symmetry off and allowing the forms to become asymmetrical in these final stages.

2. Begin by adding some compression lines to the buttocks. Notice how they radiate out from the area of greatest compression beneath the buttocks. Carry these lines lightly out to the sides of the legs (Figure 10.67).

3. Rotate to the front. Use the same brush to create striations of cloth radiating from the inner thighs out and around the legs. Don't go overboard here; just add a slight indication of fabric across the muscle forms already there (Figure 10.68).

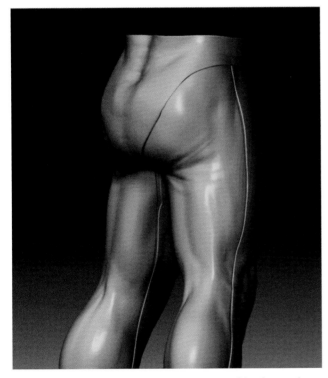

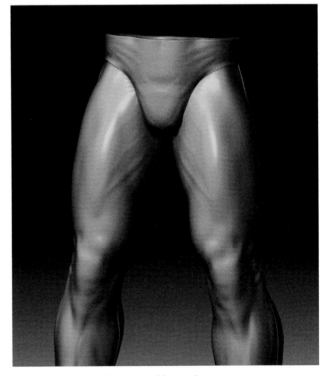

Figure 10.67 Sculpting compression wrinkles beneath the buttocks

Figure 10.68 Adding wrinkles to legs

4. Return to the back view, and radiate folds from the inner thighs across the back of the legs. Here as well, take care that the wrinkles lightly traverse over the existing muscle form. You want the impression of wrinkled fabric stretched over muscle (Figure 10.69). Also, be sure to move around the figure as you sculpt the folds. Just like sculpting any form, it will work out best if you are constantly moving around rather than working from one view. Drapery especially is defined by how it interacts with the figure in all views. Notice that I have masked the shorts in this view. This

allows me to make long strokes with the Lazy Mouse without having to worry about affecting the outer layer of fabric. This helps create the impression that the wrinkles start under the shorts and extend out into view.

5. Return to the front view, and start to cluster finer folds at the knees. Since this is an area of high mobility, it is likely the fabric will gather here in smaller folds. This is also where the pants will eventually be tucked into the boots, which would also affect the surface quality of the fabric (Figure 10.70).

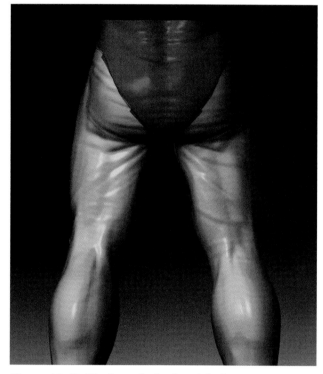

Figure 10.69 Working the backs of the legs

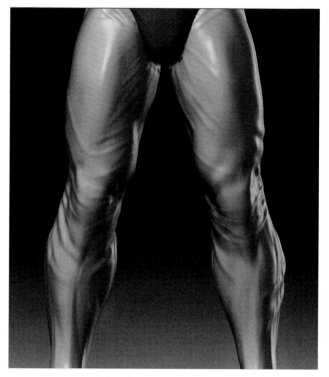

Figure 10.70 Adding bunched wrinkles to the knees

6. Complete the leg by adding more striations to the lower leg. Notice how the wrinkles flow from a high point near the back of the leg down to the front. Alternate the folds from left to right sides of the legs so they appear to interlock at the front of the shin. This interweaving helps add visual interest and create a sense of rhythm to the drapery (Figure 10.71). Be sure to use the Morph brush to blend off any areas that are too strong. Keep the Morph brush at a ZIntensity of 8 for the best results.

Figure 10.72 shows the sculpted folds, with overlay lines showing the general flow and rhythm I tried to keep in mind while sculpting. Try to find the flows on your own sculpture. Look at references of similar materials when possible, and try to remember to make the wrinkles tighter in areas of higher mobility or compression-like joints.

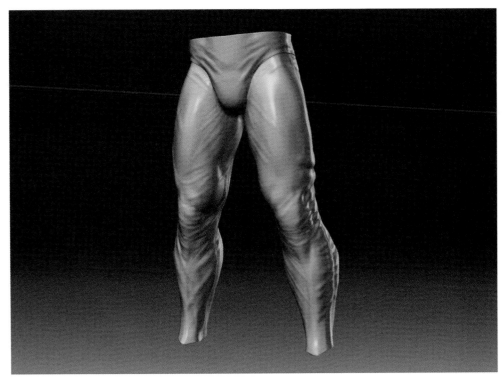

Figure 10.71 Working the shin

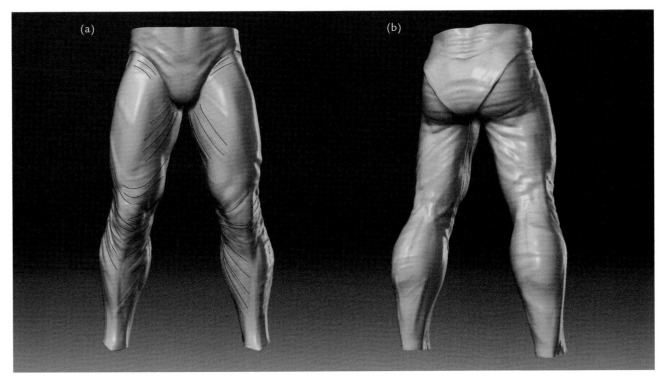

Figure 10.72 The rhythms of the wrinkles

You are now ready to start adding some finer texture details to the pants. These include features such as different panels of material, leather and weave patterns, and more seams and detail elements. Because you have taken the time to add these wrinkles to the pants, any elements you add now will conform to the sculpted surface, making them look all the more convincing.

1. The next stages will utilize a texture map that can be tiled. You can lay out the UVs on your pants manually using Maya, Headus, or another UV layout tool, or you can simply load the UVed mesh included on the DVD. To load the UVs, step down to level 1, and import `tightPantsUV.obj`.

2. You will begin by adding an overall leather texture to the pants. Select Texture → Import, and load `leatherTile.psd` from the DVD. This is a tiled leather texture (Figure 10.73). Once loaded, this texture will cover the pants and give them the appearance of cracked leather.

Figure 10.73 The `.psd` *texture on the DVD*

3. Select Tool → Masking, and choose Mask By Intensity. Then, using the Deformation → Inflate slider, inflate by −4 to create a craquelure of leather texture on the surface of the pants (Figure 10.74).

    To add visual interest to the pants, you will now mask out some areas to create panels of different materials. You can incorporate the honeycomb tiles you used on the shirt-sleeves in areas of the pants (Figure 10.75). To do this, you will mask out selections of the pants using the Lasso tool.

Figure 10.74 *The leather texture used as an Inflate mask on the pants*

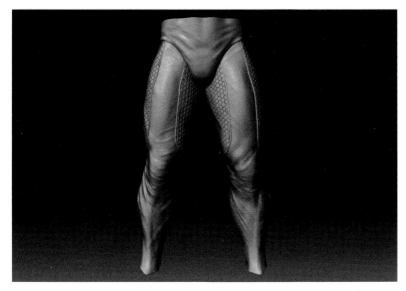

Figure 10.75 *In the next steps, you will create the appearance of multiple materials as shown here.*

4. Make sure the Lasso button on the right dock of the screen is on. Press Ctrl and drag from the side view to create the mask selections you see in Figure 10.76. You can re-create this mask pattern or create your own. Remember, you can invert the mask by Ctrl-clicking the background.

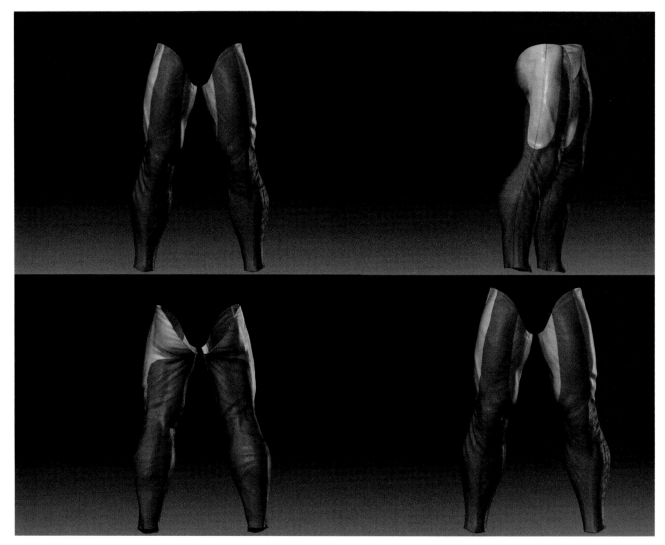

Figure 10.76 *Isolate the areas shown here with a mask.*

ZBrush allows you to store masks as alphas if you are working on a mesh with UV coordinates. The mask you see here has been stored as PanelTiles.psd on the DVD. Load this file into the Alpha palette, and select Tool → Masking → Mask By Alpha to recreate the exact masking I have here. Be sure to turn off the alpha when you are done. You will look more at loading and storing alphas later in this section.

5. You now need to clean the unmasked areas of any detail and noise. Use the Smooth brush to take down the leather texture in the unmasked areas. You want the surface to be smooth so the honeycomb tiles will appear crisp. You will also want to remove the seam on the pants in the unmasked areas (Figure 10.77).

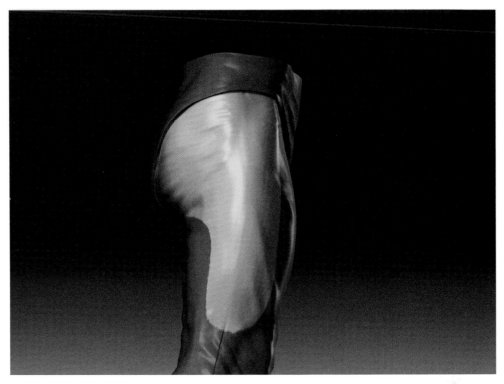

Figure 10.77 Remove the leather texture as well as the seam from the unmasked areas.

The unmasked areas will be filled with the honeycomb tile texture that you used on the shirtsleeves. To do this, you will need to create a new texture that combines both the honeycomb pattern as well as this mask you have painted. This will involve saving the mask as an alpha. If you choose to skip these steps or if you don't have Photoshop installed, I have included the final mask file panelTiles.psd on the DVD for you to use.

Storing, Recalling, and Editing Masks as Alphas

Any complex mask in ZBrush can be saved for later recall and use as long as the mesh you are working on had UVs assigned. These can be hand-laid UVs like the ones on the pants mesh or any of the ZBrush automatic solutions such as AUV, GUV, or the new PUV tiles. To save your mask as an alpha, simply select Tool → Masking → Create Alpha.

This will create a new image file in the Alpha palette that represents your mask. This image can be exported as a PSD or TIFF file for later use. You can then load the alpha at any time in the future and use the mask from the Alpha button to restore the mask on the surface of your sculpture. This can save many hours of repainting complex masks when sculpting to texture mapping. It can also assist in creating complex masks for fine details, as you will soon see. Use the following steps to combine the current mask with the honeycomb texture to create a new alpha mask:

1. You will want the alpha generated to be 2KB resolution. The default size is 1KB, unless you have a larger alpha loaded in the Alpha palette when you generate the alpha mask. To do this, go to the UV map menu under the Tool menu, and set your resolution to 2048.

2. Now open the UV Map sub-palette menu under the Tool menu. Change your resolution to 2048. Go to the Masking sub-palette and click Create Alpha. A new 2K alpha will now be created based on your mask (Figure 10.78). Export this file as `pantsMaskPanels.psd`. I have included this mask on the DVD as a PSD file.

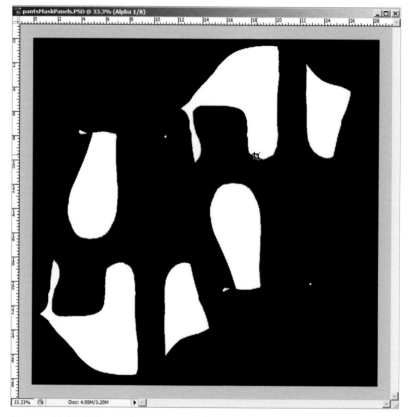

Figure 10.78 *The mask is now saved as an image file.*

3. You will now combine the mask you just exported from ZBrush with the honeycomb texture file to create a compound mask combining the two elements (Figure 10.79). This will allow you to have the unmasked areas filled with the honeycomb tiles. Open Photoshop, if you have it, and from the DVD load `honeycomb.psd` as well as the `pantsMaskPanels.psd` file you just exported from ZBrush.

Figure 10.79 These masks will combine to form the compound mask shown here.

4. With the mask.psd file open, press Ctrl+A to select all and Ctrl+C to copy. Move to honeycomb.psd, and paste the file as a new layer by pressing Ctrl+V. You can now close the pantsMaskPanel.psd file. This file will now be a layer over the honeycomb layer (Figure 10.80). Set the blending mode to Multiply, and the honeycomb texture will show through the white areas. You may now collapse the layers by selecting Layer → FlattenImage, and save this file as panelTiles.psd (Figure 10.81). Be sure not to save over the honeycomb.psd file. You can now close Photoshop.

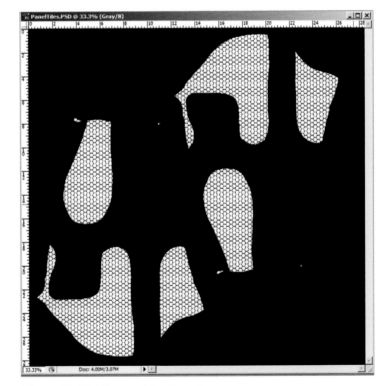

Figure 10.80 The document layers

Figure 10.81 The combined mask

5. Back in ZBrush, import `panelTiles.psd` into the Alpha palette. Select Tool → Masking → Mask By Alpha, and you will see your mask reappear on the surface with the addition of the honeycomb tiles. Using the Tool → Deformation menu, inflate the tiles by 5 (Figure 10.82).

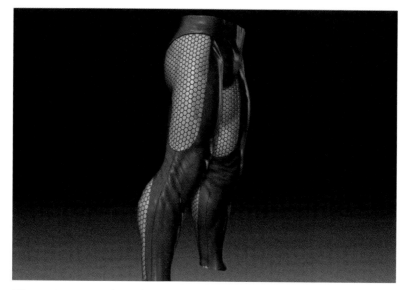

Figure 10.82 Mask applied and tiles inflated

As a final detailing to the pants, you need to add a seam between the tiles and the leather pants. This will help transition between the two materials in a more natural way, rather than the abrupt change you have now.

6. Load `pantsTiles.psd` into the Alpha palette. This is the original mask for the pants. Using Tool → Masking → Mask By Alpha, mask the pants and invert the mask so the leather is now unmasked (Figure 10.83).

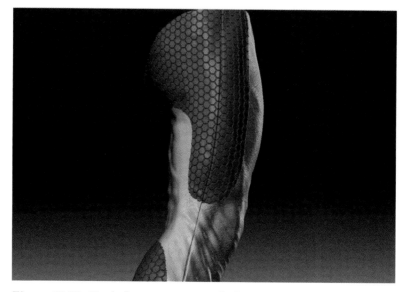

Figure 10.83 Mask the pants again with the `pantsTiles.psd` mask.

7. ZBrush has a selection of brushes especially built for making stitches and seams. Select the Stitch3 brush from the Brush menu (Figure 10.84). Stitch3 creates a stitched seam as shown in Figure 10.85. It is custom built with Roll and Lazy Mouse options already set to create one seamless stroke. If you find it hard to keep the lines smooth, you can increase the Lazy Radius value under the Stroke menu. This increases the delay of the Lazy Mouse, helping you to make a more fluid stroke.

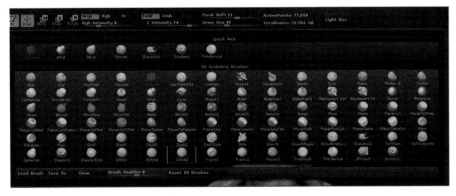

Figure 10.84 *The Stitch3 brush*

Figure 10.85 *The Stitch3 brush in action*

8. Stroke along the edge of the mask to create the seam, as shown in Figure 10.86. A useful technique (unless you're on a Mac, in which case you'll need to create your own shortcut) is to set the ZIntensity of the brush to Low, and use Ctrl+1 to repeat the stroke, building up the seam in increments. (On the Mac, the keystroke for ReplayLast is Command+1.) This helps if you find it difficult to create the seam in one brush stroke because the intensity appears too high. Continue the seams along the back of the leg as well.

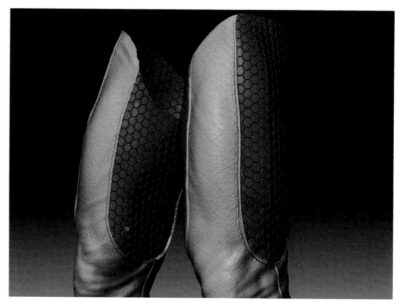

Figure 10.86 *Adding stitches to the rim with Stitch3*

9. Repeat the process by stroking along the panels on the rear of the calf. At this stage I also draw the stroke along the seams on the pants themselves (Figure 10.87).

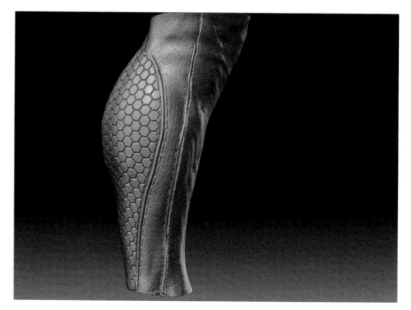

Figure 10.87 *The seams on the back of the calves*

Congratulations, you have completed the sculpting and detailing of the formfitting pants. This has involved building new geometry, capturing anatomical details, and generating a new mesh with thickness, as well as some advanced sculpting and masking techniques. Figure 10.88 shows the finished pants.

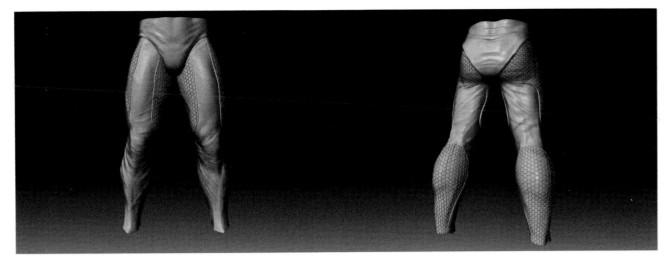

Figure 10.88 *The completed pants*

What's Next

Congratulations! You have now completed working on costume elements. In this chapter you have learned some intermediate and advanced tools and processes to create complex costume elements for any style of character. You have also looked at techniques for sculpting different kinds of fabric and how they interact with the figure.

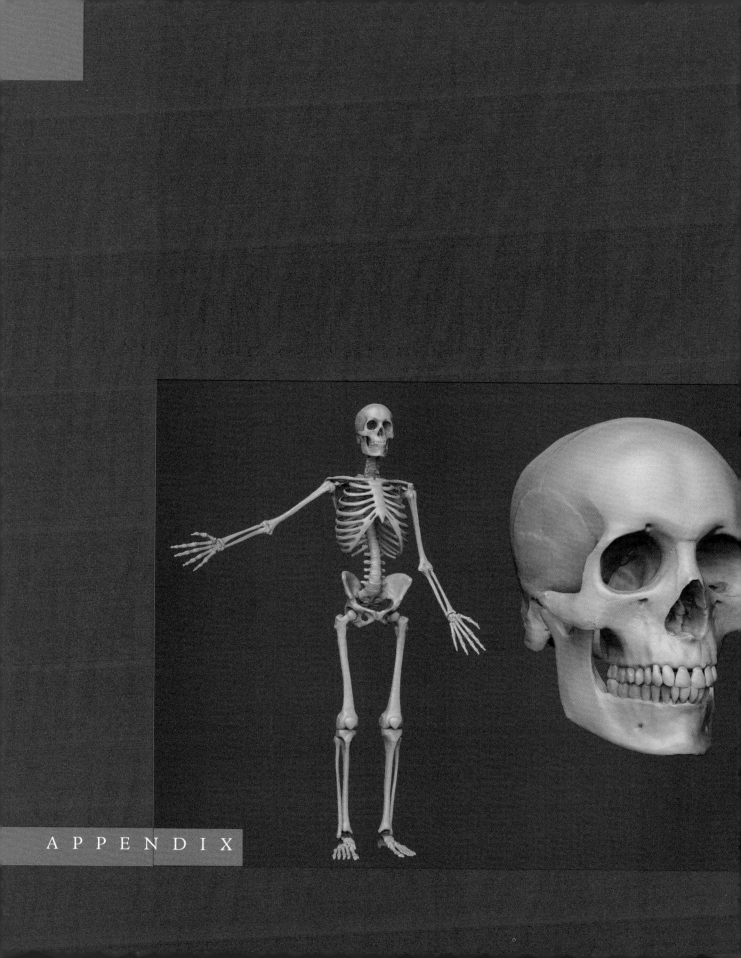

About the Companion DVD

In this Appendix, you'll find information on the following topics:

What you'll find on the DVD

System requirements

Using the DVD

Troubleshooting

What You'll Find on the DVD

The following sections are arranged by category and provide a summary of the content you'll find on the DVD. If you need help with installing the items provided on the DVD, refer to the installation instructions in the "Using the DVD" section of this appendix.

Chapter Files

In the Chapter Files directory you will find all the files for completing the tutorials and understanding concepts in this book. This includes sample files, as well as video files that provide screen recordings of the tutorials in progress. Sculpting is an artistic process that cannot always be described with words alone. You're strongly encouraged to view the movies that accompany some of the exercises in the chapters to see how the example files were created.

Some of the video files do not include audio.

Extra Videos

Please check the book's website at http://www.sybex.com/go/zbrushanatomy for updated information and new companion videos.

System Requirements

Make sure that your computer meets the minimum system requirements shown in the following list. If your computer doesn't match up to most of these requirements, you may have problems using the software and files on the companion DVD.

- Preferably a PC running Microsoft Windows XP, or Windows Vista. ZBrush requires at least Windows 2000. You can use ZBrush on an Intel-based Mac running Windows emulation software such as Boot Camp or Parallels; however, there may be some stability issues with ZBrush plug-ins such as ZMapper.

- Preferably your computer's processor should be a fast, Pentium 4 or newer (or equivalent such as AMD) with optional multithreading or hyperthreading capabilities. ZBrush requires at least a Pentium 3 processor.
- You should have at least 1024MB of RAM, preferably 2048MB for working with multi-million-poly meshes. ZBrush requires at least 512 MB of RAM.
- An Internet connection
- A DVD-ROM drive
- Apple QuickTime 7.0 or later (download from www.quicktime.com)

For the most up-to-date information, check http://www.pixologic.com/zbrush/system.

Using the DVD

To install the items from the DVD to your hard drive, follow these steps:

1. Insert the DVD into your computer's DVD-ROM drive. The license agreement appears.

Windows users: The interface won't launch if Autorun is disabled. In that case, click Start → Run (for Windows Vista, Start → All Programs → Accessories → Run). In the dialog box that appears, type *D*:**Start.exe**. (Replace *D* with the proper letter if your DVD drive uses a different letter. If you don't know the letter, see how your DVD drive is listed under My Computer.) Click OK.

---

2. Read through the license agreement, and then click the Accept button if you want to use the DVD.

The DVD interface appears. The interface allows you to access the content with just one or two clicks.

Alternately, you can access the files at the root directory of your hard drive.

Mac users: The DVD icon will appear on your desktop; double-click the icon to open the DVD and then navigate to the files you want.

Troubleshooting

Wiley has attempted to provide programs that work on most computers with the minimum system requirements. Alas, your computer may differ, and some programs may not work properly for some reason.

The two likeliest problems are that you don't have enough memory (RAM) for the programs you want to use, or you have other programs running that are affecting installation or running of a program. If you get an error message such as "Not enough memory" or "Setup cannot continue," try one or more of the following suggestions and then try using the software again:

Turn off any antivirus software running on your computer. Installation programs sometimes mimic virus activity and may make your computer incorrectly believe that it's being infected by a virus.

Close all running programs. The more programs you have running, the less memory is available to other programs. Installation programs typically update files and programs; so if you keep other programs running, installation may not work properly.

Have your local computer store add more RAM to your computer. This is, admittedly, a drastic and somewhat expensive step. However, adding more memory can really help the speed of your computer and allow more programs to run at the same time.

Customer Care

If you have trouble with the book's companion DVD-ROM, please call the Wiley Product Technical Support phone number at (800) 762–2974. Outside the United States, call +1(317) 572–3994. You can also contact Wiley Product Technical Support at `http://sybex.custhelp.com`. John Wiley & Sons will provide technical support only for installation and other general quality control items. For technical support on the applications themselves, consult the program's vendor or author.

To place additional orders or to request information about other Wiley products, please call (877) 762–2974.

Index

Note to the Reader: Throughout this index **boldfaced** page numbers indicate primary discussions of a topic. *Italicized* page numbers indicate illustrations.

Wiley Publishing, Inc.
End-User License Agreement

READ THIS. You should carefully read these terms and conditions before opening the software packet(s) included with this book "Book". This is a license agreement "Agreement" between you and Wiley Publishing, Inc. "WPI". By opening the accompanying software packet(s), you acknowledge that you have read and accept the following terms and conditions. If you do not agree and do not want to be bound by such terms and conditions, promptly return the Book and the unopened software packet(s) to the place you obtained them for a full refund.

1. License Grant. WPI grants to you (either an individual or entity) a nonexclusive license to use one copy of the enclosed software program(s) (collectively, the "Software," solely for your own personal or business purposes on a single computer (whether a standard computer or a workstation component of a multi-user network). The Software is in use on a computer when it is loaded into temporary memory (RAM) or installed into permanent memory (hard disk, CD-ROM, or other storage device). WPI reserves all rights not expressly granted herein.

2. Ownership. WPI is the owner of all right, title, and interest, including copyright, in and to the compilation of the Software recorded on the physical packet included with this Book "Software Media". Copyright to the individual programs recorded on the Software Media is owned by the author or other authorized copyright owner of each program. Ownership of the Software and all proprietary rights relating thereto remain with WPI and its licensers.

3. Restrictions On Use and Transfer. (a) You may only (i) make one copy of the Software for backup or archival purposes, or (ii) transfer the Software to a single hard disk, provided that you keep the original for backup or archival purposes. You may not (i) rent or lease the Software, (ii) copy or reproduce the Software through a LAN or other network system or through any computer subscriber system or bulletin-board system, or (iii) modify, adapt, or create derivative works based on the Software. (b) You may not reverse engineer, decompile, or disassemble the Software. You may transfer the Software and user documentation on a permanent basis, provided that the transferee agrees to accept the terms and conditions of this Agreement and you retain no copies. If the Software is an update or has been updated, any transfer must include the most recent update and all prior versions.

4. Restrictions on Use of Individual Programs. You must follow the individual requirements and restrictions detailed for each individual program in the About the CD-ROM appendix of this Book or on the Software Media. These limitations are also contained in the individual license agreements recorded on the Software Media. These limitations may include a requirement that after using the program for a specified period of time, the user must pay a registration fee or discontinue use. By opening the Software packet(s), you will be agreeing to abide by the licenses and restrictions for these individual programs that are detailed in the About the CD-ROM appendix and/or on the Software Media. None of the material on this Software Media or listed in this Book may ever be redistributed, in original or modified form, for commercial purposes.

5. Limited Warranty. (a) WPI warrants that the Software and Software Media are free from defects in materials and workmanship under normal use for a period of sixty (60) days from the date of purchase of this Book. If WPI receives notification within the warranty period of defects in materials or workmanship, WPI will replace the defective Software Media. (b) WPI AND THE AUTHOR(S) OF THE BOOK DISCLAIM ALL OTHER WARRANTIES, EXPRESS OR IMPLIED, INCLUDING WITHOUT LIMITATION IMPLIED WARRANTIES OF MERCHANTABILITY AND FITNESS FOR A PARTICULAR PURPOSE, WITH RESPECT TO THE SOFTWARE, THE PROGRAMS, THE SOURCE CODE CONTAINED THEREIN, AND/OR THE TECHNIQUES DESCRIBED IN THIS BOOK. WPI DOES NOT WARRANT THAT THE FUNCTIONS CONTAINED IN THE SOFTWARE WILL MEET YOUR REQUIREMENTS OR THAT THE OPERATION OF THE SOFTWARE WILL BE ERROR FREE. (c) This limited warranty gives you specific legal rights, and you may have other rights that vary from jurisdiction to jurisdiction.

6. Remedies. (a) WPI's entire liability and your exclusive remedy for defects in materials and workmanship shall be limited to replacement of the Software Media, which may be returned to WPI with a copy of your receipt at the following address: Software Media Fulfillment Department, Attn.: *ZBrush® Digital Sculpting Human Anatomy*, Wiley Publishing, Inc., 10475 Crosspoint Blvd., Indianapolis, IN 46256, or call 1-800-762-2974. Please allow four to six weeks for delivery. This Limited Warranty is void if failure of the Software Media has resulted from accident, abuse, or misapplication. Any replacement Software Media will be warranted for the remainder of the original warranty period or thirty (30) days, whichever is longer. (b) In no event shall WPI or the author be liable for any damages whatsoever (including without limitation damages for loss of business profits, business interruption, loss of business information, or any other pecuniary loss) arising from the use of or inability to use the Book or the Software, even if WPI has been advised of the possibility of such damages. (c) Because some jurisdictions do not allow the exclusion or limitation of liability for consequential or incidental damages, the above limitation or exclusion may not apply to you.

7. U.S. Government Restricted Rights. Use, duplication, or disclosure of the Software for or on behalf of the United States of America, its agencies and/or instrumentalities "U.S. Government" is subject to restrictions as stated in paragraph (c)(1)(ii) of the Rights in Technical Data and Computer Software clause of DFARS 252.227-7013, or subparagraphs (c) (1) and (2) of the Commercial Computer Software - Restricted Rights clause at FAR 52.227-19, and in similar clauses in the NASA FAR supplement, as applicable.

8. General. This Agreement constitutes the entire understanding of the parties and revokes and supersedes all prior agreements, oral or written, between them and may not be modified or amended except in a writing signed by both parties hereto that specifically refers to this Agreement. This Agreement shall take precedence over any other documents that may be in conflict herewith. If any one or more provisions contained in this Agreement are held by any court or tribunal to be invalid, illegal, or otherwise unenforceable, each and every other provision shall remain in full force and effect.